Defendants and Victims in International Criminal Justice

This volume considers a variety of key issues pertaining to the rights of defendants and victims at International Criminal Courts (ICTs) and explores how best to balance and enhance the rights of both in order to ensure the effectiveness and efficiency of international criminal proceedings.

The rights of victims are becoming an increasingly important issue at ICTs. Yet, at the same time, this has to be achieved without having a detrimental impact upon on the rights of the defence and the efficiency of the courts. This book provides analyses of issues on the rights of both the accused and the victims. By discussing matters concerning these two pivotal actors in international criminal justice within the same volume, the work highlights that there are intrinsic and intense conflicting and converging relationships between victims and the accused, particularly in terms of their rights. While most of the chapters focus mainly on either the accused or the victims, others discuss both at the same time. The work strikes a fine balance between, on the one hand, classic topics on the rights of the accused and the rights of the victims and, on the other, topics which have been largely unexplored and/or which require new angles or perspectives. Additionally, there are some chapters which approach both the rights of the accused and the rights of the victims in new contexts and/or under novel perspectives. The book as a whole provides a discussion of the two sides of this important coin of international criminal justice.

The work will be an essential resource for academics, practitioners and students with an interest in the field of international criminal law. It will also be of interest to human rights scholars who are working with the rights of victims and the accused.

Dr Juan-Pablo Pérez-León-Acevedo, Pluricourts, Faculty of Law, University of Oslo, Norway.

Dr Joanna Nicholson, Pluricourts, University of Oslo, Norway.

Defendants and Victims in International Criminal Justice

Ensuring and Balancing Their Rights

Edited by
Juan-Pablo Pérez-León-Acevedo and Joanna Nicholson

Routledge
Taylor & Francis Group
LONDON AND NEW YORK

First published 2020
by Routledge
2 Park Square, Milton Park, Abingdon, Oxon OX14 4RN

and by Routledge
605 Third Avenue, New York, NY 10017

First issued in paperback 2021

Routledge is an imprint of the Taylor & Francis Group, an informa business

British Library Cataloguing-in-Publication Data
A catalogue record for this book is available from the British Library

Library of Congress Cataloging-in-Publication Data
Names: Pérez-León Acevedo, Juan-Pablo, editor. | Nicholson, Joanna (Lawyer), editor.
Title: Defendants and victims in international criminal justice : ensuring and balancing their rights / [edited by] Juan-Pablo Pérez-León-Acevedo, Joanna Nicholson.
Description: 1. | New York : Routledge, 2020. | Includes bibliographical references and index.
Identifiers: LCCN 2019047221 (print) | LCCN 2019047222 (ebook) | ISBN 9780367253950 (hardback) | ISBN 9780429287565 (ebook)
Subjects: LCSH: Criminal justice, Administration of. | International criminal courts. | International Criminal Court. | Rome Statute of the International Criminal Court (1998 July 17) | Victims of crimes (International law) | Criminal liability (International law) | United Nations. Security Council. | International Tribunal for the Prosecution of Persons Responsible for Serious Violations of International Humanitarian Law Committed in the Territory of the Former Yugoslavia since 1991.
Classification: LCC K5001 .D44 2020 (print) | LCC K5001 (ebook) | DDC 345/.03—dc23
LC record available at https://lccn.loc.gov/2019047221
LC ebook record available at https://lccn.loc.gov/2019047222

ISBN 13: 978-1-03-223621-6 (pbk)
ISBN 13: 978-0-367-25395-0 (hbk)

Typeset in Galliard
by Apex CoVantage, LLC

Contents

Biographies of contributors and editors

Anthony Abato has ten years of experience in civil and criminal litigation, including public and private practice. He holds an advanced LL.M. in Public International Law from Leiden University and an LL.B. from Dalhousie University. He currently works in the Judiciary of the International Criminal Court. He is called to the bar in both Canada and the United States.

Rogier Bartels has been a legal officer in Chambers (Trial Division) of the International Criminal Court (ICC) since 2013. In July 2019, he was appointed as a judge in the District Court of Amsterdam, where he sits on criminal law cases on a part-time basis. Prior to his current positions, Rogier worked as a researcher in the Military Law Section of the Netherlands Defence Academy, and as a lawyer for the International Crimes Section of the National Prosecutor's Office of the Netherlands. Other positions include being an associate legal officer in Trial Chamber I of the International Criminal Tribunal for the former Yugoslavia, and three years as a legal adviser on international humanitarian law at the Netherlands Red Cross. Rogier is a member of the research programme on "Law of Armed Conflict and Military Operations" of the Amsterdam Center for International Law (of the University of Amsterdam) and of the Center for International Criminal Justice of the VU University Amsterdam. Rogier's publications mainly focus on international humanitarian law and international criminal law, as well as the interplay between these two branches of public international law. He regularly lectures as part of bachelor and master courses at universities, and as part of trainings for practitioners.

Kirsten Bowman is currently working to complete her PhD at Uppsala University in the field of public international law, looking at the relationship between the un Security Council and the international criminal courts from the perspectives of institutional judicial independence and the perception of legitimacy. She has previously worked as a legal officer at both the ICC and ICTR, as well as having clerked in Chambers at the ICTY. She spent time working in the Office of the Prosecutor but has primarily worked in Chambers where, at the ICC, she worked for then Vice President Blattmann on the first case to come before the Court. As well, she has taught International Criminal Law and International Courts courses at Georgetown University, was a visiting scholar at the UC Berkeley Center for Human Rights and consults for organizations focusing on ICL, including the UN, the Open Society Justice Initiative, the Women's Initiative for Gender Justice, and the International Bar Association. She holds a J.D. and is a member of the New York Bar.

Talita de Souza Dias is a DPhil candidate and Tutor in Public International Law and International Criminal Law at the Faculty of Law of the University of Oxford, where she is the recipient of the Sir Roy Goode and Planethood Foundation Scholarships. Her research focuses on the principles of legality and fair labelling in International Criminal Law. Talita is also a Teaching Fellow in Public International at Royal Holloway, University of London. She has published in some of the leading international law journals, such as the Journal of International Criminal Justice, the Leiden Journal of International Law and the International Criminal Law Review. Her article 'The Retroactive Application of the Rome Statute in Cases of Security Council Referrals and Ad hoc Declarations: An Appraisal of the Existing Solutions to an Under-discussed Problem' has recently been awarded the 2018 Journal of International Criminal Justice Prize. In 2015, she obtained her *Magister Juris degree* from Oxford with Distinction, and was awarded the Clifford Chance Prize for Best Overall Performance in the program. In 2015/2016, Talita worked as an intern at Trial Chambers I and V of the International Criminal Court. In 2017/2018, she was the co-convenor for the Oxford Public International Law Discussion Group. Talita has previously worked as a Law Clerk for an Appeals Judge and as an intern for a Federal Prosecutor in Brazil. She did her LLB at the Federal University of Pernambuco (UFPE), with a year abroad in France (Sciences-Po Lille and Pierre-Mendès Grenoble).

Andreas Føllesdal is Professor of Philosophy and Co-Director of PluriCourts (Centre for the Study of the Legitimate Roles of the Judiciary in the Global Order), Faculty of Law, University of Oslo, Norway.

Sergii Masol is a PhD researcher in law at the European University Institute, Italy. He holds an LLM in International Human Rights Law from Lund University, Sweden, and a BA (with distinction) in International Relations/International Law from the National Aviation University, Ukraine. During the PhD programme Sergii has worked as a research assistant at the European University Institute, Italy, and has been a visiting researcher at the Centre of Excellence for International Courts (iCourts) of the University of Copenhagen, Denmark. He has also been an assistant editor of the European Journal of International Law as well as a senior editor and a head of the international law section of the European Journal of Legal Studies. Previously, Sergii worked as a language assistant in the Organisation for Security and Cooperation in Europe (OSCE) Special Monitoring Mission to Ukraine. Earlier in his career, he was a volunteer at Amnesty International, Ukraine, and completed internships at the International Criminal Court, the European Court of Human Rights, the Office of the United Nations High Commissioner for Human

Rights and the Raoul Wallenberg Institute of Human Rights and Humanitarian Law.

Joanna Nicholson is a postdoctoral researcher at Pluricourts – Centre for the Study of the Legitimate Roles of the Judiciary in the Global Order, University of Oslo. Her research focuses on international criminal law, international humanitarian law and international human rights law. She is the author of *Fighting and Victimhood in International Criminal Law* (Routledge, 2018) and Editor of 'Strengthening the Validity of International Criminal Law' (Brill, 2018). Previously, she practiced law both in private law firms and as a prosecutor.

Juan-Pablo Pérez-León-Acevedo is a Post-Doctoral Researcher, Faculty of Humanities & Social Sciences, University of Jyväskylä (Finland) since March 2020. He was a Postdoctoral Fellow at PluriCourts (Research Council of Norway/Project 223274), Law Faculty, University of Oslo where he also lectured international law courses. He held positions or visiting fellowships at *inter alia* Oxford University, Max Planck Institute for Foreign and International Criminal Law, Åbo Akademi University, Pretoria University, etc. He served at *inter alia* the International Criminal Court, and the International Criminal Tribunal for the former Yugoslavia.

Rossella Pulvirenti joined the School of Law of the Liverpool John Moore University (LJMU) as lecturer in September 2018. Rossella has a PhD from the University of Nottingham with a thesis on witness and victims protective measures at the International Criminal Court. Before this, Rossella worked as a lecturer at the University of Bedfordshire and as teaching fellow at SOAS and the University of Nottingham and as research associate at the Human Rights Lab, Beacon of Excellence of the University of Nottingham. Rossella is a fully qualified lawyer in Italy and she has also interned at the Registry of the European Court of Human Rights (France).

Dejana Radisavljevic is a Doctoral Researcher at the School of Law, University of Sheffield. She has an LL.M from the University of Leicester and a number of years' professional experience with the UN International Residual Mechanism for Criminal Tribunals. Dejana has three publications to her name: 'Post-Conviction Remedies and the Residual Mechanism' in Gentian Zyberi and Colleen Rohan (eds.), *Defence Perspectives on International Criminal Justice* (Cambridge University Press 2017); 'Srebrenica and Genocide Denial in the former Yugoslavia: What has the ICTY done to address it?' in Paul Behrens, Olaf Jensen and Nicholas Terry (eds.), *Holocaust and Genocide Denial: A Contextual Perspective*(Routledge 2017); and 'Rome Statute Articles 77 and 78' in Mark Klamberg (ed.), *Commentary on the Law of the International Criminal Court* (Torkel Opsahl Academic EPublisher 2017).

Alice Riccardi is Assistant Professor of International Law at the Department of Law of University of Roma Tre, where she directs the Legal Clinic "International Protection of Human Rights". She has been representing individuals in sanctions cases before the UN Security Council Ombudsperson to the ISIL (Da'esh) and Al-Qaida Sanctions Committee since 2014. In 2018 she acted as *amicus curiae* in the case against Al-Bashir before the ICC. Prior to her current academic position, she was research fellow in international law (2013–2016 and 2017–2018) researching the interplay between UN sanctions and international criminal justice. She earned her PhD in international law *summa cum laude* at Sant' Anna School of Advanced Studies (2012). She was TLSI Fellow at the Poon School of Law of the King's College, London (2015), visiting scholar at the Max Planck Institute of International and Comparative Criminal Law (2011) and served in the ICC Office of the Prosecutor (2009–2010) and at the ICTY (2008). She writes on international criminal law, human rights law, sanctions, the law of States' responsibility and the history of international law. Her monograph on *Sentencing at the International Criminal Court: from Nuremberg to the Hague* was published in 2016.

Geir Ulfstein is Professor of Law and Co-Director of PluriCourts (Centre for the Study of the Legitimate Roles of the Judiciary in the Global Order), Faculty of Law, University of Oslo, Norway.

Michail (Michael) **Vagias** is a Senior Lecturer in Law at The Hague University of Applied Sciences and Program Manager for the ProCuria Project on Professional Legal Training (2017–2020). Following the conclusion of his Ph.D. studies in Leiden University, Michail became a lecturer and later a Senior Lecturer in Law at The Hague University of Applied Sciences. He has acted as an Expert on Mission for migration policy development, as well legal counsel in international cases. Michail's research interests focus on questions of jurisdiction in domestic and international law. In addition to his monograph (*The Territorial Jurisdiction of the International Criminal Court*, CUP, 2015), he has published extensively with leading international legal periodicals on public international and international criminal law. The author is grateful to The Research Fund of the Platform 'Good Governance for a Safe and Secure World' of The Hague University of Applied Sciences which provided financial support for the preparation of his chapter.

Tsvetelina van Benthem is a DPhil student at the University of Oxford. Her thesis, supervised by Professor Dapo Akande, explores state responsibility and individual criminal responsibility in the context of unpredictable actions of military applications using artificial intelligence. Tsvetelina is the first holder of the James Upcher Memorial Scholarship and was a Merton Lawyers' Scholar in 2016–2017. Tsvetelina holds master's degrees from Sofia University (LLM) and the University of Oxford (*MJur*, MPhil). She has taught for the Stanford in Oxford Program, Oxbridge Academic Programs and CBL, and has interned at the UN Office for the Coordination of Humanitarian Affairs.

Oliver Windridge is a lawyer specialising in international human rights law and international criminal law. He currently serves on the List of Counsel (pro bono) at the African Court on Human and Peoples' Rights (African Court). Oliver acts as counsel on cases at the African Court, African Commission on Human and Peoples' Rights as well as various UN human rights bodies. Oliver is founder of The ACtHPR Monitor website and blog dedicated to the African Court. The views expressed herein are those of the author only and are not necessarily shared by any organisations affiliated with the author.

Foreword

Whom to protect?

Geir Ulfstein and Andreas Føllesdal

How should we assess the many vocal critics against the legitimacy of international and hybrid criminal courts and tribunals (ICTs)? They claim authority to adjudicate unimaginable atrocities often committed in opaque circumstances. Defences of the ICTs cannot simply apply familiar standards known from the domestic context. One reason to be wary of such imports is the perplexing range of objectives the ICTs are tasked with – not only securing justice in a single case, but reparations, ending impunity, deterrence, reconciliation and building competence – at the same time. No wonder many parties find that these ICTs fail their legitimate yet unrealistic expectations. So, where might assessments best begin?

The editors and authors of this volume offer valuable insights and perspectives by focussing our attention on the tensions between the rights of the defendants and the victims, often addressing cases of the International Criminal Court, but with implications across other ICTs. One the one hand, ICTs must respect the human rights of the accused. But how should this be done in practice in an ICT, as opposed to domestic courts and regional human rights courts? And how should the more prominent role of victims in ICTs be implemented in light of their large number and the limited resources of the courts? May the rights of victims threaten due process guarantees of the accused?

The editors wisely warn about the possibility of drawing generalizable conclusions, insisting on the need for each ICT to handle every case with due care for the details. The impressive findings of the authors and editors of the present volume facilitates such prudent wisdom – among the judges of the ICTs and among those who observe and assess them and their institutions.

1 Introduction[1]

Juan-Pablo Pérez-León-Acevedo and Joanna Nicholson

Setting the scene and about this book

International and hybrid criminal courts and tribunals (ICTs) are not human rights courts, yet human rights are firmly embedded within their normative framework and practice. Human rights function as important standards that help both assess and enhance the legitimacy and effectiveness of ICTs. This is particularly so in relation to the, at times competing, rights of defendants and victims in the international criminal justice process.

That a defendant has received, and is perceived as having received, a fair trial is vital to the legitimacy, effectiveness, and legacy of the ICTs. Assuring the human rights of defendants at an international level is not simply a case of transposing domestic standards; rather, a host of complex considerations come into play. The particular context and mandate of ICTs requires that a mechanical application of human rights standards should be avoided. Given this, how should ICTs best assure the right of defendants to a fair trial?

At the same time, the rights of victims are becoming an increasingly important issue at ICTs. When ICTs re-emerged onto the world stage in the 1990s, victims were initially relegated to the role of witnesses, but the International Criminal Court (ICC) and subsequent ICTs have expanded their roles to participants, civil parties and/or reparations claimants, and ICTs must take their rights into account. However, how can this be achieved without having a detrimental impact upon the rights of the defence and the efficiency of the ICTs?

Within this context, the present volume considers a variety of key issues pertaining to the rights of defendants and victims at ICTs and explores how best to balance and enhance the rights of both in order to ensure the effectiveness and efficiency of international criminal proceedings. Due to its importance and global scope, the authors in this volume tend to focus on the ICC, yet, attention is also given to other ICTs, in particular the International Criminal Tribunal for the Former Yugoslavia (ICTY), the Special Tribunal for Lebanon (STL), and the International Criminal Law Section of the Prospective African Court of Justice

1 This chapter and the present book have been funded by PluriCourts – Research Council of Norway, Project 223274.

and Human Rights (ACJHR). Moreover, all chapters to a larger or lesser extent contain analysis, findings or conclusions which are relevant to, or concern, international criminal justice institutions as a whole rather than one specific court.

Against this rationale, the present volume seeks to realise two main aims. First, it provides analyses of issues on the rights of both the defendant and the victims at ICTs. By discussing matters concerning these two pivotal actors in international criminal justice within the same volume, the book aims to highlight that there are intrinsic and intense conflicting and converging relationships between victims and defendants, particularly in terms of their rights. Whereas most of the chapters in the present book focus mainly on either the defendant or the victims, others endeavour to tackle both at the same time. The book as a whole provides a discussion of the two sides of this important coin of international criminal justice.

Second, the book strikes a fine balance between, on the one hand, 'classic' topics on the rights of defendants and the rights of the victims and, on the other, topics which have been largely unexplored and/or which require new angles or perspectives. Additionally, there are some chapters which particularly endeavour to approach both the rights of the defendant and the rights of the victims in new contexts and/or under novel perspectives.

In terms of existent academic literature, this volume arguably constitutes an original addition. It complements materials which are mainly focused on either the rights of the defendant at ICTs[2] or the rights of victims at ICTs.[3] In this context, the rights of defendants and victims are addressed together in the same volume rather than in a separated or fragmented manner which has so far been the trend in existent legal academic publications. Although some materials have examined the rights of both the accused and victims at ICTs, these have primarily focused on general principles and common rules.[4] Conversely, the book chapters of the present volume engage in thorough and up-to-date discussions of specific or novel topics and issues on ensuring and balancing the rights of the defendants and victims in international criminal justice institutions.

The chapters of the book

The book begins with a chapter exploring the use of human rights law at the ICC. In Chapter 2, Sergii Masol examines Article 21(3) of the Rome Statute of

2 See, for example: Yvonne McDermott, *Fairness in International Criminal Trials* (Oxford University Press 2016); Caleb H. Wheeler, *The Right to be Present at Trial in International Criminal Law* (Brill, 2019).

3 See, for example: Brianne McGonigle Leyh, *Procedural Justice? Victim Participation in International Criminal Proceedings* (Intersentia 2011); Luke Moffett, *Justice for Victims Before the International Criminal Court* (Routledge 2014); Juan Perez-Leon-Acevedo, *Victims' Status at International and Hybrid Criminal Courts: Victims as Witnesses, Victim Participants/Civil Parties and Reparations Claimants* (Abo Akademi University Press 2014).

4 See, for example: Göran Sluiter, Håkan Friman, Suzannah Linton, Sergey Vasiliev, and Salvatore Zappalà (eds) *International Criminal Procedure. Principles and Rules* (Oxford University Press 2013).

the ICC, which obliges the court to interpret and apply the law in a consistent manner with internationally recognised human rights. The chapter provides an analytical framework to the process of identification of human rights to be considered by these institutions, particularly the ICC. As Masol states, knowledge of the contents of the rights of defendants and victims at the ICC (and certainly other international and hybrid criminal tribunals) constitutes a necessary first step in ensuring and balancing the rights of defendants and victims. Indeed, he suggests that Article 21(3) is a tool that enables the ICC to clarify diverse elements of the rights of defendants and victims via references to external human rights norms. Masol's principal focus is to determine in which legal sources the ICC can find internationally recognised human rights, including national law, international soft law and international hard law at both the universal and regional levels. Masol's main argument is that Article 21(3) of the Rome Statute empowers the Court to invoke human rights provided that these are internationally recognised. By following this premise, he sustains and finds that neither national acceptance of a norm in light of international silence, nor a soft law norm suffices. In turn, regional human rights norms can be invoked by the ICC if they are accepted within a broader normative framework. However, Masol argues that a universal human rights norm should always outweigh a regional human right norm, even if the latter provides a higher level of protection than the former does in the regime of the ICC. Conversely, universal norms meet the requirement of being internationally recognised. He emphasises that Article 21(3) of the Rome Statute refers to human rights which are both international and binding.

How are matters involving defendants and victims in international criminal justice best addressed in different institutional landscapes? This question is explored in Chapter 3, where Oliver Windridge discusses how the defence and victims are expected to fair at the first ever regional criminal court, the ACJHR, particularly its International Criminal Law Section. He focuses on two key instruments of the yet-to-be-established ACJHR, namely, the Protocol on the Statute of the ACJHR and the Protocol on Amendments to the Protocol on the Statute of the ACJHR. Windridge compares the relevant provisions with those contained in the Statutes of the ICC, the Special Court for Sierra Leone (SCSL) and the International Criminal Tribunal for Rwanda (ICTR), with the goal of determining whether the prospective ACJHR may be considered to be a progressive or retrograde institution concerning the rights of defendants and victims

The chapter begins by discussing the establishment of the ACJHR, before analysing and comparing the normative provisions on defence rights. Here, Windridge pays attention to norms that endeavour to guarantee the respect for the rights of defendants, including the formation of a defence office, the appointment of public defenders, as well as the incorporation of a 'Principal Defender'. He then examines provisions on victim participation, also paying attention to similar developments at other international criminal justice institutions. At this point, the author critically points out that there is some ambiguity in normative provisions on victims and related potential matters involving victim participation in trial proceedings. Windridge concludes with a set of observations and recommendations, including suggestions on areas that require further clarification via the adoption of additional protocols or court rules as well as judicial decision making.

The focus of the book then moves to examining particular defence rights and how these can be impacted or affected by the rights of victims. In Chapter 4, Rogier Bartels touches on the wider issue of whether parties other than the defendant, namely victims and the prosecutor, can be said to have a 'right' to a fair trial, when he explores the issue of when the ICC has found that prejudice has been caused to a party to the proceedings in procedural matters relating to the admission of evidence.

A corollary of the defendant's right to a fair trial is the requirement that a court assess whether prejudice has been caused to the defendant by the actions of the other party, for example by the late introduction of incriminating evidence by the prosecutor or the late addition of new prosecution witnesses. The court is generally required to evaluate the prosecution's request and issue a decision as to whether or not prejudice has been caused to the defendant. Evidence of prejudice is insufficient in itself, rather a certain level of prejudice must be shown to have occurred, undue prejudice.

Bartels begins by discussing how the notion of prejudice has been interpreted by the ICC in cases involving procedural decisions and how the court has determined that the prejudice was undue. He then analyses cases where the prosecution has argued that prejudice has been caused to them, for example by the late admission of defence evidence. He shows that the ICC has applied the same rules to prosecution and defence requests. While this may accord with the principle of equality of arms, Bartels wonders who is being prejudiced by late admission of defence evidence – the prosecution? The victims? The international community? He finds that the ICC has treated the prosecution as acting in the interests of victims and therefore as having a right to a fair trial, but queries whether this approach should be followed throughout the case, as while the prosecution must be able to properly present their case, this cannot be to the detriment of the rights of the defence.

How an ICT gains access to evidence and information can seriously impact a defendant's right to a fair trial. Alice Riccardi's chapter, Chapter 5, addresses the issue of smart sanction regimes, namely sanctions that are directed against particular individuals and entities. She explores the growing cooperation between the ICC and the United Nations Security Council Sanctions Committees, and asks whether this could impact the defendant's s right to a fair trial and endanger the legitimacy of the court.

The proposal that smart sanctions could be used in connection with ICC fugitives has received significant support, for example from the ICC Assembly of States Parties and the Prosecutor, in the hope that their use could lead to fugitives' arrest and surrender. While a smart sanction has yet to be issued in connection with an ICC fugitive, Riccardi finds evidence that coordination and information sharing is taking place between sanctions committees and the court. However, there is currently no legal framework or guidance concerning this information sharing process, raising concerns, both as to the potential impact upon a defendant's right to a fair trial and the impact upon the Court's overall legitimacy.

Riccardi explores the legal consequences of sanctions should they be adopted in connection with pre-trial proceedings, as well as examining the process of information sharing between the court and sanctions committees. She argues that using smart sanctions to tackle ICC arrest dilemmas would associate the court with a tool that violates the human rights of those who are targeted; would politicise court proceedings; and would ultimately affect the court's legitimacy. She recommends that the court re-think how it cooperates with these bodies in future, both as a matter of law and of policy. Consideration should be paid as to how such cooperation can impact upon a defendant's fair trial rights during the pre-trial process and how it affects victims' perception of the court as an independent, unbiased actor.

Another issue which an impact both victims and defendants is whether a case can or should proceed in the absence of the defendant. In Chapter 6, Talita de Souza Dias and Tsvetelina van Bentham focus on two ICTs which adopt contrasting approaches to this matter: the ICC, which as a general rule requires the presence of the defendant, and the STL, which allows trials *in absentia*. The authors observe that there is significant legal uncertainty as to the legal nature of the defendant's presence before these courts, with it being viewed variously as a right of the defendant, an obligation owed to victims and witnesses; an institutional demand; or a mixture of these.

The authors discuss what is meant by presence at trial and *in absentia* trials and the relationship between the two concepts, before examining the approaches of the ICC and STL in more detail. They find that the ICC conceives of presence at trial as a type of unwaivable right of the defendant. As such, *in absentia* trials are allowed only in exceptional circumstances. The STL, on the other hand, adopts a more relaxed approach to presence, whereby in cases where an accused has absconded or cannot be found, presence is treated as a waivable right, not a duty. The authors argue that neither court's approach is satisfactory: neither complies with human rights law and neither succeeds in factoring in the different interests at stake, including those of defendants and victims. In order to overcome this, they advocate that the courts follow the approach to presence adopted in human rights law, whereby presence can be waived by an unequivocal waiver of the defendant. Furthermore, the authors recommend that a more flexible and case-by-case approach should be adopted which incorporates the various interests at play in international criminal justice, particularly those of the defendant, victims and witnesses.

It is important that defendants should have effective fair trial rights, but what if the evidence shows that a challenge on the basis of a particular right is probably doomed to fail? Michail Vagias discusses just this eventuality in Chapter 7, concerning the defendant's right to challenge the jurisdiction of an ICT. This right is intended to operate as a fundamental guard against unwarranted judicial process, however, as Vagias explains, no case has ever been rejected in international criminal proceedings following a successful defence challenge to jurisdiction, begging the question of whether the defence gains any benefit from mounting such a challenge in the first place.

Vagias explores the defence success rate before four courts, the ICTY, ICTR, SCSL and the ICC, finding that less than one out of ten defence challenges to the jurisdiction of these courts has been successful. He pinpoints several possible reasons for this lack of defence success: prosecutorial caution; defence misuse of jurisdictional challenges; and inconsistency surrounding the interpretation and application of jurisdictional concepts. The author is particularly critical of the unclear jurisprudence emanating from these ICTs concerning important questions such as proof of facts, which have continually moved the goal posts for defendants seeking to challenge on jurisdictional grounds.

Although victims are not particularly visible in jurisdictional challenges, given that they occur at such an early stage in the judicial process, it is nevertheless the first time in the proceedings that the rights of defendants and victims are pitted against each other. Vagias finds that the current body of law in this area is strongly pro-institutional and pro-victim and argues that this extremely low defence success rate concerning jurisdictional challenges should give cause for serious reflection. If defendants and their advisors view a challenge based on this fundamental right as having minimal to no chances of success, making it is an 'illusory' right, it will have a severe detrimental impact upon both the procedural and sociological legitimacy of these institutions.

In carrying out their mandate, ICTs are required to fulfil a number of different goals, which encompass both the traditional goals of criminal courts, such as fair adjudication, retribution, deterrence and rehabilitation, together with other goals that are more peculiar to these special international institutions, such as peace and reconciliation. Trying to achieve this wide spectrum of objectives causes challenges for these institutions, not least when it comes to balancing the rights of different stakeholders involved in the process, including defendants and victims. Dejana Radisavljević's chapter, Chapter 8, focuses upon the ICTY's efforts to achieve traditional criminal justice objectives, while at the same time promoting broader objectives of peace and reconciliation, and explores how the tribunal dealt with the competing interests of defendants and victims in this respect.

At the ICTY it was hoped that trying and punishing individuals would help affect reconciliation within the former Yugoslavia. However, the reality of this proved to be far more complex. Radisavljević explains that the precise meaning of 'reconciliation' was not defined by the tribunal, leading to misunderstanding and heightened expectations as to what the tribunal could realistically achieve in that regard. She reflects upon what reconciliation means and requires in practice in the context of ICTs and discusses how to resolve the tension between the micro and macro objectives of these institutions. The author argues that using the defendant as a means of promoting reconciliation, and thus as no more than an object, is incompatible with retributivism and respect for the defendant's dignity. At the same time, reconciliation calls for greater participative rights for victims. Retributive justice requires a balancing of the rights of the victims and those of the defendants. Radisavljević suggests that this is not an impossible task, indeed certain domestic criminal justice objectives, particularly that of rehabilitating the offender and reintegrating them back into society, are useful ways of promoting reconciliation, and in future ICTs should give greater consideration as to how to best achieve these aims.

Currently there is a dearth of legal research concerning the rights of victims at ICTs, the remainder of the book tries to address this with a number of chapters looking at different issues in this area. One underexplored issue concerns the political dimensions of victim participation. In Chapter 9, Kirsten Bowman examines the implications of a victim's politics in ICC proceedings. She enquires whether the ICC should adopt a different approach based on the existence of such a political reality and whether victim participation at the ICC has been compromised or 'politicised' to such a level that may affect the fairness of the proceedings. The questions formulated in this chapter help explore how to balance victims' right to agency with the need and mandate of the ICC to determine the truth and deliver justice in international criminal proceedings.

Bowman conducts a comparative analysis, discussing the politics surrounding victim participants in Darfur and the related *Banda & Jerbo* case, and Kenya and the related *Kenyatta* case. Applying a socio-legal perspective, Bowman considers the issue of politics within the framework of victims in order to establish whether political actions or views have had an impact upon victim participation at the ICC, and to determine whether the political identity of victims should be taken into account when crafting the framework of victim participation at the court. This helps shed light on the assumptions embedded in the Rome Statute, and is important when examining potential issues and finding solutions to the matter of political influence in victim participation at the ICC.

The author finds that whether victim participation has been compromised or even politicised in a manner affecting fair proceedings is still an open question. The ICC avoided the issue in the *Banda & Jerbo* case and ended the Kenyan cases without tackling the political interference issue in victim participation and its alleged effect on the judicial outcome. Nevertheless, she identifies the potential for 'political' victims or the impact of the politicization of victim participation on the proceedings, all of which may compromise a defendant's right to a fair and impartial trial.

Chapter 10 considers how witnesses' testimony can be given in a safe and secure way. Rossella Pulvirenti investigates whether the ICC adequately safeguards the right to privacy of victims when they provide testimony as witnesses under Article 68(1) of the Rome Statute, and whether the ICC has appropriately balanced the rights of victims with diverse aspects of the right of the accused to a fair trial in this respect.

Pulvirenti begins by examining the scope of the right to privacy of victims under the Rome Statute. She uses an original definition of this right, which in turn shapes the content of the human rights analysis and defines protective measures ordered by the ICC to protect the privacy of the victims who participate as witnesses in the proceedings. The chapter then proceeds to examine the limitations to the right to privacy and the right to a fair trial in the Rome Statute, before carrying out an analysis of the case-law and transcripts of the ICC. In this part, the author focuses on: i) the situation in the Democratic Republic of Congo and the *Lubanga*, *Ngudjolo Chui*, and *Katanga* cases; ii) the situation in the Central African Republic and the *Bemba* case; iii) the Kenyan situation and *Ruto & Sang* and *Kenyatta* cases; and iv) the situation in Ivory Coast and the *Gbagbo & Blé Goudé* cases.

Pulivirenti concludes with recommendations as to how the ICC may better guarantee the right of victims to privacy without breaching the right of defendants to a fair trial. She finds that the ICC's practice on protective measures is, generally speaking, coherent overall with the right to privacy of victims who are witnesses at the ICC, and argues that the ICC ought to maintain its procedures whereby the need for protective measures is determined on a case-by-case basis and is justified by the need of protecting the privacy of victims. Additionally, she suggests that the ICC should: i) be as transparent as possible in making available information on protective measures; ii) improve its compliance with regard to the defendant's right to a fair, impartial and public trial in the context of protective measures; and iii) pursue additional forms of evidence, including new electronic evidence and written statements.

In the final substantive chapter of the book, Chapter 11, Anthony Abato examines the role of reparations orders in light of the rights that ICTs can provide. Focusing on the law and practice of ICC concerning reparations, particularly the *Bemba* case, he analyses reparations at international criminal justice institutions via the consideration of the perspectives of victims who claim reparations and the convicted individual. He argues that it is clear that victims hold high expectations which are in turn grounded in rights that are sometimes difficult to identify. Abato demonstrates that legal representatives of victims and the legal counsellors of the defence seemingly have fundamental disagreement concerning the set of rights and obligations held by the parties to reparations proceedings. For instance, the chapter closely follows the *Bemba* case where the accused was finally acquitted by the ICC Appeals Chamber and which gives rise to questions such as whether such an acquittal would impact Bemba's liability for reparations to victims and whether reparations could be even ordered by the ICC in case of acquittal.

At a more general level, Abato discusses the expectations of parties with regard to the outcomes of reparations proceedings. Furthermore, he provides a thoughtful discussion about ensuring and balancing the rights of individuals who are subject to reparations orders. Abato concludes that the ICC's reparations procedure must be clarified so that the convicted individuals can know the basis of their liability. Victims must be informed of their rights, meaning that they know what to expect and can trigger other remedies at other institutions. Furthermore, reparations proceedings in international criminal justice institutions should complement domestic and regional options: ICTs cannot or should not substitute states' responsibility to provide remedies, and are not suitable platforms for dealing with civil remedies.

In Chapter 12, Joanna Nicholson and Juan-Pablo Pérez-León-Acevedo (the editors of this book) provide some general and final thoughts at two levels. On the one hand, some final remarks concern the big picture of ensuring and balancing the rights of the defendant and victims at ICTs. On the other hand, some general thoughts are formulated as for either the rights of the defendant or the rights of the victims at international criminal justice institutions.

2 The content of internationally recognised human rights under the Rome Statute of the International Criminal Court

Sergii Masol

Introduction

Article 21(3) of the Rome Statute of the International Criminal Court (ICC) is at the heart of the study of human rights protection in the ICC regime. It stipulates that '[t]he application and interpretation of law (. . .) must be consistent with internationally recognized human rights'.[1] This obligation concerns all provisions of the Statute, including those laying down the rights of defendants and victims. However, the definition of 'internationally recognized human rights' is not provided: Article 21(3) is open-ended.[2] Some scholars have searched for the meaning attributed to this phrase in other international instruments.[3] Although the expression 'is extensively used in international relations (. . .) its content is neither precisely defined nor consistently detailed'.[4]

The present chapter clarifies where the ICC can find internationally recognised human rights. It begins by determining whether they can take account of domestic law. After that it proceeds to examine the issue of international soft law. The discussion continues with the consideration of international hard law at the universal and regional levels. Then four judicial approaches to the problem are inferred from the jurisprudence of the ICC. Finally, conclusions are drawn.

Domestic law

The qualifier 'internationally recognized' under Article 21(3) of the Rome Statute suggests a certain degree of acceptance by the subjects of international law,

1 Rome Statute of the International Criminal Court (adopted 17 July 1998, entered into force 1 July 2002) 2187 UNTS 90 (Rome Statute), Art. 21(3).

2 Lorenzo Gradoni, 'International Criminal Courts and Tribunals: Bound by Human Rights Norms. . . or Tied Down?' 19 *Leiden Journal of International Law* (2006) 847, p. 853.

3 Gerhard Hafner and Christina Binder, 'The Interpretation of Article 21(3) ICC Statute: Opinion Reviewed' 9 *Austrian Review of International and European Law* (2004) 163, pp. 178–83; Rebecca Young, '"Internationally Recognized Human Rights" before the International Criminal Court' 60 *International and Comparative Law Quarterly* (2011) 189, pp. 194–6; Stephen Bailey, 'Article 21(3) of the Rome Statute: A Plea for Clarity' 14 *International Criminal Law Review* (2014) 513, pp. 527–8.

4 Hafner and Binder, *supra* note 3, p. 183.

i.e. not all human rights are internationally recognised.[5] Smoking marijuana for recreational purposes as an aspect of the fundamental right to the free development of personality in Mexico[6] epitomises a right that is neither 'internationally recognized', nor even 'international' today. Is domestic law excluded altogether? Alex Davidson suggests three ways by which domestic law may become internationally recognised by the ICC: i) recognition of a human right in various national legal systems; ii) its approval by an international body; or more radically iii) *de facto* recognition by the ICC itself by a mere reference to that right.[7] The first two options resemble the formation of the classic sources of international law, viz, the general principles of law and customary international law, whereas the third option disregards the fact that 'recognized' means something that is already accomplished. Consequently, domestic law norms as such do not seem to be internationally recognised.

International soft law

While nobody denies that 'internationally recognized human rights' include international hard law, the status of international soft law is debatable. On the one hand, it is often taken for granted that it is included in Article 21(3).[8] On the other hand, some academics insist on a point-blank rejection of soft law as a source of international criminal law.[9] A more ambiguous stance is that the ICC is free, albeit not obliged, to rely thereon.[10] Unfortunately, the scholarly conclusions are seldom substantiated. Four opinions, however, deserve a closer look.

First, Volker Nerlich, relying on a literal interpretation of Article 21(3), admits that 'recognized' may not be the same as 'binding'.[11] Denis Abels also maintains

5 George E Edwards, 'International Human Rights Law Challenges to the New International Criminal Court: The Search and Seizure Right to Privacy' 26 *Yale Journal of International Law* (2001) 323, p. 376.

6 According to the National Supreme Court of Justice (Mexico), the right in question derives from the constitutional right to dignity which is also implicit in international treaties. Sentencia, No 548/2018 (31 October 2018) <www.scjn.gob.mx/sites/default/files/listas/documento_dos/2018-10/AR-548-2018-181018.pdf> accessed 5 February 2019.

7 Alex Davidson, 'Human Rights Protection before the International Criminal Court: Assessing the Scope and Application of Article 21(3) of the Rome Statute' 18 *International Community Law Review* (2016) 72, p. 89.

8 Claire Callejon, 'Article 21. Droit applicable' in Julian Fernandez and Xavier Pacreau (eds), *Statut de Rome de la Cour pénale internationale: Commentaire article par article*, vol I (Pedone, 2012), p. 777.

9 Aleksey G Kibalnik, 'Vvedenie v mezhdunarodnoe ugolovnoe pravo' in Anatoliy V Naumov and Aleksey G Kibalnik (eds), *Mezhdunarodnoe ugolovnoe pravo* (3rd edn, Yurayt, 2017), p. 33.

10 Ondřej Svaček, 'Human Rights before the International Criminal Court' 5 *Czech Yearbook of Public and Private International Law* (2014) 327, p. 330.

11 Volker Nerlich, 'Article 21(3) of the ICC Statute: Identifying and Applying "Internationally Recognized Human Rights"' in Paolo Lobba and Triestino Mariniello (eds), *Judicial Dialogue on Human Rights: The Practice of International Criminal Tribunals* (Brill Nijhoff, 2017), p. 87.

(in a more forceful manner) that being 'recognized' differs from being legally binding. In the latter scholar's view, the recognition of a norm by universal bodies, such as the United Nations (UN) General Assembly, makes it fall within the purview of Article 21(3).[12] Nevertheless, he defies the qualifier. Anything must be pronounced in public to be known, but if such a pronouncement of a right at the international level constitutes recognition, then the difference between international human rights and internationally recognised human rights amounts to naught.

Second, Volker Nerlich argues that it should be permissible for the ICC to refer to soft law instruments that formed the basis for the inclusion of certain provisions (for example, those relating to the rights of victims) in the Rome Statute at the drafting stage.[13] Nevertheless, the mandate of international judges differs fundamentally from that of lawmakers who can avail themselves of not only legal, but also non-legal tools during negotiations. The stringent requirements of Article 21(3) – 'must be consistent' and 'internationally recognized' – are not readily suitable for moral, religious, utilitarian or other factors. Still, judicial recourse to the circumstances of the conclusion of the Rome Statute is possible by exploring other avenues, notably the customary methods of treaty interpretation as reflected in the Vienna Convention on the Law of Treaties.[14]

Third, Alex Davidson believes that the word 'recognized' does not add much, because every international human right is in a way recognised.[15] The only consequence of being 'recognized' is that this right needs to be articulated in a determinable source.[16] At first sight, one might assume that this interpretation of Article 21(3) justifies the exclusion of soft law sources. Surprisingly, Alex Davidson further argues that 'internationally recognized human rights' is not the same as 'internationally recognized human rights law' and, thus, the former includes soft law.[17] In addition, this is supported by his broad reading of Article 21(3) with a reference to the *travaux préparatoires*, during which one of the delegates suggested that 'the law applied should be consistent with certain internationally recognized values'.[18] Leaving this mishmash of self-contradictory claims aside, I think that the argumentation is weak for the following reasons: i) the simultaneous presence of the words 'recognized' and 'law' would be tautological (to put it another way, what is the point of being 'recognized' then?); ii) the word 'law' does not automatically make something hard law (ironically, the expression 'soft

12 Denis Abels, *Prisoners of the International Community: The Legal Position of Persons Detained at International Criminal Tribunals* (TMC Asser Press, 2012), p. 141.

13 Nerlich, *supra* note 11, p. 87.

14 Vienna Convention on the Law of Treaties (adopted 23 May 1969, entered into force 27 January 1980) 1155 UNTS 331, Arts. 31–33, especially Art. 32.

15 Davidson, *supra* note 7, p. 84.

16 Ibid., pp. 84–5.

17 Ibid.

18 United Nations Diplomatic Conference of Plenipotentiaries on the Establishment of an International Criminal Court (Rome 15 June – 17 July 1998), Official Records, vol II, Summary Records of the Plenary Meetings and of the Meetings of the Committee of the Whole, A/CONF.183/13 (New York: United Nations, 2002), p. 222. See also Davidson, *supra* note 7, pp. 86–7.

law' itself contains the word 'law'); and iii) the preparatory work is inconclusive, as it can support both interpretations: a broad one if we, following Alex Davidson, focus on the unfixed concept of values, or a narrow one if we underscore the limitation imposed by the word 'certain' and distinguish the recommendatory 'should' in the draft text from the obligative 'must' in the final version.

Fourth, Alex Davidson presents a pragmatic argument for the 'usefulness of soft law as guidance in determining human rights standards' citing, in this regard, Jann Kleffner.[19] However, it utterly distorts both Article 21(3) and the original writings of the German scholar because: i) the mere 'guidance' discords with the obligatory message of 'must'; and ii) Jann Kleffner is discussing Article 17(2) ('the principles of due process recognized by international law') – not Article 21(3) – in the pertinent passages of his monograph.[20] Even if Article 21(3) were implied, Jann Kleffner accurately observes that the rights of defendants are international legal standards (which should, by the way, assuage Alex Davidson's concern about the word 'law') and that they are to be found in treaties, customary international law or general principles of law, i.e. hard law, while it is the interpretation and application of the legal standards in those sources by international human rights bodies that provide a useful means for the clarification of the statutory norms on admissibility.[21] Indeed, a differentiation must be made between the substance of a norm and its form.[22] The fact that a norm is contained in soft law sources (for instance, views of the UN Human Rights Committee) does not necessarily mean that the norm itself is non-binding.

Thus, none of the arguments is persuasive enough to deny that internationally recognised human rights belong only to the category of international hard law norms. At the same time, the question remains whether these norms should be universally recognised (i.e. universally binding) or whether something less than universal suffices.[23]

International hard law

Universal recognition

The ordinary meaning of the term 'universal' is 'of, affecting, or done by all people (. . .) in the world (. . .) applicable to all cases',[24] while what is meant by the

19 Davidson, *supra* note 7, p. 84, referring to Jann K Kleffner, *Complementarity in the Rome Statute and National Criminal Jurisdictions* (Oxford University Press, 2008), pp. 129–30.
20 Kleffner, *supra* note 19, pp. 129–30.
21 Ibid.
22 Robert Kolb, *Theory of International Law* (Hart Publishing, 2016), p. 152.
23 Although the Vienna Declaration and Programme of Action expressly called all human rights universal, there are salient differences regarding their substance and scope in different regions and national societies. Edwards, *supra* note 5, p. 381. Cf Nerlich, *supra* note 11, p. 83 (claiming that there is nothing 'specifically "European" about the ECtHR's jurisprudence that would be at odds with "universal" human rights law').
24 Angus Stevenson and Christine A Lindberg (eds), *New Oxford American Dictionary* (3rd edn, Oxford University Press 2010) <www.oxfordreference.com.ezproxy.eui.eu/view/10.1093/

word 'international' is 'between two or more nations' or 'all or many nations'.[25] No doubt, the universal recognition of the rights of defendants or victims is international. Hence, universal multilateral conventions such as the International Covenant on Civil and Political Rights (ICCPR)[26] – via the customary nature of their norms – and customary international law reach the threshold of being 'internationally recognized'.

One of the problems concerning universal treaties is their paucity. Stanislav Chernichenko remarked shortly after the adoption of the Rome Statute that 'there are almost no ideally universal international treaties (to which all States of the world would have been parties), especially in the field of human rights'.[27] Although the situation with ratifications of, and accessions to, human rights treaties has improved since the late 1990s, none of them can be deemed to be 'ideally universal'. Another problem is the litany of reservations made to these treaties.[28] Do such reservations preclude international recognition? The most adequate solution proposed is to assess this on a case-by-case basis.[29]

Although Adriaan Bos claims that Article 21(3) points to exclusively universal recognition,[30] most commentators debunk his view.[31] First, Article 21(3) does not expressly prohibit reliance on non-universal human rights norms.[32] Second, a contextual interpretation provides some guidance. Pursuant to the Rome Statute, crimes against humanity include '[p]ersecution (. . .) on (. . .) grounds that are *universally recognized* as impermissible under international law'.[33] If the Statute differentiates between the terms 'internationally' and 'universally', their content

acref/9780195392883.001.0001/m_en_us1302328?rskey=7eMQmZ&result=86966> accessed 5 February 2019.

25 Ibid. <www.oxfordreference.com.ezproxy.eui.eu/view/10.1093/acref/9780195392883.001.0001/m_en_us1258651?rskey=BP1wSb&result=42461> accessed 5 February 2019.

26 Göran Sluiter, 'International Criminal Proceedings and the Protection of Human Rights' (2002–2003) 37 *New England Law Review* 935, p. 940.

27 Stanislav V Chernichenko, *Teoriya mezhdunarodnogo prava*, vol II (NIMP, 1999), p. 430 (translation the author's).

28 For instance, Jordan and the Maldives made reservations to the Convention on the Rights of the Child regarding the freedom of religion. See <https://treaties.un.org/Pages/ViewDetails.aspx?src=IND&mtdsg_no=IV-11&chapter=4&lang=en> accessed 5 February 2019.

29 Hafner and Binder, *supra* note 3, p. 189.

30 Adriaan Bos, '1948–1998: The Universal Declaration of Human Rights and the Statute of the International Criminal Court' 22 *Fordham International Law Journal* (1998) 229, p. 234.

31 See, e.g., Krit Zeegers, *International Criminal Tribunals and Human Rights Law: Adherence and Contextualization* (TMC Asser Press, 2016), pp. 93–4.

32 Philippe Currat, 'L'interprétation du Statut de Rome' 20 *Revue québécoise de droit international* (2007) 137, p. 158; Daniel Sheppard, 'The International Criminal Court and "Internationally Recognized Human Rights": Understanding Article 21(3) of the Rome Statute' 10 *International Criminal Law Review* (2010) 43, pp. 63–4. But see Hafner and Binder, *supra* note 3, p. 187.

33 Art. 7(1)(h), Rome Statute (emphasis added).

should be different: the former, arguably, means something less than the latter.[34] Third, this conclusion is confirmed by the above-mentioned dictionary definitions, with the caveat that 'international' may at times mean 'all nations', thus becoming universal.

Regional recognition

When it comes to the regional systems, five arguments have been put forward as to why the Convention for the Protection of Human Rights and Fundamental Freedoms (ECHR) should be the primary source of reference. However, all of them can be rebutted.

First, it has been claimed that the ECHR provides for the highest standard of protection among its regional counterparts and, therefore, contains internationally recognised human rights.[35] As a preliminary remark, it must be stressed that the highest protection for one party to, or participant of, the ICC proceedings does not always tally with the highest possible protection for the other. Now let me conduct a brief comparative analysis of the regional human rights systems.

The African Charter on Human and Peoples' Rights (ACHPR) does not have a derogation clause,[36] while Article 4(2) of the Arab Charter on Human Rights and Article 27(2) of the American Convention on Human Rights (ACHR) contain more extensive lists of non-derogable rights than Article 15(2) of the ECHR. Moreover, the treaty-based list of non-derogable rights has been expanded by the Inter-American Court of Human Rights (IACtHR).[37] Besides this, the IACtHR has ruled that amnesty cannot be an obstacle to investigating and punishing

34 Edwards, *supra* note 5, p. 377; Gilbert Bitti, 'Article 21 and the Hierarchy of Sources of Law before the ICC' in Carsten Stahn (ed.), *The Law and Practice of the International Criminal Court* (Oxford University Press, 2015), p. 434.

35 Gudrun Hochmayr, 'Applicable Law in Practice and Theory: Interpreting Article 21 of the ICC Statute' 12 *Journal of International Criminal Justice* (2014) 655, p. 675; Davidson, *supra* note 7, p. 94.

36 This has been explicitly underlined in *Commission nationale des droits de l'Homme et des libertés v Chad*, Decision, African Commission on Human and Peoples' Rights, Communication No 74/92 (11 October 1995), para 21 (or para 36 in the French and Portuguese versions). Cf Nsongurua J Udombana, 'Toward the African Court on Human and Peoples' Rights: Better Late than Never' 3 *Yale Human Rights and Development Law Journal* (2000) 45, pp. 62–3 (claiming that the so-called 'claw-back' Charter clauses, such as references to national security or to domestic law, are worse than the well-defined derogation clauses in other human rights treaties).

37 *Habeas corpus in Emergency Situations (Arts. 27(2), 25(1) and 7(6) American Convention on Human Rights)*, Advisory Opinion OC-8/87, Inter-American Court of Human Rights Series A No 8 (30 January 1987), para 44; *Judicial Guarantees in States of Emergency (Arts. 27(2), 25 and 8 American Convention on Human Rights)*, Advisory Opinion OC-9/87, Inter-American Court of Human Rights Series A No 9 (6 October 1987), para 41. However, the derogation clause of the ACHR has a lower threshold of applicability than the one in the ECHR. See Thomas Buergenthal, 'The American and European Conventions on Human Rights: Similarities and Differences' 30 *American University Law Review* (1980) 155, p. 165.

those responsible for violations of victims' non-derogable rights.[38] As regards the defendant's right to a fair trial, it has held that civilians cannot be prosecuted in military criminal courts.[39] The IACtHR was in the vanguard of declaring forced disappearance a violation of multiple human rights despite the absence of such a provision in any of the treaties of the Inter-American system at the time.[40] The contribution of the IACtHR to the development of the rights of victims, including their right to truth, and the concept of reparations is also colossal.[41] So is the contribution of the Inter-American[42] and African[43] systems to the enhancement of the rights of indigenous peoples. The universal and other regional systems have much to learn from the African one when it comes to group rights.[44] Importantly, the ACHPR contains some justiciable rights of peoples, such as the right to a general satisfactory environment favourable to their development.[45] The ACHPR also protects a number of justiciable economic, social and cultural rights of individuals, such as the right to health.[46] It is in fact the first international treaty protecting all three so-called generations of human rights in a single document and without any distinction regarding their justiciability. Despite the

38 *Barrios Altos v Peru (Merits)*, Judgment, Inter-American Court of Human Rights Series C No 87 (14 March 2001), para 41. Cf *Marguš v Croatia* App No 4455/10 (ECtHR, 27 May 2014), para 139.

39 See, e.g., *Castillo Petruzzi and others v Peru (Merits, Reparations and Costs)*, Judgment, Inter-American Court of Human Rights Series C No 52 (30 May 1999), paras 128–9. Cf *Ergin v Turkey (No 6)* App No 47533/99 (ECtHR, 4 May 2006), para 42; UN Human Rights Committee, 'General Comment No 32' (23 August 2007), UN Doc CCPR/C/GC/32, para 22.

40 *Velásquez Rodríguez v Honduras*, Judgment, Inter-American Court of Human Rights Series C No 4 (29 July 1988), paras 155–8.

41 Jo M Pasqualucci, 'The Inter-American Human Rights System: Progress Made and Still to Be Made' (2009) 52 *German Yearbook of International Law* 181, pp. 197–9, 206–12.

42 *The Mayagna (Sumo) Awas Tingni Community v Nicaragua*, Judgment, Inter-American Court of Human Rights Series C No 79 (31 August 2001); *The Yakye Axa Indigenous Community v Paraguay (Merits, Reparations and Costs)*, Judgment, Inter-American Court of Human Rights Series C No 125 (17 June 2005); *The Kichwa Indigenous People of Sarayaku v Ecuador (Merits and Reparations)*, Judgment, Inter-American Court of Human Rights Series C No 245 (27 June 2012). See also Pasqualucci, *supra* note 41, pp. 203–5.

43 *Centre for Minority Rights Development (Kenya) and Minority Rights Group International on behalf of Endorois Welfare Council v Kenya*, Decision, African Commission on Human and Peoples' Rights, Communication No 276/2003 (4 February 2010). See also George Mukundi Wachira, 'Rights of Indigenous Peoples in Africa' in Manisuli Ssenyonjo (ed.), *The African Regional Human Rights System: 30 Years after the African Charter on Human and Peoples' Rights* (Martinus Nijhoff Publishers, 2012), pp. 195–212.

44 Basil Ugochukwu, Opeoluwa Badaru and Obiora Okafor, 'Group Rights under the African Charter on Human and Peoples' Rights: Concept, Praxis and Prospects' in Ssenyonjo, *The African Regional Human Rights System, supra* note 43, p. 117.

45 *Social and Economic Rights Action Center (SERAC) and Center for Economic and Social Rights (CESR) v Nigeria*, Decision, African Commission on Human and Peoples' Rights, Communication No 155/96 (27 October 2001), paras 52–3.

46 *Sudan Human Rights Organisation and Centre on Housing Rights and Evictions (COHRE) v Sudan*, Decision, African Commission on Human and Peoples' Rights, Communication Nos 279/03 and 296/05 (27 May 2009), paras 208–10.

generality and vagueness of the formulations of these rights, the African Commission on Human and Peoples' Rights has developed their normative content in its post-2001 jurisprudence and has even read into the text of the ACHPR some human rights not explicitly enshrined therein (e.g., the right to housing).[47] It candidly noted:

> [N]ormatively, the African Charter is an innovative and unique (. . .) document (. . .) in placing special emphasis on the rights of 'peoples.' It substantially departs from the narrow formulations of other regional and universal human rights instruments by weaving a tapestry which includes the three 'generations' of rights: civil and political rights; economic, social, and cultural rights; and group and peoples' rights.[48]

Furthermore, the Protocol to the African Charter on Human and Peoples' Rights on the Rights of Women in Africa goes beyond previous human rights treaties, both universal and regional, for the first time articulating certain rights of women in a legally binding document, particularly the prohibition of verbal and economic violence against women.[49] In conclusion, all the above-mentioned examples confirm that the standard of protection under the ECHR is not the highest with respect to every human right.

Second, the European paragon has been claimed to have the highest level of influence among all human rights protection systems[50] and to enjoy universal legitimacy, because its judgments are cited as persuasive authority by international and regional (quasi-)judicial bodies.[51] Nevertheless, a similar view has been expressed as regards not only the European Court of Human Rights (ECtHR), but also the IACtHR.[52] Moreover, the avoidance of Eurocentrism by the ICC may strengthen its own legitimacy considering the post-colonial criticism of the

47 *Social and Economic Rights Action Center (SERAC) and Center for Economic and Social Rights (CESR) v Nigeria*, *supra* note 45, para 60; Manisuli Ssenyonjo, 'Economic, Social and Cultural Rights in the African Charter' in Ssenyonjo, *The African Regional Human Rights System*, *supra* note 43, pp. 58–60, 69–81, 98–9.

48 *Centre for Minority Rights Development (Kenya) and Minority Rights Group International on behalf of Endorois Welfare Council v Kenya*, *supra* note 43, para 149.

49 Protocol to the African Charter on Human and Peoples' Rights on the Rights of Women in Africa (adopted 11 July 2003, entered into force 25 November 2005) CAB/LEG/66.6 (13 September 2000).

50 Antonio Cassese, 'The Impact of the European Convention on Human Rights on the International Criminal Tribunal for the former Yugoslavia' in Paul Mahoney and others (eds), *Protecting Human Rights: The European Perspective – Studies in Memory of Rolv Ryssdal* (Carl Heymanns Verlag KG, 2000), p. 213.

51 Nicolas AJ Croquet, 'The International Criminal Court and the Treatment of Defence Rights: A Mirror of the European Court of Human Rights' Jurisprudence?' 11 *Human Rights Law Review* (2011) 91, p. 123.

52 Emanuela Fronza, 'Human Rights and Criminal Law: Reference to the Case Law of Human Rights Bodies by International Criminal Tribunals' in Robert Kolb and Damien Scalia (eds), *Droit international penal: Précis* (2nd edn, Helbing Lichtenhahn, 2012), p. 394.

civilising mission of international criminal law.[53] A more general concern relates to any regional centrism by the ICC that can potentially make it culturally biased or make it look biased and, as a result, not truly international.[54]

Third, it has been argued that the ECHR reflects customary international law, as it 'dates from 1950 and served as a model for the ICCPR',[55] or that the ECHR 'has in large parts led to the development of global customary law' owing to the numerous cross-references among international human rights bodies and international criminal tribunals (ICTs).[56] However, neither of these explanations is tenable. First, they speciously refer to the treaty as a whole or in large parts instead of indicating the concrete norms that might indeed be customary; and, secondly, they fail to demonstrate the classic elements of customary international law: State practice and *opinio juris.* Ironically, my latter counter-argument can also be advanced against a claim that the case law of the ECtHR does not constitute customary international law on account of the Strasbourg court's coverage of 'only a limited geographical area'.[57] In my view, a regional treaty norm may reflect a regional or local custom and, at least in theory, be part of customary or general international law.[58] Alternatively, recourse to regional human rights treaties as interpreted by regional courts (e.g., the ECtHR) may – as a supplementary means – help to flag norms of customary international law.[59]

Fourth, in practical terms, it is easier to refer to the ECHR system than to the other regional courts due to the availability of thousands of cases concerning various human rights norms[60] in HUDOC, a user-friendly electronic database. As of 31 December 2017, the ECtHR had delivered around 20,600 judgments,[61]

53 Sergey Vasiliev, 'International Criminal Tribunals in the Shadow of Strasbourg and Politics of Cross-fertilisation' 84 *Nordic Journal of International Law* (2015) 371, pp. 400–1.

54 Annika Jones, 'Insights into an Emerging Relationship: Use of Human Rights Jurisprudence at the International Criminal Court' 16 *Human Rights Law Review* (2016) 701, pp. 706–7.

55 Alexander Zahar and Göran Sluiter, *International Criminal Law: A Critical Introduction* (Oxford University Press, 2008), p. 279.

56 Christophe Deprez, 'Extent of Applicability of Human Rights Standards to Proceedings before the International Criminal Court: On Possible Reductive Factors' 12 *International Criminal Law Review* (2012) 721, pp. 732–3.

57 *Zigiranyirazo v Prosecutor* (Decision on Protais Zigiranyirazo's Motion for Damages) ICTR-2001-01-073, T Ch III (18 June 2012), para 34.

58 Joe Verhoeven, 'Article 21 of the Rome Statute and the Ambiguities of Applicable Law' 33 *Netherlands Yearbook of International Law* (2002) 3, p. 14.

59 Antonio Cassese, 'The Influence of the European Court of Human Rights on International Criminal Tribunals – Some Methodological Remarks' in Morten Bergsmo (ed.), *Human Rights and Criminal Justice for the Downtrodden: Essays in Honour of Asbjørn Eide* (Martinus Nijhoff Publishers, 2003), p. 50; Jones, *supra* note 54, p. 707.

60 Cassese, 'The Impact of the European Convention on Human Rights', *supra* note 50, 216; Croquet, *supra* note 51, 128; Robert Roth and Françoise Tulkens, 'The Influence of the European Court of Human Rights' Case Law on (International) Criminal Law: Introduction' 9 *Journal of International Criminal Justice* (2011) 571, p. 574; Jones, *supra* note 54, p. 725; Nerlich, *supra* note 11, p. 83.

61 Overview, 1959–2017, ECHR, p. 4 <www.echr.coe.int/Documents/Overview_19592017_ENG.pdf> accessed 5 February 2019.

while the IACtHR had rendered only 344[62] judgments and decisions, and the African Court on Human and Peoples' Rights had finalised only 43 cases.[63] On the one hand, in this plethora of European cases, certain issues that are very relevant to the activity of the ICTs may – and, in fact, have been – dealt with by the ECtHR more frequently and more thoroughly than by the other human rights institutions (e.g. an appraisal of the prohibition of torture).[64] On the other hand, it is mainly the IACtHR and the Inter-American Commission on Human Rights that have regularly had to respond to massive breaches of human rights, i.e. the issues which are likely to amount to international crimes.[65] Regarding the African system, the unfilled docket of the African Court on Human and Peoples' Rights prevents it from realising its enormous potential.[66]

Fifth, it has been claimed that one of the advantages of the ECHR system *vis-à-vis* its regional counterparts is that its jurisprudence encompasses both common law and civil law traditions.[67] This is, however, not persuasive, because the same argument can be presented regarding the Inter-American system. In one of its advisory opinions, the IACtHR took into consideration the fact that the legal systems of some States Parties to the ACHR followed the common law tradition, whereas others belonged to the family of civil law.[68] Moreover, the European amalgamation itself can be questioned. All but four States Parties to the ECHR belong to the Romano-Germanic legal family, and, hence, there is, arguably, a jurisprudential bias regarding the interpretation of certain legal concepts, for example, the right to a fair trial in criminal proceedings.[69] Last, a haughty discussion of diversity within the parochial dichotomy in question diminishes the weight of other legal families, such as Islamic law.

As a result, notwithstanding the mainstream academic discourse or practical convenience, the ICC cannot refer to the ECHR system in the event of strong opposition to a norm which thereby precludes it from becoming 'recognized'

62 IACtHR, Decisions and Judgments <www.corteidh.or.cr/index.php/en/decisions-and-judgments> accessed 5 February 2019.

63 African Court on Human and Peoples' Rights, Contentious Matters, Finalised Cases <http://en.african-court.org/index.php/cases#finalised-cases> accessed 5 February 2019.

64 Elena Maculan, 'Judicial Definition of Torture as a Paradigm of Cross-fertilisation: Combining Harmonisation and Expansion' 84 *Nordic Journal of International Law* (2015) 456, pp. 475–6.

65 Julia Gebhard, 'Arguing Human Rights from the Bench? How Judges in International Criminal Courts Perceive International Human Rights Law' in Mayeul Hiéramente and Patricia Schneider (eds), *The Defence in International Criminal Trials: Observations on the Role of the Defence at the ICTY, ICTR and ICC* (Nomos, 2016), p. 90.

66 Rachel Murray, 'A Comparison between the African and European Courts of Human Rights' 2 *African Human Rights Law Journal* (2002) 195, pp. 213, 218–19.

67 Cassese, 'The Influence of the European Court of Human Rights', *supra* note 59, p. 25; Roth and Tulkens, *supra* note 60, p. 574.

68 *The Word 'Laws' in Article 30 of the American Convention on Human Rights*, Advisory Opinion OC-6/86, Inter-American Court of Human Rights Series A No 6 (9 May 1986), para 20.

69 Nerlich, *supra* note 11, pp. 83–4.

beyond Europe. Nor can it, for good reason, refer to any other regional system alone. The UN Human Rights Committee opined about a limitation on the exercise of the right to freedom of expression:

> '[T]he concept of morals derives from many social, philosophical and religious traditions; consequently, limitations (. . .) for the purpose of protecting morals must be based on principles not deriving exclusively from a single tradition'. Any such limitations must be understood in the light of universality of human rights.[70]

This position can, *mutatis mutandis*, be transposed to our discussion. The recognition of diversity can only bolster the universality of human rights,[71] whereas a failure to take into account various regional human rights norms – many of which are inherently linked to morality[72] – may undermine it.[73] Thus, the expression 'internationally recognized human rights' under Article 21(3) does not give the green light to references to a single regional treaty[74] unless the norm concerned exists within the broader normative framework. Moreover, regional systems of human rights protection containing regional-specific variations, even if taken together, do not represent the entire planet. Arguably, even a combined reference to the ECHR and the ACHR may not be enough, because Europe and the Americas 'have a significantly greater historical and legal affinity than either of them has with other regions'.[75] One should also remember that there is still no fully-fledged Asian system.[76]

The *travaux préparatoires* of the Rome Statute largely support this conclusion. The phrase 'internationally recognized human rights' initially related to the provision dealing with evidence.[77] These rights were, according to the commentary on the Syracuse Draft, reduced to those 'enumerated in *widely ratified* International Treaties, such as the Torture Convention',[78] which, as of 1 July 1995, had ninety States Parties. This confirms that bilateral and other agreements with few

70 UN Human Rights Committee, 'General Comment No 34' (12 September 2011), UN Doc CCPR/C/GC/34, para 32.

71 Vienna Declaration and Programme of Action, UN Doc A/CONF.157/23 (25 June 1993), para 37.

72 See, e.g., Eckart Klein, 'Zum (völker-)rechtlichen Unter- und Hintergrund von Menschenrechtsverträgen: Gibt es ein menschenrechtliches corpus iuris?' (2017) 55 *Archiv des Völkerrechts* 303, p. 304.

73 Rachel Murray, 'International Human Rights: Neglect of Perspectives from African Institutions' 55 *International and Comparative Law Quarterly* (2006) 193, p. 203.

74 Bailey, *supra* note 3, p. 532.

75 Buergenthal, *supra* note 37, p. 156.

76 Jones, *supra* note 54, p. 707.

77 Donald K Piragoff and Paula Clarke, 'Article 69. Evidence' in Otto Triffterer and Kai Ambos (eds), *The Rome Statute of the International Criminal Court: A Commentary* (3rd edn, CH Beck · Hart · Nomos, 2016), p. 1333.

78 Draft Statute for an International Criminal Court – Alternative to the International Law Commission's Draft (Syracuse – Draft) prepared by a Committee of Experts, Syracuse/Freiburg (July 1995), Art. 44(6) (emphasis added).

parties are excluded.[79] This also rebuts Daniel Sheppard's claim that – mindful of Article 21(2) of the Rome Statute which permits inconsistency in the case law – the ICC can apply different human rights standards to different defendants so long as the international obligations of the States that would normally exercise jurisdiction over a case are met.[80] The other confutations expressed in academic literature are as follows: i) the non-discrimination clause under Article 21(3) must be identical for all States;[81] ii) the coherence of international jurisprudence is important despite the wording of Article 21(2);[82] iii) the universality of human rights should preclude human rights protection in the ICC context from being geographically relative;[83] and iv) Article 21(3) would have made it crystal clear if a reading that differentiates between the various regions was intended.[84]

The Zutphen Draft of the Rome Statute spoke about 'internationally protected human rights' instead of the excised phrase 'international law', with a view to not reducing the consideration of external human rights norms to treaty law.[85] As the phrase 'internationally protected human rights' is often used interchangeably with 'internationally recognized human rights',[86] customary international law and general principles of law are covered. Finally, at the Rome Conference Article 21(3) was virtually unanimously accepted by the drafters.[87]

Judicial approaches

It has been suggested that the meaning of 'internationally recognized human rights' must have been left to the ICC to determine.[88] As most of the cases deal with certain issues in a repetitive manner, four major approaches will be canvassed.

A smorgasbord of laws

The prevalent approach of the ICC has been to enumerate many universal and regional instruments without any explanation and unabashedly declare that a

79 Putting aside the issue of customary international law, it may also indicate that there is no need for all States Parties to the Rome Statute to ratify, or accede to, an international convention. Otherwise, the only relevant human rights treaty would be the Convention on the Rights of the Child.

80 Sheppard, *supra* note 32, pp. 65–7.

81 Hochmayr, *supra* note 35, p. 674; Davidson, *supra* note 7, p. 89.

82 Bailey, *supra* note 3, pp. 531–32; Davidson, *supra* note 7, pp. 89–90.

83 Davidson, *supra* note 7, pp. 77, 89–90.

84 Ibid., p. 89.

85 Preparatory Committee on the Establishment of an International Criminal Court, Report of the Inter-Sessional Meeting from 19 to 30 January 1998 in Zutphen, the Netherlands, UN Doc A/AC.249/1998/L.13 (4 February 1998), p. 118.

86 Edwards, *supra* note 5, pp. 379–380 (admitting, however, that the former may be deemed as a subset of the latter, for instance when certain recognised rights are constantly violated).

87 The only discord concerned the definition of 'gender'. Margaret M deGuzman 'Article 21. Applicable Law' in Triffterer and Ambos, *supra* note 77, pp. 947–8.

88 Jones, *supra* note 54, p. 711.

certain right of a defendant or of a victim is internationally recognised.[89] The key criterion appears to be the mere regulation of certain legal affairs by those instruments. For example, in *Bemba*, the ICC harnessed Article 21(3) to refer to the principle of fairness of criminal proceedings 'as enshrined in international legal instruments, such as (. . .) the Universal Declaration of Human Rights, [the ICCPR, the ECHR, the ACHR and the ACHPR]'.[90]

Occasionally, the ICC has used Article 21(3) to explicitly refer to universally recognised human rights. These rulings do not, however, shed light on the term due to the medley of both universal and regional instruments. For example, in *Lubanga*, the ICC Appeals Chamber held that 'a universally recognized human right (. . .) finds expression in international and regional treaties' (referring in a footnote to the ICCPR, the ECHR, the ACHR and the ACHPR).[91] In another case, the same Chamber consisting of the same judges held that 'the [ICCPR] and many regional conventions (. . .) [give] effect to universally recognized human rights *norms*'.[92] The addition of the word 'norms' does not seem to serve any purpose here. In theory, it might suggest the exclusion of case law. However, the ICC has used Article 21(3) extensively to refer to international human rights jurisprudence.[93] It not only gives precise contours to human rights norms that are usually framed in generic terms, but also ensures that the ICC keeps track of the living body of international human rights law.[94]

The ICC's approach permits it to not delve too deeply into the problem of the relevance and (non-)binding character of an instrument. Instead, the substance of a right is brought to the forefront.[95] Such uncertainty not only imposes an enormous burden on all parties to, and participants in, proceedings, but also impairs the legitimacy of the Court.[96] Some clarification was provided by Judge Pikis: reliance on a set of international instruments may tacitly confirm that the

89 Sheppard, *supra* note 32, p. 49 (calling it a 'shotgun' method); Zeegers, *supra* note 31, pp. 94–5.

90 Decision on the Prosecutor's application for leave to appeal Pre-Trial Chamber III's decision on disclosure, *Prosecutor v Bemba*, (ICC-01/05-01/08-75), Pre-T Ch III, 25 August 2008, para 13 (emphasis omitted).

91 Reasons for 'Decision of the Appeals Chamber on the Defence application "Demande de suspension de toute action ou procédure afin de permetrre la désignation d'un nouveau Conseil de la Défense" filed on 20 February 2007' issued on 23 February 2007, *Prosecutor v Lubanga*, (ICC-01/04-01/06-844), A Ch, 9 March 2007, para 12.

92 Judgment on the Prosecutor's Application for Extraordinary Review of Pre-Trial Chamber I's 31 March 2006 Decision Denying Leave to Appeal, *Situation in the Democratic Republic of the Congo*, (ICC-01/04-168), A Ch, 13 July 2006, para 38 (emphasis added).

93 See, e.g., Fourth Decision on Victims' Participation, *Prosecutor v Bemba*, (ICC-01/05-01/08-320), Pre-T Ch III, 12 December 2008, para 40.

94 Ann Marie Thake, 'The (In)Admissibility of Unlawfully Obtained Evidence at the International Criminal Court' 28 *Hague Yearbook of International Law* (2015) 161, p. 181.

95 Bitti, *supra* note 34, p. 436.

96 Sheppard, *supra* note 32, p. 44; Zeegers, *supra* note 31, pp. 95–6.

court alludes to customary international law.[97] But this may be difficult to accept if the ICC refers to non-binding resolutions, especially regional ones.[98]

The method in question allows the ICC to avoid meticulously differentiating between international instruments. On the one hand, Antonio Cassese observes that the norms set forth in the ECHR, to a certain extent, clarify those of the Universal Declaration of Human Rights and that 'there is great commonality between the European Convention and the ICCPR'.[99] Furthermore, it has been argued that 'every human rights provision should be interpreted as being compatible with all other human rights, including through the principle of avoiding any "cracks" between human rights'.[100] On the other hand, Sergey Vasiliev stresses that the conception of a unified body of international human rights law norms is mistaken.[101] Indeed, the ostensible uniformity evanesces when it comes to the concrete formulations in the texts and especially jurisprudence because of the different institutional dynamics of the respective (quasi-)judicial bodies.[102] Let me give three illustrative examples.

The first is the right to be informed of the reasons for the arrest and of the charges. Article 5(2) of the ECHR sets a uniform threshold of 'promptness', while Article 9(2) of the ICCPR differentiates between the 'promptness' of being informed of the charges and a higher threshold of human rights protection – 'at the time of arrest' that denotes immediateness – regarding the reasons for the

97 Decision on the Prosecutor's "Application for Leave to Reply to 'Conclusions de la défense en réponse au mémoire d'appel du Procureur'", *Prosecutor v Lubanga,* (ICC-01/04-01/06-424), A Ch, 12 September 2006, Separate Opinion of Judge Pikis, para 3.

98 Decision establishing the principles and procedures to be applied to reparations, *Prosecutor v Lubanga,* (ICC-01/04-01/06-2904), T Ch I, 7 August 2012, para 185 (adding that it is merely guided by them). Cf Zeegers, *supra* note 31, p. 93 (claiming that the threshold for international recognition under Article 21(3) is lower than for customary international law).

99 Cassese, 'The Impact of the European Convention on Human Rights' *supra* note 50, p. 215. Cf John G Merrills, *The Development of International Law by the European Court of Human Rights* (2nd edn, Manchester University Press, 1993), p. 18 (noting that despite the considerable differences between various human rights treaties, 'there is a great deal of overlap, especially in the area of civil and political rights').

100 Martin Scheinin, 'European Human Rights as Universal Rights: In Defence of a Holistic Understanding of Human Rights' in Eva Brems and Janneke Gerards (eds), *Shaping Rights in the ECHR: The Role of the European Court of Human Rights in Determining the Scope of Human Rights* (Cambridge University Press, 2013), p. 259.

101 At the same time, he argues that, under Article 21(3) of the Rome Statute, the ICC judges have discretion to define the content of 'internationally recognized human rights'. Vasiliev, *supra* note 53, pp. 391ff.

102 Sheppard, *supra* note 32, pp. 53–4. In this respect, Daniel Sheppard distinguishes between binding judgments of regional human rights courts and non-binding views of the UN human rights treaty bodies. This distinction is, however, not justified. The former are binding exclusively on respondent States and not even on the courts themselves. Hence, views (and, *mutatis mutandis,* general comments and concluding observations) and judgments can, on an equal footing, be deemed as authoritative interpretations of the underlying human rights conventions for the purposes of their use by the ICC.

arrest.[103] Here, the human rights protection at the universal level appears to be better than at the regional one.

The situation can, of course, be the opposite, as is the case with the right to seek and receive asylum. The Convention relating to the Status of Refugees and its Protocol set forth the criteria for the determination of refugee status.[104] Without going into detail, it suffices to say that in the members of the Organisation of American States, as opined by the IACtHR,[105] asylum-seekers benefit from the expanded definition of 'refugee' which includes, in addition to the elements of the above-named universal treaties, 'persons who have fled their country because their lives, safety or freedom have been threatened by generalized violence, foreign aggression, internal conflicts, massive violation of human rights or other circumstances which have seriously disturbed public order'.[106]

Lastly, the third example is the right to appeal in criminal matters, which has in fact been subject to adjudication before the *ad hoc* ICTs.[107] Article 14(5) of the ICCPR, as construed by the UN Human Rights Committee,[108] guarantees a second review in cases where a person is convicted for the first time by the highest court, or where a person is convicted following an appeal against an acquittal. At the same time, Article 2(2) of Protocol No 7 to the Convention for the Protection of Human Rights and Fundamental Freedoms[109] explicitly allows for exceptions in these two scenarios. As a result, the choice between the instruments

103 Stefan Trechsel, 'Rights in Criminal Proceedings under the ECHR and the ICTY Statute – A Precarious Comparison' in Bert Swart, Alexander Zahar and Göran Sluiter (eds), *The Legacy of the International Criminal Tribunal for the Former Yugoslavia* (Oxford University Press, 2011), p. 160.

104 Art. 1, Convention relating to the Status of Refugees (adopted 28 July 1951, entered into force 22 April 1954) 189 UNTS 137; Art. 1, Protocol relating to the Status of Refugees (adopted 31 January 1967, entered into force 4 October 1967) 606 UNTS 267. For the purposes of this discussion, I assume that both treaties belong to the domain of internatonal human rights law *lato sensu*.

105 *Rights and Guarantees of Children in the Context of Migration and/or in Need of International Protection*, Advisory Opinion OC-21/14, Inter-American Court of Human Rights Series A No 21 (19 August 2014), paras 73–9.

106 Cartagena Declaration on Refugees, Colloquium on the International Protection of Refugees in Central America, Mexico and Panama (22 November 1984), section III, para 3 <www.refworld.org/docid/3ae6b36ec.html> accessed 5 February 2019.

107 See, e.g., Appeal Judgment on Allegations of Contempt against Prior Counsel, Milan Vujin, *Prosecutor v Tadić* ICTY-94-1-A-AR77, A Ch, 27 February 2001, p. 3, and Separate Opinion of Judge Wald Dissenting from the Finding of Jurisdiction, pp. 3–4; Judgment, *Rutaganda v Prosecutor*, ICTR-96-3-A, A Ch, 26 May 2003, Separate Opinion of Judge Shahabuddeen, paras 11-29, and Dissenting Opinion of Judge Pocar, pp. 1ff; Judgment, *Prosecutor v Mrkšić and Šljivančanin*, ICTY-95-13/1-A, A Ch, 5 May 2009, Partially Dissenting Opinion of Judge Pocar, paras 2ff.

108 See, e.g., UN Human Rights Committee, *Jesús Terrón v Spain*, Views (5 November 2004), UN Doc CCPR/C/82/D/1073/2002, para 7.4; 'General Comment No 32', *supra* note 39, para 47. Nevertheless, five States (Austria, Belgium, Germany, Luxembourg and Norway) made reservations or declarations regarding this Article.

109 As of 5 February 2019, it has been ratified by all but three member States of the Council of Europe.

becomes decisive. It is submitted that a universal treaty norm or a norm reflecting customary international law should always outweigh any regional human rights norm even when this would lead to a lower level of human rights protection before an ICT. In this connection, I partly disagree with the legal reasoning, albeit not the conclusion, of Judge Pocar who applied the human rights law principle of the prevalence of the highest of the diverging international standards, to the domain of international criminal law.[110] No doubt, it is a key principle in international human rights law: if a State has two diverging human rights obligations, it shall apply the one that would better protect human rights. From the standpoint of a State, the fact that one is universal and another is regional does not really matter. However, things are different before an ICT. All ICTs must comply with general and customary international law and the ICC must also comply with 'internationally recognized human rights', including a regional norm only if it is recognised within the broader normative framework.

Regional human rights law

Another common practice of the ICC has been to refer exclusively to regional instruments and jurisprudence, but again without any explanation. In her assiduous analysis of the *Lubanga* case, Annika Jones has discerned two determinants of the judicial reliance thereon, namely: i) the prior experience of the ICC judges (to be precise, only Judge Pikis) in human rights courts; and ii) the ICC's interpretation of Article 21(3).[111] Leaving the former aside, as it does not directly concern the problem under discussion, let me scrutinise the latter. In support of the argument that '[a]rticle 21(3) provides not only a legal basis, but also a requirement for judges to take regional human rights law into consideration in the interpretation of the Rome Statute'[112] two examples are given, both of which are, in my view, misread.

The first is the following statement of the Court: 'As required by Article 21(3) of the Statute, the Chamber considers [a previously reached conclusion] to be the only interpretation consistent with the "reasonable suspicion" standard provided for in [the ECHR and the ACHR]'.[113] According to Annika Jones, it points to 'an obligation to interpret the Rome Statute in accordance with regional human rights law'.[114] Here, three critical remarks need to be made. Firstly, the author mixes up a duty 'to take (. . .) into consideration in the interpretation' with a duty 'to interpret (. . .) in accordance with'. Article 21(3) of the Rome Statute deals

110 *Prosecutor v Mrkšić and Šljivančanin*, *supra* note 107, para 7.
111 Jones, *supra* note 54, pp. 713–14.
112 Ibid., p. 714.
113 Decision concerning Pre-Trial Chamber I's Decision of 10 February 2006 and the Incorporation of Documents into the Record of the Case against Mr Thomas Lubanga Dyilo, *Prosecutor v Lubanga*, (ICC-01/04-01/06-8-US-Corr), Pre-T Ch I, 24 February 2006, para 12.
114 Jones, *supra* note 54, p. 714.

with the latter type of an obligation, while the former, which leaves more room for interpretive manoeuvre, is reminiscent of the one under Article 31(3)(c) of the Vienna Convention on the Law of Treaties.[115] Secondly, although Pre-Trial Chamber I indeed used the word 'required' in the first part of the sentence, it was inseparably linked to the requirement of Article 21(3) as such, i.e. the duty imposed by the word 'must', while the references to the regional instruments appear in the second part. This reading becomes more intelligible if we look at another decision handed down by the same Chamber consisting of the same judges in the case of *Harun and Kushayb*, which, admittedly, was not part of Annika Jones' research:

> [A]s *required* by Article 21(3) of the Statute, the expression 'reasonable grounds to believe' must be interpreted and applied in accordance with internationally recognized human rights. Thus, in interpreting and applying [this] expression (. . .) the Chamber will be *guided* by the 'reasonable suspicion' standard under [the ECHR and the ACHR].[116]

However controversial this excerpt is in and of itself, the first sentence includes a paraphrase of Article 21(3), whereas the second concentrates on its operation in relation to the issue at hand. The word 'guided' reinforces my counter-argument that the ICC may – rather than must – equate regionally recognised human rights with 'internationally recognized human rights'. An *arguendo* assumption that the equation is a requirement brings us to my third remark. In both decisions in question, the ICC extracted a standard from two different regional systems of human rights protection. Annika Jones' observation is, therefore, limited to this specific scenario. It cannot easily be extrapolated if the ICC refers to only one regional instrument, which has, in fact, happened quite often, especially regarding European human rights norms. For example, in several cases, the ICC construed the 'substantial grounds to believe' standard under Article 61(7) of the Rome Statute in the light of 'the jurisprudence of the [ECtHR] to mean "strong grounds for believing", such that the Prosecution "must offer concrete and tangible proof demonstrating a clear line of reasoning underpinning its specific allegations"'.[117]

The second example given by Annika Jones is the next statement of Judge Song:

115 'There shall be taken into account, together with the context (. . .) any relevant rules of international law applicable in the relations between the parties' Art 31(3)(c), Vienna Convention on the Law of Treaties.

116 Decision on the Prosecution Application under Article 58(7) of the Statute, *Prosecutor v Harun and Abd-Al-Rahman ("Ali Kushayb")*, (ICC-02/05-01/07-1-Corr), Pre-T Ch I, 27 April 2007, para 28 (emphases added).

117 Decision on the confirmation of charges, *Prosecutor v Mbarushimana*, (ICC-01/04-01/10-465-Red), Pre-T Ch I, 16 December 2011, para 40. See also, among others, Decision on the confirmation of charges, *Prosecutor v Lubanga*, (ICC-01/04-01/06-803-tEN), Pre-T Ch I, 29 January 2007, paras 38–9.

> [The] jurisprudence [of the ECtHR and the IACtHR] ***should be taken into account*** when interpreting the term 'personal interests of the victims' in Article 68(3) of the Statute, as Article 21(3) of the Statute ***obliges*** the Court to interpret and apply the Statute in consistence with internationally recognized human rights.[118]

All three of my above-mentioned remarks are, *mutatis mutandis*, applicable thereto. Moreover, in a footnote, Judge Song also referred to a couple of non-binding documents of the UN Human Rights Commission, which shows that he had a broader picture in mind.

On the one hand, the ICC can be reproached for its over-reliance on regional instruments and cases. On the other hand, after a careful examination of the pleadings, it becomes apparent that parties to, and participants in, proceedings often use regional laws without hesitation. Such references are sporadical, but strategically aimed towards proving one's position. Let me take the situations in the Democratic Republic of the Congo and Uganda, both in Africa, as examples. In *Lubanga*, the legal representatives of the victims relied on the jurisprudence of the ECtHR and the IACtHR when advancing their submissions as to the definition of 'personal interest'.[119] In *Ngudjolo*, the defence referred to the ECHR in seeking instructions as to how to proceed with the preparations for proceedings, given that the defendant was held in the Schiphol detention centre and could not properly work with his counsel.[120] Nevertheless, in *Kony and others*, the ICC rejected the arguments based on regional jurisprudence. Repudiating the extension of the rights of an accused under Article 67 to persons who had not yet been under its control, the ICC held that '[t]he decisions of the [IACtHR] and of the [ECtHR] on which (. . .) the Defence relies are related to procedural contexts different from the instant case'.[121] Indeed, there are many differences between the ICC and human rights courts.

I think that the ICC should continue to be vigilant and to count critically on the submissions of all parties to, or participants in, proceedings, because even

118 Decision of the Appeals Chamber on the Joint Application of Victims a/0001/06 to a/0003/06 and a/0105/06 concerning the "Directions and Decision of the Appeals Chamber" of 2 February 2007, *Prosecutor v Lubanga*, (ICC-01/04-01/06-925), A Ch, 13 June 2007, Separate Opinion of Judge Sang-Hyun Song, para 16 (emphases added).

119 Decision on the defence observations regarding the right of the legal representatives of victims to question defence witnesses and on the notion of personal interest -and- Decision on the defence application to exclude certain representatives of victims from the Chamber during the non-public evidence of various defence witnesses, *Prosecutor v Lubanga*, (ICC-01/04-01/06-2340), T Ch I, 11 March 2010, para 19.

120 Decision on "Urgent application by Mathieu Ngudjolo's Defence seeking the Appeals Chamber's instructions on the modalities of preparation for the appeals procedure in view of Mathieu Ngudjolo's current situation (Article 67 of the Rome Statute)", *Prosecutor v Ngudjolo*, (ICC-01/04-02/12-67), A Ch, 24 April 2013, paras 4–5.

121 Judgment on the Appeal of the Defense against the "Decision on the Admissibility of the Case under Article 19(1) of the Statute" of 10 March 2009, *Prosecutor v Kony, Otti, Odhiambo and Ongwen*, (ICC-02/04-01/05-408), A Ch, 16 September 2009, para 66.

more disturbing problems might happen. For instance, regional human rights law should intuitively be more demanding than universal, at least because a smaller group of subjects of international law should, in principle, have the stronger sense of solidarity and common interests leading to stricter rules of conduct.[122] In practice, this is, however, not always true and may result in erroneous reliance on a regional system when the higher standard is in fact offered by the UN human rights monitoring bodies. This scenario is not imaginary. On the contrary, such a misconception regarding the right of prisoners to family life has occurred before the Residual Special Court for Sierra Leone (which, admittedly, functions in a different normative and institutional context, but still without formal prioritisation of any regional system of human rights protection). In *Taylor*,[123] both the convict and the prosecutor substantiated their claims by reference to the jurisprudence of the ECtHR, whereas the Trial Chamber was, according to Jamil Ddamulira Mujuzi, unable or unwilling to go beyond their parochial submissions and look into the relevant documentation of the UN Committee against Torture, the UN Human Rights Committee or the UN Special Rapporteurs, etc.[124]

International silence

A controversial, if not tendentious, method of the ICC is its reliance on the absence of international human rights instruments and jurisprudence as an indicator of the Rome Statute's consistency therewith. In *Katanga and Ngudjolo*, a set of victims' procedural rights in ICC proceedings was borrowed from six civil law States.[125] The Single Judge noted that the UN Human Rights Committee, the ECtHR and the IACtHR had, in this context, never found these States to be in breach of international commitments regarding the rights of an accused and the right to a fair trial.[126] Moreover, she maintained that granting the procedural rights in question had, in some States, been very effective in the fight against impunity for international crimes.[127] Nevertheless, I think that the ICC acted

122 Buergenthal, *supra* note 37, p. 156; Dominique Carreau and Fabrizio Marrella, *Droit international* (12th edn, Pedone, 2018), p. 129.

123 *In the Matter of Charles Ghankay Taylor* (Decision on Public with Public and Confidential Annexes Charles Ghankay Taylor's Motion for Termination of Enforcement of Sentence in the United Kingdom and for Transfer to Rwanda) (SCSL-03-01-ES), T Ch (30 January 2015), paras 4, 18–19, 75.

124 Jamil Ddamulira Mujuzi, 'War Criminals Transferred to Serve their Sentences in Foreign Countries and their Right to Family Life: A Comment on the Residual Special Court for Sierra Leone's Decision in *Charles Ghankay Taylor's Motion for Termination of Enforcement of Sentences in the United Kingdom and for Transfer to Rwanda*' 15 *Law and Practice of International Courts and Tribunals* (2016) 419, pp. 433ff.

125 Decision on the Set of Procedural Rights Attached to Procedural Status of Victims at the Pre-Trial Stage of the Case, *Prosecutor v Katanga and Ngudjolo,* (ICC-01/04-01/07-474), Pre-T Ch I, 13 May 2008, para 61.

126 Ibid., para 66.

127 Ibid., para 68.

ultra vires, since the domestic acceptance of a norm in the light of international silence does not necessarily lead to international recognition.[128]

First, it is submitted that the ICC erred in equating an international situation of fact with a norm of international law.[129] The absence of condemnation by international human rights bodies may simply indicate that there have so far been no (admissible) applications alleging human rights violations of a certain kind.

Second, the *Lotus* principle – i.e. what is not prohibited by international law is legally permitted[130] – implied by the ICC does not help in the case under discussion owing to the Single Judge's own acknowledgement that neither the approach of the selected national jurisdictions, nor the opposite approach of the common law States impinges on the rights of an accused or the right to a fair trial.[131] If both models of victims' participation in criminal proceedings are legally possible, the choice seems to pivot on non-legal justifications, including pragmatism or appropriateness in a particular case.[132] As for the effectiveness thesis of the Court, it is just too weak. Not only is it unsupported by any empirical evidence, but the ICC also carelessly suggests that the common law procedure is less effective in the fight against impunity. In any event, I think that non-legal reasons should be avoided, because they circumvent the obligative 'must' stipulation under Article 21(3) of the Rome Statute and, on top of that, can bring about inconsistencies in the Court's jurisprudence. Alternatively, a *non liquet* declaration could have been issued in *Katanga and Ngudjolo*, but it would not offer any guidance on how to solve the problem in question.[133]

Third, the Single Judge failed to comply with Article 21(1)(c) of the Rome Statute by relying on the national laws *per se* as opposed to general principles of national law.[134] Moreover, she cherry-picked States. One of them, Brazil, is her homeland and the rest are Western democracies. It is noteworthy that these are not even 'States that would normally exercise jurisdiction over the crime'[135] allegedly committed in the Democratic Republic of the Congo. Instead, the ICC ought to have followed the principle of the completeness of the international legal order.[136] This is based on the idea that there are no spheres of international concern left wholly unregulated by international law.[137] That being so,

128 But see Fronza, *supra* note 52, p. 385 (noting that the human rights consistency test can be used indirectly).
129 See, *mutatis mutandis*, *Case of the S.S. "Lotus"* (*France v Turkey*), 7 September 1927, PCIJ Publications, Series A No 10, Dissenting Opinion of Judge Nyholm, 59, pp. 60–61.
130 Ibid., Judgment, 3, p. 31.
131 *Katanga and Ngudjolo*, *supra* note 125, paras 66, 71, 74.
132 Helen Quane, 'Silence in International Law' 84 *British Yearbook of International Law* (2014) 240, p. 263.
133 Ibid., pp. 264ff.
134 For an emphasis on this distinction see Roger O'Keefe, *International Criminal Law* (Oxford University Press, 2015), p. 552.
135 Art. 21(1)(c), Rome Statute.
136 Quane, *supra* note 132, pp. 260–3.
137 Ibid., p. 260.

international courts should interpret and apply the existing norms of international law 'in such a manner as to render them capable of regulating the situation under consideration'.[138] In particular, the ICC should have made better use of general principles of law under Article 21(1)(c) of the Rome Statute by conducting broader and deeper comparative law analyses of national jurisdictions.[139]

International soft law

The fourth method that is open to discussion is the ICC's reliance on international soft law. Let me examine one of the notable examples. The definition of 'victims' under the Rules of Procedure and Evidence rests on a definition of 'harm', which is not provided. The ICC has noted that it must interpret the latter 'on a case-by-case basis in the light of Article 21(3)'.[140] In practice, the Court has relied on the Basic Principles and Guidelines on the Right to a Remedy and Reparation for Victims of Gross Violations of International Human Rights Law and Serious Violations of International Humanitarian Law (Basic Principles), which is a resolution of the UN General Assembly.[141] Nevertheless, in one of the decisions Judge Blattmann dissented:

> [The Basic Principles] is not a strongly persuasive or decisive authority [to legally determine] victims and in particular the definition of victims and participation. I support and follow Article 21(3) (. . .). However, the (. . .) provisions relied on in the Majority decision were specifically considered and rejected during the [*travaux préparatoires*] of the Rome Statute.[142]

Regarding his first point, it must be recalled that the inclusion of a norm in a soft law instrument does not necessarily mean that this norm is non-binding. Furthermore, the Dissenting Judge's statement that he abides by Article 21(3) implies that the norm in question has not become 'internationally recognized'. What is crucial is that even the rejection of an international human rights norm during the preparatory work of the Statute will not make it irrelevant to the ICC's consideration, unless this norm is nascent and, thus, does not meet the requirement of being internationally recognised.[143] These points notwithstanding, the Appeals Chamber in *Lubanga* upheld the majority's decision and, clarified that the Trial Chamber had merely been 'guided' by the Basic Principles and

138 Ibid.
139 Nerlich, *supra* note 11, p. 86 (stressing the importance of such an assessment).
140 *Situation in the Democratic Republic of the Congo* (Decision on the Applications for Participation in the Proceedings of VPRS 1, VPRS 2, VPRS 3, VPRS 4, VPRS 5 and VPRS 6), (ICC-01/04-101-tENG-Corr), Pre-T Ch I (17 January 2006), para 81.
141 See, e.g., ibid., paras 115–16.
142 Decision on Victims' Participation, *Prosecutor v Lubanga,* (ICC-01/04-01/06-1119), T Ch I, 18 January 2008, Separate and Dissenting Opinion of Judge Blattmann, para 4.
143 For a similar view see Sheppard, *supra* note 32, p. 51.

the decision had actually been based on the Rules of Procedure and Evidence.[144] Nevertheless, this does not elucidate whether the ICC considered the Basic Principles to be internationally recognised. If it did (via Article 21(3)), then it could not have merely been guided by them. If it was merely guided by the Basic Principles, then it could not have used Article 21(3) due to the requirement of international recognition.

Conclusions

To ensure and balance the rights of defendants and victims one must first know the content of their rights. In this respect, Article 21(3) of the Rome Statute is a useful tool for the ICC to elucidate the various aspects of the rights of defendants and victims by referring to external human rights norms.

As argued in the present chapter, the *sine qua non* of such references is that human rights are internationally recognised. Universal norms certainly meet this requirement. A nascent norm never suffices. This notwithstanding, the ICC has referred to domestic law and soft law norms, stressing that it is merely 'guided' by the latter. This reasoning is, in my opinion, wrong, because Article 21(3) speaks about human rights that are international and binding.

Regarding the non-universal recognition, it is submitted that the ICC can invoke a human rights norm from a single region, such as the Council of Europe system of human rights protection, only if it is recognised within the broader normative framework. Furthermore, a universal human rights norm should always outweigh any regional human rights norm even when this would lead to a lower level of human rights protection in the ICC regime.

144 Judgment on the appeals of the Prosecutor and the Defence against Trial Chamber I's Decision on Victims' Participation of 18 January 2008, *Prosecutor v Lubanga*, (ICC-01/04-01/06-1432), A Ch, 11 July 2008, para 33.

3 For better or worse

The rights of defendants and victims before the African Court of Justice and Human and Peoples' Rights

Oliver Windridge

Whilst the other chapters in this book look at how operational institutions address the rights of defendants and victims, this chapter is slightly different. It considers the rights of defendants and victims at an as yet to be operational international tribunal: the African Court of Justice and Human and Peoples' Rights (ACJHPR).

Once operational, the ACJHPR will be the African Union's apex judicial organ. It will contain three sections: General Affairs, Human and Peoples' Rights (currently operating as the African Court on Human and Peoples' Rights) and International Criminal Law. The latter international criminal law section is the focus of this chapter. The International Criminal Law Section will have jurisdiction over an impressive 14 crimes. In addition to the 'core' crimes of genocide, war crimes, crimes against humanity and aggression, the ACJHPR's International Criminal Law Section will have jurisdiction over allegations of, *inter alia*, piracy, corruption and trafficking of persons and drugs. With a jurisdictional reach many times greater than any current or previous international tribunal, the ACJHPR has the potential to handle many more cases, meaning many more defendants and victims.

To assess the rights of the defence and victims before the ACJHPR this chapter reviews its two foundational instruments: the Protocol on the Statute of the African Court of Justice and Human Rights and the Protocol on Amendments to the Protocol on the Statute of the African Court of Justice and Human Rights. The chapter will highlight provisions contained within the International Criminal Law Section that seek to ensure respect for the rights of defendants, such as the creation of a defence office, the appointment of public defenders and the establishment of the role of 'Principal Defender'. The chapter will then assess the participation of victims. In particular, it will consider the somewhat ambiguous terms in which victims appear, and highlight potential issues concerning victim participation during trials. In assessing both defendant and victim participation, the chapter will undertake comparative analysis between the ACJHR and current and previous international criminal statutes including the International Criminal Court (ICC), Special Court for Sierra Leone (SCSL) and International Criminal Tribunal for Rwanda (ICTR) in order to determine whether the proposed ACJHPR should be considered a progressive or retrograde tribunal. The chapter concludes by suggesting areas in need of further clarification either through additional protocols, court rules or judicial decision making. Importantly the ACJHPR can be seen as the latest attempt to develop defence and victims' rules and procedure within international criminal law. This attempt does not exist within a vacuum, but instead is part of wider process that includes the SCSL, ICTR and ICTY. Understanding this, this chapter examines the ACJHPR defence and victims' sections within the context of these previous institutions, and pinpoints where the ACJHPR has accepted previous practice as its own and areas where the ACJHPR has developed or regressed, for better or worse.

The Malabo Protocol

The African Charter on Human and Peoples' Rights (African Charter) contains many familiar rights, such as the right to fair trial and the right to freedom of expression, as well as peoples' rights such as the right to freedom of environment. Should individuals or NGOs wish to bring a case against an African Union member state for violation of one or more of the rights found in the African Charter, as well as in some circumstances other international human rights instruments, they can approach either the African Commission on Human and Peoples' Rights (African Commission) or the African Court on Human and Peoples' Rights (African Court), depending on that member states' ratification and signature of a triple layer of African Union instruments.[1] But neither the African Court or African Commission have jurisdiction over international crimes.[2] For international criminal jurisdiction within Africa, a new tranche of African Union protocols must be introduced.

In 2008 the African Union adopted the protocol for the establishment of the African Court of Justice and Human Rights (First Protocol).[3] This First Protocol contained a statute that envisioned the merger of the African Court of Justice with the African Court on Human and Peoples' Rights, creating a new court called the African Court of Justice and Human Rights.

1 Ratification of the African Charter gives access to the African Commission. For direct access to the African Court, matters are more complex. For detail on accessing the African Court see Oliver Windridge, 'Necessary Checkpoints or Immovable Roadblocks? Accessing the African Court on Human and Peoples' Rights', 35 *Wisconsin International Law Journal* (2018) 5. It should also be noted that in addition to the African Court and African Commission, individuals and NGOs also have the potential to petition regional human rights courts such as the East African Court of Justice and ECOWAS Court.

2 Much commentary has focused on the African Union's ongoing relationship with the International Criminal Court as the reason for the adoption of amendments giving the ACJHR jurisdiction over international crimes. Whilst ongoing African Union and ICC issues are undoubtedly part of the reason, it should be noted that discussion with regards to an African human rights court with jurisdiction over international crimes dates as far back as the 1970s. See Ademelo Abass, 'Historical and Political Background to the Malabo Protocol', in Gerhard Werle and Moritz Vormbaum (eds), *The African Criminal Court: A Commentary on the Malabo Protocol*, International Criminal Justice Series Volume 10 (Springer, 2017).

3 Protocol on the Statute of the African Court of Justice and Human Rights, available at https://au.int/sites/default/files/treaties/7792-treaty-0035_-_protocol_on_the_statute_of_the_african_court_of_justice_and_human_rights_e.pdf

This court would have two 'sections' equivalent to the existing courts: a Human Rights section and a General section. In June 2014 at its summit meeting in Malabo, Equatorial Guinea, the African Union adopted an additional protocol which included in its annex an amendment to the Statute (Malabo Protocol). Whilst the Malabo Protocol leaves the General section and the Human Rights section largely unchanged, crucially, it bolts on a third limb; the International Criminal Law Section. With the Malabo Protocol therefore the African Union created, on paper at least, a mega-court containing three sections: i) General Affairs; ii) Human and Peoples' Rights; and iii) International Criminal Law.[4] To enter into force, and give life to this ambitious project the Malabo Protocol requires fifteen ratifications from AU Member States. At the time of writing, whilst nine African Union Member States have signed the Malabo Protocol, none have ratified it.[5]

The Malabo Protocol sets out that the ACJHPR's International Criminal Section will have jurisdiction over an ambitious roster of 14 crimes. Joining the so-called 'core crimes' of genocide, crimes against humanity, war crimes, and the crime of aggression, are the crimes of unconstitutional change of government, piracy, terrorism, mercenarism, corruption, money laundering, trafficking in persons, trafficking in drugs, trafficking in hazardous wastes, and the illicit exploitation of natural resources.[6] Once operational, the ACJHPR's International Criminal Section will contain the widest jurisdiction of any modern day international criminal tribunal.[7]

The defence

Defence as a reality rather than concept at international criminal trials incorporates several strands, including most importantly the rights of the accused. All these strands are vitally important in upholding defendants' rights before any international tribunal, not least the ACJHPR International Criminal Section. This section will look first at the rights of the accused, followed by sentencing provisions. It will then review the creation of the defence framework including the

4 Article 16 of the Annex to the Malabo Protocol.

5 Ratifications can be checked at the African Union website, available at https://au.int/en/treaties/status

6 Article 28A, Malabo Protocol. Further details and chapeau requirements for these crimes can be found in Article 28B (Genocide), Article 28C (Crimes Against Humanity), Article 28D (War Crimes), Article 28E (The Crime of Unconstitutional Change of Government), Article 28F (Piracy), Article 28G (Terrorism), Article 28H (Mercenarism), Article 28I (Corruption), Article 28I *Bis* (Money Laundering), Article 28J (Trafficking in persons), Article 28K (Trafficking in drugs), Article 28L (Trafficking in Hazardous Wastes), Article 28L *Bis* (Illicit Exploitation of Natural Resources), Article 28M (Crime of Aggression).

7 For further discussion on the crimes under the ACJHPR jurisdiction see Charles C. Jalloh, 'A Classification of the Crimes in the Malabo Protocol', in Charles C. Jalloh, Kamari M. Clarke and Vincent O. Nmehielle (eds), *The African Court of Justice and Human and Peoples' Rights in Context: Development and Challenges,* (Cambridge University Press, 2019).

establishment of a defence office within the ACJHPR International Crime Division and the establishment of a 'Principle Defender' role.

The rights of the accused

The Malabo Protocol specifically contains rights of the accused.[8] These include the presumption of innocence,[9] the right to be tried without undue delay,[10] and the right to appeal.[11] These provisions can be seen as being broadly in line with other international tribunals including the ICC,[12] ICTR,[13] and SCSL.[14] Three issues are worthy of further examination, however.[15]

First, the Malabo Protocol appears to eliminate the possibility of trials *in absentia*. Article 46A.4(d) of the Malabo Protocol explicitly requires defendants to be present; a welcome clarification in line with the ICC, but not all internationalised tribunals.[16] Unlike the ICC Statute however, the Malabo Protocol does not explicitly provide for the continuance of an ongoing trial in the absence of an accused in situations where the defendant disrupts proceedings.[17] A small omission perhaps, but given the relatively common occurrence of defendants at international trials seeking to disrupt proceedings, for example ex-Chadian leader

8 Article 46A, Malabo Protocol.

9 Article 46A.3, Malabo Protocol.

10 Article 46A.4(c), Malabo Protocol.

11 Article 46A.4 (i), Malabo Protocol.

12 Article 67, Rome Statute of the International Criminal Court (ICC Statute), available at www.icc-cpi.int/resource-library/Documents/RS-Eng.pdf

13 Article 20, Statute of the International Tribunal for Rwanda (ICTR Statute) available at http://legal.un.org/avl/pdf/ha/ictr_EF.pdf

14 Article 17, Statute of the Special Court for Sierra Leone (SCSL Statute) available at www.rscsl.org/Documents/scsl-statute.pdf

15 See also Melinda Taylor, 'Defence and Fair Trial Rights at the African Court of Justice and Human and Peoples' Rights', in Charles C. Jalloh, Kamari M. Clarke and Vincent O. Nmehielle (eds), *The African Court of Justice and Human and Peoples' Rights in Context: Development and Challenges*, (Cambridge University Press, 2019).

16 See Article 46A.4(d), Malabo Protocol. The ICC Statute explicitly states that trials in absentia are prohibited, see Article 63 The Rome Statute ('the accused shall be present during the trial, [unless] the accused, being present before the Court, continues to disrupt the trial, [in which case] the Trial Chamber may remove the accused.. . . Such measures shall be taken only in exceptional circumstances'.). One notable exception is the Special Tribunal for Lebanon, which is currently conducting a multi accused trial *in absentia*. See Decision to Hold Trial in Absentia, *Prosecutor v Ayyash et al*, (STL-11-01), 1 February 2012 and more generally, available at www.stl-tsl.org/en/about-the-stl/unique-features

17 Article 67 (4), ICC Statute referring to Article 63(2) which states 'If the accused, being present before the Court, continues to disrupt the trial, the Trial Chamber may remove the accused and shall make provision for him or her to observe the trial and instruct counsel from outside the courtroom, through the use of communications technology, if required. Such measures shall be taken only in exceptional circumstances after other reasonable alternatives have proved inadequate, and only for such duration as is strictly required'. Similar provisions are found in the ICTR and SCSL Statutes.

Hissène Habré before the Extraordinary African Chambers, the addition of a similar provision may have been wise.[18]

Second, whilst the Malabo Protocol does mention the right not to be compelled to testify against oneself or to confess guilt,[19] it lacks the ICC's qualification that with the right to remain silent, such silence will not be used in consideration of the determination of guilt or innocence.[20] The lack of this important qualification appears to mean that whilst a defendant at the ACJHPR has the right to remain silent, such silence could be used against the defendant to infer guilt. Should this indeed be implemented in practice by a trial or appeals chamber, this would constitute a retrograde step against the generally accepted norm that silence cannot be used against a defendant to infer guilt. Similarly, the Malabo Protocol also excludes the right to make an unsworn oral or written statement in his or her defence, and not to have imposed on him or her any reversal of the burden of proof or any onus of rebuttal, a provision found explicitly within the ICC Statute.[21] Again, the absence of such terms could lead to the worrying restriction of defence rights from the very outset of a case, since unsworn statements are forbidden and at the deliberations stage of a case concerning the burden of proof to be applied. The implementation of similar terms as found in the ICC Statute and highlighted herein would go a long way to plugging these gaps.

Third, details on disclosure differ from the ICC Statute, and could be cause for apprehension. Whilst the ICC Statute contains significant details on the provision of disclosure, the Malabo Protocol does not. The absence of such detailed provision could spell concerns for defendants who are not provided with the same level of disclosure obligations from the Prosecution as defendants before the ICC are. Given that the Malabo Protocol was ratified years after the ICC Statute came into force, it must be assumed that the absence of such provisions was deliberate. Similar to the second point above, whilst the absence of disclosure provision is concerning as it currently stands, the implementation of disclosure rules and protocols by way of an additional amendment to the Malabo Protocol or through the creation of stand-alone disclosure protocols would help plug this current gap.

18 Habré's lawyers refused to appear at the opening of the trial in July 2015 because they consider the Extraordinary African Chambers to be illegitimate. The Extraordinary African Chambers then appointed three Senegalese lawyers to defend him and adjourned for 45 days so they could prepare. The first day back, on September 7, Habré was brought in to the court by force, kicking and screaming. After that, he was brought into the courtroom for each session before the doors to the public opened. Habré refused to cooperate with the court appointed lawyers and remained silent throughout his trial. See www.hrw.org/news/2016/05/03/qa-case-hissene-habre-extraordinary-african-chambers-senegal#10. For more on the Extraordinary African Chambers see www.chambresafricaines.org and www.hrw.org/blog-feed/trial-hissene-habre

19 Article 46A 4. (g), Malabo Protocol.

20 Article 67.7, ICC Statute.

21 Cf. Article 67 (8) (9), ICC Statute.

Sentencing

In terms of sentencing, the Malabo Protocol explicitly removes the death penalty as a form of sentence.[22] Whilst the exclusion of the death penalty is in line with other international tribunals, and therefore may be expected, this is a point worth noting since many AU member states still retain the death penalty in domestic legislation.[23]

The Malabo Protocol does appear however to permit the handing down of whole life sentences without the need for a minimum number of years served. This area is not fully developed in the Malabo Protocol, but it seems there is no provision for the review of sentences. Should this be the case in practice, this would be a development out of sequence with other international tribunal practice which has sought to clarify life sentences and the need for clear terms of reference for years served and the potential for early release.[24]

In addition to custodial sentences, the Malabo Protocol allows for the forfeiture of property, proceeds or any asset acquired unlawfully or by criminal conduct, and their return to their rightful owner or to an appropriate Member State.[25] Of course, with a roster of 14 crimes, flexibility in sentencing could well be important. Whilst the returning of property may not be particularly appropriate for sentencing in cases of genocide, the ability to target property or assets acquired through the commission of other crimes within the ACJHPR's jurisdiction, for example corruption or the illicit exploitation of natural resources, could be a useful provision alongside, or even instead of, custodial sentences.

Defence office

Turning now to the framework for the defence at the ACJHPR, the Malabo Protocol provides for the creation of a Defence Office within the International

22 Article 43A.1 and Article 43A.2, Malabo Protocol.

23 Within the African Union several member states are retentionist, carrying the death penalty for ordinary crimes: Botswana, Chad, Comoros, Democratic Republic of the Congo, Egypt, Equatorial Guinea, Ethiopia, Gambia, Lesotho, Libya, Nigeria, Somalia, South Sudan, Sudan, Uganda and Zimbabwe. African Union member states considered abolitionist in practice include: Algeria, Burkina Faso, Cameroon, Central African Republic, Eritrea, Ghana, Kenya, Liberia, Malawi, Maldives, Mali, Mauritania, Morocco/Western Sahara, Niger, Sierra Leone, Swaziland, Tanzania, Tunisia and Zambia see 'Death Sentences and Executions 2017', Amnesty International (2017) available at www.amnesty.org/en/latest/news/2018/04/death-penalty-sentences-and-executions-2017/

24 See for example President's Office, Reasons for the President's Decision to Deny the Early Release of Stanislav Galić and Decision on Prosecution Motion, *Prosecutor* v. *Stanislav Galić*, (MICT-14-83-ES), 23 June 2015.

25 Article 43A.4, Malabo Protocol. See also Mark A. Drumbl, 'Sentencing and Penalties', in Charles C. Jalloh, Kamari M. Clarke and Vincent O. Nmehielle (eds), *The African Court of Justice and Human and Peoples' Rights in Context: Development and Challenges* (Cambridge University Press, 2019).

Criminal Section.[26] The independence of the Defence Office is enshrined within the Malabo Protocol, making clear that it will act independently as a separate organ of the ACJHPR's International Criminal Section.[27] The aim of the Defence office is to ensure the rights of suspects, accused and 'any other person entitled to assistance'. Whilst the first two categories of persons may seem straightforward, the third at least raises the possibility of others being assisted by the Defence Office.[28] The Defence Office will provide support and assistance to defence counsel and to persons entitled to legal assistance, including legal research, collection of evidence and advice and appearing before the Chamber in respect of certain issues.[29] This provision however seems to raise the possibility that defendants will be entitled to appoint counsel of their own choosing, leading to potential overlap between the work of a Defence Office team and that of the defence team selected by a defendant.

The Malabo Protocol also makes clear that the defence shall ensure adequate facilities to defence counsel and persons entitled to legal assistance in the preparation of a case, and shall provide additional assistance as ordered by a judge or Chamber.[30] This is an interesting provision, as facilities are often severely lacking for defence teams at international tribunals. The fact that *facilities* are mentioned explicitly will likely be welcomed by many defence lawyers.

Also of note, is the establishment of a Principle Defender within the framework of the International Crime Section of the ACJHPR. The Malabo Protocol states that the Defence Office will be headed by the Principle Defender,[31] but it also provides for the possibility of additional public defenders.[32] The qualifications for the role of Principle Defender include a minimum of ten years' experience and extensive experience in the 'defence of criminal cases',[33] although it appears experience of *international* criminal cases is not necessary, leaving open at least the chance of the appointment of a principle defender with no international criminal experience. Irrespective of qualifications, whomever is appointed in the role of Principle Defender will be required to adopt regulations and practice directions, likely meaning the first Principle Defender will be handed the unenviable task of drafting these instruments from scratch.[34]

The Principle Defender will also gain a staff, appointed by the Principle Defender themselves, allowing at least the potential centralisation of power as well as the chance for nepotism and/or country or regional bias in office.[35] The Principle Defender will also enjoy equal status with the ACJHPR Prosecutor in terms

26 Article 22C, Malabo Protocol.
27 Article 22C.2, Malabo Protocol.
28 Article 22C.1, Malabo Protocol.
29 Article 22C.2, Malabo Protocol.
30 Article 22C.3, Malabo Protocol.
31 Article 22.C.4, Malabo Protocol.
32 Article 22C.2, Malabo Protocol.
33 Article 22C.4, Malabo Protocol.
34 Article 22C.5, Malabo Protocol.
35 Article 22C.6, Malabo Protocol.

of rights of audience and negotiations *inter partes*.[36] This status also includes the significant power to appear *proprio motu* in matters of 'general interest' to defence teams, the fairness of proceedings or the rights of a suspect or accused.[37] Finally, it is interesting to note that the Malabo Protocol contains provision for a Principle Defender, other public defenders, plus support for defence counsel. Since the Malabo Protocol appears to allow accused to select counsel of their own choosing, there is the distinct possibility that an accused will have a defence team, in additional to the Defence Office with a Principle Defender.

The provision of a defence office separate from other organs stands in stark contrast to the ICC. The ICC does not have an independent defence office, but rather an Office of Public Counsel for the Defence (OPCD).[38] Whilst the OPCD is, according to the ICC, an independent office falling within the ICC Registry solely for administrative purposes, by virtue of its positioning within the ICC Registry there is potentially some implication of a lack of independence, best seen perhaps as a kind of Defence Office Lite. However, the somewhat confusing situation of the ICC defence office at least gives some defence presence. With the *ad-hoc* tribunals – the ICTR and International Criminal Tribunal for the former Yugoslavia (ICTY) – no provision was made for the defence within the formal structure of the tribunals. For example, the ICTR had Chambers (Trial and Appeal), Prosecution and Registry, but no defence office.[39] Similarly, the SCSL had Chambers, Prosecutor and Registry, but no defence office.[40] As to the role of Principle Defender, no tribunal actively prosecuting international cases has included such as role. The Residual Special Court for Sierra Leone (RSCSL) includes a Principle Defender, although the precise nature of this role remains somewhat vague given the lack of details on this role within the RSCSL Statute.[41] The residual *ad-hoc* tribunal, the Mechanism of International Criminal Tribunals (MICT) has no such role. Perhaps the nearest comparison may be at the Special Tribunal for Lebanon which includes not only a Defence Office, but also a Head of Defence Office.[42]

In comparison therefore to the ICC and particularly the ICTY and ICTR, the Malabo Protocol can be seen as a progressive step in the provision of an adequate defence in international tribunals. In fact, with establishment of a Defence Office, at least one Principle Defender plus the ability to appoint counsel of one's own choosing, if the Malabo Protocol could be accused of anything it could be of over egging the pudding. Certainly, the ACJHPR will be in contention for the accolade of most defence-friendly international tribunal ever.

36 Article 22C.7, Malabo Protocol.
37 Article 22C.8, Malabo Protocol.
38 Regulation 77, ICC Court Regulations.
39 Article 10, International Criminal Tribunal for Rwanda Statute.
40 Article 11, Special Court for Sierra Leone Statute.
41 See Residual Special Court for Sierra Leone www.rscsl.org/RSCSL-Officials.html
42 See Special Tribunal for Lebanon Defence Office, available at www.stl-tsl.org/en/about-the-stl/structure-of-the-stl/defence-2

Victims

In this section, this chapter will examine provisions made for victims within the Malabo Protocol's International Criminal Law section. First, examining the possibility of victim participation at the various stages of trials. Second, reviewing the potential for reparations afforded within the Malabo Protocol.

Victim participation

Unlike the defence, with the independent defence office and the establishment of a Principle Defender, the Malabo Protocol makes no provision for a victim's unit or office. The Malabo Protocol does state that the Registry shall set up a victims and witnesses unit.[43] It also states that the Pre-Trial Chamber may issue orders to provide protection and ensure the privacy of witnesses and victims, the presentation of evidence and protection of arrested persons.[44] Concerning the office of the Prosecutor, the prosecutor shall have the power to question suspects, victims and witnesses.[45] However, all these provisions appear to be in relation to providing support and protection for victims who appear at court as witnesses rather than the participation of victims in the various stages of proceedings as parties themselves. This approach to victim participation is similar to that found at the ICTY and ICTR, as well as the SCSL.[46] This is however in sharp contrast to the ICC, where victim participation has been elevated within proceedings at the pre-trial, trial, appeals and reparations stages. In particular, the ICC Rules of Procedure and Evidence provide explicitly for the participation of victims in proceedings.[47]

There does appear to be some potential scope for victims to make representations before the Pre-Trial Chamber, where the Office of the Prosecutor requests authorization for an investigation to be commenced.[48] However, this seems restricted, in the best-case scenario, to the very limited authorization of investigation stage of proceedings. This provision also stands alone, without any guidance as to how victims may be able to approach a Pre-Trial Chamber, and would benefit from greater clarity from the ACJHPR when it becomes operational.[49] In any event, given the lack of provision for victim participation within the Malabo Protocol as it currently stands, it is difficult to envisage victim participation at the

43 Article 22B.9(a), Malabo Protocol.
44 Article 19 Bis 3, Malabo Protocol.
45 Article 22A, Malabo Protocol.
46 See Article 21, ICTR Statute, Article 16 SCSL Statute.
47 Rules 89-Rule 93, ICC Rules of Procedure and Evidence.
48 Article 46G.3, Malabo Protocol.
49 For further examination of the role of victims at the ACJHPR See Godfrey M. Musila, 'A Promise Too Dear? The Right to Reparations for Victims of International Crimes Under the Malabo Protocol of the African Criminal Court', in Charles C. Jalloh, Kamari M. Clarke and Vincent O. Nmehielle (eds), *The African Court of Justice and Human and Peoples' Rights in Context: Development and Challenges*, (Cambridge University Press, 2019).

ACJHPR on a similar level to that we have seen at the ICC, for example in the *Lubanga* case where victims participated at pre-trial, trial, appeal and even review of sentencing stages.[50]

Reparations

Whilst victim participation within the Malabo Protocol, be it in the pre-trial, trial or appeals stages, appears extremely limited, the Malabo Protocol contains far more extensive provisions for victim participation in the reparations stage of cases, although this is still not particularly clear. The Malabo Protocol requires the establishment of Rules of the Court which should contain principles relating to reparations to, or in the respect of, victims, including restitutions, compensation and rehabilitation.[51] The ACJHPR can, on request or *proprio motu*, determine the scope and extent of any damage, loss or injury to, or in respect of, victims and will state the principles on which it is acting.[52] Before making an order, the ACJHPR may invite or take account of representations from, or on behalf of, the convicted person, victims, other interested persons or interested States.[53] Within this section of the Malabo Protocol therefore, there is at least the suggestion that victims have some chance of representation if not in the trial itself, then at the reparations stage of proceedings before the International Criminal Law Section of the ACJHPR .

Linked to victims participation during reparations, the Malabo Protocol also establishes the existence of a trust fund for victims.[54] This trust fund is required to be set up for legal aid and assistance for the benefit of victims of crimes or human rights violations and their families.[55] The Court can transfer fines or forfeited property into the Victims Trust Fund.[56] The use of the Victims Trust Fund appears very broad. The wording of the relevant provisions seems to indicate that this fund can be used for legal aid, therefore raising the possibility that an accused could use these funds. It also seems to include funds for reparations for victims under the human rights division of the ACJHPR. With the participation of victims in the pre-trial, trial and appeal stages of the International Criminal Law Division is unclear, it is difficult to see how and when victims of crimes can petition the ACJHPR in a bid to secure reparations.

50 See for example Second Decision on the Review Concerning Reduction of Sentence of Mr Thomas Lubanga Dyilo, *The Prosecutor v. Thomas Lubanga Dyilo* (ICC-01/04/01/06), 3 November 2017, paras. 12–15.

51 Article 45.1, Malabo Protocol.

52 Article 45.2, Malabo Protocol.

53 Article 45.3, Malabo Protocol.

54 Article 46M, Malabo Protocol.

55 Article 46M.1, Malabo Protocol. The Trust Fund is to be managed according to criteria to be determined by the Assembly, See Article 46M.3, Malabo Protocol. It should be noted that the ICC also runs a trust for victims although its scope is more limited. See www.trustfundforvictims.org

56 Article 46M.2, Malabo Protocol.

Conclusion

The ACJHPR is at present a paper-only court. However, the entry into force of the Malabo Protocol and the creation of the ACJHPR is on the horizon. Examining its structure and operation now affords the rare opportunity to critically assess a prospective international tribunal and its likely impact on international criminal justice, but admittedly it will take institutional practice to see how these provisions will play out.

Despite this, it is clear that the Malabo Protocol allows for significant attention on the defence. There are however some areas of concern. The provisions for the rights of the accused lack some crucial elements found in comparable ICC provisions, for example a lack of guarantee that silence will not be used against the accused, the absence of disclosure provisions and no guarantee of the reversal of burden of proof. These provisions are crucial to a fair trial, and amendments to the relevant sections of the Malabo Protocol would be welcomed. Despite these reservations, overall the defence are well catered for. If anything, an analysis of the defence framework raises issues over whether the creation of a defence office and Principle Defender represent an overly ambitious stretch? The ICC copes with a Defence Office Lite, with no principle defender to speak of, whilst the ICTR and SCSL did not even have defence offices, let alone a Principle Defender. These may not be ideal precedents upon which to model the ACJHR, but the contrast between them is significant.

Victim representation however fairs less well. At present, victim participation is limited to the role played by victims as witnesses as per the role envisioned within the *ad-hoc* tribunal system. Victim participation as a party in proceedings is far less detailed, with potential access for victims at the investigation stage before the Pre-Trial Chamber and the reparations stage, but with precious little in-between. Should the ACJHPR wish to become more victim-friendly once in operation, either liberal interpretation of the current statute or significant amendments will be required. Finally, the ACJHPR must be viewed in the context of its international criminal law predecessors including the SCSL, ICTR and ICC. Seen not in isolation, but as the latest in a line of institutions tackling international crime, the ACJHPR makes further strides to address the rights of the defence, but may be seen as regressing on victim participation. The ACJHPR represents the future, rather than the past, of international criminal law in Africa, for better or worse.

4 Balancing prejudice

Fair trial rights and international procedural decisions relating to evidence

*Rogier Bartels**

Introduction

Despite the gravity of the alleged conduct in cases of aggression, genocide, crimes against humanity, or war crimes, it is – fortunately[1] – undisputed that a person accused of having committed international crimes is entitled to receive a fair trial. Shortly before the birth of international criminal law,[2] Winston Churchill favoured summary execution of all (alleged) German war criminals, referring to fair trial rights as 'complications'.[3] However, the Charter of the International Military Tribunal at Nuremberg, adopted a few months later, did include several provisions 'to ensure fair trial for the Defendants'.[4] At the International Criminal Tribunal for the former Yugoslavia (ICTY), the trial chambers had to 'ensure that a trial is fair and expeditious and that proceedings are conducted [. . .] with full respect for the rights of the accused', as stated in Article 20 of the Tribunal's Statute.[5] The International Criminal Court (ICC or Court), on which this

* The views expressed in this contribution are the author's and do not necessarily reflect does of the International Criminal Court.

1 In the early years of the *ad hoc* tribunals, Gerry Simpson observed that '[i]t is clear that in an area of law so thoroughly politicised, culturally freighted and passionately punitive as war crimes there is a need for even greater protections for the accused'. Gerry J. Simpson, 'War Crimes: A Critical Introduction', in Timothy L.H. McCormack and Gerry J. Simpson (eds), *The Law of War Crimes* (Kluwer Law International, 1997), p. 15.

2 The Charter of the International Military Tribunal at Nuremberg has been referred to as the 'birth certificate of international criminal law': Heiko Ahlbrecht, 'Foundations', in Gerhard Werle (ed.), *Principles of International Criminal Law* (T.M.C. Asser Press, 2005), p. 6.

3 Churchill is quoted in minutes of a wartime cabinet meeting on 12 April 1945 as having said: 'Agree the trial will be a farce. Indictment: facilities for counsel. All sorts of complications ensue as soon as you admit a fair trial. I would take no responsibility for a trial – even though U.S. wants to do it. Execute the principal criminals as outlaws – if no Ally wants them.' Peggy McGuinness, 'Churchill on War Crimes Trials', *Opinio Juris* (23 January 2006), relying on Thomas Vinciguerra, 'The Private Thoughts of a Public Man', *The New York Times* (22 January 2006).

4 Section IV ('Fair Trial for Defendants') of the Charter of the International Military Tribunal.

5 Article 20 of the ICTY Statute. The next provision (Article 21), sets out the "[r]ights of the accused". Its sister tribunal, the International Criminal Tribunal for Rwanda (ICTR), contained similar provisions. The ICTY and ICTR have now been replaced by the International Residual Mechanism for Criminal Tribunals (IRMCT), but the relevant provisions of the IRMCT Statute are virtually the same: see Articles 18 and 19 of the IRMCT Statute.

contribution focusses, naturally also acknowledges the accused's right to a fair trial. The Court's legal texts do not explicitly refer to this right as such, but its various components are incorporated in several provisions of the Rome Statute of the International Criminal Court (Rome Statute),[6] such as Articles 22,[7] 23,[8] 55,[9] and 67.[10] In addition, some provisions of the Rome Statute more generally address the need for trial to be 'fair'[11] or refer to associated concepts, for instance the 'integrity of the proceedings'.[12] However, as discussed below, the phrase 'integrity of the proceedings', as well as the phrase 'in the interests of justice', are often used to justify the placing of certain limitations on the rights of an accused. Whereas the fair trial rights explicitly laid down in the various statutes of international criminal institutions mostly concern fundamental principles, such as *nullum crimen sine lege* and *ne bis in idem*, or the right not be tried in secret, the present contribution focusses specifically on evidentiary matters, and the related fair trial rights, such as due notice and the principle of equality.

One of the corollaries of the right to fair trial is the assessment of prejudice to the accused caused by certain actions of the other party – that is, the Office of the Prosecutor (Prosecution) – and/or actions by participants to the proceedings – that is, at the ICC, mainly the Legal Representatives of Victims – or prejudice resulting from decisions taken by the chamber seised of the case. Examples of such actions by the Prosecution are the late disclosure of materials that it intends

6 E.g., Articles 20, 22, 23, 24, 55, 64, 67, 68, and 69 of the Rome Statute. Naturally, the catch-all clause of Article 21(3), which requires the Court to bear 'internationally recognized human rights' in mind, can also be seen as incorporating fair trial rights.

7 Article 22 incorporates the principle of *nullum crimen sine lege*, albeit specifically in relation to the conduct in question being criminalised by the Rome Statute, as opposed to the law applicable to the alleged perpetrator at the time. However, Article 21(3), referred to in the previous footnote, provides that the Court is to apply and interpret the law in a manner consistent with internationally recognised human rights standards. Therefore, even if Article 22 does not provide the required protection, the Court would still be held to apply the broader *nullum crimen sine lege* principle as included in international human rights law, including, for example, the International Covenant on Civil and Political Rights. See Rogier Bartels, 'Legitimacy and ICC Jurisdiction following Security Council Referrals', in Nobuo Hayashi and Cecilia M. Bailliet (eds), *The Legitimacy and Effectiveness of International Criminal Tribunals* (Cambridge University Press, 2017), pp. 159–61; and Dapo Akande, 'Sources of International Criminal Law', in Antonio Cassese *et al.* (eds.), *The Oxford Companion to International Criminal Justice* (Oxford University Press, 2009), pp. 46–7.

8 Article 23 sets out the principle of *nulla poena sine lege*: 'A person convicted by the Court may be punished only in accordance with this Statute'.

9 Article 55 sets out the rights of persons during an investigation into alleged criminal conduct. At the time of an investigation, the relevant person is not yet an 'accused', which someone only becomes after the confirmation stage, but the relevant safeguards include traditional fair trial rights, such as the right not to be compelled to incriminate oneself, and the right to legal assistance.

10 Article 67 is entitled 'Rights of the accused' and provides that 'the accused shall be entitled [. . .] to a fair hearing conducted impartially', and sets out 'minimum guarantees', such as '[t]o be tried without undue delay' (Article 67(1)(c)).

11 E.g., Article 68(1), (3), and (4); and Article 69(4) of the Rome Statute.

12 Article 69(7) of the Rome Statute.

to introduce as incriminating evidence, or the addition of (new) witnesses to the Prosecution's list of witnesses after the relevant deadline imposed by the chamber, or after the trial proceedings have commenced.[13] Generally, a request will have to be made to do so, and in deciding on any such request the relevant chamber will evaluate the prejudice caused. That is to say, not merely whether prejudice is caused, but rather the level of prejudice that would be caused should the request be granted, since any decision by a trial chamber admitting incriminating evidence is, of course, prejudicial to the accused. Every witness testifying against the accused, and any piece of incriminating evidence admitted, as well as any day less to prepare because of late disclosure,[14] causes a certain inconvenience, or may have another negative impact on the work of the defence, and thus on the accused. Therefore, what has to be assessed, and thus the language that ought to be used by the relevant chamber, is whether any 'undue prejudice'[15] is caused.[16] There may be some prejudice, but it must not be too much.[17]

Other procedural decisions may affect the rights of the accused in another way, thereby causing prejudice, such as the granting of a request to rely on anonymous witnesses at the pre-trial stage,[18] or the granting of other, less far reaching, types of protective measures for witnesses that nonetheless limit the defence's ability to investigate these persons for the purposes of impeachment.[19] Both impact on

13 See, for example, ICC, Decision on prosecution requests to add witnesses and evidence and defence requests to reschedule the trial start date, *Prosecutor v. William Samoei Ruto and Joshua Arap Sang*, (ICC-01/09-01/11), 3 June 2013; ICC, Decision on the Prosecution's Requests to Add New Witnesses to its List of Witnesses, *Prosecutor v. William Samoei Ruto and Joshua Arap Sang*, (ICC-01/09-01/11), 3 September 2013; and ICC, Decision on Prosecution Request to Add Items to its List of Evidence, to include a Witness on its List of Witnesses and to Submit Two Prior Recorded Testimonies under Rule 68(2)(b) and (c), *Prosecutor v. Dominic Ongwen*, (ICC-02/04-01/15), 22 November 2016.

14 This is especially so when the preparation had initially started without the relevant items or witnesses in mind.

15 Other phrases used include 'unfair prejudice' or 'material prejudice'.

16 It is therefore important to observe that a decision granting any of the abovementioned requests by, *inter alia*, stating that 'no prejudice is caused' is incorrect.

17 Rule 136 of the ICC Rules of Procedure and Evidence mandates that cases against persons who are jointly accused must bet ried seperately if doing so is necessary 'to avoid serious prejudice to the accused'. It is not explained what would amount to 'serious prejudice', however.

18 See, e.g., Public Redacted Version of 'Decision on the Prosecution Motion for Authorization to File an Anonymous Summary concerning Witness MLI-OTP-P-P0113', *Prosecutor v. Al Hassan Ag Abdoul Aziz Ag Mohamed Ag Mahmoud*, (ICC-01/12-01/18), 13 September 2018 (public redacted version filed on 27 September 2018).

19 Article 8(4) of the ICC Code of Professional Conduct for counsel states, for example, that 'Counsel shall not reveal the identity of protected victims or witnesses, or any confidential information that may reveal their identity and whereabouts, unless he or she has been authorized to do so by an order of the Court'. In *Ruto and Sang*, the defence team for Mr Ruto argued that it was hampered in its ability to effectively investigate Prosecution witnesses because most of them had been granted protective measures. At the same time, the Prosecution was concerned that the methods of investigations used by the defence for Mr Ruto did not sufficiently protect the security and identity of some of its witnesses. See ICC, Decision

the accused's ability to confront the witnesses against him or her. In practice, however, the fact that one of the fair trial rights is impeded upon will still be considered in terms of prejudice. It is clear that any limitation on a fair trial right, such as the right to effectively test and challenge incriminating evidence, causes prejudice. Also in these cases, the assessment therefore is whether the amount of prejudice is not undue, and whether the prejudice is sufficiently mitigated.

This chapter analyses whether it can be assessed if undue prejudice will be suffered, or has been suffered, when it concerns procedural matters before the ICC relating to evidence. The present edited volume addressed the balancing of the rights of accused persons and of victims of crimes allegedly committed by these persons. When a chamber assesses the potential prejudice for the purposes of procedural decisions, it is effectively carrying out a balancing exercise. As discussed below, it makes this assessment by looking at the interest of the accused on one side and those of the Prosecution and victims on the other. The present chapter further discusses whether prejudice can only be suffered by the accused, or also by others, namely the Prosecutor or – through their legal representatives – victims.

What is prejudice?

The notion of prejudice is mentioned in various provisions of the Rome Statute and the Rules of Procedure and Evidence,[20] but it is not explained by these instruments. Indeed, Trial Chamber II, in *Katanga and Ngudjolo*, observed that 'as with probative value, it is not possible to define the meaning of prejudice exhaustively'.[21] The concept of prejudice has been referred to in many ICC decisions, including explanations of what must be understood as undue prejudice, or what remedies may be taken to prevent an act from becoming unduly prejudicial. These explanations will be discussed below.

The present contribution does not discuss the assessment whether any irreparable prejudice has been caused by intentional breaches of the fair trial rights of accused. In *Lubanga*, for example, the existence of irreparable prejudice was alleged by the defence for Mr Lubanga as a result of the use of intermediaries to obtain witnesses, and the non-disclosure by the Prosecution of United Nations documents.[22] This led to a temporary stay of proceedings of the trial, but not – as requested by Mr Lubanga – a permanent stay, which would effectively have

---

Related to Defence Submission of Confidential Defence Investigation Materials, *Prosecutor v. William Samoei Ruto and Joshua Arap Sang*, (ICC-01/09-01/11), 6 June 2014.

20 Articles 68 and 69 of the Rome Statute; and Rules 68, 72(2) and 136 of the Rules of Procedure and Evidence. It appears either as 'prejudice' or 'prejudicial'. Most references to either of these words are made in a different, unrelated context.

21 ICC, Decision on the Prosecutor's Bar Table Motions, *Prosecutor v. Germain Katanga and Matthieu Ngudjolo Chui*, (ICC-01/04-01/07), 17 December 2012, para. 38.

22 ICC, Judgment on the appeal of the Prosecutor against the decision of Trial Chamber I entitled "Decision on the consequences of non-disclosure of exculpatory materials covered by Article 54(3)(e) agreements and the application to stay the prosecution of the accused, together with certain other issues raised at the Status Conference on 10 June 2008"*Prosecutor v.*

meant the end of the trial. As a result, it has been observed that the 'threshold' warranting a definite stay of proceedings as a result of a violation of the rights of the accused is very high and 'almost impossible to meet'.[23]

More recently, in *Ntaganda*, the defence team for Mr Ntaganda requested an 'indefinite stay of proceedings'.[24] In the Defence's submission, the Prosecution had obtained access to phone conversations of Mr Ntaganda with third persons which the trial chamber had decided should not be given to the Prosecution in unredacted form, and thereby it had become privy to information about the defence strategy and defence witnesses, as a result of which the Prosecution allegedly 'gained an undue and unfair advantage causing grave prejudice to the accused and the fairness of the proceedings'.[25] Although the *Ntaganda* Trial Chamber found that Mr Ntaganda had suffered prejudice as a result of the Prosecution's actions,[26] it considered that the prejudice did not rise to the level that would warrant a stay of proceedings. The Trial Chamber was 'not convinced' that the prejudice identified reached the 'threshold for a stay of proceedings'.[27] Instead, it held that 'any prejudice may be remedied, retroactively and prospectively, through alternative, less drastic measures' than a stay of proceedings.[28]

The aforementioned two decisions assess the amount of prejudice caused as a result of actions by the Prosecution, but do so by considering whether the negative impact on the accused's rights was so disproportionate that it could not be remedied in any other way than by staying the proceedings.[29] While relevant to

---

Lubanga, (ICC-01/04-01/06), 21 October 2008; and ICC, Decision on Intermediaries, *Prosecutor v. Lubanga*, (ICC-01/04-01/06), 31 May 2010.

23 Masha Federova, Sten Verhoeven and Jan Wouters, 'Safeguarding the Rights of Suspects or Accused Persons in International Criminal Proceedings', *Leuven University Institute for International Law Working Paper No. 27* (June 2009), p. 25.

24 Interestingly, in light of the topic of this contribution, the Defence phrased it motion as a request for a 'stay of the proceedings against Mr Ntaganda *with prejudice to the Prosecutor*'. ICC, Public redacted version of the Defence Request for stay of proceedings with prejudice to the Prosecutor, *Prosecutor v. Bosco Ntaganda*, (ICC-01/04-02/06), 21 March 2017, paras 3, 12–13, 93–4 and p. 31.

25 Ibid.

26 The Chamber found that 'the fact that the Prosecution has had access to such information is prejudicial to the accused as it places the Prosecution in an unduly advantageous position vis-à-vis the Defence.' However, it continued to note that '[w]hile the Chamber is of the view that the Prosecution's access to such information is in itself prejudicial, the Chamber considers that, on the basis of the submissions made so far, the information which may be relevant to defence strategy appears to be limited.' (ICC, Decision on Defence request for stay of proceedings with prejudice to the Prosecution, *Prosecutor v. Bosco Ntaganda*, (ICC-01/04-02/06), 28 April 2017, paras 42–3).

27 Ibid., para. 43.

28 Ibid.

29 The various chambers of the ICC have consistently held that the remedy of a permanent stay of proceedings serves situations where it would be 'repugnant or odious to the administration of justice to allow the case to continue, or where the rights of the accused have been breached to such an extent that a fair trial has been rendered impossible'. Yet, a stay of proceedings constitutes 'an exceptional remedy to be applied as a last resort', and 'not every violation of fair trial rights will justify the imposition of a stay'. See, for example, ICC, Public

mention in a chapter dealing with the concept of prejudice, this type of request will not be further addressed. The present contribution focusses on regular procedural decisions, in situations where it is clear that any level of prejudice does not warrant a stay of proceedings, but rather the question is whether granting the procedural request may cause certain prejudice, and whether – as a result of the prejudice being 'undue' – the request ought to be rejected, or granted with conditions, to mitigate the prejudice.

In assessing whether any such 'undue prejudice' would occur in a particular circumstance, one must differentiate between prejudice and mere inconvenience. Lawful actions, such as including a large number of witnesses on the Prosecution's witness list, can cause the same form and level of inconvenience to the defence (and thereby the accused) as would be the case with actions that may be found to be unduly prejudicial. Yet, in the case of the former, the inconvenience is not prejudicial in the legal sense, as it has been contemplated and accepted by the legal process. Since the very nature of a criminal trial, as well as the Prosecution's role in the process, involves the bringing of incriminating evidence before judges, the presentation of evidence as such cannot be seen as prejudicial. By way of example, if the Prosecution places 60 witnesses on its list, who it seeks to examine for an average of six hours each, this obviously causes more work for the defence, in terms of investigations and preparation, than would be the case if the Prosecution's list of witnesses only included ten persons, each called to testify for a similar average of examination time. Yet, the placing of 50 more witnesses on its list, does not make the Prosecution's action prejudicial to the accused. It would be different if the Prosecution seeks to add additional witnesses after the disclosure deadline, thereby impeding the time provided to the defence to prepare for the testimonies, or even more so if the request to add witnesses is made while the trial has already commenced. As will be shown below, prejudice can therefore arise with regards to a fair right, such as the right to examine a witness providing incriminating evidence,[30] but also more generally with regards to the accused organising a proper defence, including having sufficient time to prepare – although the latter is, of course, also guaranteed through the right '[t]o have adequate time and facilities for the preparation of the defence'.[31]

Actions out of the ordinary, including failing to abide by timelines set by a chamber, such as the late addition of witnesses to the list of witnesses, do result in prejudice. As mentioned in the introduction, an example of a non-ordinary situation is the use of anonymous witnesses. Interestingly, in the early years of the ICC, its Appeals Chamber noted that the use of summaries without disclosure of the identities of the relevant witnesses to the defence, at the pre-trial stage, 'may affect the ability of the accused to challenge the evidence presented by the

---

redacted version of Decision on Defence application for a permanent stay of the proceedings due to abuse of process, 5 December 2013, *The Prosecutor v. Uhuru Muigai Kenyatta*, (ICC-01/09-02/11), para. 14, and the case law referred to therein.

30 As included for the ICC in Article 67(1)(e) of the Rome Statute.

31 Article 67(1)(b) of the Rome Statute.

Prosecutor at the confirmation hearing in two respects', the witnesses' identities are unknown to the defence and because it does not receive the underlying material 'the ability of the defence to evaluate the correctness of the summaries is restricted', yet it found that the use of such summaries of anonymous witnesses is 'not [. . .] necessarily prejudicial to or inconsistent with the rights of the accused and a fair and impartial trial'.[32] The Appeals Chamber appears to have accidentally mashed the concepts of prejudice to the accused, (in)consistency with the rights or the accused, and the concept of a fair and impartial trial, together.[33] Whereas the two aspects identified by the Appeals Chamber show that the use of summaries, and lack of disclosure of the identities and witness statements of witnesses, will negatively impact on the defence's ability to challenge this evidence, and thus is *per se* prejudicial, so long as the reliance on these summaries is sufficiently counterbalanced, the accused's rights – while affected – may not be *violated*, and the trial may still be fair.[34]

The difference between prejudice and undue prejudice is shown by admission of prior recorded testimony. As a result of the principle of orality, 'in-court personal testimony [is] the rule' at the Court.[35] For any request to admit non-oral testimony, as one of the exceptions provided for under Article 69(2) of the Rome Statute, 'a Chamber must ensure that doing so is not prejudicial to or inconsistent with the rights of the accused or with the fairness of the trial generally', and any decision on allowing the admission of prior recorded testimony therefore has to be made 'cautious[ly]'.[36] The ICTY Appeals Chamber had on an earlier occasion recalled that '[t]he principle of orality is intended principally to ensure

32 ICC, Judgment on the appeal of Mr. Thomas Lubanga Dyilo against the decision of Pre-Trial Chamber I entitled "First Decision on the Prosecution Requests and Amended Requests for Redactions under Rule 81", *Prosecutor v. Thomas Lubanga Dyilo*, (ICC-01/04-01/06), 14 December 2006, para. 50.

33 It is noted, however, that the same paragraph contains another sentence with similar, combined wording: 'is not *per se* prejudicial to or inconsistent with the rights of the accused and a fair and impartial trial'.

34 See ibid., para. 51. See also, Public Redacted Version of 'Decision on the Prosecution Motion for Authorization to File an Anonymous Summary concerning Witness MLI-OTP-P-P0113, *Prosecutor v. Al Hassan Ag Abdoul Aziz Ag Mohamed Ag Mahmoud*, (ICC-01/12-01/18), 13 September 2018 (public redacted version filed on 27 September 2018), paras 35-36, in which the Pre-Trial Chamber recalled that 'Pre-Trail Chambers have consistently stated that they attached lesser probative value to summaries of statement than to evidence given by witnesses whose identities were known to the defence, that the summaries had to be corroborated, and that no conclusions could be drawn exclusively on the basis of anonymous hearsay evidence.'

35 As concluded by the Appeals Chamber on the basis of Article 69(2) of the Rome Statute: ICC, Judgment on the appeals of Mr Jean-Pierre Bemba Gombo and the Prosecutor against the decision of Trial Chamber III entitled "Decision on the admission into evidence of materials contained in the prosecution's list of evidence", *Prosecutor v. Jean-Pierre Bemba Combo*, (ICC-01/05-01/08), 3 May 2011, para. 76.

36 Ibid., para. 78. Recalled by the Appeals Chamber in ICC, Judgment on the Decision on the Admission of Prior Recorded Testimony under Rule 68, *Prosecutor v. William Samoei Ruto and Joshua Arap Sang*, (ICC-01/09-01/11), 12 February 2016, para. 85.

the accused's right to confront the witnesses against him'.[37] By not being able to cross-examine a witness, the accused will suffer prejudice.[38] Trial Chamber II therefore, in a time before the amendment of Rule 68, which now allows for the admission of prior recorded testimony even with the accused's opposition, held that 'unless the accused persons have either waived their right to examine the witness or had the opportunity to do so when the testimony was recorded', admission of prior recorded testimony of a witness would necessarily be 'unduly prejudicial to the right of the accused to examine, or have examined, adverse witnesses'.[39] While the aforementioned right, as contained in Article 67(1)(e) of the Rome Statute, remains unchanged, the amendment of Rule 68[40] has now introduced legal limitations to this right. Interestingly, the level of prejudice resulting from the introduction of evidence against the will of the accused has changed as a result. Whereas, as found by Trial Chamber II, this would initially be unduly prejudicial, now that – following the amendment of the Rules of Procedure and Evidence – the admission of prior recorded testimony has become an institutionalised practice,[41] a decision with the same outcome would no longer be unduly prejudicial by definition, but may only be merely 'prejudicial' – to such a level that it does not prevent the introduction of prior recorded testimony into evidence.

The relevant legal framework still recognises that any prior recorded testimony that 'goes to proof of acts and conduct of the accused' would be more prejudicial and as such 'may be a factor against its introduction, or part of it'.[42] However, such indications to assist the assessment of the chamber are not generally included in the Rules of Procedure and Evidence. So how can chambers assess in practice whether any prejudice is caused; and if so, whether it can be sufficiently mitigated or whether the relevant decision would lead to undue prejudice? This is discussed next.

37 ICTY, Decision on interlocutory appeal concerning admission of record of interview of the accused from the bar table, *Prosecutor v. Sefer Halilovic*, (IT-01-48-AR73.2), 19 August 2005, para. 17.

38 E.g., ICC, Judgment on the appeals of Mr Jean-Pierre Bemba Gombo and the Prosecutor against the decision of Trial Chamber III entitled "Decision on the admission into evidence of materials contained in the prosecution's list of evidence", *Prosecutor v. Jean-Pierre Bemba Combo*, (ICC-01/05-01/08), 3 May 2011, para. 78.

39 ICC, Decision on the Prosecutor's Bar Table Motions, *Prosecutor v. Germain Katanga and Mathieu Ngudjolo Chui*, (ICC-01/04-01/07), 17 December 2010, paras 50–1.

40 Rule 68 of the ICC Rules of Procedure and Evidence was amended by the Assembly of States Parties in 2013 (Resolution ICC-ASP/12/Res.7) to include the possibility to admit evidence of witnesses who are either not examined by the Prosecution, but available for cross-examination, or who do not appear in person at all, for example because they are deceased or have been threatened. The amendments reflect the rules as included for the ICTY as Rules 92 *bis*, *ter*, *quater* and *quinquies*.

41 Arguably, as a result of the amendment, the admission of prior recorded testimony could be seen as no longer being out of the ordinary, but the fact that the amended rule continues to state that any such admission may only be done, 'provided that this would not be prejudicial to or inconsistent with the rights of the accused' shows that this is not the case.

42 Rule 68(2)(c) and (d) of the ICC Rules of Procedure and Evidence.

Assessing whether the prejudice is undue

The Court's case law has given some guidance how to assess prejudice. In relation to the admission of evidence, as mentioned above, and aptly noted by Trial Chamber I in *Lubanga*, 'it is trite to observe that all evidence that tends to incriminate the accused is also "prejudicial" to him'.[43] A chamber, in deciding on requests for admission into evidence, must ensure that it is not unfair to admit the disputed material. Trial Chamber I clarified that this could be so 'for instance because evidence of slight or minimal probative value has the capacity to prejudice the Chamber's fair assessment of the issues in the case'.[44] In *Katanga and Ngudjolo*, Trial Chamber II, after first noting that '[t]he existence and extent of prejudice must be ascertained on a case-by-case basis' and that it therefore would 'serve little purpose for the Chamber to discuss all possible forms of prejudice in general terms',[45] did set out some criteria to consider when deciding on so-called bar table motions (requests for the admission of documentary evidence not tendered through a witness). It also clarified that 'when addressing issues of prejudice, the Chamber will consider two questions: a) what causes the prejudice; and b) what suffers the prejudice'.[46] Trial Chamber II held that unduly prejudicial would be admission of evidence that would affect the right to be tried without undue delay, as enshrined in Article 67(1)(c) of the Rome Statute,[47] because the relevant evidence would require a disproportionate time to be presented to, or considered by, the chamber, as compared to its probative value.[48] As examples, one can think of the admission of very lengthy videos, or of entire books, even though they contain only a limited amount of relevant information. Trial Chamber II further highlighted the rather obvious situation that admission of evidence obtained in violation of the right to remain silent and not to be compelled to incriminate him- or herself, or the right to counsel, would be unduly prejudicial.[49] In relation to the same rights, it clarified that in a multi-accused trial, the admission of evidence on behalf of one of the accused, which would violate the rights of a co-accused, would also be unduly prejudicial; albeit not to the accused requesting the admission, but rather to his or her co accused.[50]

43 ICC, Decision on the admissibility of four documents, *Prosecutor v. Lubanga*, (ICC-01/04-01/06), 13 June 2008, para. 31.
44 Ibid.
45 ICC, Decision on the Prosecutor's Bar Table Motions, *Prosecutor v. Germain Katanga and Mathieu Ngudjolo Chui*, (ICC-01/04-01/07), 17 December 2010, para. 40.
46 Ibid., para. 38.
47 Interestingly, in *Mugiraneza* at the ICTR, first the trial chamber and then the Appeals Chamber considered that 'prejudice to the accused, if any' was only one of five factors of the 'determination of whether an accused person's right to be tried without undue delay has been violated': ICTR, Decision on Prosper Mugiraneza's Interlocutory Appeal from Trial Chamber II Decision of 2 October 2003 Denying the Motion to Dismiss the Indictment, Demand Speedy Trial and for Appropriate Relief, *Prosecutor v. Mugiraneza*, (ICTR–99–50–AR73), 27 February 2004, p. 3.
48 Ibid., para. 41.
49 Ibid., paras 55–65.
50 Ibid., paras 52–4.

In the same decision, as noted above, Trial Chamber II, in a time before the amendment of Rule 68 to allow for the admission of prior recorded testimony even with the accused's opposition, further held that the admission of prior recorded testimony of a witness would be unduly prejudicial.[51]

Prejudicial to whom?

As a result of the mostly adversarial system adopted for the trial proceedings at the Court,[52] the same legal framework is – perhaps unintentionally – generally used to decide on requests for both the phase in which the Prosecution presents its evidence[53] and the phase during which the Defence does so.[54] For example, the rule that in deciding on relevance or admissibility of any items, the trial chamber should take into account 'the probative value of the evidence and any prejudice that such evidence may cause to a fair trial or to a fair evaluation of the testimony of a witness',[55] is applied to requests for admissions into evidence by the Prosecution, as well as to such requests made by the Defence.[56] Similarly, the admission of prior recorded testimony for Defence witnesses is assessed on the basis of the same criteria as comparable requests by the Prosecution.[57] Although understandable from the perspective of the principle of equality of the parties,[58]

51 Ibid., paras 50–1. See the discussion above on Rule 68 of the ICC Rules of Procedure and Evidence.

52 Trial Chamber V(A) of the ICC observed in this regard that 'the [Rome] Statute does not prescribe a fixed structure for the manner or order in which evidence should be presented at trial.' It notes, however, 'the general practice in the administration of international criminal justice, which involves an arrangement in which the defence presents its own case following the conclusion of the case for the prosecution.' ICC, Decision No. 5 on the Conduct of Trial Proceedings (Principles and Procedure on 'No Case to Answer' Motions), *Prosecutor v. William Samoei Ruto and Joseph Arap Sang*, (ICC-01/09-1/11-1334), Trial Chamber V(A), 3 June 2014, para. 17.

53 Generally referred to as the 'Prosecution case'.

54 Referred to as the 'Defence case'. If the Legal Representative of Victims is permitted to present evidence, there is also a so-called 'Victims case'.

55 Article 69(4) of the Rome Statute.

56 Compare, for example, ICC, Decision on Prosecution's request for admission of documentary evidence, *Prosecutor v. Ntaganda*, (ICC-01/04-02/06), Trial Chamber VI, 28 March 2017, para. 6 with ICC, Decision on second Defence request for admission of evidence from the bar table, *Prosecutor v. Ntaganda*, (ICC-01/04-02/06), Trial Chamber VI, 21 February 2014, para. 5.

57 E.g., ICC, Public redacted version of 'Decision on Defence request for admission of prior recorded testimony of Witnesses D-0001, D-0013, D-0123, D-0134, D-0148, D-0150, D-0163, and D-0179 pursuant to Rule 68(2)(b), *Prosecutor v. Ntaganda*, (ICC-01/04-02/06), Trial Chamber VI, 4 December 2017, para. 8, which incorporates by reference the applicable law as set out in decisions on similar requests for admission of prior recorded testimony made by the Prosecution.

58 See, for example, ICTY, Decision on the Prosecutor's Appeal on Admissibility of Evidence, *Prosecutor v. Aleksovski*, (IT-95-14/1-AR73), 16 February 1999, para. 27, in which the principle of the equality of the parties is referred to justify treating a request by the defence similar to a similar one by the prosecution.

one can wonder how admission of evidence at the request of the Defence can be prejudicial to a fair trial. The admission of any incriminating item of evidence will cause certain prejudice to the accused, and it is therefore correct for chambers to assess whether the admission of evidence that was disclosed late or is admitted in a different manner than the orality requirement, causes 'undue prejudice' to the accused. However, who would be prejudiced by the admission of Defence evidence? Would that be the Prosecution, the victims, or perhaps the international community? Article 69(4) can be read as referring to a 'prejudice [. . .] to a fair evaluation of the testimony of a witness', but it is unclear who would be prejudiced by an 'unfair' evaluation of such testimony? An incorrect or unfair reflection of evidence impacts on the ability to reflect the truth, but as parties generally put forward their version of the truth,[59] and given that witness testimonies are evaluated by the trial chamber, is the prejudice perhaps caused to the Judges?

Whether it is correct to treat the Defence request in the same manner as Prosecution requests, will be discussed below. First it is worth noting in what manner the similar treatment is done. In *Ntaganda*, for example, the ICC Prosecution, in response to a request by the defence team for Mr Ntaganda to add witnesses to the Defence's witness list, submitted that 'the extent to which the Chamber may grant such requests has a direct impact on the degree of undue prejudice to the Prosecution and the need for adequate time to prepare'.[60] The Prosecution made this argument referring to two decisions by the *Ntaganda* Trial Chamber on a similar request by the Prosecution. In arguing that the Chamber should apply the same assessment to the Defence request, the Prosecution averred that the 'required' case-by-case assessment should lead the Chamber to conclude that prejudice to the Prosecution and the victims caused by granting the Defence request would 'far outweigh' the justifications for granting out forward by the Defence.[61] In deciding on the Defence request, Trial Chamber VI, seised of the *Ntaganda* case, did consider the 'potential prejudice' arising from the request – albeit not explicitly referring to the Prosecution.[62]

The same trial chamber, in later decisions on Defence requests to admit documentary evidence, applied the same 'applicable law' as it did to decide on similar requests by the Prosecution, which had been made during the phase of the trial in which the Prosecution presented its evidence.[63] It therefore analysed the

59 See, for example, Thomas Weigend, 'Should We Search for the Truth and Who Should Do It?', 36 *North Carolina Journal of International Law and Commercial Regulation*, (2011) pp. 401–16; Sergei Vasiliev, *International Criminal Trials: A Normative Theory* (Vol I, University of Amsterdam 2014), pp. 245–54.

60 ICC, Public redacted version of "Prosecution response to the Defence 'Request to add D-0251 and D-0257 to the Defence List of Witnesses, *Prosecutor v. Ntaganda*, (ICC-01/04-02/06, ICC-01/04-02/06-2052-Conf), 16 October 2017, para. 4.

61 Ibid, para. 27.

62 ICC, Decision on Defence Request to add Witnesses D-0251 and D-0257 to its List of Witnesses, *Prosecutor v. Ntaganda*, (ICC-01/04-02/06), 20 October 2017, para. 24.

63 ICC, Public redacted version of "Decision on Defence request for admission of evidence from the bar table", *Prosecutor v. Ntaganda*, (ICC-01/04-02/06), 31 January 2018, para. 4,

admissibility of documents, *inter alia*, 'on the basis of its relevance, probative value, and any prejudice that its admission may cause to a fair trial or to the evaluation of the testimony of a witness'.[64] In its analysis, the trial chamber indeed considered whether any 'undue prejudice' would arise from admission of the requested documents.[65] The trial chamber did not state that the potential undue prejudice would be against the accused, and given its reliance on the wording of Article 69(4) of the Rome Statute, the prejudice assessed could have been 'to the evaluation of the testimony of a witness' and not to the Prosecution, but given that the admission request mostly concerned documents, such as reports and internal documents of the organisation the accused was a member of, it is more likely that the Chamber was assessing potential undue prejudice to the Prosecution.

In case of requests for admission of evidence submitted by the legal representatives of victims, the relevance of the items must similarly be considered and their probative value weighed against the prejudice admission would cause to the accused. Whereas the relevance and related probative value concern the crimes the accused is charged with, admission of the item is in the interest of the victims, as without proof of any crimes (and any conviction) there are no 'victims' in the procedural sense of the term.[66]

Fair trial rights for the Prosecution and victims

While the accused's right to a fair trial, as noted above, is undisputed, one can debate whether the Prosecution has a similar right to fair trial – and, consequently, whether the Prosecution can suffer any prejudice. The Appeals Chamber of the ICTY held in *Prlić et al.* that the requirement that the trial be fair was 'not uniquely predicated on the fairness accorded to any one party'.[67] As a result of the Appeals Chamber's ruling, the Prosecution was not held to the deadline for the presentation of evidence initially set by the trail chamber, and took approximately eight months longer.[68] Treating the Prosecution as having fair trial rights may thus have a big impact on the right of the accused to an expeditious trial. Yet, in another ICTY case, its Appeals Chamber noted in relation to fair trial rights that the Prosecution acts on behalf of victims and the international community,[69]

---

referring to ICC, Decision on Prosecution's first request for the admission of documentary evidence, *Prosecutor v. Ntaganda*, (ICC-01/04-02/06), 19 February 2016, paras 6–7.

64 Ibid.

65 Ibid, e.g., paras 11, 14, and 15.

66 Rule 85(a) of the ICC Rules of Procedure and Evidence explains that '"[v]ictims" means natural persons who have suffered harm as a result of the commission of any crime within the jurisdiction of the Court.'

67 ICTY, Decision on Prosecution Appeal Concerning the Trial Chamber's Ruling Reducing Time for the Prosecution Case, *Prosecutor v. Prlić et al.*, (IT-04-74-AR73.4), Appeals Chamber, 6 February 2007, para. 14.

68 Yvonne McDermott, *Fairness in International Criminal Trials* (Oxford University Press, 2016), p. 109.

69 ICTY, Decision on Appeal against the Trial Chamber's Decision on the Evidence of Witness Milan Babić, *Prosecutor v. Martić*, (IT-95-11-AR73.2), Appeals Chamber, 14 September 2006, para. 13.

while a trial chamber in a further case explicitly referred to the Prosecution having a right to fair trial.[70] A trial chamber of the Special Tribunal for Lebanon similarly explicitly recognised a 'right to a fair trial' for the Tribunal's prosecution.[71]

At the Court, Judge Herrera Carbuccia, albeit in dissenting opinions,[72] has twice expressed her view that fair trial rights 'do not only belong to the accused'.[73] According to her,

> the right to a fair trial must be interpreted in a flexible and comprehensive manner, as fairness pertains to all parties: on the one hand the accused, and on the other, the Prosecutor, who acts on behalf of the international community, including the victims.[74]

In Judge Herrera Carbuccia's view, chambers must ensure respect for the interests of justice also with regards to the Prosecution, as

> [w]ithout these fundamental rights the Prosecutor's obligation to act before the court pursuant to Article 42(1) of the Statute and on behalf of the international community is hindered. Victims' right to seek justice and ultimately reparations is equally thwarted.[75]

This judge therefore clearly links the Prosecution's right to a fair trial to its role in acting on behalf of victims. However, if – as held by the ICTY Appeals Chamber in *Martić* – the ICTY Prosecution was considered to have a right to fair trial (in part) because it represented victims, one may wonder what this means for the ICC, where victims are represented by separate counsel. Does the difference in system mean that the victims, through their Legal Representative(s), have such a right, and the Prosecution does not?

In a series of decisions addressing the meaning of 'fairness' within the context of interlocutory appeals submitted pursuant to Article 82(1)(d) of the Rome Statute, the early ICC pre-trial chambers had defined 'fairness' in broad terms. Article 82(1)(d) requires a chamber to consider whether the issue a party wishes to appeal has the potential to affect the fair and expeditious outcome of the

70 ICTY, Retrial Judgment, *Prosecutor v. Haradinaj et al.*, (IT-04-84bis-T), Trial Chamber, 29 November 2012, para. 3.

71 STL, Decision on Prosecution Motion to Amend its Exhibit List and Oneissi Defence Request to Stay the Proceedings, *Prosecutor v. Ayyash et al.*, (STL-11-01/T/TC), 13 April 2015, para. 47.

72 The majority opinions to which her dissenting opinions relate, did not pronounce on this issue.

73 ICC, Dissenting Opinion to the Chamber's Oral Decision of 15 January 2019 (Judge Herrera Carbuccia), *Prosecutor v. Laurent Gbagbo and Charles Blé Goudé*, (ICC-02/11-01/15), 15 January 2019, para. 35.

74 ICC, Dissenting Opinion of Judge Herrera Carbuccia, *Prosecutor v. William Samoei Ruto and Joshua Arap Sang*, (ICC-01/09-01/11), 5 April 2016, para. 27.

75 ICC, Dissenting Opinion to the Chamber's Oral Decision of 15 January 2019 (Judge Herrera Carbuccia), *Prosecutor v. Laurent Gbagbo and Charles Blé Goudé*, (ICC-02/11-01/15), 15 January 2019, para. 35.

proceedings. In this context, Pre-Trail Chamber II held in 2005 that '[f]airness is closely linked to the concept of "equality of arms", or of balance, between the parties during the proceedings.'[76] It continued to explicitly 'recognise' that 'the requirement of fairness exists for all participants in the proceedings and therefore also operates to the benefit of the Prosecutor'.[77] In 2006, also linking it to the equality of the parties, Pre-Trial Chamber I explained that

> [t]he term "fairness" (*equite*) from the Latin "*equus*" means equilibrium, or balance. As a legal concept, equity or fairness "is a direct emanation of the idea of justice." Equity of the proceedings entails equilibrium between the parties, which assumes both respect for the principle of equality and the principle of adversarial proceedings.[78]

This Chamber held that 'fairness of the proceedings includes respect for the procedural rights of the Prosecutor, the Defence, and the Victims as guaranteed by the relevant statutes (in systems which provide for victim participation in criminal proceedings).'[79]

In a 2007 decision, also dealing with a request for leave to file an interlocutory appeal, Pre-Trial Chamber II considered that the right to fair trial, as set out in the major human rights treaties,

> has two main components: 'a general one', applicable to various types of proceedings (civil, criminal or administrative), and a specific one, related to the rights of the defence in criminal proceedings. With regard to criminal proceedings, it is usually understood that the right to a fair trial applies first and foremost to a defendant or to the defence. However, the Chamber wishes to recall that 'the general component' of fairness should be preserved to the benefit of all participants in the proceedings, including the Prosecutor.[80]

Pre-Trial Chamber I held that

> within the context of the Statute, respect for the fairness of the proceedings with regard to the Prosecutor, at the investigation phase of a situation,

76 ICC, Decision on Prosecutor's application for leave to appeal in part Pre-Trial Chamber's II's decision on the Prosecutor's applications for warrants of arrest under Article 58, *Situation in Uganda*, (ICC-02/04-01/05), Pre-Trial Chamber II, 21 August 2005, para. 30 (footnotes omitted).

77 Ibid, para. 31.

78 ICC, Decision on the Prosecutor's Application for Leave to Appeal the Chamber's Decision of 17 January 2006 on the Application for Participation in the Proceedings of VPRS1, VPRS 2, VPRS 3, VPRS 4, VPRS5 and VPRS6, *Situation in the Democratic Republic of Congo*, (ICC-01/04), Pre-Trial Chamber I, 31 March 2006, para. 38.

79 Ibid.

80 ICC, Decision on Prosecutor's applications for leave to appeal dated the 15th day of March 2006 and to suspend or stay consideration of leave to appeal dated the 11th of May 2006, *Situation in Uganda*, (ICC-02/04-01/05), Pre-Trial Chamber II, 10 July 2006, para. 24.

means that the Prosecutor must be able to exercise the powers and fulfil the duties listed in Article 54.[81]

One can wonder then, whether the fair trial rights only attach to the Prosecution during the investigation phase, when victims are not yet participating in a case before the Court, and the Prosecution therefore may be seen as representing their interests during these early stages of what may later become actual trial proceedings. In this regard, the decisions discussing fair trial rights of the Prosecution in the context of interlocutory appeals are not of much assistance, as victims, through their legal representatives, are participants to the proceedings and therefore do not have a right to appeal.[82] Consequently, they cannot ask for leave to appeal decisions, even if a decision directly impacts on them. In requesting leave to start interlocutory appeal proceedings, the Prosecution therefore has to also represent the interest of the victims in the situation or case. In assessing the fairness for the purposes of Article 82(1)(d), the right to a fair trial awarded to the Prosecution may therefore, in whole or in part, be derived from its role in representing victims.

81 ICC, Decision on the Prosecutor's Application for Leave to Appeal the Chamber's Decision of 17 January 2006 on the Application for Participation in the Proceedings of VPRS1, VPRS 2, VPRS 3, VPRS 4, VPRS5 and VPRS6, *Situation in the Democratic Republic of Congo*, (ICC-01/04), Pre-Trial Chamber I, 31 March 2006, para. 38.

82 Article 82 of the Rome Statute only refers to '[e]ither party'. The Court's case law has confirmed that victims may request to participate in an interlocutory appeal, but may not themselves request leave to appeal. See in this regard the interesting filings in the Afghanistan situation before Pre-Trial Chamber II of the ICC, including the various victim representatives' requests for leave to appeal and direct appeals before the Appeals Chamber (see, e.g., ICC, Victims' Notice of Appeal of the 'Decision Pursuant to Article 15 of the Rome Statute on the Authorisation of an Investigation into the Situation in the Islamic Republic of Afghanistan, *Situation in the Islamic Republic of Afghanistan*, (ICC-02/17-36), 10 June 2019, and the Prosecution's reaction to these requests (ICC, Observations concerning diverging judicial proceedings arising from the Pre-Trial Chamber's decision under Article 15 (filed simultaneously before Pre-Trial Chamber II and the Appeals Chamber), *Situation in the Islamic Republic of Afghanistan*, (ICC-02/17-36), 12 June 2019). The Prosecution's observation were afterwards heavily criticised on Twitter. On 17 September 2019, Pre-Trail Chamber II, by majority, while granting the Prosecution leave to appeal its decision, rejected the requests for leave to appeal filed by the various groups of victim. It held that 'the individuals who submitted the Victims' Request only qualify as potential victims, whose procedural rights are limited to those expressly bestowed on them', and that 'allowing (potential)victims to request leave for an appeal review of the decision adjudicating those proceedings would subvert [the] legislative choice [of th drafters not to expressly grant (potential) victims the option to appeal Article 15 decisions] and thus unduly interfere with the delicate balance underlying the provision as a whole.' ICC, Decision on the Prosecutor and Victims' Requests for Leave to Appeal the 'Decision Pursuant to Article 15 of the Rome Statute on the Authorisation of an Investigation into the Situation in the Islamic Republic of Afghanistan', *Situation in the Islamic Republic of Afghanistan*, (ICC-02/17-36), paras 20 and 24. In his partially dissenting opinion to the aforementioned decision, Judge Mindua expressed his view that, in specific circumstances, victim, and even 'potential victims', ought to be permitted to appeal such a decision, especially in case the Prosecution would not seek lave to appeal.

The ICC Prosecution evidently considers that it independently possesses fair trial rights, also during the rest of the proceedings. The Deputy Prosecutor, referring to the ICTY case law discussed above, stated that the Prosecution is 'entitled to be treated fairly in proceedings before the ICC, pursuant to Article 64(2) of the Rome Statute. Just as the accused and victims participating in the proceedings are entitled to a fair trial, so too fairness includes respect for the procedural rights of the Prosecutor.'[83] He averred that '[t]he guarantee of a fair trial attracts [. . .] the protection of the ability of the Prosecutor to fulfil her mandate under the Rome Statute.'[84] This argument is based on the provisions and case law of the ICC legal framework that relate to the equality of the parties, but also on the 'strong societal interest' in a fair trial.[85] Although it is correct that '[a] fair process serves the truth-finding function of a trial and offers greater assurance that the final judgment will be accurate',[86] this does not support a finding that the Prosecution itself has fair trial rights under the ICC's legal framework. Moreover, one can wonder how the Prosecution's opposition to Defence evidence being admitted, or Defence witnesses being added, alleging that this would be prejudicial to the Prosecution, can be justified when the purpose is to find the truth.

Certainly, the Prosecution is entitled to have the case it brings before a chamber considered in a serious and impartial manner, but basic fair trial rights have developed in order to guard the accused in a system where the opposing side has a full State machinery at its disposal. The European Commission on Human Rights explained that

> in any criminal proceedings brought by a state authority, the prosecution has at its disposal, to back the accusation, facilities deriving from its powers of investigation supported by judicial and police machinery with considerable technical resources and means of coercion. It is in order to establish equality, as far as possible, between the prosecution and the defence that national legislation in most countries entrusts the preliminary investigation to a member of the judiciary or, if it entrusts the investigation to the Public Prosecutor's Department, instructs the latter to gather evidence in favour of the accused as well as evidence against him. It is also, and above all, to establish that same equality that the 'rights of the defence' [. . .] have been instituted.[87]

That fair trial rights cannot be applied 'in reverse', that is, to the other party, was expressed early in the existence of the ICTY. As part of the Tribunal's first case,

83 James Stewart, *Fair Trial Rights under the Rome Statute from a Prosecution Perspective*, presentation at the ICTR Symposium (Arusha, 7 November 2014), p. 14. See also p. 2 of the same. Mr Stewart's speech is included in the online 'Compendium on the Legacy of the ICTR and the Development of International Law', produced by the ICTR, available at http://unictr.irmct.org/en/compendium-legacy-ictr-and-development-international-law.

84 Ibid, p. 2.

85 Ibid, pp. 14–15.

86 Ibid, p. 16.

87 *Jespers v. Belgium*, No. 8493, Report of the European Commission on Human Rights, 27 D.R. [1981] 61 at 87.

Judge Vohrah expressed the view that fair trial rights and the principle of equality of arms only aim to protect the accused, not the prosecution.[88]

A scholar, who critically discusses the *ad hoc* tribunals' case law in which the Prosecution is found to have a right to fair trial, convincingly shows the problems that may arise from such an approach.[89] Indeed, the 'perception of the fair trial as a balancing exercise between the rights of the accused and the interests of the prosecution can only result in inequity in practice, considering the prosecution's already privileged position.'[90] Moreover, entering into a balancing exercise is dangerous, as it allows for the accused's rights to be outweighed by other factors.[91] Another academic submits that 'application of the concept of a fair trial in favour of both parties is understandable', because the Prosecution acts on behalf of the international community and in the interest of victims.[92] From this perspective, he argues, relying on an early ICTY Appeals Chamber decision, 'it is difficult to see how a trial could ever be considered to be fair where the accused is favoured at the expense of the Prosecution beyond a strict compliance with those fundamental protections'.[93] However, a 'strict compliance' with the rights of the accused actually requires precisely that the accused be favoured, for example, in relation to the burden of proof, or generally in relation to the application of the principle of *in dubio pro reo*.[94]

Concluding remarks

Procedural decisions can cause an impact upon an accused's fair trial rights, either by negatively affecting his or her defence team's ability to provide for an effective defence, or because a matter directly impinges on another fair trial right, such as the right to be tried without undue delay. If the impact amounts to undue prejudice, the request concerned should not be granted or the procedural action ought not to be permitted. In cases where a fair trial right would be directly violated,

88 ICTY, Decision on Prosecution Motion for Production of Defence Witness Statement, Separate Opinion of Judge Vohrah, *Prosecutor v. Tadić*, (IT-96-1-T), 27 November 1996.

89 McDermott, *supra* note 67, pp. 109–15; and Yvonne McDermott, 'Rights in Reverse: A Critical Analysis of Fair Trial Rights Under International Criminal Law', in William A. Schabas, Yvonne McDermott, and Niamh Hayes (eds), *The Ashgate Research Companion to International Criminal Law: Critical Perspectives* (Ashgate, 2013), pp. 165–80.

90 Ibid, p. 111.

91 Ibid.

92 Vladimir Tochilovsky, *Jurisprudence of the International Criminal Courts and the European Court of Human Rights: Procedure and Evidence* (Brill, 2007), p. 276.

93 *Ibid*, quoting ICTY, Decision on the Prosecutor's Appeal on Admissibility of Evidence, *Prosecutor v. Aleksovski*, (IT-95-14/1-AR73), 16 February 1999, para. 27.

94 Incorporated in the Rome Statute in Articles 66(2) and 22(2), respectively. The principle of *in dubio pro reo*, as included in the Rome Statute, relates only to the definition of a crime, but as the ICTY Appeals Chamber has clarified, this principle is 'a corollary to the presumption of innocence, and the burden of proof beyond a reasonable doubt, [and therefore] applies to findings required for conviction, such as those which make up the elements of the crime charged: ICTY, Judgment, *Prosecutor v. Limaj et al.*, (IT-03-66-A), Appeals Chamber, 27 September 2007, para. 21.

determining that prejudice arises to the accused is straightforward. However, if it concerns a weighing of probative value and prejudice, or an assessment of how much additional work a certain decision will cause, thereby potentially affecting the effectiveness of the defence, there is a lot of room for the bench to exercise discretion when considering whether the prejudice is undue. Such discretion is necessary since the level of prejudice will depend upon many factors that may change throughout the trial. For a request for late disclosure, the various factors to take into account include the amount of disclosure; the content and to what extent it relates to the acts and conduct of the accused or whether it relates to matters that witnesses have already testified about;[95] the time left before a witness related to the disclosure will appear; and many other issues that require a full understanding of the case and the specifics of the trial proceedings concerned.

The practice of the ICC shows that chambers often apply the same regime to adjudicate procedural requests by the Prosecution and the Defence. This enables the Prosecution to allege that it would suffer undue prejudice if the Defence request would be granted,[96] *inter alia*, by calling upon a right to fair trial for the Prosecution. The Prosecution's right to fair trial is said to derive from the principle of equality of the parties, or from the Prosecution's stated role in representing the victims and international community.

Treating the Prosecution as having to act in the interest of victims and thereby being entitled to a right to fair trial may be appropriate in relation to certain aspects of a case, such as requests for interlocutory appeals, or certain stages, such as during the investigation stage, when no actual case against an identified accused yet exist. However, it would generally be more appropriate to not take such an approach, as any decision that considered the Prosecution's (alleged) fair trial rights in denying all or part of the relevant Defence request will by way of its outcome have negatively affected the accused. Assessing whether the Prosecution will suffer prejudice will thus generally lead to a reverse prejudice to the accused.

The Prosecution must have an opportunity to properly present its case,[97] or to put it differently, it must 'not be unduly hampered in the presentation of its case',[98] but the rights of the accused must not be breached when doing so. If the Prosecution presents a strong case in an effective manner, this will have a negative impact on the accused but it is not unduly prejudicial, as the presentation of incriminating evidence is an inherent feature of criminal trials. Or, alternatively,

95 Meaning that they could not be cross-examined on the information contained in the disclosure, unless the witnesses would be recalled.

96 As shown above, the Prosecution may also, prior to being aware of the regime that the relevant chamber will apply to Defence requests, make submissions that indicate that in its view the Defence should be held to the same standard.

97 See, e.g., ICTY, Decision on Prosecution's Request for Certification of Rule 73bis Issue for Appeal, *Prosecutor v. Milutinović et al.*, (IT-05-87-T), 30 August 2006, para. 10.

98 ICTR, Decision on Prosecution Joint Motion for Re-Opening its Case and for Reconsideration of the 31 January 2006 Decision on the Hearing of Witness Michel Bagaragaza via Video-Link, *Prosecutor v. Zigiranyirazo*, (ICTR-2001-73-T), 16 November 2006, para. 18.

if the Prosecution is prevented from presenting certain evidence, because doing so would violate the accused's fair trial rights or otherwise be unduly prejudicial to him or her (e.g. because disclosure took place too late or because the identity of a source or witness could not be provided to the Defence and the accused), the Prosecution is not unduly hampered, as upholding the rights of the accused cannot be contrary to a fair trial.

5 UNSC sanctions regimes and the ICC

Arguments against cooperation for arrest and investigative purposes in light of defendants' rights

Alice Riccardi

Article 41 of the United Nations (UN) Charter empowers the UN Security Council (UNSC or Council) to adopt measures not involving the use of force in order to maintain or restore international peace and security. Until the 1990s, the UNSC used these measures, commonly known as sanctions, to comprehensively target States threatening or breaching the peace. The catastrophic humanitarian consequences of state-oriented sanctions imposed in the aftermath of the Cold War (e.g. in the cases of 1990 Iraq and 1994 Haiti) prompted the Council to modify their scope *ratione personae*: sanctions became 'targeted' or 'smart', namely directed against the persons functionally in a position to trigger the sanctions in the first place, as in the case of measures inflicted against members of the military junta in 1997 Sierra Leone. The emergence of the Al-Qaeda terrorism threat and the fight against the proliferation of arms of mass destruction convinced the Council to de-territorialize sanctions, which today can target individuals and entities irrespective of any link with a given State. When an individual is sanctioned, he/she is usually hit by a temporally unlimited travel ban, an asset freeze and an arms embargo. At the time of writing, 709 individuals (and 302 entities) are listed under 14 sanctions regimes.[1] The vast majority of legal scholars agree that sanctions blatantly violate the rights of those targeted,[2] most notably their due process rights, as affected individuals and entities are not accorded a forum for review at the UN level nor informed of the information substantiating the sanctions. In 2013, the European Court of Justice (ECJ) – when meting out its final decision in the *Kadi* saga – factored in that UNSC smart sanctions infringe upon targeted individuals' due process rights.[3]

Notwithstanding the despicable human rights record of smart sanctions, practice shows that since at least 2012 an idea has been floated to formalise a relationship between the International Criminal Court (ICC or the Court) and UNSC

1 UNSC, 'Consolidated Security Council Sanctions List' (3 March 2020) <www.un.org/securitycouncil/content/un-sc-consolidated-list> accessed 3 March 2020.

2 The doctrinal production on this issue is gargantuan. Above all see Bardo Fassbender, 'Targeted Sanctions Imposed by the UN Security Council and Due Process Rights' 3 International Organizations Law Review (2006), p. 437.

3 Joined Cases C-584/10 P, C-593/10 P and C-595/10 P *Commission and others v Kadi* [2013] ECLI:EU:C:2013:518.

Sanctions Committees (SCs) – i.e. the UNSC sub-organs managing sanctions.[4] This proposal is widely supported today: in 2018, the proposal was expressly encouraged by the ICC Assembly of States Parties (ASP);[5] endorsed by the Prosecutor;[6] and welcomed by various States.[7] In a nutshell, such proposed formalisation aims at inflicting smart sanctions upon persons fleeing ICC arrest. The underlying idea is that sanctions could function as 'negative incentives'[8] directed against fugitives, thereby 'enhanc[ing] the prospect that requests of the Court for the[ir] arrest and surrender are expeditiously executed'.[9] At the time of writing, only Kony has been sanctioned by the UNSC after the issuance of an ICC arrest warrant against him, although almost 15 years after the warrant was unsealed. Accordingly, there is currently no evidence of UNSC sanctions being imposed immediately following the issuance of an ICC arrest warrant.[10]

However, some coordination between SCs and the Court is happening: for instance, in 2017, roughly one month before the Prosecutor affirmed that she was 'collaborating and sharing information with a network of national and international agencies' on the issue of the crimes committed against migrants attempting to transit through Libya,[11] the President of the Libya SC affirmed that: 'I

4 UNSC 6849th meeting (17 October 2012) UN Doc S/PV.6848 23, statement of France.

5 ASP 'Strengthening the International Criminal Court and the Assembly of States Parties' (6 December 2019) ICC-ASP/18/Res.6, para 32(c). For earlier accounts see: ASP 'Strenghtening the International Criminal Court and the Assembly of States Parties' (17 December 2018) ICC-ASP/17/Res.5, paras 40(c), 51; ASP 'Report on the draft Action Plan on arrest strategies, submitted by the Rapporteur' (16 November 2015) ICC-ASP/14/26/Add.1 (Draft Action Plan), paras 31(a), 36(b), 40(a)(ix)(d); ASP 'Strengthening the International Criminal Court and the Assembly of States Parties' (14 December 2017) ICC-ASP/16/Res.6, para 35(c).

6 Office of the Prosecutor, 'Statement of the Prosecutor of the International Criminal Court, Fatou Bensouda, at first Arria-formula meeting on UNSC-ICC relations' (6 July 2018) (Statement of the Prosecutor). For earlier accounts see UNGA 'Report of the International Criminal Court' (28 August 2015) UN Doc A/70/350, paras 95–8.

7 UN Web TV, 'UNSC-ICC relations: achievements, challenges and synergies – Security Council, Arria formula meeting' (6 July 2018) <http://webtv.un.org/meetings-events/watch/unsc-icc-relations-achievements-challenges-and-synergies-security-council-arria-formula-meeting/5806377792001/?term=> accessed 3 March 2020, 01h.03min, 02h.13min, statements of France and Mexico. For earlier accounts see UNSC: 6849th meeting (17 October 2012) UN Doc S/PV.6848 28, statement of Estonia and UN Doc S/PV.6848 (Resumption 1) 6, 14, 17, statements of Australia, Lithuania and Costa Rica; 7285th meeting (23 October 2014) UN Doc S/PV.7285 (Resumption 1) 3, statement of Romania; 7323th meeting (25 November 2014) UN Doc S/PV.7323 16, statement of Luxembourg; 'Annex, Assessment report. Achievements, challenges and opportunities resulting from the recommendations of the Compendium of the High-Level Review of United Nations Sanctions' (23 June 2017) UN Doc S/2017/543 9.

8 Draft Action Plan, *supra* note 6. See also Office of the Prosecutor, 'Strategic Plan 2019–2021' (17 July 2019), para 31.

9 ASP Resolution 3 (27 November 2013) ICC-ASP/12/Res. 3, para 15. Also, the infliction of sanctions may be used to secure reparation. This paper does not discuss this issue.

10 Although some other ICC fugitives are blacklisted, their listing predates the issuance of arrest warrants.

11 Office of the Prosecutor, 'Statement of the ICC Prosecutor to the UNSC on the situation in Libya' (9 May 2017), para 25.

recently floated the idea with the Chief Prosecutor of the International Criminal Court as to whether it would be possible to consider human trafficking as a crime against humanity'.[12] In June 2018, the Libya SC added six individuals to its sanctions list due to their involvement with transnational trafficking networks.[13] One of these is the Commander of the Libyan Coast Guard in Zawiya.[14] The status of ICC investigations is at present unknown to this author.

This recent episode reveals that a relationship between the Office of the Prosecutor (OTP) and SCs, albeit informal, already exists. Further instances show that this relationship is not limited to mere exchanges of views (as in the above example), but that information is also exchanged for investigative purposes.[15] UNSC documents clearly demonstrate that a binary information sharing channel is operating between SCs and the OTP. There is indeed evidence that the OTP and SCs have routine contacts either directly[16] or indirectly, i.e. through so-called sanctions expert monitoring bodies,[17] namely those bodies created by the UNSC to undertake field investigations with the aim of overseeing the implementation of sanction regimes. According to the Court, the 'increasing dialogue'[18] with these bodies is of high value for the OTP, as the latter '*often obtain, very early on, valuable information* on situations of interest to the Office' (emphasis added).[19] In its 2017 Report to the UN, the Court affirmed that it 'continues to work

12 UNSC 7927th meeting (19 April 2017) UN Doc S/PV.7927 21.

13 UNSC 'Security Council Committee concerning Libya Adds Six Individuals to its Sanctions List' (7 June 2018) UN Doc SC/13371.

14 UNSC, 'Narrative summary of reasons for listing of LYi.026 Abd Al Rahman Al-Milad' (7 June 2018) <www.un.org/securitycouncil/sanctions/1970/materials/summaries/individual/abd-al-rahman-al-milad> accessed 3 March 2020.

15 UNSC 'Annex. Compendium of the High-Level Review of United Nations Sanctions' (12 June 2015) UN Doc S/2015/432 (HLR Compendium), 67.

16 E.g. with the Libya SC (UNSC: 7706th meeting (6 June 2016) UN Doc S/PV.7706 4; 'Report of the Security Council Committee established pursuant to resolution 1970 (2011) concerning Libya' (30 December 2016) UN Doc S/2016/1078, 4).

17 Including with: i) the Panel of Experts of the Libya SC (UNSC 'Final report of the Panel of Experts on Libya established pursuant to resolution 1973 (2011)' of: (5 September 2018) UN Doc S/2018/812 para 12; (1 June 2017) UN Doc S/2017/466 8; (9 March 2016) UN Doc S/2016/209 8; (20 March 2012) UN Doc S/2012/163 57); ii) the Group of Experts of the Democratic Republic of Congo SC (UNSC: UN Doc S/2004/551 34; UN Doc S/2005/30 50; UN Doc S/2008/773 123; UN Doc S/2012/845; UN Doc S/2013/433; UN Doc S/2014/42; UN Doc S/2016/466 48); ii) the Monitoring Group of the ISIL (Da'esh) & Al-Qaida SC (UNSC UN Doc S/2003/669 31); iii) the Panel of Experts of the Central African Republic SC (UNSC 'Final report of the Panel of Experts on the Central African Republic established pursuant to Security Council resolution 2127 (2013)' (29 October 2014) UN Doc S/2014/762 58); and iv) the Group of Experts of the Côte d'Ivoire SC (UNSC 'Letter dated 22 February 2016 from the Group of Experts on Côte d'Ivoire addressed to the Chair of the Security Council Committee established pursuant to resolution 1572 (2004)' (17 March 2016) UN Doc S/2016/254 49, and para 202).

18 UNGA 'Report of the International Criminal Court' (18 September 2014) UN Doc A/69/321, 17.

19 UNGA 'Report of the International Criminal Court' (28 August 2015) UN Doc A/70/350, para 88.

towards strengthening cooperation' with SCs.[20] Although it is clear that information is shared among the two international organisations, neither the UN nor the Court have provided any legal basis for this, nor have they published guidelines regulating their relationship or clarified how they use shared information.[21] As will be shown below, however, such sharing may have far-reaching negative consequences on the respect of the rights of ICC defendants.

Against this background, the present chapter aims to test the partially *in fieri* relationship between the Court and SCs in light of the rights of ICC defendants, particularly the right to a fair trial and its corollaries. This chapter thus contributes to the broader debate fostered by this book by specifically looking at an under-investigated albeit crucial issue impacting on the rights of defendants and potentially undermining the legitimacy of the Court and of the international criminal justice project as a whole. Accordingly, the next section discusses the prospective infliction of UNSC sanctions against individuals sought by the Court, and the following one challenges the operation of an information sharing channel between the OTP and SCs. The chapter concludes by arguing that the Court – both as a matter of law and as a matter of policy – should re-think any current or future cooperation with the UNSC in light of the legal framework within which the former operates, with the aim of not frustrating the right to a fair trial of ICC defendants.

Enforcing ICC arrest warrants through UNSC smart sanctions

It is still unclear how the infliction of smart sanctions against ICC fugitives should happen in practice. First, whereas some argue that the UNSC should only act upon referrals of serious instances of States' non-compliance pursuant to Article 87(7) ICC Statute,[22] others believe that the Council should be free to act irrespective

20 UNGA 'Report of the International Criminal Court' (17 August 2017) UN Doc A/72/349, para 92.

21 Generally speaking, those supporting an ICC/SCs relationship justify it in the following legal terms: the UNSC's competence to enforce the peace may overlap with the purpose of enforcing the law; hence, respective SCs' and ICC's "jurisdictions" naturally intersect (Enrico Carisch, Sue Eckert and Loraine Rickard-Martin, 'High Level Review of UN Sanctions. Background Paper' (*Watson Institute for International Studies/Compliance & Capacity Skills International*) <www.hlr-unsanctions.org/20140706_HLR_Background.pdf> accessed 3 March 2020, 12; Kirsten Boon, 'Jurisdictional Overlap: Security Council Sanctions and the ICC' (*Opinio Juris*, 25 July 2014) <http://opiniojuris.org/2014/07/25/jurisdictional-overlap-security-council-sanctions-icc/> accessed 3 March 2020; Art. 3 of the Relationship Agreement between the ICC and the UN (Negotiated Relationship Agreement between the ICC and the UN (adopted 4 October 2004, entered into force 4 October 2004) 2283 UNTS 196) provides for the obligations to cooperate and consult on matter of mutual interest; said broadly-phrased obligations may serve as the legal basis for inflicting smart sanctions against individuals warranted by the ICC and allow for reciprocal exchanges of information on situations of interest.

22 Larissa van den Herik, 'The Individualization of Enforcement in International Law' in Tiyanja Maluwa, Max du Plessis and Dire Tladi (eds), *The Pursuit of a Brave New World in International Law* (Brill, 2017), pp. 234, 256–7.

of the judicial findings of States' inaction.[23] Second, among those supporting the latter scenario, some maintain that sanctions should automatically follow arrest warrants;[24] others instead affirm that the Council should be left with 'sufficient flexibility' in adopting sanctions.[25] Third, there is no agreement as to whether sanctions should be adopted only in the context of cases emerging from situations referred to the Court by the UNSC, or otherwise. The present author has dealt with these issues elsewhere,[26] and accordingly, this chapter does not delve into these questions. Rather, given that a clear picture is still lacking, the present analysis considers the law as it stands today, namely, it: first, postulates that UNSC determinations are discretionary,[27] thus a scenario in which smart sanctions are inflicted automatically upon an ICC arrest warrant is currently unconceivable; second, assumes that smart sanctions would be adopted within the context of existing sanctions regimes;[28] third, hypothesises that sanctions would be adopted *after* the issuance of ICC arrest warrants and with the *purpose of facilitating arrest.* Against this framework of analysis, the next two sections attempt to define such new type of UNSC sanctions and then discuss their legal consequences.

Attempting a definition

Generally speaking, the UNSC has always steadfastly affirmed that smart sanctions are 'preventative in nature and not reliant upon criminal standards',[29] as they 'do not impose a criminal punishment or procedure, such as detention, arrest or extradition'.[30] Accordingly, doctrine commonly portrays them as administrative

23 Deborah Ruiz Verduzco, 'The Relationship between the ICC and the United Nations Security Council' in Carsten Stahn (ed), *The Law and Practice of the International Criminal Court* (Oxford University Press, 2015), pp. 30, 61.

24 *Inter alia*: statement of France, *supra* note 7; HLR Compendium, *supra* note 15, 58; Statement of the Prosecutor, *supra* note 6; ASP 'Report of the Court on the status of ongoing cooperation between the International Criminal Court and the United Nations, including in the field' (14 October 2013) ICC-ASP/12/42, para 49.

25 Draft Action Plan, *supra* note 5, paras 11–13.

26 Alice Riccardi, 'On the Use of UN Smart Sanctions in Connection with ICC Proceedings: A (Human Rights-Oriented) Rebuttal' 1 *Diritti umani e diritto internazionale* (2018) 77, pp. 88–97.

27 Nico Krisch, 'Article 39' in Bruno Simma et al (eds), *The Charter of the United Nations*, vol. II (Oxford University Press, 2012), pp. 1272, 1275.

28 It may indeed be argued that the UNSC could develop an autonomous sanctions regime where to list ICC defendants.

29 *Inter alia* UNSC Res: 1735 (22 December 2006) UN Doc S/RES/1735 preamble para 10; 2083 (17 December 2012) UN Doc S/RES/2083 preamble para 14; 2253 (17 December 2015) UN Doc S/RES/2253, paras 44, 58.

30 UNSC 'Third report of the Analytical Support and Sanctions Monitoring Team appointed pursuant to resolution 1526 (2004) concerning Al-Qaeda and the Taliban and associated individuals and entities', (9 September 2005) UN Doc S/2005/572 para 41; Office of the Ombudsperson, 'Approach and Standards' <www.un.org/securitycouncil/ombudsperson/approach-and-standard> accessed 3 March 2020 (Ombudsperson, Approach and Standards). In critical terms see Lisa Ginsborg, 'UN sanctions and counter-terrorism strategies: moving towards thematic sanctions against individuals?' in Larissa van den Herik (ed), *Research Handbook on UN Sanctions and International Law* (Elgar, 2017), pp. 73, 89.

measures not subject to criminal fair trial guarantees for they are not intended to be punishment for criminal conduct.[31] Would this classification still hold if sanctions were inflicted in connection with ICC arrest warrants? It is argued that the answer to this question is in the negative. In such a scenario, smart sanctions would work as a (hereto unknown) pre-trial tool to enforce ICC arrest warrants *substantially connected* to the proceedings before the Court. This 'substantial connection' is demonstrated by two factors, namely the sanctions' rationale and evidentiary standard.

First, whereas normally sanctions overlook the criminal proceedings in which the target may be involved, in the case at hand they would be inflicted *because* a criminal charge is brought against him/her. Hence, sanctions would have a clear criminal law enforcement rationale (i.e. to force fugitives into custody or in any case facilitate their arrest). Accordingly, they would lose their preventative character. In this respect, it should also be underlined that sanctions would not be imposed as a reaction to alleged violations of international law (specifically, of the ICC Statute) with the aim of 'hamper[ing] access to resources in order to impede, impair, isolate and incapacitate . . . and encourage a change of conduct.'[32] UNSC sanction regimes indeed already commonly provide for the listing of individuals who commit crimes under international law, with a deterrent aim. In contrast, in cases involving the new procedure, sanctions would be imposed with the purpose of inducing the target to surrender to the Court – which is not currently a legal obligation – and stand trial.

Second, whereas in 'ordinary' sanctions cases the criminal proceedings to which the target may be subjected form only a part of the assessment of whether to list, in the scenario at hand an arrest warrant would be *the* basis for listing. It follows that SCs would 'import' the standard enshrined in Article 58(1)(a) of the ICC Statute, and inflict sanctions relying upon the evidentiary threshold of 'reasonable grounds to believe that a person has committed a crime within the jurisdiction of the Court'.

Legal consequences

The 'substantial connection' of smart sanctions with ICC pre-trial proceedings would cause three main sets of consequences related to sanctions' i) adoption, ii) review and iii) implementation.

There are three main consequences related to the modalities of sanctions' adoption: first, sanctions would violate the principle of separation of power. Indeed, although adopted as pre-trial tools of criminal law enforcement, they would be inflicted by an executive body, i.e. the UNSC. Notably, sanctions would escape the

31 *Contra*, above all: Ian Cameron, 'The European Convention on Human Rights, Due Process, and United Nations Security Council Counter-Terrorism Sanctions' *Council of Europe*, 6 February 2006, 10; UNGA 'Report of the Special Rapporteur on the promotion and protection of human rights and fundamental freedoms while countering terrorism' (16 August 2006) UN Doc A/61/267, paras 34 ff.

32 Ombudsperson, Approach and Standards, *supra* note 30.

judicial control of the very court managing the proceedings which should benefit from them, i.e. the ICC, whose judges would have no right to review sanctions' adoption, implementation, suspension and termination. Second, an inherent consequence of allowing the Council to officially become a law enforcement pillar of individual criminal responsibility is that such enforcement will be subject to the Council's dynamics, including the exercise of its permanent members' veto power. SCs' decisions are indeed adopted by consensus; however, if consensus cannot be reached, the matter may be submitted directly to the UNSC.[33] This would inescapably entail unequal treatment of different ICC defendants, depending on whether any permanent UNSC member had an interest in the situation from which the case stems from. As the law stands,[34] it is hardly imaginable that permanent members who are not party to the ICC Statute will not veto the infliction of sanctions against, at a minimum, their citizens, or persons acting on their behalf, direction or control in cases stemming from e.g. the Afghan,[35] Ukrainian[36] and Georgian situations.[37] Third, by blurring the line between executive and judicial powers, the infliction of sanctions as ICC pre-trial enforcement tools will further exacerbate anti-ICC sentiments of those States lacking the political leverage to resist the adoption of sanctions against persons entangled with them. This would disrupt the intention of the ICC Statute's drafters to protect the Court from the UNSC dynamics even further. Evidence of this is already emerging: the Assembly of the African Union directed its member States parties to the ICC Statute to reject the adoption of the draft Action Plan proposed by the ASP Special Rapporteur on Arrest Strategies, in the light of the novel powers in enforcing sanctions (and arrests) that such document calls upon the UNSC to assign to peacekeeping missions.[38]

A second group of consequences of smart sanctions derive from the general principle of international law that fair trial guarantees are applicable throughout

33 See: ISIL (Da'esh) & Al-Qaida SC 'Guidelines of the Committee for the conduct of its work' (23 December 2016) (ISIL (Da'esh) & Al-Qaida SC Guidelines), para 4(a); DRC SC 'Guidelines of the Committee for the conduct of its work' (6 August 2010) (DRC SC Guidelines), para 4(c); Sudan SC 'Guidelines of the Committee for the conduct of its work' (23 December 2013) (Sudan SC Guidelines), para 4(c); Libya SC 'Provisional Guidelines of the Committee for the conduct of its work' (25 October 2011) (Libya SC Guidelines), para 4(c); CAR SC 'Guidelines of the Committee for the conduct of its work' (20 March 2017) (CAR SC Guidelines), para 4(a); Mali SC 'Guidelines of the Committee for the conduct of its work' (29 January 2018) (Mali SC Guidelines), para 4(c).

34 See Art. 27, UN Charter.

35 Judgment on the appeal against the decision on the authorisation of an investigation into the situation in the Islamic Republic of Afghanistan, *Situation in the Islamic Republic of Afghanistan* (ICC-02/17 OA4), Appeals Chamber, 5 March 2020, paras 65 ff, on crimes allegedly committed by members of the US armed forces and members of the CIA.

36 OTP 'Report on Preliminary Examination Activities 2017' (4 December 2017), p. 19 ff.

37 Decision on the Prosecutor's request for authorization of an investigation, *Situation in Georgia* (ICC-01/15-12), Pre-Trial Chamber I, 27 January 2016, paras 24–35.

38 AU Assembly 'Decision on the International Criminal Court' (29 January 2018) Assembly/AU/Dec.672(XXX), para 5(vi); AU Assembly 'Decision on the International Criminal Court' (18 July 2016) Assembly/AU/Dec.616(XXVII).

the proceedings for the determination of a criminal charge, including at the pre-trial stage.[39] If the argument is accepted that sanctions are pre-trial tools to facilitate the arrest of ICC fugitives, minimum fair trial guarantees shall be extended to them, including procedural rights, such as the right to judicial review before an independent and impartial court within a reasonable time, and the rights of the defence, including the right to be heard. Judicial review should be particularly aimed at establishing whether sanctions' severity is justified against the aim sought (facilitating arrest), given that sanctions immensely compress the freedom of movement of those affected (as per the travel ban), their right to private and family life (as per the travel ban and the assets freeze), and their right to property (as per the assets freeze). Sanctions are indeed indefinite and permanent measures which may be exempted from only under specific circumstances.[40] Absent said guarantees, the ICC would 'benefit' from measures which gravely infringe upon fair trial rights, the gist of which may be said to be part of *jus cogens.*

Last, sanctions are implemented by States, which are under a legal obligation – stemming from Article 25 UN Charter – to freeze the assets and impede the travel of targets. Lacking a forum for review at the UN level, sanctions' implementing measures may be impugned by targeted individuals before domestic courts. Within the EU legal order, *inter alia*, the ECJ made it generally clear that, upon impugnation, EU courts shall conduct i) a legal review of the lawfulness of the grounds substantiating the sanction and ii) a factual review to verify whether the sanction has 'sufficiently solid factual basis'.[41] The same two-step test would equally apply in the case at hand, should an ICC fugitive targeted with a UNSC sanction impugn the sanction's national implementing measure. Two scenarios may emerge. First, national authorities may agree with the argument that sanctions are 'substantially connected' with ICC proceedings. In such case, they could either annul the sanction for it is a criminal law enforcement measure unknown to the legal order of the given State – and this, in terms of the ICC's legitimacy, is particularly worrying;[42] or, in any case, test it *vis-à-vis* the standard proper to criminal pre-trial proceedings. Second, national authorities may still consider the sanction to be an administrative measure and test it *vis-à-vis* the 'sufficiently solid factual basis' standard. In both scenarios, however, domestic courts will indirectly scrutinise the evidence brought by the ICC Prosecutor to

39 Among many: *Imbroscia v Switzerland* (App no 13972/88), ECtHR, 24 November 1993, para 36; *Vera Fernandez-Huidobro v Spain* (App no 74181/01) ECtHR, 6 January 2010, para 109.

40 It seems that, for instance, the Libya SC denied a UN member State's request for authorisation to unfreeze part of Al-Senussi's assets to pay for his legal representation before the ICC. See UNSC 'Final report of the Panel of Experts established pursuant to resolution 1973 (2011) concerning Libya' (9 March 2013) UN Doc S/2013/99, paras 250 ff. In other situations, relevant SCs lifted travel bans to allow witnesses and accused to travel to the Hague (e.g. UN Doc: S/2006/1048; S/2012/3) or to afford basic expenses when detained under the ICC custody (e.g. UN Doc S/2013/747).

41 *Kadi, supra* note 3, paras 117–19.

42 See Antonios Tzanakopoulos, *Disobeying the Security Council* (Oxford University Press, 2011), pp. 154ff.

substantiate her request for an arrest warrant. This would entail fragmentation of enforcement and de-legitimisation of the Court. Indeed, although domestic scrutiny of ICC arrest warrants may not be a problem in the courts of ICC 'like-minded' States, it would certainly be before the courts of States opposing ICC arrest warrants, e.g. in Sudan.[43]

In conclusion, the use of UN smart sanctions to tackle the ICC arrest dilemma will associate the Court with a tool that unequivocally violates the rights of targets. Hence, as the law stands today, the infliction of smart sanctions to induce surrender must be resisted, unless – at a minimum – appropriate procedures to guarantee ICC defendants' human rights are put in place. In any case however, the infliction of sanctions would inherently entail a (further) politicisation of ICC proceedings and may trigger de-legitimisation spirals: thus, such use may be counter-productive in achieving universality of the ICC Statute and rather confirm the perception of the Court as an organisation prone to the most powerful States.

UNSC-OTP information sharing

As anticipated in the introduction, it appears that SCs and the OTP are already informally exchanging information for investigative purposes.[44] This relationship is grounded in the idea that it is 'highly useful for the Prosecutor, when investigating a situation in which targeted sanctions have been imposed . . . to expeditiously access information and documents of the relevant sanctions committee';[45] and that, vice versa, SCs could make use of the situation-specific information gathered by the Prosecutor.[46] This chapter does not discuss the latter stream of the interaction, but rather focuses on the former, as it is particularly worrying *vis-à-vis* the rights of ICC defendants. Accordingly, the following sections describe the SCs' information gathering processes, and then discuss questions arising from the use of information retrieved from SCs in the proceedings before the Court.

UNSC's processes of information gathering

SCs are UNSC subsidiary bodies,[47] to which the Council delegates a form of secondary normative power.[48] Hence, they are 'as much as political organs as the

43 Revealingly, although the Sudan sanctions regime allow for the listing of individuals who 'commit violations of international humanitarian law or human rights law or other atrocities' (UNSC Res 1591 (2005) UN Doc S/RES/1591 para 3(c)), President Al-Bashir was never added to the list.

44 See practice mentioned in *supra* notes 16–20.

45 Marina Mancini, 'UN Sanctions Targeting Individuals and ICC Proceedings: How to Achieve a Mutually Reinforcing Interaction' in Natalino Ronzitti (ed), *Coercive Diplomacy, Sanctions and International Law* (Brill, 2016), p. 228, 230. See also France statement, *supra* note 7, 01h.03min; HLR Compendium, *supra* note 15, 68.

46 S/2005/30, *supra* notes 17, 50; EU statement, *supra* note 7, 02h.27 min.

47 See Art. 29, UN Charter.

48 Laura Picchio Forlati and Linos-Alesander Sicilianos (eds), *Economic Sanctions in International Law* (Brill-Nijhoff, 2004), p. 568.

Security Council itself'.[49] This is reflected in SCs' methods of information gathering, which are political rather than judicially focused. Notably, SCs mainly utilise two channels to gather the information upon which they adopt listing decisions.

First, each SC relies upon monitoring bodies.[50] The ISIL (Da'esh) & Al-Qaida sanction regime is the only one allowing listed individuals and entities to submit a petition for delisting to an Ombudsperson.[51] It is difficult to classify the activities of said bodies. Indeed, although they share some characteristics with fact-finding (e.g. they are composed of experts), they do not aim at dispute settlement and are rather political in terms of their agenda, focus and operation – *inter alia*: the scope of their mandates mirrors that of the corresponding SC, they meet in closed sessions and do not undertake comprehensive investigations. Furthermore, the majority of the information that monitoring bodies provide to SCs is not made public. Notably, monitoring bodies do not disclose information on individuals proposed for listing (for the evident reason of not forewarning targets).[52] As to the information that is made public, there is no real elaboration on the evidentiary standards employed. Although monitoring bodies usually affirm in a standardized manner[53] that they use the 'evidentiary standard' of basing their 'findings on documents and, wherever possible, on first-hand, on-site observations by the experts themselves' and, when impossible, they 'corroborate information by using at least three independent and reliable sources',[54] it is clear that these indications do not point to any evidentiary standard, but rather concern the methodology of information gathering. In turn, these bodies do not make clear which standard they use, nor if they have one. The Ombudsperson to the ISIL (Da'esh) & Al-Qaida SC is the only one which affirms that it adopts the standard of 'sufficient information to provide a reasonable and credible basis for the listing'. However, the Ombudsperson's reports are confidential and only shared with the relevant SC. Evidentiary standards cannot be deduced from SC's reports. The reports indeed do not employ language recalling judicial concepts (e.g. expressions/terms such as 'reasonable suspicion', 'balance of probabilities', 'certainty', etc.); furthermore, when they affirm having 'evidence' that a fact occurred, they do not provide for a threshold (e.g. 'credible', 'sufficient', 'reasonable', 'convincing', etc.).

An example may help in illustrating the lack of clear evidentiary standards and methodology of information gathering. An individual recently sanctioned by the

49 Alain Pellet and Alina Miron, 'Sanctions' in Rudger Wolfrum (ed), *MPEPIL* (Oxford University Press, 2013), para 40.

50 See, *supra* note 17.

51 UNSC Res 1904 (17 December 2009), UN Doc S/RES/1904 (2009), paras 20–7.

52 UNSC 'Final report of the Panel of Experts on Libya established pursuant to resolution 1973 (2011)' (1 June 2017) UN Doc S/2017/466 69, where information on individuals meeting designation criteria are 'provided separately'.

53 Following the recommendation of UNSC 'Report of the Informal Working Group of the Security Council on General Issues of Sanctions' (22 December 2006) UN Doc S/2006/997 (Report of the Informal Working Group), paras 21–3.

54 UNSC 'Final report of the Group of Experts on the Democratic Republic of Congo' (4 June 2018) UN Doc S/2018/531 (Final report 2018), para 5.

Democratic Republic of Congo (DRC) SC is Guidon Shimiray Mwissa.[55] Mwissa is said to be the commander of the armed group Nduma défense du Congo-Rénové (NDC-R). Mwissa's Narrative Summary of Reasons for Listing (i.e. the public document published on the UNSC website constituting the only information released to the target providing the reasons for his listing) indicates that '[t]he NDC-R, led by Guidon Shimiray Mwissa, uses child soldiers and deployed them in armed conflict.'[56] This information may be of high relevance for the OTP, which also seeks Sylvestre Mudacumura, the FDLR army commander,[57] namely the group against whom Mwissa is said to be fighting.[58] Hence the OTP may want to use the DRC SC's Group of Experts' public reports for investigative/prosecutorial aims. However, the only information that can be retrieved from said reports concerning the allegation that Mwissa's armed group recruits and uses children is a general reference to 'the continued use of children by armed groups' in eastern DRC.[59] In a report published after Mwissa's sanctioning, the Group added that 'ex-combatants told the Group that there were many children present in the movement and that several were considered to be combatants. According to MONUSCO officials, there were 46 documented cases of child recruitment by NDC-R in 2017'.[60]

Evidently, the DRC SC's reports fall short of containing information that may be useful for the OTP: they are not detailed;[61] the specific sources of the information are not identified, hence it is impossible to verify them;[62] there is no indication as to whether evidence (e.g. interviews with ex-combatants) was preserved, nor is it said whether interviews were conducted under oath;[63] the Group does not indicate its confidence in the findings; there appears to have been no effort made to corroborate the MONUSCO statements,[64] nor to collect information

55 UNSC, 'Narrative Summary of reasons for listing of CDi.033, Guidon Shimiray Mwissa' (1 January 2018) <www.un.org/securitycouncil/sanctions/1533/materials/summaries/individual/guidon-shimiray-mwissa> accessed 3 March 2020.

56 Ibid.

57 Decision on the Prosecutor's Application under Article 58, *Prosecutor v Sylvestre Mudacumura* (ICC-01/04-01/12), Pre-Trial Chamber II, 13 July 2012.

58 UNSC 'Final report of the Group of Experts on the Democratic Republic of the Congo' (23 May 2016) UN Doc S/2016/466, para 77.

59 UNSC 'Midterm report of the Group of Experts on the Democratic Republic of the Congo' (28 December 2016) UN Doc S/2016/1102, para 97.

60 Final report 2018, *supra* note 54, para 79.

61 Hence they may be hardly defined as fact-finding. See: UNGA 'Declaration on Fact-Finding by the United Nations in the Field of the Maintenance of International Peace and Security' (9 December 1991) UN Doc A/RES/46/59 para I(2); Stephen Wilkinson, 'Standards of Proof in International Humanitarian and Human Rights Fact-Finding and Inquiry Missions' (*Adh Genève*, 2012).

62 As required in Report of the Informal Working Group, *supra* note 53, para 21.

63 See Dov Jacobs and Cathering Harwood, 'Can International Criminal Investigators and Prosecutors Afford to Ignore Information from United Nations Human Rights Sources?' in Morten Bergsmo (ed), *Quality Control in Fact-Finding* (Torkel Opsahl Academic Epublisher, FICHL Publication Series 2013), pp. 325, 338.

64 It should be highlighted in this respect that there is evidence that peacekeeping missions use private military contractors especially in the field of intelligence gathering. cf Lindsey

from different parties, etc. Above all, there is no reference to exculpatory evidence. This is an overwhelmingly important issue. Although SCs have also been called upon to investigate exculpatory information,[65] their reports usually include no indication to this end. Notably, no Narrative Summary of Reasons for Listing published on the UNSC website includes exculpatory information.[66] Overall, these considerations run in favour of the opinion that SCs are not neutral, but 'conceived or viewed as political tools . . . to achieve geo-political ends'.[67]

This brief overview suffices to rule out the hypothesis that the OTP may use SCs monitoring bodies' public documents. However, as anticipated, these bodies also possess confidential information. Furthermore, they are not the only entities supplying information to SCs. Above all, SCs rely heavily upon information channelled directly by States. States are indeed the entities empowered to request SCs to list individuals, and in such case they shall:

> provide [SCs] a detailed statement of case in support of the proposed listing that forms the basis or justification for the listing.. . . The statement of case should provide as much detail as possible . . . including: (1) specific findings and reasoning demonstrating that the criteria are met; (2) the nature of supporting evidence (e.g., reports by the Group of Experts, intelligence, law enforcement, judicial, media, admission by subject, etc.); and (3) supporting evidence or documents that can be supplied.[68]

However, only a minimal part of the statements of case is made publicly available in the Narrative Summary of Reasons for Listing substantiating each listing. This is due to the classified (intelligence) nature of the information upon which sanctioning is usually grounded.[69] Notably, the ISIL (Da'esh) & Al-Qaida SC may refuse to share its information with no less that the Ombudsperson.[70] Furthermore, SCs may grant anonymity to the very State proposing the listing.[71] This entails that information provided by States cannot be externally verified, as

---

Cameron, *The Privatization of Peacekeeping: Exploring Limits and Responsibilities under International Law* (Cambridge University Press, 2017), pp. 27–9. On the use of contractors by US in particular see Simon Chersterman, '"We Can't Spy . . . If We Can't Buy!": The Privatization of Intelligence and the Limits of Outsourcing "Inherently Governmental Functions"' 9 *European Journal of International Law* (2008) 1055.

65 High Level Review of United Nations Sanctions and Compliance & Capacity Skills International 'Assessment Report' (August 2017) 11, Annex 24–5.

66 UNSC, 'Narrative Summaries of Reason for Listing' <www.un.org/securitycouncil/sanctions/narrative-summaries> accessed 3 March 2020.

67 Dan Saxon, 'Purpose and Legitimacy in International Fact-Finding Bodies' in Morten Bergsmo (ed), *supra* note 63, pp. 211, 222.

68 DRC SC Guidelines para 5(c). In similar terms see: ISIL (Da'esh) & Al-Qaida SC Guidelines para 6(h); Sudan SC Guidelines para 5(c); Libya SC Guidelines para 5(c); CAR SC Guidelines para 6(f); Mali SC Guidelines para 6(f), all quoted in *supra* note 33.

69 See, e.g., Libya SC Guidelines para 5(c); Sudan SC Guidelines para 5(c); ISIL (Da'esh) & Al-Qaida SC Guidelines paras 6(h)(5) and 4(c), all quoted in *supra* note 33.

70 Ibid., para 7(aa).

71 Ibid., para 6(j).

the sharing is made in a closed session. It is known that some individuals sanctioned by the ISIL (Da'esh) & Al-Qaida SC challenged their listing, claiming that the intelligence substantiating it was obtained through torture.[72] The overall process lacks transparency, and not even SCs can verify information provided by States, over which they have no control.

In conclusion, public information contained in monitoring bodies' reports is generally not credible, reliable or accurate, and hence would be of little or no use to the Prosecutor.[73] Still, she may be interested in having access to confidential information held by SCs either supplied to them by their monitoring bodies or by States. This is a particularly complex issue, dealt with in the following sub-section.

On the use by the OTP of UNSC confidential information

Should the OTP be interested in obtaining confidential information held by SCs, it should enter (if it is not already doing so) into confidentiality agreements/arrangements with the UNSC under Article 54(3)(e) of the ICC Statute,[74] which places non-disclosure obligations upon the OTP. It is a given that the Prosecutor would be (or is) forced to agree to not disclose such information, following the so-called 'originator control' principle, according to which the sharing of intelligence may happen only if the receiving entity ensures the information's secrecy by guaranteeing that no external scrutiny of the originator's decision to classify the information will be exerted upon sharing. This is the usual condition upon which the UNSC shares information, and in no court proceedings known to this author has the UNSC agreed to lift the 'originator control', thereby allowing the receiving entity to share sanctions information with the reviewing court, due to the risk that the latter could decide to disclose it to the parties in its entirety.[75] As a matter of law, agreements/arrangements concluded in such a fashion would blatantly violate the ICC Statute, as follows.

First, the Appeals Chamber in *Lubanga* clarified that confidentiality agreements cannot be routinely concluded by the OTP but shall only be relied upon

72 See UNHRC 'Report of the Special Rapporteur on the promotion and protection of human rights and fundamental freedoms while countering terrorism' (21 February 2017) UN Doc A/HRC/34/61 para 19; Office of the Ombudsperson, 'Approach to Analysis, Assessment and Use of Information' <www.un.org/securitycouncil/ombudsperson/assessment-information> accessed 3 March 2020 para 2.2; Case T-248/13 *Al-Ghabra v Commission* [13 December 2016] ECLI:EU:T:2016:721; *Youssef v Secretary of State for Foreign and Commonwealth Affairs* [2016] UKSC 3 on appeal from [2013] EWCA Civ 1302.

73 UN Interagency Working Group on Sanctions 'High Level Review of UN Sanctions' (*United Nations*, 2014) 12, according to which 'there is continuing concern about the performance of experts panels, specifically with regard to evidentiary standards, due process, and independent review of listing and de-listing'.

74 According to which '[t]he Prosecutor may . . . enter into such arrangements or agreements, not inconsistent with this Statute, as may be necessary to facilitate the cooperation of a State, intergovernmental organization or person'.

75 Case C-27/09 P *Council v PMOI* [2011] ECLI:EU:C:2011:853, para 75.

exceptionally.[76] The plan to formalise the SCs-ICC relationship suggests the opposite of this.

Second, it is argued that *ad hoc* arrangements would also be inconsistent with the Statute, namely, with the principle that Trial Chambers shall review *ex parte* confidential material held by the OTP in order to discern 'which counter-balancing measures can be taken to ensure that the rights of the accused are protected and that the trial is fair'.[77] The right to disclosure is not absolute as it may be at odds with competing public interests, such as the security of States and international organisations, or the protection of the individual providing the information. In this respect, the ICC Appeals Chamber decided to align itself to the European Court of Human Rights[78] and ECJ case-law,[79] in affirming that Trial Chambers shall adopt adequate safeguards on a case-by-case basis to protect the interests of the accused, including the right to disclosure of exculpatory material.[80] Accordingly, the ICC has held that confidential material *shall be handed* to the ICC judges who will decide:[81] i) prior to trial, whether such material must or must not be disclosed to the defence (in the latter event, the OTP cannot then introduce the material into evidence at trial without prior disclosure);[82] (ii) during trial, how to accommodate competing interests, e.g. by disclosing summaries of the original information. This approach is completely unacceptable to the UNSC, which, as discussed above, would never agree to share these details with ICC judges and thereby risk full disclosure.

Ad absurdum, should the UNSC decide to disclose some material to the Court, the latter would not be satisfied with mere summaries of relevant information,[83]

76 Judgment on the appeal of the Prosecutor against the decision of Trial Chamber I entitled 'Decision on the Consequences of Non-disclosure of Exculpatory Material Covered by Article 54(3)(e) Agreements and the Application to Stay the Prosecution of the Accused, Together with Certain Issues Raised at the Status Conference on 10 June 2008', *Prosecutor v Lubanga* (ICC-01/04-01/06-1401 OA 13), Appeals Chamber, 21 October 2008, para 55.

77 *Ibid*, para 51; cf. ICC RPE Rules 77, 81(2)-(4).

78 *Van Mechelen and others v the Netherlands* (App nos 21363/93, 21364/93, 21427/93 and 22056/93), ECtHR, 23 April 1997, para 58.

79 See Joined Cases C-402 & 415/05 P *Kadi & Al Barakaat International Foundation v Council and Commission* [2008] ECLI:EU:C:2008:461 para 326.

80 See Article 67(2), ICC Statute; Decision on the Consequences of Non-Disclosure of Exculpatory Materials Covered by Article 54(3)(e) Agreements and the Application to Stay the Prosecution of the Accused, Together with Certain Other Issues Raised at the Status Conference on 10 June 2008, *Prosecutor v Lubanga* (ICC-01/04-01/06-1401), Trial Chamber I, 13 June 2008, paras 88-89. See also UNHRC 'Concluding observations of the Human Rights Committee. Canada' (20 April 2006) UN Doc CCPR/C/CAN/CO/5 para 13, where the UNHRC clarified that the right of access to documents covers all materials 'that are exculpatory', irrespective of 'exceptional circumstances'; UNHRC 'General Comment No. 32' (23 August 2007) UN Doc CCPR/C/GC/32 para 33.

81 *Lubanga, supra* note 76, para 46.

82 Rule 81(2), ICC RPE.

83 Which is, in the author's experience in litigating UNSC sanctions, the only form in which SCs' intelligence is disclosed.

for they lack details allowing for the identity of the source to be traced. Indeed, the Appeals Chamber has already clarified that 'it is the evidence and not the summaries which should be provided to the court'.[84] Hence, the material should be handed to the Court in its original form and entirety.[85] This is in order not to frustrate i) the power of the Trial Chambers to decide on disclosure[86] and ii) defence rights, in particular the right to access facilities (a right which encompasses also access to evidence) and the right to call/examine witnesses.[87]

Notwithstanding this, should the OTP still conclude confidentiality agreements with the UNSC to merely gather so-called 'spring-board' evidence (i.e. evidence leading to the discovery of further, so-called 'lead' evidence, where only the latter is admitted into evidence at trial), it would violate the principle of equality of arms and the right to adversarial proceedings, both constitutive elements of the concept of a fair trial. The former means that each party shall not be placed at a substantial disadvantage *vis-à-vis* the opponent.[88] The latter, that in principle each party shall have knowledge of, and comment upon, all evidence adduced by the other party, with the view of influencing the court in its decision.[89] The conclusion of confidential agreements with the UNSC to gather 'spring-board' evidence may violate both principles from a threefold viewpoint. First, these agreements may allow (or are allowing) the OTP to conceal large amounts of information, thereby creating 'dossiers of secret information concerning the situation and the conduct of the accused'.[90] Second, the OTP would (or is) taking advantage of a privileged relationship with the UNSC to which defence teams have no access at all.[91] Both these occurrences would place defences at a substantial disadvantage *vis-à-vis* the Prosecutor. Third, defence teams would not be able to challenge the authenticity of the information and oppose its use by the OTP. In this respect, it should be highlighted that, as already demonstrated, the quality of the information held by SCs is very low due to the circumstances in which it is obtained: its intelligence provenance, coupled with the non-existent evidentiary standards employed by SCs, cast serious doubt on its reliability, accuracy and credibility. In turn, non-disclosure in this scenario would violate the core of the principle of equality of arms and the right to adversarial proceedings,

84 *Lubanga, supra* note 80, para 86.
85 Ibid., paras 76, 82–4.
86 Ibid., para 73.
87 Public redacted version of the "Decision on the Thirteen Documents Obtained under Article 54(3)(e) of the Statute and Not Yet Disclosed to the Defence" dated 19 June 2009, *Prosecutor v Katanga and Ngudjolo Chui* (ICC-01/04-01/07), Trial Chamber II, 26 June 2009, para 12.
88 *Foucher v France* (App no 22209/93) ECtHR, 18 March 1997, para 34.
89 *Koupila v Finland* (App no 27752/95) ECtHR, 27 April 2000, para 38.
90 Kai Ambos, 'Confidential Investigations (Article 54(3)(e) ICC Statute) vs. Disclosure Obligations: The Lubanga Case and National Law' 12 *New Criminal Law Review* (2009) 543, p. 555.
91 Decision on Appellant's Notice and Supplemental Notice of Prosecution's Non-Compliance with its Disclosure Obligation Under Rule 68 of the Rules, *Prosecutor v Kordic & Cerkez* (IT-65-14/2-A), Appeals Chamber, 11 February 2004, para 17.

i.e. mitigating the fact that the OTP has greater logistical and strategic resources compared to the defence.[92]

Conclusively, if – as practice suggests – the OTP is already receiving information from SCs, the former should immediately halt such a relationship and promote a transparent reflection meant to test whether sharing contrasts in any way with the law applicable before the Court, with the further aim to secure future prosecutions from accusations of unfairness and illegality.

Conclusions

The ICC was envisaged by the Statute's drafters as a system that should be as separated and independent as possible from executive powers, particularly from the UNSC.[93] This was clearly done in order to boost the Court's legitimacy, protect it from accusations of politicisation and underline its consent-based nature, as evidenced by the Statute's preparatory works[94] and a number of the Statute's provisions.[95] At the same time, it is true that the ICC cannot effectively function without the cooperation of the international community, particularly when it comes to the arrest and surrender of individuals sought (as evidenced by the *Al-Bashir* case) and access to information for investigative purposes (as demonstrated by the case against Kenyatta).[96] The necessity to explore ways to actively involve the UNSC in the Court's activities is thus a real one, and efforts made in this direction should be taken seriously.

In this regard, in light of the issues discussed in this chapter, the following question arises: is there a risk that current proposals meant to enhance the UNSC's engagement with the ICC could turn cooperation into dependency upon/deference to executive powers? The analysis undertaken here indicates that this risk is real. Notwithstanding this, doctrine and 'like-minded' States seem to unreservedly support the formalisation of an ICC-SCs relationship, disclosing an understanding of the law as a policy instrument.[97] Very little is said on the legal-

92 See Kai Ambos, *Treaties on International Criminal Law* (Vol. III) (Oxford University Press, 2016), p. 532.

93 William Schabas, 'United States Hostility to the International Criminal Court: It's All About the Security Council' *European Journal of International Law* (2004) 701, p. 720.

94 *Inter alia*: PrepComm, 'Proposals by States on Articles 51 and 52' (3 December 1997) 2 where a delegation warned against UNSC 'veto power [which] may be abused to shield criminals'; PrepComm, 'Comments on the background paper prepared by the Secretariat entitled "Establishment of the Court and Relationship with the United Nations"' (18 March 1998) A/AC.249/1998/WG-7/DP-1 2-3; Rome Conference, 'Press Release: United States declares at Conference that UN Security Council must play important role in proposed International Criminal Court' (18 June 1998) L/ROM/11.

95 E.g. Art. 42(1), ICC Statute, according to which the OTP 'shall not seek or act on instructions from any external source'.

96 See OTP, 'Statement of the Prosecutor of the International Criminal Court, Fatou Bensouda, on the status of the Government of Kenya's cooperation with the Prosecution's investigations in the Kenyatta case' (4 December 2014).

97 Carisch, Eckert and Rickard-Martin, *supra* note 21; Boon, *supra* note 21; Mancini, *supra* note 45.

ity and legitimacy of such a relationship.[98] As anticipated in the introduction, this starkly contrasts with the severe criticisms moved against smart sanctions regimes in light of sanctioned individuals' human rights. Although it is true that '[a] major purpose of law is to constrain power, and yet, law requires power to be enforced',[99] this should not persuade the Court to abdicate to respect for the rule of law. In this regard, the research undertaken here suggests that it is possible to draw a demarcation line between cooperation and deference: i.e. cooperation meets the limits of the respect for fundamental human rights of those standing trial before the Court. This stems from the fact that, as an entity created to promote some identity values within the international community, the ICC cannot fail to use them as ordering factors in its practice. The present chapter thus confirms one of the main posits of this book: that defendants receive, and are perceived to receive, a fair trial is vital to the legitimacy of the Court and of the international criminal justice project as a whole. This entails that the transposition of human rights standards within the Statute does not suffice to assure the human rights of defendants: the respect of said rights must also be effectively ensured at all procedural phases, including the pre-trial stage. This chapter has unveiled that in the two scenarios discussed here a vital right (corresponding to a strong identity value of international criminal justice) is at stake: namely, the right to a fair trial (and its various corollaries, including the right to judicial review, to be heard and defend oneself, to disclosure, to adversarial proceedings and equality of arms). The Court should therefore seriously reflect upon the ways it is currently exploring possibilities of fostering cooperation with the UNSC, as the danger of altering the ICC's original project is particularly high. Moreover, as a matter of policy, any further empowerment of the Council *vis-à-vis* the Court will increase, rather than reduce, the perception that the Court is politicised and biased.

98 van den Herik, *supra* note 22.

99 Darrel Robinson, 'Inescapable Dyads: Why the International Criminal Court Cannot Win' *Leiden Journal of International Law* (2015) 323, p. 338.

6 The presence of the accused during trial

Bridging the gap between mandatory presence and *in absentia* trials

Talita de Souza Dias and Tsvetelina van Bentham

Introduction

The question of whether or not the accused shall be present during trial occupies a prominent place in the statutes and procedural rules of most international criminal tribunals (ICTs). Indeed, presence during trial is considered a fair trial right of the accused in various human rights instruments and under customary international law (CIL). Yet there is great discrepancy in the legal treatment of presence across the various ICTs. At one end of the spectrum, the International Criminal Court (ICC) requires the presence of the accused at each and every trial, allowing excusals only in exceptional circumstances, such as disruptive behaviour in the courtroom, individuals exercising extraordinary public duties and health considerations, including accused persons that are unfit to stand trial. At the other end, the Special Tribunal for Lebanon (STL) permits what has been broadly referred to as trials *in absentia*, i.e. the possibility of holding the entirety of criminal proceedings without the accused's presence. More worryingly, there is significant uncertainty as to the legal nature of the accused's presence *across and within each of those tribunals*. This is a reflection of the diverse interests that ICTs seek to balance: presence is perceived as either a right of the accused, an obligation owed to victims and witnesses, an institutional demand, or a complex amalgamation of those three, and perhaps other legal interests.

The purpose of this chapter is to compare the two principal approaches to presence, clarify its legal nature and propose an alternative approach that bridges the existing gap between mandatory presence and trials *in absentia*. In particular, our proposed approach incorporates the various interests that permeate the issue of presence, together with its overriding human right pedigree, to arrive at a flexible solution that focuses on the specific demands of each case.

With this general aim in mind, we will first provide some preliminary clarifications on the concepts of presence at trial and trials *in absentia*, the interplay between them, and on their classification as rights and/or duties. The next section will provide a critical appraisal of presence and *in absentia* trials in the ICC and STL and consider to what extent these are in line with international human rights law (IHRL). Following this, we will seek to identify the underlying causes of the conflicting treatment of presence among those two tribunals, and between them and IHRL. The final section will propose an interpretation of presence and *in absentia* trials that seeks to harmonise the conflicting approaches of the ICC and STL, and to ensure that these are consistent with IHRL. This interpretation is grounded on the idea that, under IHRL, presence is a *right* which is binding on both the ICC and STL, under CIL and key provisions of their statutes. This justifies a primary consideration of the interests of each individual accused when deciding whether presence should be required. At the same time, the interests of victims, witnesses, institutional demands and broader international criminal justice aims should also be given some weight when establishing the more specific conditions and parameters of the accused's presence at trial. Bringing all these strands together, the legal framework of presence can help ensure that all relevant interests are factored in and, importantly, that a balance is struck between the rights of defendants and victims in the context of international criminal justice.

Presence at trial versus *in absentia* trials, and the right *versus* duty dichotomy: some preliminary clarifications

Before going into the specific legal treatment of presence at trial in the context of the ICC and the STL, two preliminary clarifications are necessary in order to fully grapple with the approach adopted by each tribunal and their compatibility with IHRL. First, what do we actually mean by presence at trial and *in absentia trials*, and what is the relationship between these two concepts?

Presence at trial has been generally understood as the *physical* presence of the accused in the courtroom during the course of criminal proceedings that are being held against her/him, starting from the trial phase onwards.[1] By extension, presence has also been interpreted to cover the participation of the accused her or himself through video technology.[2] This contrasts with the idea of presence as mere participation in, or monitoring of, the trial by the accused *through counsel* and/or other legal representation.[3]

When it comes to trials *in absentia*, their exact meaning has caused confusion in the literature and case-law.[4] The term has been loosely and broadly used to

1 Veronique Caruana and William A Schabas, 'Art. 63: Trial in the Presence of the Accused' in Otto Triffterer and Kai Ambos (eds), *Rome Statute of the International Criminal Court: A Commentary* (Beck/Hart, 2016), at 1572–3, 1575–6; Paola Gaeta, 'Trial In Absentia Before the Special Tribunal for Lebanon' in Amal Alamuddin, Nidal N Jurdi and David Tolbert (eds), *The Special Tribunal for Lebanon: Law and Practice* (Oxford University Press, 2014), at 233–4; William Schabas, 'Art.63 Trial in the Presence of the Accused', *The International Criminal Court: A Commentary on the Rome Statute* (Oxford University Press, 2016), at 968.

2 Caruana and Schabas, *supra* note 1, at 1572–3; Rule 134*bis,* ICC Rules of Procedure and Evidence, ICC-ASP/1/3 and Corr1 (2002) (ICC RPE).

3 See Decision on Mr Ruto's Request for Excusal from Continuous Presence at Trial, *Prosecutor v Ruto and Sang* (ICC-01/09-01/11-777) Trial Chamber V(A), 18 June 2013, at para. 18 ('*Ruto's Excusal Decision*').

4 Gaeta, *supra* note 1, at 230–231; Nicolo Pons, 'Some Remarks on in Absentia Proceedings before the Special Tribunal for Lebanon in Case of a State's Failure or Refusal to Hand over the Accused', 8 *Journal of International Criminal Justice* (2010) 1307, at 1309–10.

cover all types of criminal proceedings where the (physical or virtual) presence of the accused in the courtroom is not required in part(s) of the trial or during its entirety. This includes, firstly, trials in which the accused has been *personally served* of the charges, and voluntarily chooses not to appear in court from the outset of the trial or later on, either by explicit or implicit waiver.[5] Implicit waivers comprise disruptive behaviour in the courtroom,[6] and instances where the accused has subsequently absconded from justice.[7] Some have also included within the umbrella of '*in absentia* trials' proceedings at which the accused is unable to be present because of her/his mental or physical state, i.e. when the accused is *unfit to stand trial*.[8] However, given the accused's inability to meaningfully participate in the proceedings, these trials may be indefinitely suspended or adjourned, and so should be treated separately.[9] Lastly, trials in which the accused has *not been personally served* of the charges, either because s/he absconded to escape notification or cannot otherwise be found, have also been treated as types of *in absentia* trials.[10] Nonetheless, because there is uncertainty as to whether she or he is actually aware of the trial, these trials have been more appropriately characterised as 'trials by default'.[11]

Thus, although the term '*in absentia*' has covered a variety of trials, only the first type, where there is personal notification of the charges, and the accused is fit to attend the proceedings, can be *properly* considered as a trial in her/his absence. They have been rightly described as trials *in absentia* proper.[12]

The second clarification relates to the more general concepts of *right* and *duty*, which have both been associated with presence at trial. As we will discuss later on, while the majority of ICTs, human rights bodies and commentators have conceived presence as a (fair trial) *right* of the accused, in the context of some tribunals, especially the ICC, presence has been treated simultaneously as a right of the accused and as a duty that s/he owes to victims, the tribunal itself and other participants.[13] Some have taken issue with this classification and have criticised it

5 Caleb H Wheeler, 'Right or Duty? Is the Accused's Presence at Trial a Right or a Duty Under International Criminal Law?', 28 *Criminal Law Forum* (2017) 99, at 102–3, 106; Caruana and Schabas, *supra* note 1, at 1579–85; Schabas, 'Art.63', *supra* note 1, at 958, 963–4; Gaeta, *supra* note 1, at 231–3, 237–8.

6 Caruana and Schabas, *supra* note 1, at 1578–1579; Gaeta, *supra* note 1, at 233, 238; Wheeler, *supra* note 5, at 114–16, 118, 120, 124.

7 Caruana and Schabas, *supra* note 1, at 1585–6; Gaeta, *supra* note 1, at 233, 237–8; Wheeler, *supra* note 5, at 107, 111.

8 Rule 135, ICC RPE, *supra* note 2; Caruana and Schabas, *supra* note 1, at 1576–7; Schabas, 'Art.63', *supra* note 1, at 968–71.

9 Caruana and Schabas, *supra* note 1, at 1576–8.

10 Wheeler, *supra* note 5, at 102, 109; Caruana and Schabas, *supra* note 1, at 1565; Gaeta, *supra* note 1, at 231, 237; Pons, *supra* note 4, at 1310–11; Art 22(1)(b), (c), Statute of the International Criminal Tribunal for Lebanon, UNSCR 1757 (2007) (STL Statute); *Sejdovic v Italy* (App no 56581/00), ECtHR, 1 March 2006).

11 Gaeta, *supra* note 1, at 231, 237–8; Caruana and Schabas, *supra* note 1, at 1565.

12 Gaeta, *supra* note 1, at 231.

13 Wheeler, *supra* note 5, at 107–12; Caruana and Schabas, *supra* note 1, at 1569–72; Judgment on the appeal of the Prosecutor against the decision of Trial Chamber V(a) of 18 June

for being contradictory.[14] This is based on the idea that, if an obligation covers the same ground as a right, then the right is deprived of its core feature and main practical effect, which is the ability of being voluntarily waived or renounced by the consent of its holder.[15] In the same vein, viewing presence as a right negates the notion of an 'excusal from duty', which has been employed at the ICC.[16] There is indeed merit to this criticism: for waivable rights, making their exercise an obligation would remove the right-holder's freedom to choose how to exercise her/his own right.

However, there is nothing wrong in principle with conceiving presence as both a right and a duty. Indeed, the notion of 'unwaivable' or 'unavailable' rights, i.e. rights that cannot be simply waived by consent, or by consent only, has been employed in various legal fields, including, in particular, human rights law.[17] The freedom of their beneficiaries to waive such rights is limited and perfectly compatible with the idea that there is a parallel obligation to exercise those rights, the purpose of which is to protect the bearer's own interests or those of another relevant stakeholder.

Overall, there does not seem to be a strict dichotomy between what is a right and what is a duty, especially when it comes to presence at trial. Rather, the various international and domestic judicial or quasi-judicial bodies have construed different and often complex models for depicting and regulating the issue of presence and its relationship with trials *in absentia*. Four principal (and by no means exhaustive) models can be identified.

First, presence can be perceived as an 'unavailable' or 'unwaivable' right, i.e. as a 'dual right and obligation of the accused. Under this model, trials *in absentia* could not result from waiver and trials by default are completely ruled out.[18] Second, presence can be conceived as an *available right* belonging to the accused, and the accused only, which can be explicitly or implicitly waived by her/him. Under this model, although trials *in absentia* are not the general rule, they can

---

2013 entitled 'Decision on Mr Ruto's Request for Excusal from Continuous Presence at Trial', *Prosecutor v Ruto and Sang* (ICC-01/09-01/11-1066), Appeals Chamber, 25 October 2013, at paras 48–51, 54; *Ruto's Excusal Decision*, *supra* note 3, at paras 35–7, 39–42; Decision on Defence Request for Conditional Excusal from Continuous Presence at Trial, *Prosecutor v Kenyatta* (ICC-01/09-02/11-830), Trial Chamber V(B), 18 October 2013, at paras 82–3, 124 ('*Kenyatta's Excusal Decision*').

14 Wheeler, *supra* note 5, at 112–13; Decision on the Prosecution's motion for reconsideration of the decision excusing Mr Kenyatta from continuous presence at trial, Dissenting Opinion of Judge Eboe-Osuji, *Prosecutor v Kenyatta* (ICC-01/09-02/11-863-Anx-Corr), Trial Chamber V(B), 26 November 2013, para 35.

15 Wheeler, *supra* note 5, at 100–2, 107–8.

16 Decision on the Prosecution's motion for reconsideration of the decision excusing Mr Kenyatta from continuous presence at trial, Dissenting Opinion of Judge Eboe-Osuji, *Prosecutor v. Kenyatta supra* note 14, at para. 35.

17 Examples include freedom from torture or inhuman and degrading treatment, and the prohibition of slavery.

18 Arts 60(1), 63(2), Rome Statute of the International Criminal Court (last amended 2010) UN Doc A/CONF.183/9 (17 July 1998) (Rome Statute); Rules 134*bis*, *ter*, *quater* and 135, ICC RPE, *supra* note 2; Wheeler, *supra* note 5, at 107–12; Gaeta, *supra* note 1, at 232–3.

be justified whenever the accused waives her/his right to presence. Thus, in a way, conceiving presence as an available or waivable right means that the accused also has a right to be absent. Third, presence can be framed as solely or chiefly an *obligation*, subject to sanctions and forfeitures which are applied to avoid trials *in absentia* to the greatest possible extent.[19] Fourth and last, presence can be conceived as an obligation *of the accused*, combined with *in absentia* or by default trials as *punishment for failure to appear before the court*.[20]

Under IHRL, it is relatively uncontroversial that presence is a *right* of the accused,[21] which can be set aside by an *unequivocal waiver*.[22] This includes both explicit waivers made in writing and waivers implied from the accused's conduct, such as in the case of disruptive behaviour in the courtroom or an accused that has absconded after appearing in court or to escape an arrest.[23] However, according to the consistent case-law of the European Court of Human Rights

19 *Ruto's Excusal Decision*, *supra* note 3, at para. 42; Wheeler, *supra* note 5, 108, 111.

20 Wheeler, *supra* note 5, at 101, 125; Pons, *supra* note 4, at 1308–1309; Art 22(1)(b), (c), STL Statute, *supra* note 10.

21 See Art 14, International Covenant on Civil and Political Rights (adopted 16 December 1966, entered into force 23 March 1976) 999 UNTS 171; art 6(3)(c), Convention for the Protection of Human Rights and Fundamental Freedoms (European Convention on Human Rights, as amended); Art. 8(2)(d), American Convention on Human Rights (signed 22 November 1969, entered into force 18 July 1978) 1144 UNTS 123; Art 7(1)(c), African Charter on Human and People's Rights (adopted 27 June 1981, entered into force 21 October 1986) (1982) 21 ILM 58. See also ICRC, 'Customary IHL - Practice Relating to Rule 100. Fair Trial Guarantees, Section I. Presence of the Accused at the Trial' <https://ihl-databases.icrc.org/customary-ihl/eng/docs/v2_rul_rule100_sectioni> accessed 18 October 2019. For the related jurisprudence, see *Alex Thomas v Tanzania* (App no 005/2013) ACtHPR, 20 November 2015, paras. 86–99; *Demebukov v Bulgaria* (App no 68020/01) ECtHR, 28 February 2008, at para. 47; *Case of Valle Jaramillo et al v Colombia* (Merits, Reparations and Costs) Inter-American Court of Human Rights Series C No 192 (27 November 2008), para 165; Human Rights Committee, 'General Comment No 32, Art. 14: Right to Equality before Courts and Tribunals and to a Fair Trial' (2007), CCPR/C/GC/32, at para. 31; *Sejdovic*, *supra* note 10, at paras 82, 86; *Stoichkov v Bulgaria* (App No 9808/02) ECtHR, 24 June 2005, at paras 54–56; *Avocats Sans Frontières (on behalf of Gaëtan Bwampamye) v Burundi* No 231/99 (ACommHPR, 6 November 2000), at para. 28; *Maleki v Italy* (13 September 1999) Communication No 699/1996 CCPR/C/66/D/699/1996 paras 9.2–9.3; *Brozicek v Italy* (App No 10964/84) ECtHR, 19 December 1989, paras 45–6; *Colozza v Italy* (App no 9024/80) ECtHR, 12 February 1985, at paras. 45–6; Human Rights Committee, 'CCPR General Comment No. 13: Art. 14 (Administration of Justice) Equality before the Courts and the Right to a Fair and Public Hearing by an Independent Court Established by Law' (1984), at para. 11.

22 *Stoyanov v Bulgaria* (App no 39206/07) ECtHR, 30 April 2012, at paras 31–2; *Kounov v Bulgaria* (App no 24379/02) ECtHR, 23 May 2006, para 48; *Sejdovic*, *supra* note 10, at para. 86; *Colozza*, *supra* note 21, at para. 28; *Håkansson and Sturesson v Sweden* (App no 11855/85) ECtHR, 21 February 1990, at para. 66; *Miango v Zaire* (27 October 1987) Communication No 194/1985 CCPR/C/18/D/16/1977, at para 14.1. See also Gaeta, *supra* note 1, at 240–2; W Jordash and T Parker, 'Trials in Absentia at the Special Tribunal for Lebanon: Incompatibility with International Human Rights Law', 8 *Journal of International Criminal Justice* (2010) 487, at 489–93; Pons, *supra* note 4, at 1315–17.

23 *Stoyanov*, *supra* note 22, at 31; *Sejdovic*, *supra* note 10, at para. 99; Gaeta, *supra* note 1, at 237, 241; Jordash and Parker, *supra* note 22, at 490–1.

(ECtHR) and the Human Rights Committee (HRC), for a waiver to be considered unequivocal, the accused must have made an *informed choice*, i.e. s/he must have had been aware of the *opportunity* to exercise the right to presence.[24] This means that s/he must have been notified of the charges, either in person or by indirect means, or must otherwise have *actual notice* of the charges. Indeed, even in the absence of official notification, certain established facts might constitute unequivocal proof that the accused is aware of the existence of criminal proceedings against her/him and does not intend to be present therein.[25] These facts include, for instance, public or written statements by the accused or materials 'brought to the attention of the authorities' that unequivocally point to the accused's awareness of the proceedings.[26]

While there has been some academic debate as to what 'actual notice of charges' means,[27] it seems clear that the jurisprudence of human rights bodies requires *more* than an attempt or a best effort by the relevant state to notify the accused. Rather, *actual* notice of the charges by the accused must be proved by direct or circumstantial evidence.[28] It is important to note that under IHRL, even if the authorities have not satisfied the requirement of due notification, an effective remedy could be an opportunity to obtain a 'fresh determination of the merits of the charge'.[29] Thus, if a person has been convicted *in absentia* without proper notification, and is subsequently deprived of the possibility to obtain a fresh determination of charges, a denial of justice, and therefore a violation of fair trial rights, has occurred.[30]

Two approaches: the ICC and the STL

While the approaches adopted by the two tribunals towards presence of the accused could be seen as occupying the two extremities of a spectrum, they provide useful insights into the regulation of this legal issue.

Presence and in absentia *trials at the ICC*

In the Statute of the ICC, the general principle of presence is recognised in three main provisions, namely, Articles 60(1), 63 and 67(1)(d). The first provision

24 *Stoyanov*, *supra* note 22, at para. 31–32; *Kounov*, *supra* note 22, at para. 48; *Sejdovic*, *supra* note 10, at paras 87, 99, 101; *Colozza*, *supra* note 21, at para. 28; *Håkansson and Sturesson*, *supra* note 22, at para, 66; *Maleki*, *supra* note 21, at paras 9.2–9.4; *Miango*, *supra* note 22, at paras 14.1.

25 *Stoyanov*, *supra* note 22, at para. 31.

26 *Sejdovic*, *supra* note 10, at para. 99.

27 E.g., Gaeta, *supra* note 1, at 240–1, 245–6; Pons, *supra* note 4, at 1315–17, 1321; Jordash and Parker, *supra* note 22, at 491–6.

28 *Stoyanov*, *supra* note 22, at paras 31–2; *Kounov*, *supra* note 22, at para. 48; *Sejdovic*, *supra* note 10, at paras 99, 101; *Maleki*, *supra* note 21, at paras 9.2–9.4; *Miango*, *supra* note 22, at para 14.1.

29 *Colozza*, *supra* note 21, at para. 29.

30 *Sejdovic*, *supra* note 10, at para. 82.

precludes the commencement of *trial* if the accused has not appeared in person, voluntarily or not, at the Confirmation of Charges Hearing.[31] Article 63, in turn, appears to frame presence as a *duty* that *the accused* must fulfil: s/he '*shall* be present during trial' (paragraph 1).[32] The only explicit exception to this duty is when the accused continuously disrupts the trial, in which case s/he will be removed, but will remain observing the trial and instructing counsel 'through the use of communications technology, if required' (paragraph 2). This effectively rules out trials by default before the ICC.[33]

At the same time, Article 67(1)(d) seems to conceive presence as a 'right' or an 'entitlement' belonging to the accused.[34] This is because Article 67 is not only entitled 'Rights of the accused', but its *chapeau* covers some of the 'minimum guarantees' that the accused is 'entitled to', including presence.

Interestingly, Article 61(2) of the ICC Statute, when dealing with the procedure for the Confirmation of Charges, seems to allow a hearing to be held in the absence of the accused, even if s/he has not yet appeared in court.[35] This is subject to two alternative conditions, namely a) that the accused has waived her/his right to be present; or b) has '[f]led or cannot be found and all reasonable steps have been taken to secure his or her appearance before the Court and to inform the person of the charges and that a hearing to confirm those charges will be held'. These conditions are similar to, and even laxer than, the ones that presently exist for holding *in absentia* trials under IHRL. Indeed, under Article 61(2) of the Statute, waivers need not be unequivocal and actual notice of the charges is not necessary, only reasonable steps to inform the accused or secure her/his presence need be taken. Nevertheless, this possibility only applies to *one* single hearing and one that takes place *before trial*, i.e. during the Confirmation of Charges stage. Thus, it has been argued that its regulation should be kept strictly separate from the one applying to *trial* hearings.[36] However, given the importance of the factual and legal issues decided in the Confirmation Hearing,[37] one might question whether it is justifiable to have a different legal regulation of presence for trial and confirmation hearings.

If the Statute's text wasn't confusing enough, the ICC's case-law has further muddied the waters when it comes to presence and *in absentia* trials. First, in the

31 Gaeta, *supra* note 1, at 232.
32 Emphasis added.
33 Gaeta, *supra* note 1, at 232–3.
34 Caruana and Schabas, *supra* note 1, at 1570–1572; Yvonne McDermott and William A Schabas, 'Art. 67: Rights of the Accused' in Otto Triffterer and Kai Ambos (eds), *Rome Statute of the International Criminal Court: A Commentary* (Beck/Hart, 2016), at 1664; Wheeler, *supra* note 5, at 121–2.
35 Rule 123, ICC RPE, *supra* note 2; William Schabas, *The International Criminal Court: A Commentary on the Rome Statute* (Oxford University Press, 2016), at 929.
36 Schabas, *The International Criminal Court*, *supra* note 35, at 929.
37 See Art 61(7), ICC Statute, *supra* note 18. See also ibid., at 925–6; Mohamed M El Zeidy, William A Schabas and Eleni Chaitidou, 'Art. 61: Confirmation of the Charges before Trial' in Otto Triffterer and Kai Ambos (eds), *Rome Statute of the International Criminal Court: A Commentary* (Beck/Hart, 2016), at 1486–7.

Ruto and Sang case, Trial Chamber V(A) decided to exceptionally grant Ruto's request to be excused from being physically present at certain portions of the trial, in order to allow him to attend his duties as Deputy President of Kenya.[38] In reaching this decision, the Chamber conceived presence as not only a *right* of the accused, closely connected to the presumption of innocence,[39] but also, and mainly, as a duty *of the accused* owed primarily *to the Court itself*.[40] Thus, the Trial Chamber extended the possibility of holding *in absentia* trials, at least partly, beyond the text of Article 63.[41] In particular, it left the issue to be decided on a case-by-case basis, after balancing all the interests concerned, including those of victims and witnesses.[42] However, it also constrained the excusal to the strict exercise of Ruto's important functions of an extraordinary dimension,[43] and specified a number of important hearings in which his presence was required.[44]

Similarly, in the *Kenyatta* case, Trial Chamber V(B) was faced with a request for excusal from continuous presence at trial by the serving President of Kenya, Uhuru Kenyatta. It reached exactly the same conclusion as Trial Chamber V(A) in the *Ruto and Sang* case: presence was *both a right and a duty*,[45] and excusal was granted as a reasonable and exceptional accommodation to Kenyatta's demanding office, and was conditioned upon his presence in some key hearings.[46]

Before the Appeals Chamber, the question of excusal of continuous presence at trial was given a slightly more restrictive interpretation than the one reached by the Trial Chambers. Indeed, on Appeal of the Decision on Ruto's Request of Excusal, the Chamber implicitly held that presence was a *duty* of the accused, referring to it as a 'requirement' that was justified by her/his central role in the proceedings and the wider significance of her/his attendance to victims, witnesses and the administration of justice.[47] At the same time, the Appeals Chamber did seem to emphasise the nature of presence as a right of the accused, given that s/he could voluntarily waive such right by behaving in a way that would continuously disrupt the trial, as foreseen in Article 63(2) of the Statute.[48] Significantly, the Chamber relied on the preparatory works of Article 63 to conclude that *mandatory* presence had the purpose of *reinforcing* the *right* of the accused to be present at trial, and, in particular, to preclude a presumption that failure to

38 *Ruto's Excusal Decision*, *supra* note 3, at paras 1–3.
39 Ibid., at paras 32, 35, 48.
40 Ibid., at paras 38–42.
41 Ibid., at paras 47, 53.
42 Ibid., at paras 3, 47, 49, 103–4, 110.
43 Ibid., at paras 3(b), 27, 49–53, 104(b), 109.
44 Ibid., at paras 3(a), 104(a).
45 *Kenyatta's Excusal Decision*, *supra* note 13, at para. 124.
46 Ibid., at paras 4–6, 116, 124.
47 *Ruto's Excusal Appeal Judgement*, *supra* note 13, at paras 49–50. See also Caruana and Schabas, *supra* note 1, at 1571–2.
48 *Ruto's Excusal Appeal Judgement*, *supra* note 13, at para. 51. See also Decision on the Prosecution's motion for reconsideration of the decision excusing Mr Kenyatta from continuous presence at trial, Dissenting Opinion of Judge Eboe-Osuji, *Prosecutor v. Kenyatta*, *supra* note 14, at para. 35.

appear for trial amounted to an implicit waiver of presence.[49] Thus, the Appeals Chamber concluded that disruptive behaviour was not the sole exception to the requirement of presence and that Chambers could, on a case-by-case basis, use their discretion to grant excusals in other scenarios.[50]

Nevertheless, the Appeals Chamber also considered that the Trial Chamber had granted too broad an excusal to Ruto, effectively turning the exception (absence) into the general rule.[51] According to the Appeals Chamber, presence could only be excused in certain hearings if six stringent conditions were met, namely: 1) the existence of exceptional circumstances; 2) the excusal was a measure of last resort, i.e. only if other reasonable alternatives have proved inadequate; 3) it could only be adopted for such duration as strictly necessary; 4) the accused must have explicitly waived her/his right to be present at trial; 5) her/his rights must be fully ensured in her/his absence, in particular through representation by counsel; and 6) any decision must be taken on a case-by-case basis, with due regard to the subject-matter of the specific hearings in which the accused would be absent.[52]

Following this decision, the Assembly of States Parties to the Rome Statute adopted three amendments to the Rules of Procedure and Evidence (RPE).[53] Rule 134*bis* now allows the accused to be present through video technology in part(s) of her/his trial, to be decided on a case-by-case basis. Rule 134*ter* codifies the Appeals Chamber's interpretation of Article 63(1) and is identical to its general conclusion on the conditions of an excusal of presence. Rule 134*quater* is the more controversial amendment, which applies specifically to accused persons in charge of extraordinary public duties. Unlike Rule 134*ter*, Rule 134*quater* does *not* require exceptional circumstances, strict necessity or a case-by-case basis analysis.[54] This has led some to believe that the amendments, especially Rule 134*quater*, open too wide a door for holding *in absentia* hearings, and unjustifiably favour senior state officials.[55] But despite these allegations, Trial Chamber

49 *Ruto's Excusal Appeal Judgement*, *supra* note 13, at paras 52–4.
50 Ibid., at paras 55–6.
51 Ibid., at paras 61, 63.
52 *Ibid.*, at paras 61–2.
53 Caruana and Schabas, *supra* note 1, at 1574–5; Schabas, 'Art.63 Trial in the Presence of the Accused', *supra* note 1, at 965–7; Steven Arrigg Koh, 'Presence and Politics at the International Criminal Court' 19 *ASIL Insights* (2015) 2 <www.asil.org/insights/volume/19/issue/11/presence-and-politics-international-criminal-court> accessed 18 October 2019; Abel S Knottnerus, 'The International Criminal Court on Presence at Trial: The (In)Validity of Rule 134quater' 5 *International Crimes Database Brief* (2014) 1–4, <www.internationalcrimesdatabase.org/upload/documents/20140904T143535-ICD%20Brief%20-%20Abel%20S%20%20Knottnerus.pdf> accessed 18 October 2019.
54 Reasons for the Decision on Excusal from Presence at Trial under Rule 134quater, *Prosecutor v Ruto and Sang* (ICC-01/09-01/11-1186), Trial Chamber V(A), 18 February 2014, at para. 50.
55 See Wheeler, *supra* note 5, at 121–122; Caruana and Schabas, *supra* note 1, at 1584, Schabas, 'Art. 63 Trial in the Presence of the Accused', *supra* note 1, at 966; Knottnerus, *supra* note 53, at 7–8, 10–11; Abel Knottnerus, 'Emerging Voices: Extraordinary Exceptions at the ICC–What Happened with Rule 134quater?' (*Opinio Juris*, 18 July 2014) <http://opiniojuris.

V(A) has considered the amendments to be subsequent agreements to the Statute, in accordance with Article 31(3)(a) of the Vienna Convention on the Law of Treaties (VCLT).[56]

The judicial controversy over presence and *in absentia* trials has lost some of its pungency since the indefinite suspension of the *Kenyatta*[57] and *Ruto and Sang* cases.[58] However, the question has been implicitly raised in the *Gbagbo and Blé Goudé* case, in the context of Gbagbo's fitness to stand trial.[59] In this instance, the key question which seems to have been side-stepped by the Court is what health considerations, short of 'unfitness to stand trial',[60] could justify the continuation of the trial in the absence of the accused.

For our present purposes, this judicial and political saga over the treatment of presence before the ICC yields two preliminary conclusions:

Firstl, it appears that the ICC follows the fourth model of presence described earlier, i.e. it conceives presence at trial as a type of *unwaivable* or *quasi-absolute* right of the accused. As a consequence, *in absentia* trials proper are allowed *only in those exceptional circumstances* envisioned in Rules 134*bis*, *ter* and *quater*. Paradoxically, presence at the *Confirmation Hearing* has been treated as a *relative right* of the accused.

Secondl, while both Trial Chambers have taken into account relevant rules of international law when interpreting Articles 63 and 67(1)(d), they have *not* followed the model of presence under IHRL. Indeed, even if the ICC's case-law has tried to read into the Statute and RPE additional grounds for holding trials *in absentia*, these clearly fall short of the standard developed by human rights bodies, i.e. that any unequivocal waiver of presence, followed by actual notice of the charges, suffices to justify *in absentia* trials. On the other hand, the requirements for holding *in absentia* Confirmation Hearings are much less stringent than those under IHRL.

---

org/2014/07/18/emerging-voices-extraordinary-exceptions-icc-happened-rule-134 quater/> accessed 18 October 2019; Kevin Jon Heller, 'Will the New RPE 134 Provisions Survive Judicial Review? (Probably Not.)' (*Opinio Juris*, 28 November 2013) <http://opinio juris.org/2013/11/28/will-new-rpe-134-provisions-survive-judicial-review/> accessed 18 October 2019.

56 Reasons for the Decision on Excusal from Presence at Trial under Rule 134*quater*, *Prosecutor v. Ruto and Sang*, *supra* note 54, at para. 56.

57 Decision on the withdrawal of charges against Mr Kenyatta, *Prosecutor v Kenyatta* (ICC-01/09-02/11-1005) Trial Chamber V(B), 13 March 2015.

58 Decision on Defence Applications for Judgments of Acquittal, *Prosecutor v Ruto and Sang* (ICC-01/09-01/11-2027-Red-Corr) Trial Chamber V(A), 5 April 2016.

59 Decision on the fitness of Laurent Gbagbo to stand trial, *Prosecutor v Gbagbo and Blé Goudé* (ICC-02/11-01/15-349), Trial Chamber I, 27 November 2015, at paras 44–6; Decision on the fitness of Laurent Gbagbo to take part in the proceedings before this Court, *Prosecutor v Gbagbo* (ICC-02/11-01/11-286-Red) Pre-Trial Chamber I, 2 November 2012.

60 See Rule 135(4), ICC RPE, *supra* note 2; Caruana and Schabas, *supra* note 1, at 1578.

Presence and in absentia *trials at the STL*

Presence under the STL Statute is explicitly recognised as one of the minimum guarantees forming the core of the rights of the accused: s/he is entitled, 'to be tried in his or her presence, and to defend himself or herself in person or through legal assistance of his or her own choosing'.[61] Yet this is the first Tribunal since the International Military Tribunal at Nuremberg to allow full trials *in absentia*. Indeed, the trial of Ayyash, Mehri, Oneissi and Sabra was the first *in absentia* trial conducted by an internationally established tribunal[62] since the trial of Martin Bormann, who was sentenced to death in 1946.

According to Article 22 of the Statute:

> 1 The Special Tribunal shall conduct trial proceedings in the absence of the accused, if he or she:
>
> a) Has expressly and in writing waived his or her right to be present;
> b) Has not been handed over to the Tribunal by the State authorities concerned;
> c) Has absconded or otherwise cannot be found and all reasonable steps have been taken to secure his or her appearance before the Tribunal and to inform him or her of the charges confirmed by the Pre-Trial Judge.

The Statute lists three alternative scenarios, which, if present, would *require* the STL to conduct a trial *in absentia*.[63] From a linguistic perspective, the employment of the verb 'shall' indicates the mandatory character of the provision, obviating discretionary judgment. It is interesting to contrast this approach with the one provided under Rule 138 of the STL's RPE where the Trial Chamber has the *discretion* to remove a disruptive accused.

Since trials *in absentia* tread a fine line between the fair trial rights of the accused, the interests of the victims and society, and institutional demands, their regulation encompasses a set of guarantees. Thus, the STL must certify, in all circumstances, that the 'accused has been notified, or served with the indictment, or notice has otherwise been given of the indictment through publication in the media or communication to the State of residence or nationality', as well as that a defence counsel has been assigned – whether chosen by the accused or appointed by the Defence Office.[64] The RPE envision an additional safeguard procedure for cases falling within Art. 22(1)(b), requiring a consultation with the

61 Art 16(4)(d), STL Statute, *supra* note 10.

62 Decision to Hold Trial *In Absentia*, *Prosecutor v Salim Jamil Ayyash, Mustafa Amine Badreddine, Hussein Hassan Oneissi & Assad Hassan Sabra* (STL-ll-OI/I/TC) Trial Chamber, 1 February 2012.

63 Jordash and Parker, *supra* note 22, at 495.

64 Art 22(2), STL Statute, *supra* note 10; Decision on Defence Appeals Against Trial Chamber's Decision on Reconsideration of the Trial *In Absentia* Decision, *Prosecutor v Ayyash*

President of the Tribunal in view of ensuring that '*all necessary steps*' are taken in order to allow the participation of the accused 'in the most appropriate way'.[65] Finally, the Statute and RPE regulate the consequences of the appearance of the accused both during and after the proceedings *in absentia*, granting a broad right to retrial in *all cases* in which the accused has been absent and not represented by counsel of her/his choice.[66]

Criticism surrounding the introduction of *in absentia* proceedings at the STL has not run out of steam.[67] In particular, it has been contended that Article 22 introduces a procedure that is neither consistent with IHRL nor desirable, allowing the STL to engage in selective story-telling.[68] First, Jenks affirms that the 'notice otherwise given' provision does not ensure that the accused is aware of the proceedings and of the consequences of her/his absence.[69] Second, Jordash and Parker argue that even the right to a retrial could not remedy the initial breach of the right of the accused to be present, since the STL is a Tribunal of limited duration – the right to a retrial is thus severely time-constrained.[70]

It is important to analyse the STL in context. While the criticism levelled against the Tribunal is not without merit, it omits to place sufficient emphasis on the rationale for the existence of the STL. Five clarifications are warranted. One, the STL's *raison d'être* is confined to the events surrounding 'the attack of 14 February 2005 resulting in the death of former Lebanese Prime Minister Rafik Hariri and in the death and injury of other persons',[71] as well as other connected attacks.[72] Two, none of the attackers were apprehended after the events and their whereabouts are, to this day, unknown.[73] It is clear that, without the possibility of conducting *in absentia* proceedings, the operation of the STL would have been

---

et al. (STL Case No STL-11-01/PT/AC/AR126.1) Appeals Chamber, 1 November 2012, at paras 25, 31.

65 Rule 106(B), STL Rules of Procedure and Evidence, STL-BD-2009-01-Rev.9 (2017) (STL RPE).

66 Art. 22, STL Statute, *supra* note 10; Rules 108, 109, STL RPE, *supra* note 65.

67 Jordash and Parker, *supra* note 22; Chris Jenks, 'Notice Otherwise Given: Will in Absentia Trials at the Special Tribunal for Lebanon Violate Human Rights?', 33 *Fordham International Law Journal* (2009) 57; Bjorn Elberling, 'The Next Step in History-Writing through Criminal Law: Exactly How Tailor-Made Is the Special Tribunal for Lebanon?', 21 *Leiden Journal of International Law* (2008) 529. See contrary views: Gaeta, *supra* note 1; Maggie Gardner, 'Reconsidering Trials In Absentia at the Special Tribunal for Lebanon: An Application of the Tribunal's Early Jurisprudence', 43 *George Washington International Law Review* (2011) 91; Ralph Riachy, 'Trials in Absentia in the Lebanese Judicial System and at the Special Tribunal for Lebanon. Challenge or Evolution?', 8 *Journal of International Criminal Justice* (2010) 1295; Cecile Aptel, 'Some Innovations in the Statute of the Special Tribunal for Lebanon' 5 *Journal of International Criminal Justice* (2007) 1107.

68 Elberling, *supra* note 67, at 7.

69 See generally Jenks, *supra* note 67.

70 Jordash and Parker, *supra* note 22, at 499.

71 Art. 1, STL Statute, *supra* note 10.

72 Ibid.

73 Gardner, *supra* note 67, at 116.

frustrated.[74] Three, the STL applies Lebanese domestic law under which trials *in absentia* are permissible. Four, although the Statute does leave some ambiguity as to how *in absentia* proceedings would be carried out, the Report of the Secretary-General on the establishment of the STL is explicit that the Tribunal is meant to be 'based on the highest international standards of criminal justice'.[75] Article 28 of the STL Statute, together with Rule 3(A) RPE, provide for a general rule of interpretation of the Rules in accordance with the highest standards of international criminal procedure and international standards of human rights. This bolsters the statutory presumption that the intention of the drafters was to ensure compliance with IHRL.[76] Five, the practice of the STL in its two decisions to hold trials *in absentia* under Art. 22(1)(c) fortifies the view that the Tribunal *seeks* to follow IHRL.

In order to understand the approach of the STL, two separate questions need to be addressed. First, does the legal approach of the STL accord with IHRL? Second, is the approach compliant with IHRL in its practical implementation?

At the outset, it is important to clarify that the various hypotheses of *in absentia* trials listed in Article 22(1) can either be classified as *in absentia* proper or by default, depending on the type of notification provided to the accused.[77] If any of the scenarios contemplated is preceded by personal or direct notification of the charges, the trial will be one that is *in absentia* proper. Conversely, when notice is provided by indirect means, in accordance with Article 22(2)(a) of the STL Statute and Rules 76(E) and 76*bis* RPE, the trial will be one by default. Since notice of the charges is required in *all circumstances*,[78] the STL is not authorised to hold trials by default without the knowledge of the accused.[79] As the STL has not yet addressed situations concerning defendants who have either explicitly waived their right to be present or have not been handed by authorities of a State, the present examination will focus on cases in which the accused 'has absconded or otherwise cannot be found'.[80]

In these cases, the STL embarks on a three-prong enquiry. It assesses whether: i) *reasonable efforts* have been taken to notify the accused personally; ii) the evidence as to notification satisfies the Trial Chamber that the accused *actually knew* of the proceedings against them; and that, iii) it does so with such *degree of specificity* that the accused's absence means they *must have elected not to attend* the hearing and therefore have waived their right to be present.[81] Considering the

74 Report of the Secretary-General on the Establishment of a Special Tribunal for Lebanon (2006) U.N. Doc. S/2006/893, at 32.
75 Ibid., at 2.
76 Jordash and Parker, *supra* note 22, at 496.
77 Gaeta, *supra* note 1, at 237–8.
78 Art. 22(2)(a), STL Statute, *supra* note 10; Decision on Defence Appeals Against Trial Chamber's Decision on Reconsideration of the Trial In Absentia Decision, *Prosecutor v Ayyash et al*, *supra* note 64, at paras 25, 31.
79 Gaeta, *supra* note 1, at 238–239, 243–247.
80 Art. 22(1)(c), STL Statute, *supra* note 10.
81 Decision on Defence Appeals against Trial Chamber's Decision on Reconsideration of the Trial in absentia Decision, *Prosecutor v. Ayyash et al*, *supra* note 64, at para 31; Decision to

potentially severe consequences arising from a decision to hold a trial *in absentia*, the Appeals Chamber has considered that this enquiry must be conducted on the basis of a high evidentiary standard.[82]

The possibility to hold *in absentia* proceedings does not give the Tribunal *carte blanche* to try non-notified individuals. The STL has required either direct or indirect notification of the charges to be provided *in all cases before it*, including where the accused has absconded *before* being personally served (and precisely to evade that!), or cannot otherwise be found. Given this requirement of prior notice, Art. 22(1)(c) has been interpreted as envisaging the *implied waiver* of the right to be present. As mentioned earlier, IHRL does not prohibit *in absentia* trials in cases of waiver conveyed tacitly yet unequivocally.[83]

In order to assess whether notice has been given, the STL test can be reduced to two main limbs: the reasonable steps taken by the authorities and evidence of actual notice indicating an informed choice to be absent from the proceedings. Additionally, the STL affords any accused tried *in absentia* the right to a retrial.[84] Even if the STL is not a permanent institution, its Statute *can be read* as allowing such a retrial to be carried out by a domestic court, Lebanese or not.[85] This approach draws upon the practice of the HRC and ECtHR.[86] Although the test is *prima facie* adequate to address fair trial rights concerns, the specific sub-tests adopted by the STL leave much to be desired.

On reasonable measures, the test is that 'reasonable efforts have been taken to notify the accused personally'.[87] Basing itself on the totality of circumstances, the STL examines publicity, advertisements, wanted posters and social media reporting.[88] There has been a troubling lowering of the standard adopted by the Tribunal from the *Ayyash in absentia* decision to the decision in *Merhi*. In *Merhi*, the STL, while acknowledging that the Lebanese authorities did not fulfil all the notification requirements under the domestic Code of Criminal Procedure, was satisfied that the requirement of reasonableness was met when judged in light of the *prevailing circumstances*.[89]

Turning to knowledge-through-notification criterion, the formulation of this sub-test is two-fold: 'the evidence as to notification satisfies the Trial Chamber that the accused actually knew of the proceedings against them' and 'it does

Hold Trial in Absentia, *Prosecutor v Hassan Habib Merhi* (STL-13-04/I/TC) Trial Chamber, 20 December 2013), at para. 88.

82 Decision on Defence Appeals Against Trial Chamber's Decision on Reconsideration of the Trial In Absentia Decision, *Prosecutor v Ayyash et al*, *supra* note 64, at para. 33.

83 *Sejdovic*, *supra* note 10; *Maleki*, *supra* note 21; *Stoyanov*, *supra* note 22.

84 Art. 22(3), STL Statute, *supra* note 10.

85 Gaeta, *supra* note 1, at 249; Paola Gaeta, 'To Be (Present) or Not to Be (Present): Trials *In Absentia* before the Special Tribunal for Lebanon', 5 *Journal of International Criminal Justice* (2007) 1172–3. Contra: Jordash and Parker, *supra* note 22, at 498.

86 *Maleki*, *supra* note 21, at 9.5; Gaeta, *supra* note 1, at 240–1, 243–4, 246–9.

87 *Prosecutor v Merhi*, *supra* note 81, at para. 89.

88 Ibid.

89 Ibid., at para. 93.

so with such degree of specificity that the accused's absence means they must have elected not to attend the hearing and therefore have waived their right to be present'. The STL has found an interesting way to ascertain implicit waiver where there is no indication of informed choice. Relying on the heavy publicity of the case, the Tribunal concludes that '*almost every adult*'[90] in Lebanon was notified of the indictment. In the *Merhi* decision, the chain of assumptions resembles the last moves of a Jenga game: 1) almost every adult knew of the Ayyash indictment;[91] 2) even before the formal indictment of Merhi, a number of news outlets quoted 'insider sources from the Tribunal', connecting an individual with the initials H. M. to the assassination of Prime Minister Hariri;[92] 3) there was massive publicity concerning the formal charges brought against Merhi; 4) there was massive publicity on the possibility of holding trials *in absentia* and on the *in absentia* trials of the initial four accused.[93] Therefore, the Tribunal finds that Merhi was on actual notice, falls within Art. 22(1)(c) of the Statute and can, as a consequence, be tried in his absence. Evidence related to the accused's actual knowledge is noticeably lacking.

Three conclusions can be drawn:

> First, in cases where the accused has absconded or cannot otherwise be found, the STL treats presence as a waivable right, not as a duty. The holding of *in absentia* trials is not punishment, but the effect of the non-exercise of a right.
>
> Second, while the STL has endorsed an IHRL-based approach, its implementation is superficial and relies on too many assumptions.
>
> Third, it appears from the STL's case-law, its Statute and the latter's drafting history, that the *main* interest justifying the treatment of presence as a waivable right is an *institutional* one.[94]

Both the approaches of the ICC and the STL raise two fundamental questions. Firstly, what interests have been left out of the picture in the presence/absence approaches? Secondly, how can we achieve a more complete picture of the interests involved and, at the same time, ensure consistency with IHRL? We now turn to these questions.

Explaining the disparities: what is missing from the ICC's and STL's conflicting models of presence?

As the foregoing analysis has demonstrated, the ICC's and STL's approaches to presence lie at two extremities – while the ICC's grounds for holding *in absentia*

90 Ibid., at para. 96.
91 Ibid., at para. 100.
92 Ibid., at para. 54 in connection to 100.
93 Ibid., at para. 107.
94 Riachy, *supra* note 67, at 1297, 1304.

trials are numerically limited and heavily circumscribed by added conditionality, the STL adopts a relaxed approach towards presence. For the ICC, presence seems to be a right with quasi-absolute status. For the STL, presence is a waivable right, but with very slim guarantees in practice: it can be limited by what the Tribunal *infers* from the accused's passive behaviour. Neither approach is satisfactory.

It is undisputed that both tribunals are faced with a multitude of inter-weaved interests: those of the accused, the victims and public at large, and those of the institution itself. It is argued here that the ICC and the STL have not factored these interests in an optimal fashion.

First, the interests of the accused are central to any trial – it is her/his presence that is at stake, and, ultimately, her/his rights throughout the proceedings and her/his status following the trial. Presence is thus a guarantee that the procedural and substantive rights of the accused will be respected. This is why IHRL treats presence as a right – and, as a non-absolute right, one that can be waived as a result of informed choice.

In this light, one of the underlying problems with the ICC's approach is the failure to consider that the accused might not be interested in attending the trial, or even in ensuring that her/his procedural or substantive rights are protected. For instance, s/he might believe that her/his interests might be better pursued through her/his counsel or another representative. Alternatively, the accused might simply refuse to take part in the proceedings, especially if s/he considers that these are not fair or legitimate. None of those interests are recognised at the ICC. Indeed, under the ICC framework, the decision to hold *in absentia* trials rests entirely with the Court.

Conversely, the STL readily accepts circumstances extraneous to the behaviour of the accused as evidence of notification and tacit waiver of the right to be present. In practice, by relying on a set of assumptions, this approach does not accord with the exigencies of IHRL, which places significant weight on actual proof of informed choice.

Second, the administration of justice, the smooth conduct of the proceedings and the tribunal's own legitimacy are important institutional interests. At the ICC, the Appeals Chamber and two Trial Chambers have duly considered that the interests of the proper administration of justice have been held to either require or excuse presence, depending on the circumstances. However, the ICC's line of reasoning does not *explicitly* include any consideration of the administration of justice. Conversely, in the STL, it seems that the institutional demands of the Tribunal have not only directly motivated the recognition of *in absentia* trials, but still seem to be silently informing the Tribunal's interpretation of implicit waivers. One of the primary objectives of the Tribunal is to ensure the expeditious and efficient completion of judicial activities.[95] However, the STL seems to act under a faulty assumption that the conduct of trials *in absentia* proper, and especially by default, would not undermine its public reputation. For many

95 STL Ninth Annual Report (2017–2018) 51.

victims and members of the general public, trials that run entirely in the absence of the accused are simply show trials.

Third, the interests of victims and witnesses also play a role. For the victims, criminal trials are the publicised version of their stories. The evidence gathered for the trials acts as a 'permanent judicial record' of events.[96] Even so, the interests of victims do not blankly require the conduct of trials – a tribunal that does not respect the rights of the accused cannot build its own legitimacy and credibility, thus weakening the legitimacy of the stories it narrates.

The STL attributes significant value to the interests of victims.[97] In the proceedings, victims have the status of 'participating victims' and are allowed to present their views.[98] As recognised by a press release from February 2018, '[t]he trial is making it possible for the Lebanese people to see evidence being presented and challenged, as well as witnesses testifying and being cross-examined in public.'[99]

In conclusion, the balancing of divergent interests in the jurisprudence of both the ICC and the STL has not been unproblematic. Although each of the three ICC Chambers have sought to balance all the competing interests in the presence of the accused,[100] it appears that they have conceived some of those interests in a unidimensional way. For instance, all three Chambers that have dealt with the issue appear to have assumed that victims and witnesses would *always* prefer the accused to be present at trial,[101] except when the accused's absence would delay the proceedings[102] or where direct confrontation would be detrimental to the testimony of vulnerable victims or witnesses.[103] Accordingly, the ICC does not seem to consider that victims might actually *prefer* to proceed in the absence of the accused, where her/his fair trial rights are guaranteed. Conversely, the STL has tried to balance institutional demands, the interests of victims and the interests of the accused, in practice only paying lip service to the latter. It is indeed striking to consider that the Prosecution in the *Ayyash* case has presented evidence from

96 Transcript of 9 October 1995, *Prosecutor v. Dragan Nikolic* (ICTY-94-2) Trial Chamber, 9 October 1995, at 59.

97 STL Seventh Annual Report (2015–2016), at 42.

98 Ibid., at 6; Art. 17, STL Statute, *supra* note 10.

99 The Prosecution completes the presentation of evidence in the Ayyash et al. case (*STL Press Release*, 7 February 2018) <www.stl-tsl.org/en/media/press-releases/6201-the-prosecution-completes-the-presentation-of-evidence-in-the-ayyash-et-al-case> accessed 18 October 2019.

100 *Ruto's Excusal Appeal Judgement*, *supra* note 13, at paras 49, 51; *Kenyatta's Excusal Decision*, *supra* note 13, at paras 119, 123–124; *Ruto's Excusal Decision supra* note 3, at paras 3, 47, 92, 103–4, 110.

101 *Ruto's Excusal Appeal Judgement*, *supra* note 13, at para. 49; Reasons for the Decision on Excusal from Presence at Trial under Rule 134quater, *Prosecutor v. Ruto and Sang*, *supra* note 54, at paras 72–3, 79(2)(6)(7); *Kenyatta's Excusal Decision*, *supra* note 13, at paras 5(a)(iii)(vii)(viii), 90, 119, 121–2; *Ruto's Excusal Decision*, *supra* note 3, paras 3(a)(iii)(vii)(viii), 47–8, 107.

102 Reasons for the Decision on Excusal from Presence at Trial under Rule 134quater, *Prosecutor v Ruto and Sang*, *supra* note 54, at para. 68; *Kenyatta's Excusal Decision*, *supra* note 13, at para. 103.

103 *Ruto's Excusal Decision*, *supra* note 3, at para. 73.

over 260 individual witnesses and about 2470 exhibits in documentary form,[104] while the *Oneissi* Defence (the only team to mount a Defence case) advanced one expert witness and a political witness.[105] This shows the inherent limitations in attempting to construct a defence without meaningful input from the accused. It further shows the need to adequately balance the three interests outlined above – if one of them is left without adequate protection, the remaining two would lose their meaning through an overall erosion of legitimacy.

Bridging the gap: a human rights-oriented and case-by-case solution

After having identified the underlying causes of the ICC's and STL's unidimensional and conflicting approaches to presence, and of their controversial relationship with IHRL, the final step of our analysis is to find a way to tackle those problems. Two key questions arise at this point. Firstly, how can we ensure that the treatment of presence and *in absentia* trials at the ICC and STL are consistent with IHRL and, thus, more uniform? Secondly, how can we incorporate into the regulation of presence and *in absentia* trials in those tribunals' consideration of all relevant stakeholders and interests that we discussed earlier, whilst still ensuring consistency with IHRL?

The first question revolves around the broader issues of fragmentation and hierarchy of norms in international law. In particular, the core issue is to what extent the ICC and STL are bound by IHRL, and, consequently, to what extent IHRL prevails over the Statutes and procedural rules of those tribunals. Two interrelated answers can be advanced.

First, regardless of any formal hierarchy in international law, both the ICC and the STL are bound by the customary rule of interpretation reflected in Article 31(3)(c) of the VCLT to *interpret* their Statutes in accordance with relevant rules of general international law, including, in particular, IHRL.[106]

Second, beyond interpretation, i.e. when the texts of the relevant Statutory provision cannot reasonably accommodate a construction that is consistent with IHRL, both the ICC and the STL have an *obligation* to *comply* with IHRL that is grounded on more than one legal basis. As subjects of international law, both

104 'The Prosecution completes the presentation of evidence in the Ayyash et al. case', *STL Press Release*, 7 February 2018, <www.stl-tsl.org/en/media/press-releases/6201-the-prosecution-completes-the-presentation-of-evidence-in-the-ayyash-et-al-case> accessed 18 October 2019.

105 'Trial Chamber schedules filing of final briefs and oral closing arguments in June 2018 in the Ayyash et al. case', *STL Press Release*, 12 April 2018, <www.stl-tsl.org/en/media/press-releases/6271-trial-chamber-schedules-filing-of-final-briefs-and-oral-closing-arguments-in-june-2018-in-the-ayyash-et-al-case> accessed 18 October 2019.

106 *Alleged Violations of Sovereign Rights and Maritime Spaces in the Caribbean Sea (Nicaragua v Colombia)* (Preliminary Objections) [2016] ICJ Rep 1, at para 35; International Law Commission, 'Fragmentation of International Law: Difficulties Arising from the Diversification and Expansion of International Law, Report of the Study Group of the International Law Commission' (2006) (A/CN.4/L.682 410–415), at 427.

tribunals are *bound by general international law*, i.e. CIL and general principles of law.[107] Since the right to be present at trial, as interpreted by human right supervisory bodies, is now part of CIL,[108] both the ICC and the STL are bound by it. In addition, the two tribunals have specific provisions in their Statutes or RPE requiring them to interpret and/or apply their provisions in accordance with human rights standards.

In the context of the ICC, this provision is Article 21(3) of the Rome Statute, which states that the 'interpretation and application' of the Court's applicable law 'must be consistent with internationally recognized human rights'. There is general agreement that this includes customary human rights law,[109] particularly fair trial rights.[110]

In the context of the STL, Article 28(2) of the Statute directs the judges to obtain guidance from 'the highest standards of international criminal procedure' when adopting and amending the RPE. More specifically, Rule 3(A) of the STL RPE requires the Rules to be interpreted in accordance with Articles 31-33 of the VCLT and 'international standards on human rights'. In fact, customary human rights are not only binding on the tribunal but *shall* also be taken into account when interpreting the STL Statute and RPE, in accordance with Article 31(3)(c) of the VCLT. In addition, going back to the preparatory works of the STL, recall that the Report of the Secretary-General on the establishment of the tribunal explicitly directed that the Tribunal be 'based on the highest international standards of criminal justice'. Accordingly, it is fair to say that the STL has a statutory duty to *interpret* its Statute and RPE in accordance with IHRL, or, at the very least, that there is *presumption* that the Statute and RPE are consistent with IHRL.[111]

For our purposes, all of this means that both the ICC and the STL are bound under both general international law, particularly CIL and their own Statutes, to follow the approach to presence and *in absentia* trials that exists under IHRL. As we demonstrated in Section 1, the prevailing interpretation under IHRL is that the right to presence can be waived by an unequivocal waiver of the accused, i.e. by an explicit and tacit waiver that follows from actual notice of the charges.

107 See, e.g., Christoph Deprez, 'Art. 21(3) of the ICC Statute and "Internationally Recognized Human Rights" as a Source of Mandatory Judicial Dialogue' in Paolo Lobba and Triestino Mariniello (eds), *Judicial Dialogue on Human Rights The Practice of International Criminal Tribunals* (Brill, 2017), at 92; Daniel Sheppard, 'The International Criminal Court and "Internationally Recognized Human Rights": Understanding Art. 21(3) of the Rome Statute', 10 *International Criminal Law Review* (2010) 43, at 57.

108 ICRC Customary IHL, *supra* note 21.

109 E.g., Deprez, *supra* note 107, at 92, 99; Leena Grover, *Interpreting Crimes in the Rome Statute of the International Criminal Court* (Cambridge University Press, 2014), at 118; Stephen Bailey, 'Art. 21(3) of the Rome Statute: A Plea for Clarity', 14 *International Criminal Law Review* (2014) 513, at 531; Rebecca Young, '"Internationally Recognized Human Rights" before the International Criminal Court', 60 *International and Comparative Law Quarterly* (2011) 189, at 192, 199; Sheppard, *supra* note 107, at 54.

110 Grover, *supra* note 109, at 115; Bailey, *supra* note 109, at 530; Young, *supra* note 109, at 198.

111 Jordash and Parker, *supra* note 22, at 496–7.

Significantly, even if one does not agree that this is the correct interpretation of the right to presence under IHRL, the application of *in dubio pro reo* would lead to the same result. This is because the current interpretation under IHRL seeks to prioritise the interests of the accused to the greatest possible extent and, therefore, appears to be the most beneficial to him/her.

The second question we proposed to answer in this final section is how to take into account all the interests that are relevant to the issue of presence and *in absentia* trials in a way that is tailored to the circumstances of each case and still consistent with the tribunals' obligation to observe IHRL and *in dubio pro reo.* Indeed, it appears that the jurisprudence of the most prominent human rights supervisory bodies has already implicitly provided the answer. This answer lies in the concepts of 'interests of justice', 'interests of the (proper) administration of justice' or 'important public interests' which have informed the interpretation of when it is permissible to limit the right to presence and, consequently, to hold *in absentia* trials under IHRL.[112] The formula 'interests of justice' and variations thereof have been used in both domestic and international courts to allow discretionary decisions to be made on a case-by-case basis. In particular, they have afforded judges some flexibility when deciding issues of criminal procedure that involve a balancing of different interests, such as prosecutorial discretion, admissibility of evidence, and the appointment of counsel to defendants against their will.[113]

Significantly, in the context of presence and *in absentia* trials, 'interests of justice' can be the key to an interpretation that, while prioritising the IHRL approach and the interests of the accused, still allows for the consideration of other competing interests, as they arise in each particular case. These include all the interests we have identified in the previous section, such as the interests of victims, witnesses, and the reputation of the institution itself. Most importantly, 'interests of justice' has also been interpreted as an umbrella term covering broader interests or aims of international criminal justice as a whole. These include traditional criminal law purposes, such as retribution, deterrence and crime prevention. But they also cover alternative functions which have been specifically associated with the international criminal justice system, such as international peace and security, truth and reconciliation, symbolic or expressive justice, and reparations and vindication for victims.[114]

112 *Sejdovic*, *supra* note 10, at para. 86; *Håkansson and Sturesson*, *supra* note 22, at para. 66; *Miango*, *supra* note 22, at para. 14.1. See also Pons, *supra* note 4, at 1314, 1317.

113 Schabas, *The International Criminal Court*, *supra* note 35, at 836; William A Schabas, 'Prosecutorial Discretion v. Judicial Activism at the International Criminal Court', 6 *Journal of International Criminal Justice* (2008) 731, at 748; Chris Gallavin, 'Art. 53 of the Rome Statute of the International Criminal Court: In the Interests of Justice?', 14 *King's Law Journal* (2003) 179, at 187–90. See also Arts. 51(1)(c), 2(c), 61(2), 65(4), 67(1)(d), Rome Statute, *supra* note 18; Arts. 15(c), 16(4)(d), 20(2), 30, STL Statute, *supra* note 10.

114 See, e.g., Talita De Souza Dias, '"Interests of Justice": Defining the Scope of Prosecutorial Discretion in Art. 53(1)(c) and (2)(c) of the Rome Statute of the International Criminal Court', 30(3) *Leiden Journal of International Law* (2017) 731, at 739–42; Conor

Given the overriding obligation to follow the approach under IHRL and its stringent requirements, the place of those interests would be limited within the legal framework of presence and *in absentia* trials. In particular, a waiver of the right to presence must still be *unequivocal*, even if implicit, and must be accompanied by *actual notice* of the charges. However, the 'interests of justice', and the more specific considerations that those interests carry with them, could play a role when interpreting what circumstances, aside from an explicit waiver, may amount to *an unequivocal waiver* of the right to presence, and thus justify holding *in absentia* trials (provided that actual notice is present!). The interests of justice could also be used to justify a decision *not* to hold a trial even if there is an unequivocal waiver to the right of presence, if that is also in the interests of the accused. For instance, the interests of victims and the tribunal's credibility would justify interpreting the refusal of an accused to appear in Court, after having actual notice of the charges, as a tacit waiver. On the other hand, the 'interests of justice' could justify *not* allowing what might appear to be an unequivocal waiver to justify an *in absentia* trial if that is contrary to some of the interests mentioned earlier.[115] For example, even if an accused has absconded after being notified of the charges, interpreting this as an unequivocal waiver and holding an *in absentia* trial might be contrary to the interests of victims, the institutional demands of the tribunals and broader international criminal justice purposes, particularly symbolic justice and truth-telling. We are mindful that some of these hypotheses have already been considered in the relevant literature and jurisprudence. However, the novelty of our approach lies in providing a structured and yet flexible framework for the evaluation any possible scenario that might arise before the ICC, STL and other tribunals in the future.

Conclusion

Throughout this chapter, we have sought to demonstrate that different international and domestic courts and tribunals follow different models on the issue of the accused's presence or absence during the trial. We have tried to classify those models based on the nature of presence as a right or an obligation and according to the limits that have been imposed upon it. We have dedicated the bulk of this chapter to a comparative analysis of two principal models of presence that are in sharp opposition to each other, namely, the ones adopted by the ICC and the STL. In particular, we have shown that these models not only differ between themselves, but are also inconsistent with IHRL, either in the abstract or in practice. In addition, it is our view that the underlying causes of such a contrasting treatment of presence lie within each tribunal's incomplete approach to the various interests at stake.

McCarthy, 'Victim Redress and International Criminal Justice. Competing Paradigms, or Compatible Forms of Justice?', 10 *Journal of International Criminal Justice* (2012) 351, at 365.

115 *Sejdovic*, *supra* note 10, at para. 86; *Håkansson and Sturesson*, *supra* note 22, para. 66.

We have argued that both the ICC and the STL have failed to perceive that, depending on the circumstances of each case, those interests can militate either against or in favour of the accused's presence (or absence), rather than in one single direction. Significantly, this is what has given rise to conflicting approaches to *in absentia* trials, and inconsistencies with IHRL. In order to remedy this, we have proposed an interpretation of presence and *in absentia* trials that is not only in line with the prevailing IHRL model, but also leaves some room for consideration of the various interests at stake in each specific case. The key or core element of this interpretation is the concept of 'interests of justice', which has been used for discretionary decision-making in other significant issues of procedural law. Specifically, we propose that the notion of 'interests of justice' be used to interpret or resolve ambiguities as to whether there has been an unequivocal waiver of the right to presence, or whether such waivers justify holding an *in absentia* trial. By doing so, different ICTs can align themselves with IHRL and observe all relevant interests, including broader international criminal justice aims. Overall, this leads us to believe that, although the accused's presence can be an important aspect of the trial, it is not decisive. Not for the defence, the victims, the general public, the tribunal, or for broader aims of international criminal justice. Rather, it is through the adoption of a more flexible approach to the legal institution of presence that a holistic assessment, including all relevant interests, can be made. Importantly, by adopting this approach, different ICTs can ensure that the rights of both victims and accused are adequately balanced.

7 Useful in theory, useless in practice?

The right of the defence to challenge the jurisdiction of international criminal courts and tribunals

Michail Vagias

Introduction

Consider this fictional situation; a defence lawyer visits his client at the Detention Centre in Scheveningen. The lawyer holds the view that a defence challenge to the jurisdiction of the court should be filed. The defendant is uncertain. His pottery classmates/fellow inmates in the Scheveningen detention centre told him that challenges to jurisdiction are notoriously ill-fated; that international criminal institutions are political institutions set up to try people, not to let them go; and filing a challenge was just 'a waste of time'. The defendant is therefore worried that a challenge to jurisdiction is doomed to fail and will only prolong his pre-trial detention unnecessarily.

Is this worry justified? Obviously, the answer to this question can never be divorced from the specific circumstances of each case. With that in mind, this study attempts to address the concern of our imaginary defendant by conducting an in-depth examination of all defence challenges to the jurisdiction filed before the International Criminal Tribunal for the former Yugoslavia (ICTY) (1993–2013), the International Criminal Tribunal for Rwanda (ICTR) (1994-2015), the Special Court for Sierra Leone (SCSL) (2000–2013) and the International Criminal Court (ICC) (2002–date), the four principal international criminal courts of the day.

It finds that no case has ever been rejected in international criminal proceedings following a successful defence challenge to jurisdiction. At best, the handful of successful challenges were accepted only in part and led to procedural adaptations that may – or may not – have had an impact on the final outcome of the trial. Any secondary benefits remain difficult to connect causally to a successful challenge on jurisdiction. As such, this study contends that our defendant's reservations concerning the filing of a defence challenge are not entirely misplaced. Absent extraordinary circumstances, defendants are in principle right to harbour low expectations from defence challenges to jurisdiction.

To make its point clear, this chapter starts with a short presentation of the research findings in the success rates of jurisdictional challenges before the ICTY, the ICTR, the SCSL and the ICC. It then analyses the reasons for the low success rate of defence challenges to jurisdiction. Third, the chapter contemplates the possibility that a defence challenge to jurisdiction holds ancillary benefits for the accused, for example by shedding light on the weaknesses of the prosecution's case and ultimately leading to the dismissal of the case at an early stage of the process, or by leading to an acquittal by removing part of the case from consideration. The record shows that these ancillary benefits are too rare and too haphazard or context-specific to form any specific patterns or support concrete conclusions. Therefore, it is understandable that against such an overwhelmingly negative history, these incidental ancillary benefits may prove too little to sustain a positive outlook for the future of defence challenges to jurisdiction.

This analysis further demonstrates that on the surface, jurisdictional questions appear focused on the competence of an institution, where the interplay between the defence and victims' rights is not immediately visible. However, a look beneath the surface shows that the jurisdictional battles are the first time when the rights of the accused and the victims are pitted against one another, albeit in less obvious forms than in subsequent stages of the process. The exercise of the defence right to challenge jurisdiction has led to the formation of a body of law with a strongly pro-institutional and essentially pro-victim approach, where the *telos* of ending impunity appears prevalent. Considering the fundamental importance of jurisdictional law and procedure for the legitimacy of international criminal proceedings in the eyes of the public, this track record would suggest a need to recalibrate the approach of all actors involved in this process, in order to avoid allegations portraying international criminal proceedings as thinly-veiled politicised prosecutions by illegitimate international courts.

Success rates of defence challenges to jurisdiction before the ICTY, the ICTR, the SCSL and the ICC: facts and figures

The legal framework of the four institutions under examination explicitly provides for the possibility to file a challenge to jurisdiction.[1] This possibility is justified on the premise of procedural economy and the protection of the accused

1 Rule 73(A) of the ICTY Rules of Procedure (RPE), IT/32, 14 March 1994, available at www.icty.org/x/file/Legal%20Library/Rules_procedure_evidence/IT032_original_en.pdf (last visited 23 October 2019). In the 50th revision, the rule is 72(a)(i). Rules of Procedure and Evidence, 8 July 2015, Rev. 50, available at www.icty.org/x/file/Legal%20Library/Rules_procedure_evidence/IT032Rev50_en.pdf (last visited 23 October 2019). Rule 73(A)(i) of the ICTR Rules of Procedure and Evidence (RPE), 29 June 1995, available at http://unictr.irmct.org/sites/unictr.org/files/legal-library/950629-rpe-en.pdf (last visited 23 October 2019). ICTR, Rules of Procedure and Evidence, 29 June 1995, Rule 73(A)(i), available at http://unictr.irmct.org/sites/unictr.org/files/legal-library/950629-rpe-en.pdf (last visited 23 October 2019)

Rule 72(B) of the SCSL Rules of Procedure and Evidence, 12 April 2002, available at www.rscsl.org/Documents/RPE.pdf (last visited 23 October 2019)

Article 19(2)(a) of the Rome Statute of the International Criminal Court, 17 July 1998, available at www.icc-cpi.int/NR/rdonlyres/EA9AEFF7-5752-4F84-BE94-0A655EB30E16/0/Rome_Statute_English.pdf (last visited 23 October 2019).

from an unjustified judicial process.[2] In the ICC's terms, the defence right to challenge jurisdiction is 'a special remedy enshrined in Article 19 of the Statute, as such autonomous and independent from any other remedy which the suspect might have by virtue of other statutory provisions'.[3]

Defence teams have availed themselves of this possibility in many instances. The table below is the result of the author's research in all case-law relating to jurisdiction before the four courts. The results are telling.

	Defence challenges	*Accepted*	*Rejected*
ICTY (1993–2013)	56	4 (1 overturned on appeal)	52
ICTR (1994–2015)	37	2 (1 overturned at reconsideration)	35
SCSL (2000–2013)	39	0	39
ICC (2002 till 2018)	5	0	5
Totals	137	6 (2 overturned on appeal) (5%)	131 (95%)

In the context of the ICTY, during the Court's operation from 1993–2013, a total of 57 defence challenges to jurisdiction were filed. None of them led to the dismissal of the case; only four were accepted in part.[4] In 2003, the Hadžihasanović defence successfully challenged the subject-matter jurisdiction of the Tribunal as regards command responsibility for crimes committed prior to the establishment of the superior-subordinate relationship.[5] In 2004 the Šešelj defence objection to jurisdiction on the existence of an armed conflict in Vojvodina and its connection to the alleged crimes attributed to the accused was accepted in part by the Trial Chamber.[6] As a result, the Prosecutor was ordered to 'clarify the ambiguity in the pleadings in relation to Vojvodina, Serbia, and the issue of armed conflict'.[7] However, it was subsequently defeated following the Prosecutor's appeal to the Appeal

2 Decision on the Defence Motion for Interlocutory Appeal on Jurisdiction, *Prosecutor v. Tadić*, 2 October 1995, para. 5.

3 Pre-Trial Chamber I, Decision on the 'Defence Challenge to the Jurisdiction of the Court', *Prosecutor v. Mbarushimana*, (ICC-01/04-01/10-451), 26 October 2011, para. 11.

4 Decision on Interlocutory Appeal Challenging Jurisdiction in Relation to Command Responsibility, *Prosecutor v. Enver Hadžihasanović, Mehmet Alagic and Amir Kubura*, (IT-01-47-AR72), 16 July 2003 (hereinafter: the *Hadžihasanović* Appeal Decision); Decision on motion by Vojislav Šešelj challenging jurisdiction and form of the indictment, *Prosecutor v. Vojislav Šešelj*, (IT-03-67/PT), 26 May 2004, filed on 3 June 2004 (hereinafter: the *Šešelj* Trial Decision); Decision on Ojdanić's Motion Challenging Jurisdiction: Indirect Co-perpetration, *Prosecutor v. Milan Milutinović, Nikola Šainović, Dragoljub Ojdanić, Nebojša Pavković, Vladimir Lazarević, Vlastimir Djordjević and Sreten Lukić*, (IT-05-87-PT), 22 March 2006 (hereinafter: the *Ojdanić* Appeal Decision); Decision on Petković's Appeal on Jurisdiction, *Prosecutor v. Jadranko Prlić, Bruno Stojić, Slobodan Praljak, Milivoy Petković, Valentin Ćorić and Berislav Bušić*, (IT-04-74-AR72.3), 23 April 2008 (hereinafter: *Petković* Appeal Decision).

5 *Hadžihasanović* Appeal Decision, ibid., para. 51.

6 *Šešelj* Trial Decision, *supra* note 4.

7 Ibid., para. 40.

Chamber, which held that the jurisdictional requirements of Article 5 of the ICTY Statute did not require proof of an armed conflict within the state where the crime was allegedly committed.[8] The 2006 decision on Ojdanić's defence challenge to jurisdiction led to the removal of indirect co-perpetration from the indictment; the Appeals Chamber accepted that this form of responsibility did not form part of customary law at the time and ordered that the relevant part of the indictment be stricken out.[9] Finally, in 2008, the Petković motion on jurisdiction led the Appeals Chamber to reprimand the Trial Chamber for failing to clarify the form of individual criminal responsibility and instructed that the necessary clarification be made.[10]

Before the ICTR, the only successful defence challenge to jurisdiction was filed in the *Kanyabashi* case, but it is questionable whether this was a jurisdictional issue proper, since it concerned the division of authority between two trial chambers to decide on a certain motion.[11] In *Barayagwiza*, the 1999 Appeals Chamber decision upheld the defence challenge to personal jurisdiction on the grounds of an egregious delay in Barayagwiza's pre-trial arrest, transfer and charging.[12] However, approximately one year later the Appeals Chamber reconsidered its decision, ostensibly due to new evidence, which suggested that the delay was owed to shortcomings attributable to a state and not to the Tribunal.[13] In the context of the SCSL, no challenge to jurisdiction was accepted, and the Court proceeded to try and convict all individuals in the handful of cases it decided. Finally, as regards the ICC, defence challenges to jurisdiction have so far been very rare and uniformly unsuccessful.[14]

In closing, this part has demonstrated that on the basis of the judicial decisions on jurisdiction issued in contemporary international criminal law, only a handful of challenges have been successful, most of which focused on subject-matter jurisdiction. Many different reasons appear to have caused this overwhelmingly negative history on the fate of defence challenges to jurisdiction. It is therefore time to discuss some of these reasons and assess how the Prosecutor, the defence and the judges have all contributed to this state of affairs.

8 Decision on the Interlocutory Appeal Concerning Jurisdiction, *Prosecutor v. Vojislav Šešelj*, (IT-03-67-AR72.1), 31 August 2004, para. 14.
9 *Ojdanić* Appeal Decision, *supra* note 4, paras. 39–40.
10 Ibid.
11 Decision on the Defence Motion for Interlocutory Appeal on the Jurisdiction of Trial Chamber I, *Prosecutor v. Joseph Kanyabashi*, (ICTR-96-15-0031 (A)), 3 June 1999. For a further discussion see below under 3.3.1.
12 Decision, *Jean-Bosco Barayagwiza v. the Prosecutor*, (ICTR-99-17-AR72), 3 November 1999, paras. 71–2.
13 Decision on Prosecutor's Request for Review and Reconsideration, *Jean-Bosco Barayagwiza v. the Prosecutor*, (ICTR-99-17-AR72), 31 March 2000. Further see, M. Shahabudeen, *International Criminal Justice at the Yugoslav Tribunal: A Judge's Recollection* (Oxford University Press, 2012), pp. 102–3.
14 In *Ntaganda* OA2 the defence succeeded in having the challenge classified as 'jurisdictional', although in the end the Appeals Chamber rejected the complaint in substance. Judgment on the appeal of Mr Bosco Ntaganda against the 'Decision on the Defence's challenge to the jurisdiction of the Court in respect of Counts 6 and 9', *Prosecutor v Bosco Ntaganda*, (ICC-01/04-02/06-1225), 22 March 2016.

Identifying the reasons

The research findings provided above demonstrate that less than one out of ten defence challenges to the jurisdiction of an international criminal court have been successful from 1992 to date. Different causes have contributed to this situation, such as prosecutorial caution, defence misuse of jurisdictional challenges, and the inconsistency surrounding the interpretation and application of important jurisdictional concepts. Each will be now addressed in turn.

Prosecutorial caution

An important reason underpinning the lack of success in jurisdictional challenges is prosecutorial caution. Admittedly, piercing the confidentiality surrounding prosecutorial choices is not easy and this is not an 'insider's account'. The conclusions presented here are drawn from public statements. With that caveat in mind, prosecutorial caution on matters of jurisdiction have taken many shapes over the years.

First, in cases of doubt, international prosecutors asked for guidance and confirmation. In the ICTY context, Prosecutor del Ponte claimed that she did not proceed with investigations into the alleged crimes committed against Serbians and ethnic Albanians in Kosovo by the Kosovo Liberation Army from 1999–2001 due to doubts about the Tribunal's jurisdiction. She asked for an explicit mandate to that effect by the Security Council, which was not forthcoming and therefore did not proceed with the investigations.[15] In the ICC context, the Prosecutor requested the opinion of Pre-Trial Chamber I. The Rohingya deportation from the territory of Myanmar (a state non-party) to Bangladesh (a state party) was the first case where a trace of jurisdictional ambivalence emerged, insofar as the Court's Statute does not explicitly provide for 'objective territoriality' or 'ubiquity'.[16] The Prosecutor asked effectively for an advisory opinion from the Court prior to making a decision to open an investigation.[17] In the status conference of 20 June 2018, Deputy Prosecutor James Stewart made clear the motivation underpinning the Prosecutor's request for a ruling on jurisdiction;

> First, the Prosecutor will assume full responsibility for any decision she must take in relation to the situation affecting the Rohingya. But she does not wish to announce a preliminary examination, create expectations, and invest her limited resources *unless she is confident that she is on solid jurisdictional*

15 Matthias Holvoet, 'The Continuing Relevance of the Hybrid or Internationalized Justice Model: The Example of the Kosovo Specialist Chambers', 28 *Criminal Law Forum* 35 (2016), pp. 43–4, with references to Carla del Ponte, *Madame Prosecutor, Confrontations with Humanity's Worst Criminals and the Culture of Impunity*, (Other Press, 2008), pp. 275–6 *et seq*.

16 The terms denote the exercise of territorial jurisdiction when an offence occurs only partly within a state's territory.

17 Application under Regulation 46(3), Prosecution's Request for a Ruling on Jurisdiction under Article 19(3) of the Statute, (ICC-RoC46(3)-01/18-1), 9 April 2018.

> *ground*. And that is why we have taken the unusual step of seeking from you a ruling on jurisdiction in this unique situation.[18]
>
> [emphasis added]

The Pre-Trial Chamber granted the Prosecutor's request and ruled that the Court had jurisdiction, in spite of the many valid objections raised by the dissenting judge concerning the Chamber's power to issue such decision.[19]

Second, the ICC Prosecutor has actively solicited self-referrals by States Parties and presented cases within very narrow and jurisdictionally clear confines.[20] As regards situations, the governmental letters conferring jurisdiction on the Court were confirmed with subsequent governmental correspondence[21] and declarations of jurisdiction specifically designed to dispel any ambiguity concerning the Court's jurisdiction.[22] As a result, the Prosecutor could present cases that fell squarely within the scope of a situation. Jurisdictional certainty was further guaranteed by the strict and narrow delimitation of the cases brought before the Court. In *Katanga*, for example, the Prosecution charged the accused with participating in the commission of serious crimes committed on 24 February 2003 during the attack on the village of Bogoro in Ituri.[23]

Last but not least, it may well be that cumulative charging was resorted to as a cure for jurisdictional ambivalence. This may have been the case especially

18 Matter under Regulation 46(3) of the Regulations of the Court, (ICC-RoC46(3)-01/18), ex parte status conference, 20 June 2018, Transcript p. 4, lines 15–20.

19 Pre-Trial Chamber I, Request under Regulation 46(3) of the Regulations of the Court, 'Decision on the "Prosecution's Request for a Ruling on Jurisdiction under Article19(3) of the Statute"', (ICC-RoC46(3)-01/18-37), 6 September 2018, Dissenting Opinion of Judge Perrin de Brichambaut.

20 B. Kloss, *The Exercise of Prosecutorial Discretion at the International Criminal Court* (Herbert Utz, Munchen, 2016), pp. 129–130, Ph. Clark, 'Chasing Cases: The ICC and the Politics of State Referral in the Democratic Republic of Congo and Uganda', in C. Stahn and M. El Zeidy (eds) *The International Criminal Court and Complementarity*, (Cambridge University Press, 2011), pp. 1180–203.

21 *Situation in the Republic of Cote d'Ivoire*, Decision Pursuant to Article 15 of the Rome Statute on the Authorisation of an Investigation in the Situation in the Republic of Côte d'lvoire, 3 October 2011, (ICC-02/11-14-Corr), paras. 10-12. The Chamber refers to the letters accepting the jurisdiction of the Court under Article 12(3) submitted by the Government of Côte d'Ivoire on 18 April 2003, on 14 December 2010 and on 3 May 2011. The 18 April 2003 letter accepted the jurisdiction of the Court from 19 September 2002 for an unspecified period of time. The 14 December 2010 letter confirmed the earlier letter's acceptance of jurisdiction, whereas the 3 May 2011 letter referred specifically to the need to investigate possible crimes against humanity connected to the 2010 presidential elections in that country.

22 In the Situation in Uganda, the Government of Uganda submitted an additional 'Declaration on Temporal Jurisdiction' under Article 12(3), in order to make sure that the Court would have jurisdiction also in the period between 1 July 2002 and 1 September 2002. Situation in Uganda, Warrant of Arrest for Joseph Kony issued on 8 July 2005 as amended on 27 September 2005, (ICC-02/04-01/05-53), 13 October 2005, para. 32.

23 Decision on the Confirmation of Charges, *Prosecutor v. Germain Katanga and Mathieu Ngudjolo Chui*, (ICC-01/04-01/07-717), paras. 20–6.

before the *ad hoc* tribunals, where the existence of a crime or mode of liability in customary law could be seriously contested. The ICTY Appeals Chamber accepted that cumulative charging is permissible, because 'prior to the presentation of all of the evidence, it is not possible to determine to a certainty which of the charges brought against an accused will be proven'.[24] However, cumulative charging addressed uncertainty not only as regards proof of fact, but also proof of law; namely, the existence of a crime in customary law as the essential jurisdictional prerequisite for the Tribunal's subject-matter jurisdiction. In *Naletilić and Martinović* the Trial Chamber justified cumulative charging as a permissible tactic, considering that 'the crimes over which the Tribunal has jurisdiction are frequently broad and yet to be clarified in the jurisprudence of the Tribunal'.[25] Therefore, cumulative charging acted as a valid prosecutorial precaution against jurisdictional uncertainty.

This part has shown that the Prosecutor had many strategies available to cope with jurisdictional uncertainty and did not hesitate to use them. As a result, the question of jurisdiction was to all intents and purposes settled before the defence had a realistic opportunity to seriously challenge it. Nonetheless, this does not appear to have dissuaded defence teams from challenging jurisdiction, as the next part will show.

Defence confusion and (mis-)use of jurisdictional challenge

Arguably, defence counsel have also contributed to this overwhelmingly negative history of jurisdictional challenges. As the record shows, defence teams filed 'motions challenging the jurisdiction' of an international criminal court or tribunal, even when it was reasonably clear that they had no chance of success or they sought to achieve objectives other than a finding on jurisdiction.

A good example is defence challenges to the jurisdiction of the *ad hoc* tribunals due to the illegal arrest and detention of the suspect. In 1999, the ICTR accepted that such motions were jurisdictional in nature.[26] However, in 2000 the ICTR and ICTY Rules of Procedure (RPE) were amended, to the effect that under the new Article 72 (H) ICTR and 72 (B) ICTY RPE:

> a motion challenging jurisdiction refers exclusively to a motion which challenges an indictment on the ground that it does not relate to:
>
> i) any of the persons indicated in Articles 1, 6, 7 and 9 of the Statute;
> ii) the territories indicated in Articles 1, 8 and 9 of the Statute;

24 Appeals Chamber Judgement, *The Prosecutor v. Delalić, et al.*, (IT-96-21-A), 20 February 2001, para. 400.

25 Decision on Vinko Martinovic's Objection to the Amended Indictment and Mladen Naletilic's Preliminary Motion to the Amended Indictment, *Prosecutor v. Naletilić & Martinović*, (IT-98-34), 14 February 2001.

26 Decision and Scheduling Order, *Prosecutor v. Jean-Bosco Barayagwiza*, (ICTR-97-19-72), 5 February 1999, p. 3.

iii) the period indicated in Articles 1, 8 and 9 of the Statute;
iv) any of the violations indicated in Articles 2, 3, 4, 5 and 7 of the Statute.[27]

This rule made abundantly clear that any other challenge would not qualify as jurisdictional and would be dismissed as inadmissible. As a result, many defence challenges pending at the time, on precisely this issue, were caught by the change in the rules and were dismissed.[28]

However, other challenges were filed on exactly the same grounds *years* after the amendment of the rules – only to be summarily dismissed as inadmissible. For example, in 2003 the ICTY Appeals Chamber rejected the *Dragan Nikolić* jurisdictional challenge, explaining that complaints due to the conditions of arrest and surrender of a suspect are not enumerated in Rule 72(D) and therefore are not jurisdictional, but require leave to appeal.[29] Therefore, it may well be that sometimes challenges to jurisdiction were used to achieve objectives other than the ones they were designed for. To tackle the problem of abusive defence motions, the judges used many different mechanisms, such as short time limits.[30]

That said, it is nonetheless interesting to discuss the various objectives behind such use of jurisdictional motions. These seem to coalesce around three main points: the use of challenges to clarify the law; the use of challenges to acquire evidence; and, finally, the use of challenges to obtain direct access to the Appeals Chamber on legal issues.

First, defence teams appear to have used jurisdictional challenges to clarify the law and filter the case before the trial. This became important in the law and practice of the *ad hoc* tribunals, especially when the Prosecution brought charges on the basis of unwritten/customary law. In these circumstances, the law was not necessarily clear to any of the parties appearing before the judges.[31] Therefore, it

27 ICTR Rules of Procedure and Evidence with the 7th revision of 21 February 2000, under Rule 72(H). ICTR Rules of Procedure and Evidence as amended on 21 February 2000, available at http://unictr.irmct.org/sites/unictr.org/files/legal-library/000221-rpe-en.pdf (last visited 23 October 2019). The same rule was introduced verbatim in the Rule 72(B), ICTY, Rules of Procedure and Evidence, Revision 19, 1 and 13 December 2000, available at www.icty.org/x/file/Legal%20Library/Rules_procedure_evidence/IT032_rev19_en.pdf (last visited 23 October 2019).

28 Decision (Appeal against Dismissal of Motion concerning Illegal Arrest and Detention), *Prosecutor v. André Rwamakuba*, (ICTR-98-44-A), 11 June 2001, p. 4; Arret (appel de la decision du 13 mars 2001 rejetant la 'Defence motion objecting to the jurisdiction of the tribunal'), *Prosecutor v. Juvenal Kajelijeli*, (ICTR-98-44A), 16 November 2001, p. 3; Decision on the Defence's Motion to Dismiss the Indictment in toto for lack of subject-matter jurisdiction and for lack of fundamental fairness for the accused, *Prosecutor v. Hassan Ngeze*, (ICTR-97-27-I), 10 May 2000, p. 2.

29 Decision on Notice of Appeal, *Prosecutor v. Dragan Nikolić*, (IT-94-2-AR72), 9 January 2003, considerations 4 and 5.

30 K. Oellers-Frahm, 'Comments on the Pre-Trial Proceedings in the Milosevic Case before the International Criminal Tribunal for the Former Yugoslavia', 45 *German Yearbook of International Law* 203 (2002), p. 207.

31 *Prosecutor v. Naletilić and Martinović*, *supra* note 25. G. Boas, J. Jackson, B. Roche and D. Taylor III, 'Appeals, Reviews and Reconsideration', in G. Sluiter, H. Friman, S. Linton, S. Vasiliev and S. Zappala (eds), *International Criminal Procedure – Principles and Rules*

is plausible that defence challenges to jurisdiction were used to remove charges unfounded under customary law or to clarify the content of the accusation. This is evident particularly in the jurisprudence of the ICTY, where many defence challenges to jurisdiction focused on the challenge of subject-matter jurisdiction with emphasis on the existence of modes of liability under customary law at the time of the commission of the offence.

Second, defence teams may have used jurisdictional challenges to force the disclosure and production of evidence and highlight weaknesses in the prosecution's case. In the ICC context, it is clear that

> In order to effectively challenge jurisdiction, it must be ensured that the suspect has been granted access to documents that are essential for the preparation of his or her defence.[32]

Using this prerogative effectively can reveal early in the process the weaknesses of the prosecution case and contribute to the dismissal of the case at the stage of the confirmation of charges for lack of evidence. For example, the *Mbarushimana* defence filed a challenge to jurisdiction that was ultimately rejected. However, the defence successfully forced a 'trial within a trial', which arguably led to the dismissal of that case at the stage of the confirmation of charges hearing. Specifically, on 14 December 2010 the defence notified of its intention to submit a challenge to jurisdiction.[33] On 19 July 2011, the challenge to jurisdiction was finally filed.[34] Within this period of time, the defence requested the disclosure of documents from the Democratic Republic of the Congo and the Prosecution and when such disclosure was not forthcoming, it filed requests for orders to comply.[35] Ultimately, the jurisdictional challenge was rejected.[36] However, it may well be that this protracted litigation contributed to the dismissal of the case at the confirmation of charges stage, as it became apparent that the Prosecution did not

(Oxford University Press, 2013) p. 968 note that the clarification of the law and judicial economy were important considerations also for prescribing interlocutory appeals on jurisdictional rulings as a matter of right.

32 Decision on the Confirmation of Charges Pursuant to Article 61(7)(a) and (b) of the Rome Statute, Dissenting Opinion of Judge Kaul, *Prosecutor v. William Samoei Ruto and Joshua Arap Sang*, (ICC-01/09-01/11-373), 23 January 2012, para. 35.

33 Defence Request for Disclosure, *Prosecutor v. Mbarushimana*, (ICC-01/04-01/10-29), 14 December 2010.

34 Defence Challenge to the Jurisdiction of the Court, *Prosecutor v. Mbarushimana*, (ICC-01/04-01/10-290), 20 July 2011.

35 Defence Request for Disclosure, *Prosecutor v. Mbarushimana*, *supra* note 33, operative paragraph; Defence Request under Article 57(3)(b) of the Rome Statute for State Cooperation from the Democratic Republic of the Congo, *Prosecutor v. Mbarushimana*, (ICC-01/04-01/10 30), 28 December 2010, paras. 1, 5, and 15; Defence Request for the Compliance of the Democratic Republic of the Congo with ICC-01/04-01/10-56-Conf-Exp, *Prosecutor v. Mbarushimana*, (ICC-01/04-01/10-123), 27 April 2011, para. 5.

36 Decision on the 'Defence Challenge to the Jurisdiction of the Court', *Prosecutor v. Mbarushimana*, *supra* note 3.

have at its disposal sufficient evidence to meet the relevant threshold to proceed to trial. The judges – extraordinarily – noted the following:

> there were significant oversights and mistakes regarding vital aspects of the case. Among these, the 'errors, internal inconsistencies, omissions and duplications' identified by the Prosecution in the version of the DCC [Document Containing the Charges] and LoE [List of Evidence] originally filed stand out as particularly unfortunate. The Defence's request to readmit evidence it had previously successfully sought to exclude on grounds of violation of the Suspect's rights' caused unnecessary further delays in the proceedings. Such problems have not helped in streamlining the proceedings: in most cases they triggered additional petitioning and litigation, such as when the Chamber was encumbered by the Prosecution with the unnecessary burden of authorising redactions to a document which had already been previously disclosed in unredacted form. (footnotes omitted)[37]

Third, defence challenges to jurisdiction may have been mislabelled intentionally as such, in an effort to acquire access to the Appeals Chamber by right, i.e. without requiring a prior leave to appeal. It is difficult to establish the truth of such allegations at all times;[38] regardless, even if they were true in part, the defence is not alone to blame for this state of affairs. Arguably, defence teams would not feel the need to resort to such practices, if the Chambers adopted a less restrictive approach to requests for leave to appeal pre-trial issues.[39]

Judicial legislation and interpretation

In addition to the prosecution and the defence, the judges also played a role in this state of affairs. Two points stand out: first, changes to the meaning of jurisdiction and second the lack of clarity as regards the question of burden and standard of proof of facts in jurisdictional proceedings.

The definitional difficulties of 'jurisdiction'

One of the most frequent grounds for the rejection of a defence challenge to jurisdiction has been its misclassification. The root of the problem in these determinations has been mainly the lack of clarity as regards the definition of 'jurisdiction'.

37 Decision on the Confirmation of Charges, *Prosecutor v. Callixte Mbarushimana*, (ICC-01/04-01/10-465-Red.), 16 December 2011, para. 36.

38 For a rare example see, Decision on the Confirmation of Charges Pursuant to Article 61(7)(a) and (b) of the Rome Statute, *Prosecutor v. William Samoei Ruto,Henry Kiprono Kosgey, and Joshua Arap Sang*, *supra* note 32, para. 34 ('the Chamber observes that the Defences' submissions disputing the legal findings of the 31 March 2010 Decision are actually an attempt to obtain a right to appeal on this point of law and at this stage of the proceedings').

39 H. Friman, 'Interlocutory Appeals in the Early Practice of the International Criminal Court' in C. Stahn and G. Sluiter (eds), *The Emerging Practice of the International Criminal Court* (Brill, 2009), at p. 559.

This definition proved controversial in the formative stages of international criminal procedure. In the *Tadić* case, for example, it was only after the Appeals Chamber issued its ground breaking decision that motions challenging the power of the Security Council to establish the tribunals were considered to be jurisdictional in nature.[40] The Appeals Chamber thus noted that the Trial Chamber's view on jurisdiction comprising only territorial, temporal, subject-matter and personal parameters, was a narrow approach that did not exclude a broader view, which included also the legality of the creation of the Tribunal.[41]

In the 1999 *Kanyabashi* case, the Appeals Chamber was split over the question whether a challenge against the authority of a recomposed trial chamber to decide on a prosecutorial request after the initial appearance of the accused qualified as jurisdictional.[42] The majority held that it did and decided to grant the motion in part.[43] As a result, the Prosecutor's request for leave was adjudicated by Trial Chamber II. On the other hand, the minority disagreed. Judges Wang Tieya and Nieto-Navia held that the composition of the bench is a matter of judicial administration that is not jurisdictional in nature. They took the view that

> [i]n the practice of the Tribunal, to allow jurisdictional challenges to be based on re-composition is, ultimately, to allow the parties to question the validity of the portion of the Rules regarding judicial administration. If this is a matter of jurisdiction, whose and which jurisdiction would be questioned: that of the relevant Trial Chamber to follow the Rules or of the Plenary Meeting of the Judges to design and amend the Rules?[44]

The lack of a uniform understanding of the concepts of jurisdiction and defence challenge or objections to jurisdiction became forcefully evident in *Šešelj*. The Trial Chamber accepted that the existence of an armed conflict in Bosnia and/or Croatia and its connection to the alleged crimes against humanity in Vojvodina at the critical time was a jurisdictional issue.[45] However, the Appeals Chamber reversed this finding. Upon the Prosecutor's appeal, it considered that the Trial Chamber committed a serious error of law because – among others – the connection between the armed conflict in Bosnia and the alleged crimes against humanity in Vojvodina was not a jurisdictional matter, but rather a question of fact to be determined at trial.[46]

40 *Prosecutor v. Tadić*, *supra* note 2, paras. 10–12.
41 Ibid., para. 12.
42 Decision on the Defence Motion for Interlocutory Appeal on the Jurisdiction of Trial Chamber I, *Prosecutor v. Joseph Kanyabashi*, *supra* note11, para. 14.
43 Ibid., Joint and Separate Opinion of Judge McDonald and Judge Vohrah, para. 4.
44 Ibid., Joint Separate and Concurring Opinion of Judge Wang Tieya and Judge Rafael Nieto-Navia, para. 22.
45 Decision on Motion by Vojislav Seselj Challenging Jurisdiction and Form of Indictment, *Prosecutor v. Vojslav Šešelj*, *supra* note 4, paras. 39–40.
46 Decision on the Interlocutory Appeal Concerning Jurisdiction, *Prosecutor v. Vojslav Šešelj*, *supra* note 8, para. 14.

Further evidence of judicial ambivalence concerning the concept of jurisdiction emerged from ICTR jurisprudence. In the 1999 *Barayagwiza et al.* litigation before the ICTR, the Tribunal held that the legal nature of defence complaints of illegal arrest or detention of the accused was jurisdictional.[47] As a result, a number of defence teams lodged similar, *Barayagwiza*-type complaints. Within a year, the judges proceeded to amend the ICTY and the ICTR Rules of Procedure.[48] The new Rules restricted motions 'challenging jurisdiction' to objections attacking the territorial, temporal, personal and subject-matter scope of a case.[49] As a result, all pending jurisdictional complaints that did not meet this definition were rejected as inadmissible.[50] This affected particularly defence complaints of illegal arrest or detention.[51]

The Special Court for Sierra Leone was troubled with the meaning of jurisdiction in the *Fofana* case as regards the meaning of persons bearing 'the greatest responsibility'.[52] The Court interpreted the Statute on the basis of its preparatory works.[53] It ruled that the relevant terms actually introduced a jurisdictional requirement that was subject to an extremely low evidentiary threshold.[54] In the ICC context, in the 2006 *Lubanga* ruling, the Appeals Chamber restricted the concept of jurisdiction to challenges on the four main aspects of the Court's authority and considered defence motions alleging illegal arrest or detention as *sui generis* motions of human rights violations.[55]

47 *Prosecutor v. Jean-Bosco Barayagwiza*, *supra* note 26. See also, Decision on Petition for a Writ of Habeas Corpus on behalf of Radoslav Brdanin, *Prosecutor v. Br anin*, 8 December 1999, para. 6 accepted the possibility that a defence challenge of lawfulness of detention may amount to a challenge to jurisdiction.

48 New Rules 72(B) ICTY RPE and 72(H) ICTR RPE, *supra* note 1.

49 Ibid. K. A. A. Khan and R. Dixon, *Archbold International Criminal Courts – Practice Procedure and Evidence*, (Sweet and Maxwell, 3rd edn, 2009), p. 111 (in their view, such challenges remained an issue of jurisdiction 'in a wide sense', but did not fall within the scope of Rule 72).

50 Ibid. For the authority of judges of the ad hoc tribunals to amend the Rules of Procedure, see Rule 6, ICTY RPE, *supra* note 1.

51 Appeal Against Dismissal of Motion Concerning Illegal Arrest and Detention, *André Rwamakuba v. The Prosecutor*, *supra* note 28; Decision on the Defence's Motion to Dismiss the Indictment in toto for lack of subject-matter jurisdiction and for lack of fundamental fairness for the accused, *Prosecutor v. Hassan Ngeze*, *supra* note 28, p. 2 (freedom of speech); *Arret* (appel de la decision du 13 mars 2001 rejetant la 'Defence motion objecting to the jurisdiction of the tribunal'), *Prosecutor v. Juvenal Kajelijeli*, *supra* note 28; Decision on Notice of Appeal, *Prosecutor v. Dragan Nikolić*, *supra* note 29.

52 Decision on the Preliminary Defence motion on the lack of personal jurisdiction filed on behalf of the accused Fofana, *Prosecutor v. Norman, Fofana and Kondewa*, (SCSL-04-14-PT), SCSL Trial Chamber, 3 March 2004, paras. 22–5.

53 Ibid., paras. 26–7.

54 Ibid. For the evidentiary threshold, see next part.

55 Judgment on the Appeal of Mr. Thomas Lubanga Dyilo against the Decision on the Defence Challenge to the Jurisdiction of the Court pursuant to Article 19 (2) (a) of the Statute of 3 October 2006, *Prosecutor v. Thomas Lubanga Dyilo*, (ICC-01/04-01/06-772), 14 December 2006, para. 24.

In closing, this part has shown that the lack of clarity on the meaning of jurisdiction affected the fate of defence challenges to jurisdiction. The difference of opinion in *Tadić* between the narrow and broad meaning of jurisdiction adopted by the Trial and Appeals Chambers respectively, the dissenting opinions in *Kanyabashi*, the change in the Rules of Procedure in 2000, as well as the difference of opinion between the Trial and Appeals Chambers in *Šešelj* show that judges themselves faced difficulties with the notion and fluctuated considerably in its interpretation.

As time went by, the definition of jurisdiction crystallized. In turn, this appears to have diminished the significance of this cause for the rejection of defence challenges to jurisdiction. However, jurisprudential oscillation has continued to plague defence challenges to jurisdiction to this day, albeit in a different context: the assessment of facts in the context of jurisdictional proceedings. We will now turn our attention to this important issue.

Is it allowed to dispute facts by means of a defence challenge to jurisdiction?

This has proved to be a controversial question in international jurisprudence. It is not an exaggeration to say that it constitutes one of the main reasons for the rejection of defence challenges to jurisdiction today. Each system has given its own answer to this question.

THE *AD HOC* TRIBUNALS (ICTY, ICTR)

The *ad hoc* tribunals took the view that defence challenges to jurisdiction raising issues requiring proof of facts are inadmissible and should be reserved for the merits of the case. A challenge would qualify as jurisdictional only if it challenged at least one of the four aspects of the scope of the Court's jurisdiction. For example, in *Boškoski and Tarculovski*, the ICTY discussed and rejected the defence challenge that the Court lacked territorial jurisdiction over crimes allegedly committed in the territory of the Former Yugoslav Republic of Macedonia at the time.[56] The *Đorđević* defence challenges to the temporal and territorial jurisdiction of the ICTY met with the same fate; the tribunal ruled that it had jurisdiction over crimes committed in Kosovo after the Dayton Peace Agreement in 1995 under the relevant provisions of the ICTY Statute.[57] In cases of doubt, the challenge was relegated for consideration in the trial proper. For example, in *Kordić and Čerkez*, the Trial Chamber rejected the defence challenge to jurisdiction as a non-jurisdictional motion, because the question of the accused's

56 Decision on Johan Tarculovksi's Motion Challenging Jurisdiction, *Prosecutor v. Ljube Boskoski and Johan Tarculovski*, (IT-04-82-PT), 1 June 2005, para. 9.

57 Decision on Vlastimir Đorđević's Preliminary Motion on Jurisdiction, *Prosecutor v. Vlastimir Đorđević*, (IT-05-87/1-PT), 6 December 2007; the issue concerning the Tribunal's jurisdiction over Kosovo was addressed in the earlier Ojdanic motion, *supra* note 4.

superior responsibility for failure to punish raised 'mixed questions of law and fact which should be dealt with during trial'.[58]

The defence challenges to subject-matter jurisdiction proved much more controversial. Typically, the defence would challenge the modes of liability or the existence of a crime under customary law at the critical time. The path most travelled in that jurisprudence was the rejection of challenges as inadmissible: the rationale was that they raised essentially evidentiary matters reserved for the merits of the case. In *Karadžić* the Tribunal ruled that none of the six defence challenges on modes of liability and the scope of the crimes in question qualified as jurisdictional and rejected them.[59] The Appeals Chamber agreed with the Trial Chamber's approach.[60] The same outcome was reached in the *Gotovina*[61] and *Tolimir*[62] cases, where the Trial and the Appeals Chambers ruled that the motions in question did not raise issues of jurisdiction, but matters pertaining to the merits of the case.

That said, however, it is telling that all defence challenges to jurisdiction that were granted in part related to subject-matter jurisdiction. As regards the *Šešelj* motion, the Prosecutor successfully appealed and quashed the decision on jurisdiction in favour of the defence.[63] In the 2008 *Petković* motion on jurisdiction, the Appeals Chamber accepted that 'the Trial Chamber's failure to address the persistent ambiguity in the forms of liability charged in the Indictment before the start of the Defence case violates Articles 20(1) and 21(4) of the Statute'.[64] As a result, the Appeals Chamber ordered the Trial Chamber to direct the Prosecution to amend the indictment according to its instructions and proceed with the trial.[65]

Finally, in two cases, the ICTY accepted the defence challenges and as a result it dismissed the case in part against the accused for lack of subject-matter jurisdiction. In *Milutinović et al.*, the Ojdanić defence successfully argued before the Trial chamber that indirect co-perpetration as alleged in the indictment did not form part of customary law at the time of commission of the offence. The Trial

58 Decision on the Joint Defence Motion to Dismiss for lack of jurisdiction portions of the amended indictment alleging 'failure to punish' liability, *Prosecutor v. Dario Kordić and Mario Ćerkez*, 2 March 1999, para. 16.

59 Decision on 6 preliminary motions challenging jurisdiction, *Prosecutor v. Radovan Karadžić*, (IT-95-5/18-PT), 28 April 2009, paras. 29–32.

60 Decision on Radovan Karadžić's motions challenging jurisdiction (omission liability, JCE-III – Special Intent Crimes, Superior Responsibility), *Prosecutor v. Radovan Karadžić*, (IT-95-5118-AR72.1), 25 June 2009, paras. 33–7.

61 Decision on Ante Gotovina's Interlocutory Appeal Against Decision on Several Motions Challenging Jurisdiction, *Prosecutor v. Ante Gotovina et al.*, (IT-06-90-AR72.1), 6 June 2007, para. 24.

62 Decision on Tolimir's 'Interlocutory Appeal Against the Decision of the Trial Chamber on the Part of the Second Preliminary Motion Concerning the Jurisdiction of the Tribunal', *Prosecutor v. Zdravko Tolimir*, (IT-05-88/2-AR72.1), 25 February 2009, paras. 7, 10.

63 *Šešelj* Trial Decision, *supra* note 4.

64 *Petković* Appeal Decision, *supra* note 4, para. 20.

65 Ibid.

Chamber therefore accepted that the tribunal did not have subject-matter jurisdiction to decide these accusations. It proceeded to strike out the parts of the indictment that invoked Ojdanić's responsibility as an indirect co-perpetrator.[66] The trial proceeded on the rest of the charges and Ojdanić was eventually convicted for aiding and abetting crimes against humanity and sentenced to 15 years imprisonment. In the *Hadžihasanović et al.* case, the Appeals Chamber agreed with the defence that customary international law at the critical time did not provide for the criminal responsibility of a commander over acts that took place prior to the establishment of a superior-subordinate relationship.[67] As a result, the trial proceeded on the other counts and concluded with the conviction of the accused for war crimes to short prison sentences.

THE SPECIAL COURT FOR SIERRA LEONE

In contrast to the *ad hoc* tribunals and the ICC, the SCSL took a more lenient approach to the admissibility of defence challenges to jurisdiction. It allowed a wide range of challenges: from the constitutionality of the establishment of the Court, to the criminalization of child recruitment under customary law, and the exclusion of responsibility due to the amnesty clause of the Lomé Agreement.[68]

As regards proof of facts in jurisdictional proceedings, the matter was addressed in the *Fofana* case, albeit the ruling was not very clear. In that case, the defence argued that the accused was not a person who bore 'the greatest responsibility' under Article 1(1) of the SCSL Statute and therefore his case fell beyond the Court's personal jurisdiction.[69]

The Chamber rejected the complaint, although with somewhat contradictory reasoning. On the one hand, it considered that the Prosecutor's mere allegation was sufficient and that the rest of the claim was 'an essentially evidentiary matter to be determined at the trial stage'.[70] This would suggest that the Court took a leaf out of the *ad hoc* tribunals' book and followed their example.

Yet, at the same time, the Court asserted that it had jurisdiction, provided that 'sufficient information existed to provide reasonable grounds for believing' that the crime alleged fell within its jurisdictional parameters.[71] This is clearly an evidentiary threshold, which the Prosecutor should meet to convince the Chambers on facts disputed at the stage of jurisdictional hearings. Neither this case, nor subsequent jurisprudence shed any further light on point.

66 *Ojdanić* Appeal Decision, *supra* note. 4.
67 *Hadžihasanović* Appeal Decision, supra note 4, paras. 45, 51–3.
68 Decision on Challenge to Jurisdiction: Lomé Accord Amnesty, *Prosecutor v. Kallon and Kamara*, (SCSL-2004-15-AR-72(E)), 13 March 2004, paras. 69, 71.
69 Decision on the Preliminary Defence motion on the lack of personal jurisdiction filed on behalf of the accused Fofana, *Prosecutor v. Norman, Fofana and Kondewa*, *supra* note 52, para. 5.
70 Ibid., para. 44.
71 Ibid., para. 41.

THE INTERNATIONAL CRIMINAL COURT

The issue of the value of facts in jurisdictional proceedings emerged before the ICC in the very first defence challenge to jurisdiction. In *Mbarushimana*, the contentious issue was the temporal connection between the referral (2004) and the case (2009). At the stage of issuing the arrest warrant, the Pre-Trial Chamber adopted a *prima facie* standard and concluded on the basis of UN Security Council Presidential Statements and Resolutions that the case fell within the temporal scope of the situation of crisis.[72] Once the accused was in custody and made his initial appearance, the defence proceeded to challenge the Court's jurisdiction. In this context, the defence asked for clarification on the applicable burden and standard of proof, to which the Pre-Trial Chamber ruled that as regards the burden of proof, each party has the burden to prove its own claims.[73] However, as regards the standard of proof, it ruled that

> the present challenge is based, and its determination will thus depend, *much more* on issues of a legal nature than on whether a given fact can or cannot be considered by the Chamber as properly established. There is thus no need for the Chamber to address the issue as to the nature of the 'standard of proof' to be satisfied by the party bringing a jurisdictional challenge.
>
> [emphasis added][74]

Therefore, while there was a burden of proof, there was no standard available, since the issue was 'much more' legal than factual. However, 'much more' did not mean exclusively. Specifically, there were real factual issues in dispute concerning the atrocities allegedly committed by the FDLR in the Kivus in the relevant window in time and the connection of the suspect to those alleged activities.[75] Thus, when it came to the assessment of facts and the temporal connection of the case to the situation, the Chamber was once again satisfied by recourse to Security Council Resolutions and Presidential Statements.[76] The *Mbarushimana* decision did not meet with the approval of other chambers. The subsequent Kenyan cases confirmed that the relevant standard was 'a degree of certainty'.[77] The defence

72 Warrant for the Arrest of Callixte Mbarushimana, *Prosecutor v. Mbarushimana*, (ICC-01/04-01/10-2), 11 October 2010, para. 7.

73 Decision on the 'Defence Challenge to the Jurisdiction of the Court', *Prosecutor v. Callixte Mbarushimana*, *supra* note 3, para. 4.

74 Ibid., para. 5.

75 M. Klamberg, *Evidence in International Criminal Trials: Confronting Legal Gaps and the Reconstruction of Disputed Events* (Brill, 2013), p. 143.

76 Decision on the 'Defence Challenge to the Jurisdiction of the Court', *Prosecutor v. Callixte Mbarushimana*, *supra* note 3, paras. 44–5.

77 Decision on the Prosecutor's Application for Summonses to Appear for Francis Kirimi Muthaura, Uhuru Muigai Kenyatta and Mohammed Hussein Ali, *Prosecutor v. Francis Kirimi Muthaura, Uhuru Muigai Kenyatta and Mohammed Hussein Ali*, (ICC-01/09-02/11-1), 18 July 2012, para. 9; Decision on the Prosecutor's Application for Summons to Appear for William Samoei Ruto, Henry Kiprono Kosgey and Joshua Arap Sang, *Prosecutor v. William*

seized the Pre-Trial and subsequently the Appeals Chamber with an alleged challenge to subject-matter jurisdiction.[78] The Pre-Trial Chamber was divided. While the majority ruled that the question whether the Mungiki qualified as an 'organisation' for the purposes of the *chapeau* of Article 7 of the ICC Statute was not a jurisdictional issue, Judge Kaul dissented.[79] Nonetheless, all judges accepted that 'the degree of certainty' standard was properly deduced from the terms of Article 19(1) of the Statute that 'the Court must satisfy itself that it has jurisdiction'.[80] Upon appeal, the Appeals Chamber agreed with the majority of the Pre-Trial Chamber and ruled that the defence challenges to jurisdiction were not jurisdictional, insofar as their main complaint raised an issue subject to evidentiary scrutiny.[81] In so ruling, the Appeals Chamber seems to follow in the footsteps of the ICTY, insofar as the latter introduced and observed a distinction between challenges concerning the absence of material in support of an indictment – a matter for the trial proper – and challenges on the legal basis of the Tribunal's authority – an issue of jurisdiction.[82] Therefore, the Appeals Chamber seemed to consider the issue moot, insofar as the relevant issues formed part of the trial proper.

The second view is that facts can never be fully divorced from jurisdiction. From this perspective, some facts will always be important for the purposes of jurisdiction, such as the nationality of a perpetrator, or the location of the offence. Accordingly, jurisdictional challenges raising issues that require proof are admissible and must be considered in substance.

Samoei Ruto, Henry Kiprono Kosgey and Joshua Arap Sang, (ICC-01/09-01/11-1), 8 March 2011, para. 9; Decision on the Confirmation of Charges Pursuant to Article 61(7)(a) and (b) of the Rome Statute, *Prosecutor v. Francis Kirimi Muthaura, Uhuru Muigai Kenyatta and Mohammed Hussein Ali*, (ICC-01/09-02/11-382-Red), 23 January 2012, para. 23; Decision on the Confirmation of Charges Pursuant to Article 61(7)(a) and (b) of the Rome Statute, *Prosecutor v. William Samoei Ruto, Henry Kiprono Kosgey, and Joshua Arap Sang*, *supra* note 32, para. 25.

78 Joint Defence Challenge to Jurisdiction, *Prosecutor v. Ruto et al.*, (ICC-01/09-01/11-30), 30 August 2011.

79 Decision on the Confirmation of Charges Pursuant to Article 61(7)(a) and (b) of the Rome Statute, *Prosecutor v. Ruto et al., supra* note 32 and see Judge Kaul's Dissenting Opinion.

80 Decision Pursuant to Article 61(7)(a) and (b) of the Rome Statute on the Charges of the Prosecutor Against Jean-Pierre Bemba Gombo, *Prosecutor v. Bemba Gombo*, (ICC-01/05-01/08-424), 15 June 2009, para. 24.

81 Decision on the appeals of Mr William Samoei Ruto and Mr Joshua Arap Sang against the decision of Pre-Trial Chamber II of 23 January 2012 entitled 'Decision on the Confirmation of Charges Pursuant to Article 61(7)(a) and (b) of the Rome Statute', *Prosecutor v. Ruto and Sang et al.*, (ICC-01/09-01/11-414), 24 May 2012 (*Ruto* Appeals Decision); Decision on the appeal of Mr Francis Kirimi Muthaura and Mr Uhuru Muigai Kenyatta against the decision of Pre-Trial Chamber II of 23 January 2012 entitled 'Decision on the Confirmation of Charges Pursuant to Article 61(7)(a) and (b) of the Rome Statute', *Prosecutor v. Muthaura et al.* (ICC-01/09-02/11-425), 24 May 2012 (*Kenyatta* Appeals Decision).

82 Decision on Motion to Dismiss, *Prosecutor v. Brđanin*, (IT-99-36-PT), 5 October 1999, paras. 9–12. G. McIntyre, 'Defining Human Rights in the Arena of International Humanitarian Law: Human Rights in the Jurisprudence of the ICTY', in G. Boas and W. A. Schabas (eds), *International Criminal Law Developments in the Case-Law of the ICTY*, (Brill, 2003), pp. 208–9.

This position has been defended forcefully by the late Judge Kaul at the ICC. He noted that facts cannot be clinically separated from jurisdiction. In his view, facts can be contested at any stage of the proceedings and therefore will need to be established.[83] While this position was not discussed or adopted in the Kenyan cases, a few years later the Appeals Chamber agreed with Judge Kaul. It held that:

> challenges, which would, if successful, eliminate the legal basis for a charge on the facts alleged by the Prosecutor may be considered to be jurisdictional challenges. Accordingly, some verification as to whether the facts alleged correspond in law to the crimes charged may be necessary, depending on the circumstances, in order to determine whether the Court has jurisdiction over such crimes.[84]

Therefore, it would seem that today factual evaluations may legitimately form part of the jurisdictional challenge. If that is the case, then the immediate follow-up questions concern the burden and standard of proof of such facts. The Appeals Chamber has accepted that 'some verification' may be required, however, to this day it has refrained from spelling out its implications in terms of the standard and burden of proof.

This issue resurfaced recently in a different context, namely in proceedings on questions of jurisdiction put to the Court by the Prosecutor. In its recent *Rohingya* ruling, the Court made the following determination.[85] On the one hand, it held that a question of jurisdiction can be 'a pure question of law', because a Chamber is not called to make any specific findings of fact and its ruling is without prejudice thereto.[86] On the other hand, the Chamber noted that since it cannot issue advisory opinions, a jurisdictional question cannot be purely hypothetical and divorced from its factual context.[87] Yet, at the same time the Chamber did not explain the extent to which the Prosecutor should prove the relevant facts. This decision corroborates the sensitivity of the issue and the uncertainty surrounding the proof of facts in the context of jurisdictional proceedings.

Be that as it may, in the context of defence challenges to jurisdiction the best view on point seems to be the one advocated by Judge Kaul on 'the degree of certainty'. Logic and procedural economy require early and clear determinations on jurisdiction. Correspondingly, this entails that pre-trial chambers should undertake an exhaustive fact-finding mission to assess the veracity of certain facts critical for the existence and exercise of the Court's authority until it is certain

83 Decision on the Confirmation of Charges Pursuant to Article 61(7)(a) and (b) of the Rome Statute, *Prosecutor v. Ruto et al.*, *supra* note 32, Judge Kaul's Dissenting Opinion, para. 37.

84 Judgment on the appeal of Mr Bosco Ntaganda against the 'Decision on the Defence's challenge to the jurisdiction of the Court in respect of Counts 6 and 9', *Prosecutor v. Bosco Ntaganda*, *supra* note 14, para. 39.

85 Pre-Trial Chamber I, Decision on the 'Prosecution's Request for a Ruling on Jurisdiction under Article19(3) of the Statute', (ICC-RoC46(3)-01/18-37), 6 September 2018.

86 Ibid., para. 50.

87 Ibid., para. 33.

of the facts establishing its jurisdiction. After all, jurisdiction either exists or does not; a Court cannot have 'a little' or 'some' jurisdiction.[88]

Secondary benefits?

The above brief foray into the maze of defence challenges to the jurisdiction of the ICTY, the ICTY, the SCSL and the ICC shows that to date there have been no fully successful challenges to jurisdiction. The reasons may vary from one tribunal to the other. Some important considerations have proven to be prosecutorial caution, defence misuse and definitional uncertainty stemming from the shifting sands of jurisdictional rulings.

It would seem therefore that, barring exceptional circumstances, the chances of a successful challenge to jurisdiction seem slim. Nonetheless, it is worth asking whether these challenges had any clearly identifiable secondary benefits for the accused: for example, did they lead to dismissal of the case for lack of evidence, or a shorter sentence for the accused?

As regards the first possibility, a good example is the *Mbarushimana* case before the ICC. The defence caused a 'trial within the trial' that lasted for 9 months and included a series of disclosure requests and other procedural findings aiming at collecting evidence prior to the filing of the challenge. The challenge was rejected as unfounded,[89] but the charges were not confirmed and the case did not proceed to trial.[90] Is it possible that the evidentiary process preceding the filing of the jurisdictional challenge contributed to this state of affairs?

It is difficult to answer this question in the affirmative with any confidence. First, the emphasis was not on a specific piece of evidence, but rather on the evidence taken as a whole. In the words of the Chamber, the assessment was guided by:

> the intrinsic coherence of each item of evidence in light of the whole of the evidence submitted for the purposes of the confirmation hearing.[91]

Moreover, it is unclear whether the disclosure process led to the production of any evidence that could not have been acquired by the defence with subsequent disclosure requests in the confirmation hearing. Finally, the Pre-Trial Chamber in the confirmation decision castigated the sloppiness of the presentation of the

88 Judge Kaul Dissenting Opinion Arrest Warrant decisions in *Ruto*, *supra* note 77 and *Muthaura*, *supra* note 83. In favour of the 'degree of certainty', see K. Ambos, *Treatise on International Criminal Law*, (Oxford University Press, 2016, Vol. III) 254; and for opinions against see C. Hall, D. Ntanda, D. Nsereko and M. Ventura, 'Article 19', in O. Triffterer/K. Ambos (eds), *Rome Statute of the International Criminal Court – A Commentary*, (Nomos, 2016,) mn. 11, 859–60, advocating for a 'reasonable grounds to believe' test.

89 *Prosecutor v. Callixte Mbarushimana*, *supra* note 3.

90 Decision on the confirmation of charges, *Prosecutor v. Callixte Mbarushimana*, *supra* note 37, para. 340.

91 Ibid., para. 47.

Prosecution and Defence cases.[92] It would therefore appear that, in light of many other factors that may be legitimately responsible for the dismissal of the case, it is important not to overemphasize the contribution of the protracted jurisdictional stage.

Nonetheless, can the success of a challenge to jurisdiction – even in part – be directly connected to an acquittal or a lower sentence? Again, it is not possible to answer this question with any confidence; the most likely conclusion is probably not.

First, the jurisdictional hearing stage typically takes place very early on in the relevant process. As a result, it is causally connected as part of the entire process, but is too far removed from the final disposition of a case to allow for the identification of clear connections. Second, in the handful of successful defence challenges to jurisdiction, all the accused were convicted.

In *Hadžihasanović* and *Kubura*, the first accused was convicted to three and a half years and the second to two years for their role in the commission of war crimes.[93] In the 2008 *Petković* appeal decision on jurisdiction, the Appeals Chamber ruled that the Trial Chamber erred by failing to instruct the Prosecutor to amend the indictment in order to remove certain modes of liability charged in this case, but dismissed by the Appeals Chamber in other cases as jurisdictionally invalid.[94] Accordingly, the Appeals Chamber ordered the Trial Chamber to instruct the Prosecutor to amend the Indictment according to its instructions.[95] Regardless, at the end the accused was sentenced to 20 years imprisonment.[96] Finally, while the *Ojdanić* challenge to jurisdiction successfully excluded indirect co-perpetration charges,[97] the accused was still found guilty and convicted to 15 years imprisonment.[98] In the *Kanyabashi* case, the accused was finally convicted to 20 years imprisonment for incitement to genocide.[99] In the ICC context, while the first Appeals Chamber decision accepted that the *Ntaganda* defence challenge qualified as jurisdictional and was therefore admissible,[100] the second decision upheld the charges on sexual offences committed against the accused's own armed forces as properly falling within the Court's jurisdiction.[101] The case is still ongoing.

92 *Supra* note 37 and text.

93 Judgment, *Prosecutor v. Enver Hadžihasanović and Amir Kubura*, (IT-01-47-A), 22 April 2008, paras. 357–8.

94 *Petković*,Appeal Decision, *supra* note 4., para. 21.

95 Ibid., para. 22.

96 Judgment (Vol. III), *Prosecutor v. Prlić et al.*, (IT-04-74-A), 29 November 2017, p. 1403, disposition.

97 *Ojdanić* Appeal Decision, *supra* note 4.

98 Judgment (Vol III), *Prosecutor v. Milutinović et al.*, (IT-05-87-T), 26 February 2009, para. 1209.

99 Judgment, *Prosecutor v. Nyiramauhuko et al.*, (ICTR-98-42-A), 14 December 2015, paras. 3534–5.

100 Judgment on the appeal of Mr Bosco Ntaganda against the 'Decision on the Defence's challenge to the jurisdiction of the Court in respect of Counts 6 and 9', *Prosecutor v Bosco Ntaganda*, *supra* note 14, para. 40.

101 Judgment on the appeal of Mr Ntaganda against the 'Second decision on the Defence's challenge to the jurisdiction of the Court in respect of Counts 6 and 9', *Prosecutor v Bosco Ntaganda*, (ICC-01/04-02/06-1962), 15 June 2017, paras. 63–5.

Finally, in the relevant sentencing analysis, the judges balanced specific aggravating and mitigating factors, such as the gravity of the offence and the role of the accused, good behaviour and voluntary surrender.[102] The favourable decisions on jurisdiction do not appear to have played any role in the determination of the sentence. Against this backdrop, it would appear too speculative to suggest that, had the Tribunal affirmed its jurisdiction also for the other charges, they would be proven on the facts or lead to a different criminal treatment of the accused.

Concluding remarks

International jurisprudence considers the defence right to challenge the jurisdiction of an international criminal court or tribunal an important independent remedy against unwarranted judicial process. However, while in theory that may well be the case, in practice the exercise of this defence right does not appear to have led to the dismissal of a case for lack of jurisdiction. This may well fuel accusations that the theoretical usefulness of defence challenges to jurisdiction is not borne out by international criminal practice.

This study argues that this state of affairs is attributable to many reasons, some more legitimate than others. A particularly troublesome situation has proven to be the shifting sands of jurisdictional jurisprudence on important questions such as the proof of facts. Moving the goal posts from one jurisdictional decision to the next hardly increases the chances of a successful challenge and does no favours to the legitimacy of international criminal proceedings.

Against this backdrop, any ancillary benefits ostensibly acquired by the defence through the filing of a challenge to jurisdiction appear too speculative and context-specific to support concrete and consolidated conclusions. Therefore, it may well be that defence lawyers are right to advise their clients that, barring exceptional circumstances, they should harbour limited expectations from the filing of a challenge to the jurisdiction of an international criminal institution.

This conclusion shows the need to reconsider jurisdictional challenges and the relevant proceedings as a discourse neutral to the defence-victims debate. Both defence and victims have a real stake in the outcome of these proceedings. Jurisdictional proceedings therefore are not a mere 'technicality' that should be relegated to the *Tadic* 1995 ruling and left at that. They have real implications for both the accused and the victims, as duly acknowledged by the relevant jurisprudence.

To date, jurisdictional proceedings seem to result almost uniformly in conclusions favourable for the institution and the victims. This rather conclusive practice should give pause for a measure of reflection on the part of all judicial actors. After all, it is no less unfair that defence counsel attempt to derail the judicial process by abusing a right than it is for judges or prosecutors to disregard a valid defence complaint on jurisdiction arguably in the name of the victims.

102 See *Hadžihasanović and Amir Kubura*, *supra* note 93, para. 356, *Prlić et al.*, *supra* note 96, paras. 3277–80, *Nyiramauhuko et al.*, *supra* note 99, paras. 3533–5, *Milutinović et al.*, *supra* note 98, paras. 1185–9.

In-depth, critical reflection is called for as regards the effective exercise of the right of the defence to challenge jurisdiction, because jurisdictional proceedings affect directly the public perception of an international criminal institution as a legitimate agent of justice. Failure to do so risks transforming the defence right to challenge jurisdiction into a 'waste of time' in the eyes of the defence, thus rendering it illusory – with all the attendant legitimacy costs this may entail for international criminal institutions.

8 The ICTY and the balancing act

Reconciliation as rehabilitation

*Dejana Radisavljević**

Introduction

In the mid-1990s, the International Criminal Tribunal for the former Yugoslavia (hereinafter referred to as the 'ICTY' or 'Tribunal') was established to respond to the grave crimes committed in the former Yugoslavia. The Tribunal's mandate was to prosecute the "persons responsible for serious violations of international humanitarian law" – a mandate that connected the Tribunal's life span to the restoration of peace.[1] Although most clearly a punitive criminal justice mechanism, and despite the lack of references to the promotion of national reconciliation, the Tribunal's inextricable connection to peace gives it a further objective of promoting reconciliation.

This chapter will discuss the ICTY's intention to promote reconciliation through punitive justice; the challenges faced by the Tribunal in aiming at such an ambitious objective; and, the delicate balancing act that the promotion of reconciliation through punitive justice requires. First, I will outline how the ICTY is connected to the promotion of reconciliation and consider what this term means in the context of international criminal justice. Second, I will consider what is required for reconciliation to be effectively promoted – including considering the needs of the victims and the post conflict society as a whole – and the interplay between these needs and the rights of the offender. Finally, I will suggest how the rights of these two different parties can be balanced with the intention of promoting reconciliation.

Ultimately, this chapter's argument is two-fold: first, despite the difficulties that arise from a court of law promoting reconciliation, this was not an objective the ICTY could avoid; and second, the promotion of reconciliation was a feasible goal for the ICTY. In making this argument, I will suggest ways whereby the ICTY could have promoted reconciliation whilst nevertheless respecting the rights of the offender, particularly by viewing reconciliation as rehabilitation. This chapter feeds into the debate of how to balance the rights of the different stakeholders in international criminal justice and links this to discussion concerning how to achieve both the micro and macro level objectives of international

* The views expressed herein are solely those of the author and may not represent the position of the United Nations.

1 UNSC Res 827 (25 May 1993) UN Doc S/RES/827, para 2.

criminal courts and tribunals. Rather than being a stocktaking exercise on the ICTY, this chapter aims to contribute to the larger debate on how international criminal justice can balance the rights of victims and defendants, using the ICTY as an example for other international courts and tribunals.

Reconciliation: how did the ICTY set out to promote it and how is it defined?

In Resolution 827, the UN Security Council stated its conviction that "the prosecution of persons responsible for serious violations of international humanitarian law [. . .] would contribute to the restoration and maintenance of peace."[2] This linked the ICTY's mandate directly to the restoration of peace. Broadly speaking, peace can be either negative or positive. The starting point post-conflict is often negative peace, which is synonymous with a cessation of violence and a notable sense of negativity in terms of negative emotions towards individuals or groups of different ethnicity or religion. Positive peace, on the other hand, is more closely linked to understanding, acceptance and tolerance of previously conflicting individuals or groups. This positive peace is more akin to harmonious relations and denotes a vision of a shared future.

The fact that the ICTY's work was closely linked to the restoration of peace ties it to reconciliation, because without beginning the process towards reconciliation, any efforts to restore and maintain peace are unlikely to be successful. That is, whilst reconciliatory efforts are not necessarily required for negative peace, any deeper and more stable sense of peace requires making efforts at reconciliation.[3]

Negative peace is by far the most realistic objective in a post-conflict situation, but it is a transitional state, because it is also more superficial: whilst the parties to the conflict refrain from violence, they also do not communicate or interact with each other in any significant way. Hence, a non-eruption of violence requires sustainable peace and this in turn requires the parties to communicate, rather than seeing each other through eyes of hatred.

Early on, the ICTY itself recognised reconciliation among its objectives. In the case of *Erdemović* the Trial Chamber noted,

> The International Tribunal's objectives as seen by the Security Council – i.e. general prevention (or deterrence), reprobation, retribution (or "just deserts"), as well as collective reconciliation – fit into the Security Council's broader aim of maintaining peace and security in the former Yugoslavia.[4]

2 Ibid.

3 Janine Natalya Clark, 'The Impact Question: The ICTY and the Restoration and Maintenance of Peace' in Bert Swart, Alexander Zahar and Goran Sluiter (eds), *The Legacy of the International Criminal Tribunal for the Former Yugoslavia* (Oxford University Press, 2011), p. 78; Donna Pankhurst, 'Issues of Justice and Reconciliation in Complex Political Emergencies: Conceptualising Reconciliation, Justice and Peace', 20 *Third World Quarterly* (1999) 239, p. 254.

4 Trial Sentencing Judgment, *Prosecutor v Erdemović* (ICTY-96-22-T), 29 November 1996, para 58.

The ICTY intended to make its contribution to reconciliation through the fight against impunity; bringing those responsible for the crimes to trial; deterring future offences; and, giving the victims a sense of justice having being served.[5] It was therefore hoped that punitive justice – trial and punishment of individuals – would contribute to reconciliation on the ground. What does this mean in practice? Aside from being a recognition of the ICTY's intended contribution to reconciliation, this is also indicative of a broader failure to specify what reconciliation as an objective means, or indeed the role that the objective can have in sentencing.[6] Whilst this chapter is concerned only with reconciliation, the question of how any specific micro- or macro-level objective is to be achieved through sentencing is not made clear during the judicial process.[7] In fact, sentences are so disconnected from the expectations of the post-conflict society that they are difficult to justify locally and appear to have no connection to any of the objectives enumerated at the sentencing or enforcement stage.[8]

A starting point when considering the Tribunal's intended contributions to reconciliation is delineating whether the ICTY in referring to reconciliation intended to promote national reconciliation or global reconciliation in terms of promoting global peace and security by fighting impunity. In this regard, the fact that Resolution 827 stated that the then situation in Yugoslavia constituted 'a threat to international peace and security' linked its work more directly to global peace and security. Whilst the post-conflict society and victims, in particular, are more likely to be interested in remedying the past than ensuring global peace, the ICTY aligned itself more with the international community than with its local stakeholders. Consequently, promoting reconciliation within the post-conflict society was seen as a desirable, though incidental, objective.[9] This perhaps explains somewhat the ICTY's half-hearted attempts at promoting its work towards reconciliation. At the same time, the Tribunal did recognise the post-conflict society in the former Yugoslavia as its constituency and stated its conviction that its work would have reconciliatory impact on the ground.[10]

This failure to define reconciliation and how it is to be promoted by the Tribunal is particularly damaging, because it leaves ample room for misunderstandings and excessive expectations. This includes a risk that influential individuals

5 ICTY website available at www.icty.org/en/about accessed 8 March 2019.

6 James Meernik and Kimi King, 'The Sentencing Determinants of the International Criminal Tribunal for the former Yugoslavia: An Empirical and Doctrinal Analysis', 16(4) *Leiden Journal of International Law* (2003) 717, p. 723.

7 Mirko Bagaric and John Morss, 'International Sentencing Law: In Search of a Justification and Coherent Framework', 6(2) *International Criminal Law Review* (2006) 191, p. 207.

8 Ralph Henham, 'International Sentencing in the Context of Collective Violence', 7 *International Criminal Law Review* (2007) 249, p. 451.

9 For a similar argument in regard to the ICTR see Jean Marie Kamatali, 'From the ICTR to ICC: Learning from the ICTR Experience in Bringing Justice to Rwandans', 12(1) *New England Journal of International and Comparative Law* (2005) 99.

10 Gabrielle Kirk McDonald, 'Achievements of the ICTY' 2 *Journal of International Criminal Justice* (2004) 569.

in post-conflict States will misuse the term and define it in a way that suits their agenda, which in the case of the ICTY has proven to be ill fitting with the Tribunal's mandate.[11] Indeed, the local political elites in the States of the former Yugoslavia have consistently interpreted the court's mandate with reinforcing their beliefs of the conflict, and peace before rendering justice. This understanding is not in line with the wording of the UNSC resolution that established the Tribunal, and instead gives peace and reconciliation a much broader and more significant a role than they could possibly play by a court of law. As such, it is important not only to define what is understood by the term 'reconciliation', but also to do so in a way that is suitable for a court of law, because to be overly ambitious damages the legitimacy of the Tribunal and its potential restorative impact.[12]

The ICTY is not alone in failing to define reconciliation; indeed the ambiguity surrounding the term is well documented. It will suffice here to reiterate that reconciliation: refers to a process, outcome or goal; can be thin or thick; and, can be both on the individual and collective level.[13] How reconciliation is understood greatly affects the extent to which it is given a place in retributive justice; that is, reconciliation through retribution.

First, a thin definition of reconciliation is more akin to a cessation of violence and so-called negative peace, as introduced above. Indeed, this notion of negative peace is particularly relevant for Bosnia and Herzegovina, where there is a notable lack of inter-ethnic communication and interaction, and instead the prewar rhetoric is in some instances gaining tract some 20 years post-conflict.[14] The wounds within society from the war give no indication of healing, and the local politicians refer back to the conflict on a regular basis, particularly in Bosnia and Herzegovina. Nevertheless, the peoples of Bosnia and Herzegovina have come to accept thin reconciliation as a fact. Since there is no alternative to peaceful co-existence in a multi-ethnic State, as is the case in Bosnia and Herzegovina;

11 Melody Mirzaagha, 'Striving Towards a Just and Sustainable Peace: The Role of Reconciliation' *FICHL Policy Brief Series* No. 73 (2016), 3; Fernando Atria, 'Reconciliation and Reconstitution' in Scott Veitch (ed.), *Law and the Politics of Reconciliation* (Routledge, 2007), p. 34.

12 Nicos Trimikliniotis, 'Sociology of reconciliation: Learning from comparing violent conflicts and reconciliation processes', 61(2) *Current Sociology* (2012) 244, p. 256.

13 David Bloomfield, 'On Good Terms: Clarifying Reconciliation', Berghof Report Center for Constructive Conflict Management, (2006), 20, available at www.berghof-foundation.org/fileadmin/redaktion/Publications/Papers/Reports/br14e.pdf accessed 8 March 2019; David Bloomfield, Teresa Barnes and Luc Huyse (eds), *Reconciliation After Violent Conflict: A Handbook* (International Institute for Democracy and Electoral Assistance, 2003), 12; Julija Bogoeva, 'Prosecuting War Criminals as the Basis for Reconciliation Policy' FICHL Policy Brief Series No. 42 (2015), p. 2; David A Crocker, 'Reckoning with Past Wrongs: A Normative Framework' 13(1) *Ethics and International Affairs*, (1999) 43–64; Donna Pankhurst, *supra* note 3, p. 254.

14 Paul B Miller, 'Contested Memories: The Bosnian Genocide in Serb and Bosnian Minds', 8(3) *Journal of Genocide Research* (2006) 311, p. 313; Marko Milanović, 'The Impact of the ICTY on the Former Yugoslavia: An Anticipatory Post-Mortem', 110(2) *American Journal of International Law* (2016) pp. 233–59, 258.

the different religious communities have to share the State whether they like it or not. As I have noted above, the biggest criticism of a thin conception of reconciliation is precisely this lack of inter-communal, inter-ethnic communication, because, in essence, it relies on maintaining pretence and lack of interaction between different individuals and groups.[15]

Thicker understandings of reconciliation focus on restoring broken relationships in a meaningful way, with emphasis on finding a shared way forward and a shared future. This deep notion of reconciliation requires empathy and respect between individuals and communities, acceptance that others too were victimised, and a willingness to rebuild trust.[16] In this regard, the ICTY's work had the potential to build trust by removing those most responsible for the crimes in the former Yugoslavia from the region and trying them in The Hague, particularly where this was accompanied by stigmatisation by the Tribunal and the local stakeholders in the region.[17] However, in practice this was not the case, and there is no indication of inter group trust or understanding on a community scale.[18]

Aside from being thin or thick, reconciliation is also multi-level, meaning that it can be at the individual, community, societal or political level. Each of these levels requires different actions, engaging with different actors and using creative methods. The ICTY, in its references to reconciliation, often referred to the victims and the potential of international criminal justice, and more precisely prosecutions and stigmatisation, to begin the healing process for victims and be cathartic – which is the most common understanding of reconciliation at the individual level. This created challenges for the ICTY, because its core mandate was not to satisfy victims, but to try individuals accused of international crimes in the former Yugoslavia and thereby bring some relief to the victims and to the post conflict society. This in turn caused misperceptions, mistrust in the Tribunal, and disappointment on the part of the victims, and made contributions to reconciliation all the more difficult.[19]

This is closely linked to the fact that once there is an accepted definition of reconciliation, the ensuing challenge is to delineate how it should be promoted. The question to ask, then, is whether the definition of, and mechanism for, the promotion of reconciliation should be chosen by the post-conflict society or imposed upon them: is reconciliation a bottom up or a top down approach? As a court of law, the ICTY had objectives aside from promoting reconciliation, and as such, could not place undue importance thereon. A bottom up concept to

15 Birju Kotecha, 'The Complexity of Reconciliation', FICHL Policy Brief Series No. 79 (2017), p. 2.

16 Ibid.

17 Bogoeva, *supra* note 13, p. 2.

18 Milanović, *supra* note 14.

19 Janine Natalya Clark, 'The 'Crime of Crimes': Genocide, Criminal Trials and Reconciliation', *14 Journal of Genocide Research* (2012) 55, p. 64; 'Exporting Justice: Perceptions of the ICTY Among the Serbian, Croatian, and Muslim Communities in the Former Yugoslavia', 4(4) *Journal of Human Rights* (2005) 559–72, pp. 563–4.

reconciliation, whilst the most likely to gain acceptance in a post-conflict State, is incompatible with respect for the rights of those brought before international courts such as the ICTY. Moreover, a bottom-up approach assumes that there is consensus as to what reconciliation means, requires, and how it should be promoted, which will often not be the case in a fragile post-conflict situation. There will undoubtedly be different understandings as to what reconciliation means or entails, and as such, it would be too cumbersome, inconsistent and contentious for international criminal justice to approach reconciliation promotion in this way. Instead, a bottom up approach to reconciliation should be left to other mechanisms and processes better suited to it, such as truth and reconciliation commissions.

Despite its inadequacies, the fight against impunity through retributive justice is a necessary response to international crimes, such as those prosecuted by the ICTY, despite the fact that any such response may well be found to be inadequate. Removing the offenders from the State – demonstrating that their crimes will not go untried and unpunished – and international, as well as, ideally, local, stigmatisation, is an important post-conflict response.

Moreover, a court of law also has other objectives aside from its broader restorative goals. As such, the ICTY, much the same as any subsequent international courts or tribunals, could not, have disregarded its micro-level objectives that respect the rights and individuality of the offender, because this is a cornerstone of the rule of law, and, as such, is important to the court and the post-conflict reconciliation process. For some cultures, such as in the former Yugoslavia, it is accepted that retribution is important for reconciliation, but even without this recognition I would agree that retribution "will always be a significant component of justice since it not only focuses on the individual offender's need to atone for the harm done, it is the legal authority's symbolic affirmation of a moral disapproval which resides in the wider community."[20] Prosecution is then a necessary response to international crimes and the respect of a court's retributive mandate, but at the same time the ICTY's work was integrally linked to the promotion of reconciliation. Rather than questioning whether reconciliation is a suitable objective for an international court, it is therefore more fitting to ask how such a court could promote reconciliation on the ground. This brings me to the question of what is required in order to promote reconciliation, and what the challenges are for a court such as the ICTY.

How can a court of law promote reconciliation and what are the challenges?

Elucidating what the promotion of reconciliation means and requires in practice is unsurprisingly not a straightforward affair, particularly for a court of law. The problem for courts such as the ICTY is often that they consider themselves as essentially extensions of national courts, and because the work of national

20 Henham, *supra* note 8, p. 463, footnote 62.

courts is neither tied to, nor evaluated through, reconciliation efforts, they shirk away from actively promoting this objective. However, dealing with mass conflict crimes meant that the ICTY had a broader mandate, if for no other reason than because it was created through Chapter VII of the Charter of the United Nations, which tied it to the restoration of peace and security. At the same time, the ICTY was first and foremost a court of law and therefore the means of promoting reconciliation must be seen through the lens of retributive justice and the limits that this type of justice imposes.

This is indicative of the greater disparity between achieving the broad aims of international criminal justice and the narrower goals of sentencing and other post-conviction practices. At both levels, these goals relate to the international and the local, the collective and the individual. The ICTY recognised both the international community and the post-conflict society as stakeholders of its work,[21] whilst being concerned with the individual offender, which created an additional tension. The academic response as to how to manage this disconnect between the traditional role of a court of law and post-conflict reconstruction is polarised. Some argue for a minimalistic role for international criminal courts such as the ICTY,[22] whereby objectives such as reconciliation should be abandoned insofar as they conflict with the domestic aims of criminal justice. Conversely, others argue that domestic aims should remain dominant, but nonetheless modestly compromised in favour of international goals such as peace and reconciliation.[23] At the farther end of the spectrum, others have advocated for a re-conceptualisation of international sentencing and criminal justice,[24] including: combining criminal and civil law;[25] giving restorative justice a more prominent role;[26] and proposing the development of international criminal justice on the basis that the more effective a court is in engaging with post-conflict societies, the more legitimate its work will be.[27] This final position places the most emphasis on reconciliation and the needs of the post-conflict society; however, this raises

21 Yuval Shany, 'Assessing the Effectiveness of International Courts: A Goal Based Approach', 106(2) *American Journal of International Law* (2012) 225, p. 240; Frédéric Mégret, 'In Defense of Hybridity: Towards a Representational Theory of International Criminal Justice', 38 *Cornell International Law Journal* (2005) 725, p. 742.

22 Mirjan Damaška, 'What is the Point of International Criminal Justice?', 83(1) *Chicago-Kent Law Review* (2008) 329.

23 Eric Posner, 'Political Trials in Domestic and International Law', 55 *Duke Law Journal* (2005) 75, p. 151.

24 Mark A Drumbl, *Atrocity, Punishment and International Law* (Cambridge University Press, 2007); Ralph Henham, *Punishment and Process in International Criminal Trials* (Ashgate Publishing, 2005).

25 Ibid.

26 Ibid.; Mark Findlay and Ralph Henham, *Transforming International Criminal Justice: Retributive and Restorative Justice in the Trial Process* (Routledge, 2005); Ralph Henham, 'Towards Restorative Sentencing in International Criminal Trials', 9 *International Criminal Law Review* (2009) 809.

27 Ralph Henham, 'Evaluating the Contribution of Sentencing to Social Justice: Some Conceptual Problems', 12 *International Criminal Law Review* (2012) 361; Ralph Henham and Mark Findlay, *Exploring the Boundaries of International Criminal Justice* (Ashgate, 2011).

questions concerning the role of courts in response to international crimes. If we accept the necessity of courts of law in such circumstances, we need to consider the fact that courts are unable to place emphasis on the victims at the expense of the offenders, or of promoting one objective at the expense of others.

This brings me to the question of the role that courts can realistically play in promoting reconciliation. A useful starting point is to consider what the victims, and the post-conflict communities more broadly, have said in this regard. There have been numerous empirical studies carried out in the former Yugoslavia and particularly in Bosnia and Herzegovina, asking victims and witnesses what exactly it is they need and feel they have received from the ICTY's justice. One of the things that is evident from these studies is that victims express a wish for retribution.[28] The majority of victims recognised as such by the ICTY want all of those responsible to be tried, convicted and sentenced by the tribunal. As for the sentences, victims often unsurprisingly state that they wish for the harshest sentences to be handed down, which in practice means that anything less than a sentence of life imprisonment is deemed insufficient.[29] Similarly, victims and victim groups often appear in the press complaining about the conditions of imprisonment, which they claim are too comfortable.[30]

In this regard, a number of scholars have suggested that victims have participatory rights and to an extent, this is largely uncontroversial, as the ICTY relied heavily on witness testimony. It is argued that in order for courts to promote reconciliation on the ground they need to encourage empowerment of the victims, which they can most clearly achieve through victim participation.[31] The reason for this is that some, including the ICTY, believe that bearing witness permits victims to commence healing their wounds, which is a stepping-stone towards reconciliation. However, it remains empirically unclear whether trial participation will have a positive or negative impact on victims and the post-conflict reconciliation process, as testifying can be a second victimisation and more traumatic than cathartic for victims. Provided we accept that victim participation has a positive effect on the victims, it can also have such effects on the post-conflict society, because victims have not just their individual identity, but also that of the broader society to which they belong. As those most harmed by the crimes, the rehabilitation and empowerment of victims is a necessity for broader reconciliation to take root.

28 Frédéric Mégret, 'The Legacy of the ICTY as Seen Through Some of its Actors and Observers', *3 Goettingen Journal of International Law* (2011) 1011, p. 1050.

29 Mirko Klarin, 'The Impact of the ICTY Trials on Public Opinion in the Former Yugoslavia', 7 Journal of International Criminal Justice (2009) 89, p. 90; Dan Saxon, 'Exporting Justice: Perceptions of the ICTY Among the Serbian, Croatian, and Muslim Communities in the Former Yugoslavia', 4(4) *Journal of Human Rights* (2005) 559, p. 564.

30 Nancy Amoury Combs, '*Prosecutor v. Biljana Plavšić*: Case No. IT-00-39&40/1-S', 97 *American Journal of International Law* (2003) 929, p. 936; Roland Kostic, *Ambivalent Peace: External Peacebuilding, Threatened Identity and Reconciliation In Bosnia and Herzegovina* (Uppsala University, 2007), p. 268.

31 Mark Findlay and Ralph Henham, *Beyond Punishment: Achieving International Criminal Justice* (Palgrave Macmillan, 2010).

Furthermore, acknowledging that victims have participatory rights means little if we do not elucidate precisely what these rights mean: how are these rights to be given effect? The rights of the victim in this regard can mean anything from having a right to testify and recount their story, to having a right to voice an opinion on the appropriate sentence to be handed down against the offender. The problem then becomes not whether victims have a right to participate in international criminal justice as actors and not just benefactors, but the detrimental effect that putting this into practice might have on the fairness of the proceedings for the offender. Greater victim participation means encroaching upon the rights of the offender, who then has to defend himself or herself against prosecution and the allegations of victims. Moreover, there is a risk that greater participation might unfairly affect the judges' judgment of the offender's culpability if they are faced with emotional testimony that is not necessarily relevant to the trial.[32] Providing for substantive victim participation means concretely connecting justice with victim satisfaction, not only for the benefit of the victims themselves, but also for the good of the post-conflict society to which they belong.

However, where justice is evaluated for its promotion of reconciliation and giving victims what they want, it takes away the emphasis of retributive justice. At the same time, it is evident that international criminal justice as it was put into practice by the ICTY was based on a punitive understanding of justice. The punitive nature of international criminal justice means it is primarily concerned with determining the guilt of the individual before it and rendering a sentence against that individual as is appropriate and just in the circumstances. This means sentencing an individual in a manner commensurate with his or her culpability. Consequently, the ICTY, as with subsequent international courts, has focused on the individual offender, which is not easily reconcilable with the needs of the victims and the post-conflict society more broadly.

It is, therefore, important to explore further the challenges of promoting reconciliation through punitive justice and the related rights of the offender and their compatibility with the promotion of reconciliation. The offender's main right in this regard is to have his or her treatment be specific to him or her as an individual, his or her actions, and his or her guilt. Whilst the victims, and therefore by proxy the post conflict society, might wish to have a say in the offender's sentence of imprisonment, giving victims such a decisive role is not fair on the offender – nor is it in the interests of justice, the rule of law or the procedures of the court. Giving victims a voice concerning sentencing would also lead to inconsistency, and this would put an unfair burden on the offender whose fate would be uncertain. He or she would have no way of knowing what the sentence against them could be, because it would largely depend on the desires of the victims and this he or she could not foresee. As such, there would be no foresight of the law. Moreover, whilst perhaps conducive to the rehabilitation of the victim or

32 Mirjan Damaška, 'The Competing Visions of Fairness: The Basic Choice for International Criminal Tribunals' 36 *North Carolina Journal of International Law and Commercial Regulation* (2010) 365, p. 373.

the post-conflict society as a whole, to give victims such an instructive role and to give reconciliation such a decisive role is not desirable.

It would be wholly wrong to utilise the offender as a means to an end; that is, as an object to promote reconciliation. Not only is this incompatible with the retributive focus of international criminal justice, it is also incompatible with respect for the offender's dignity.[33] Although a particular sentence in a particular case, requested by victims, might be precisely what they need, placing such importance on promoting reconciliation through victim satisfaction might mean the sentence is not commensurate with the guilt of the offender, whether it be too light or too heavy a burden.[34] This is most clearly evident in the unhappiness of some victims that a sentence of capital punishment is not an available option for an international criminal tribunal.[35]

A further problem with focusing on victims is that it is an oversimplification of the detrimental effects of mass crimes. Such crimes do not only affect the victims, but are harmful to the entire society. Reconstructing a society and resuming relationships and contact between previously warring communities requires dialogue and inclusion of different individuals and communities from the society, including the offender. In this sense, it is important to consider the offender not only as an individual whose actions hinder reconciliation, but also as someone whose participation is vital in reconciliation efforts. This is particularly so in the case of the former Yugoslavia, where the great majority of offenders return to the communities they lived in prior to and during the war.

Courts have a duty to protect the offender too through the law, and ensure his rights are respected.[36] This means that courts have a responsibility to ensure that their treatment of the offender causes him or her least harm, as the individual is already losing their freedom.[37] In fact, I would argue that handing out fair treatment to the offender by means of a fair trial and proportionate punishment is the most suitable way to 'convince the perpetrator, the victim and the general public that the criminal justice system has been upheld and enforced in a just way'.[38] This conviction, in turn, is necessary if the local stakeholders are to trust the

33 Denis Abels, 'Limiting the Objectives of the Enforcement of International Punishment' in Róisín Mulgrew and Denis Abels, *Research Handbook on the International Penal System* (Edward Elgar Publishing, 2016), p. 269; Sergey Vasiliev, 'International criminal trials: A normative theory' (PhD thesis, Amsterdam Center for International Law 2014), available at http://dare.uva.nl/search?arno.record.id=472731 accessed on 8 March 2019, 170.

34 Ibid.

35 Robert Sloane, 'The Expressive Capacity of International Punishment: The Limits of the National Law Analogy and the Potential of International Criminal Law', 43 *Stanford Journal of International Law* (2006) 39, p. 82.

36 Darryl Robinson, 'The Identity Crisis of International Criminal Law', 21(4) *Leiden Journal of International Law* (2008) 925, p. 939.

37 Abels, *supra* note 33, p. 250.

38 Jan Christoph Nemitz, 'The Law of Sentencing in International Criminal Law: The Purposes of Sentencing and the Applicable Method for the Determination of the Sentence', 4 *Yearbook of International Humanitarian Law* (2001) 87, p. 100.

court and the facts it has established, which is an important step if the court is to promote reconciliation through its work.

What this makes clear is that a balancing act is needed – on the one hand, the promotion of reconciliation, and on the other hand, the respect for the limits of a court of law and the rights of the offender. The next section will consider how the ICTY could have, and other international courts could, undertake this balancing act.

Undertaking the balancing act: reconciliation as rehabilitation

As I emphasised in the first section of this chapter, the promotion of reconciliation through punitive justice was not a matter of choice for the ICTY. Restoring peace and therefore promoting reconciliation was inextricably linked to the Tribunal's mandate.

The ICTY should have conceptualised reconciliation from the start. As has been explained, one way of viewing the difference between conceptions of reconciliation is thin reconciliation as a starting point of the process of post conflict reconstruction and reconciliation, and thick reconciliation as the end state – the outcome. It is the understanding of reconciliation as this final stage, the outcome so to speak, that is incompatible with international criminal justice through punishment, because it is too ambitious and ill-fits the role and objectives of a criminal court of law.

A better approach is to adopt an understanding of reconciliation as a process that will often take a very long time, and indeed may never reach an end goal. This would be much more manageable as a macro-level objective.[39] Moreover, understanding reconciliation as a process makes it not only more manageable, but also more measurable.[40] In my view, the ICTY, as a court of law, could not have hoped to promote deep national reconciliation: it is too ambitious an undertaking that is incompatible with the mandate of a court of law and impossible without the support of key political and religious leaders in the region (which for the ICTY has never been the case). Instead, the ICTY should have aimed (and the United Nations International Residual Mechanism for Criminal Tribunals and other international courts and tribunals should aim) to promote reconciliation whilst nonetheless respecting their retributive ethos. The ICTY could only ever have hoped to *start* the reconciliation process, but it could have done so in a more consistent, thorough and comprehensive manner.

How long the reconciliation process lasts, and whether a society ever reaches the end state of deep reconciliation, will depend on the society itself and the post-conflict context in the society. In the States of the former Yugoslavia, this transitional phase from negative to positive peace and deeper reconciliation is at a

39 Rachel Kerr, 'The 'Art' of Reconciliation' FICHL Policy Brief Series No. 78 (2017), p. 2.
40 Ibid.

standstill. There is currently little hope of a positive move towards reconciliation, trust, and inter-ethnic communication and interaction. It is not surprising that empathy is too ambitious an objective in this case, because of the gravity of the offences and particularly in view of the continuing and deepening denial in the States of the former Yugoslavia.

In order for a foreign, distanced court such as the ICTY to successfully restore peace and promote societal reconciliation, the peoples of the former Yugoslavia need to be convinced of its work. Empirical studies have found that it is much more likely that individuals will accept the court's establishment of the facts if they believe the court to be fair.[41] This is where the court's acknowledgment of its limitations and its demonstration of sincerity and transparency become very important, because establishing clear limits leaves less room for individuals to believe that the court has been biased against those whom it convicted from their own ethnic or religious community.[42] This is an integral way for courts to manage expectations, and acknowledge that victims are often given the role of beneficiaries of court-promulgated justice, rather than being full actors in the criminal justice system.[43]

Such openeness would have been particularly important for the ICTY, which has been plagued with perceptions of bias and unfair treatment.[44] As Marko Milanović has convincingly argued, no communication or outreach strategy alone could have convinced all ethnic groups in the former Yugoslavia of its work.[45] The influence of the local political elite as published by loyal journalists was simply too strong and negative, and the ICTY's outreach work was too little, too late. Thus, to focus on the wishes of the post-conflict society would be overly ambitious in the case of the former Yugoslavia. In this regard, it is interesting to note that two States from the former Yugoslavia, Croatia and Serbia, are collectivist societies – that is, people in Croatia and Serbia identify themselves primarily as members of a particular community of the Croatian or Serbian society, rather than primarily as individuals.[46] Although the study did not include an evaluation of the society in Bosnia and Herzegovina, it is safe to assume that as Croatia and Serbia are collectivist societies, Bosnia and Herzegovina is likely to be one too. I would suggest that this was for the ICTY, and remains so for the IRMCT,[47] a particularly important consideration, and an indication that individuals are

41 Mirko Klarin, 'The Elusive Reconciliation in the Former Yugoslavia: Role of the ICTY' FICHL Policy Brief Series No. 31 (2015), p. 3.

42 Aleksandar Fatic, *Reconciliation via the War Crimes Tribunal?* (Ashgate, 2000), p. 28.

43 Sara Kendall, 'Commodifying Global Justice: Economies of Accountability at the International Criminal Court', 13 *Journal of International Criminal Justice* (2015) 113, p. 130.

44 See for example Klarin, *supra* note 29, p. 90.

45 Marko Milanović, 'Establishing the Facts about Mass Atrocities: Accounting for the Failure of the ICTY to Persuade Target Audiences', 47(4) *Georgetown Journal of International Law* (2016) 49.

46 See www.hofstede-insights.com/country-comparison/croatia/ accessed 8 March 2019; www.hofstede-insights.com/country-comparison/serbia/ accessed 13 August 2018.

47 The United Nations International Residual Mechanism for Criminal Tribunals, mandated to continue the work of the ICTY since 1 July 2013.

unlikely to be convinced of the ICTY's work where the community to which they belong entertains doubts.

Nevertheless, courts such as the ICTY also play a role in shaping norms, so local stakeholders' dissatisfaction is not necessarily disastrous for the promotion of peace and reconciliation in the long-term.[48] One way for the Tribunal to manage expectations and leave less room for arguments as to the court's bias, is by making clear its intention to focus on the offender before it. As a court of law this focus comes more naturally to it, and is a clearer and perhaps more realistic objective than aiming to satisfy a whole society and convince it of the court's work. Starting with those who caused the most damage in the war, particularly those who were leaders, is an important and more logical point from which to begin. Although, starting with the offenders themselves would be a deeply challenging endeavour, and not one we could expect of a very nascent international criminal justice system (as was the case when the ICTY was established), it is certainly something that needs to be considered now. We need to take a step back and reflect upon the direct and broader objectives we are trying to achieve with these sentences, and how we can attempt to achieve them.

Since the ICTY was a retributive court of law, understood as focusing on rendering justified sentences that are commensurate with the guilt of the accused,[49] its promotion of reconciliation is most closely linked through its fight against impunity, its search for the truth, and by acting in a fair manner. As such, a court's focus on providing fair and efficient justice is not a hindrance to reconciliation, but is instead an important means of promoting this broad objective.[50] The clearest way a court can promote reconciliation is precisely by ensuring that trials are fair and efficient and sentences are in accordance with the guilt of the individual before the court. As such, it would have been wholly mistaken to focus on the macro level objectives of the ICTY at the expense of its micro-level objectives, directly related to the objectives of punishment and respect of the individual offender.[51]

The balancing act between reconciliation and the rights of the offender is of equal importance to the victims and the post-conflict society, as well as the offender, because it is unfair treatment that breeds the ground for discontentment and conflict. The fair, predictable and consistent treatment of offenders is necessary for the promotion of reconciliation itself.[52] Essentially, this would make courts victim-oriented, as members of a post-conflict society rather than victim-centred,[53] and reflect the view of justice as 'an ongoing dialogue between those

48 Sloane, *supra* note 35, p. 85.
49 Nemitz, *supra* note 38, pp. 92–3.
50 Vasiliev, *supra* note 33, p. 217.
51 Darryl Robinson, 'International Criminal Law as Justice', 11 *Journal of International Criminal Justice* (2013) 699, p. 701.
52 Vasiliev, *supra* note 33, p. 190.
53 Sergey Vasiliev, 'Victim Participation Revisited: What the ICC is Learning about Itself' in C. Stahn (ed.), *The Law and Practice of the International Criminal Court* (Oxford University Press, 2015), p. 66.

who seek justice and those tasked with delivering it'.[54] Dialogue requires transparency, and this would in turn help the local constituency to comprehend why and how post-conviction decisions are made so at least they are fully informed, and do not have overly grand expectations of the court.

The ICTY's potential for a restorative impact on the post-conflict society through its retributive ethos is most clearly evident in focusing efforts on the offender's rehabilitation and reintegration into society. Rehabilitation is not only beneficial to the offender, but also to the victims and the post-conflict society that the offender returns to upon release. If the rehabilitation process has had some effect upon the offender, it will make him or her less likely to pose a threat to the society and the sustainability of its fragile peace, as is the case in Bosnia and Herzegovina. This is why I would argue that rehabilitation is important for reconciliation.

The term rehabilitation conjures up different meanings, including a close link to specific deterrence as well as deep, psychological change in the offender.[55] Notably, the ICTY has failed to define its understanding of reconciliation,[56] but has referred to resocialisation, reintegration into the society and acceptance of the offender's personal responsibility in the crimes committed. This might include remorse, but would commence with acknowledgment of the crimes and his or her role in them.

Moreover, when should rehabilitation be an objective: at the sentencing stage or during the imprisonment and in preparation for the early release of the prisoner? Whilst the ICTY predominantly referred to retribution and deterrence as sentencing objectives, there was a visible move towards referencing rehabilitation and the ensuing potential social utility of punishment.[57] At the same time, rehabilitation remained an objective that was regarded with some scepticism by the ICTY.[58]

Despite arguments against the suitability of rehabilitation at the international level, European and international penal policy is such that to imprison for the sole sake of punishment is unacceptable. As international courts such as the ICTY are to set an example for national courts, it would now be unthinkable to suggest

54 Henham, *supra* note 27, p. 373.

55 Sonja Meijer, 'Rehabilitation as a Positive Obligation', 25 *European Journal of Crime, Criminal Law and Criminal Justice* (2017) 148.

56 Barbora Holá and Joris van Wijk, 'Rehabilitating international prisoners' in Roisin Mulgrew and Denis Abels, *Research Handbook on the International Penal System* (Edward Elgar Publishing, 2016), p. 274.

57 Trial Sentencing Judgment, *Prosecutor v Erdemović,* (IT-96-22-T), 5 March 1998, para 21; Trial Judgment *Prosecutor v Kupreškić et al.,* (IT-95-16-T), 14 January 2000, para 848; Stuart Beresford, 'Unshackling the Paper Tiger - the Sentencing Practices of the ad hoc International Criminal Tribunals for the former Yugoslavia and Rwanda' 1 *International Criminal Law Review* (2001) 33-90, 44; Trial Judgment, *Prosecutor v Kupreškić et al.,* (IT-95-16-T), 14 January 2000, para 848.

58 Trial Sentencing, *Prosecutor v Kunarac et al.,* (IT-96-23-T)and (IT-96-23/1-T), 22 February 2001, para 806.

that these international courts should simply make clear that their only intention is to punish. Rehabilitation has become an increasingly important penal objective, particularly in the case of lengthy sentences.[59] At the same time, because courts have to pronounce proportionate sentences, a focus on rehabilitation and reconciliation (which denotes victim satisfaction) would lead to unfair treatment and sentences that do not necessarily fit with the crimes committed, whether it be overly lenient or harsh sentences depending on the court's appreciation of the need to rehabilitate and resocialise the offender.[60] As such, a focus on rehabilitation at the expense of other objectives at the sentencing stage is unsuitable.

Instead, rehabilitation should be seen as an important imprisonment objective. Unfortunately, for the ICTY, the term rehabilitation has been synonymous with good behaviour during imprisonment, with no thought as to how such behaviour actually helps the offender come to terms with and acknowledge the crimes he or she committed and to consider why they did so.[61] The ICTY granted early release to many individuals who were clearly not rehabilitated, who continued to loudly deny their crimes, and returned to the relevant post-conflict State to pick up their lives where they had left them. The fact that benefiting from early release is almost a certitude after having served two thirds of the sentence rendered, despite the lack of demonstrations of rehabilitation or clear acknowledgment of the crimes committed, nor of the individual's responsibility, is worrying. In the case of the Bosnia and Herzegovina, these individuals return to a State with a very fragile peace, and this could be all too easily disrupted by the return of offenders whose beliefs have not changed.

At the same, in referring to rehabilitation, the ICTY asserted its volition for a restorative function of justice, for something greater than retribution and punishment for the crimes committed. Yet, this is another thing the court has done half-heartedly at best. This reflects the various international standards and guidelines for penitentiary authorities as to the importance and role of rehabilitation.[62] In this sense, it is important to consider the offender not only as an individual whose actions hinder reconciliation, but also as someone whose participation is vital in reconciliation efforts, particularly in the case of the former Yugoslavia,

59 Meijer, *supra* note 55, p. 145.

60 Nemitz, *supra* note 38, p. 88.

61 Barbora Holá, Jessica Kelder and Joris van Wijk, 'Effectiveness of International Criminal Tribunals: Empirical Assessment of Rehabilitation as Sentencing Goal' in Nobuo Hayashi and Cecilia M Bailliet (eds), *The Legitimacy of International Criminal Tribunals* (Cambridge University Press, 2017), p. 351.

62 International Covenant on Civil and Political Rights (19 December 1966) U.N.T.S. 171, 16 (entered into force 23 March 1976); UNSMR (1955). Adopted by the First UN Congress on the Prevention of Crime and the Treatment of Offenders, held at Geneva in 1955, and approved by the Economic and Social Council by its resolutions 663 C (XXIV) of 31 July 1957 and 2076 (LXII) of 13 May 1977; Recommendation of the Committee of Ministers to Member States on the European Prison Rules Council of Europe: Committee of Ministers (11 January 2006) Rec(2006) 2, Rule 6, 103.

where the great majority return to the communities they lived in prior to, and during, the war.

The lack of deeper reflection in the ICTY's references to rehabilitation is not without reason. Considering how difficult it is to be faced with such heinous crimes, it is only natural to shy away from facing them head on. Rehabilitation is challenging in international criminal justice, because it is questionable how open to rehabilitation an individual, such as Radovan Karadžić and Ratko Mladić, can be. Such individuals are ideologically and politically motivated to commit mass crimes, and do not fit the 'common' criminal profile, but are instead highly intelligent, successful individuals who were well integrated into the pre-war society. Whilst it is very often difficult to see these international offenders as corrigible personalities,[63] it would be wrong to see them as not requiring rehabilitation. It is instead all the more important to consider what led these individuals to commit such heinous crimes that have had such disastrous effects upon society. However difficult the task is to envisage, rehabilitation remains a worthy and important objective. Moreover, resocialisation is necessary, because the offenders often return to the post-conflict state and the context is not the same as the one they lived in prior to the crimes: the situation will have changed and they will need to adapt to it. Some sort of preparation for the offenders is necessary, particularly as they serve their sentences in different European States that are culturally and linguistically different to their own. In order for reintegration to be smooth and also less painful for the victims, consideration needs to be taken as to how to prepare these individuals for a changed post-conflict state, most likely with a fragile peace.

This does not mean that the ICTY, or any other court, would be evaluated through its ability to rehabilitate: it is 'an obligation of means, not of result'.[64] It is important to remember that being seen to attempt rehabilitation is just as important as achieving it: the process and attempt to rehabilitate is also important, and not just whether a court has in fact managed to rehabilitate a particular offender or not. The perception of just, fair treatment that aims to help the offender psychologically and prepare him or her for the society he or she will return to upon release cannot be overemphasised.

In this regard, rehabilitation programmes need to be considered and one of the issues that has been documented by academics is the lack of such programmes,[65] and any mechanism to ensure that offenders are rehabilitated before they are released.[66] One of the reasons for this, of course, is the inability of prison officials to comprehend the crimes that were committed and how to confront the offender with them, often preferring not to mention them through a lack of understanding as to how to do so. This is understandable. A second issue is that international offenders form only a tiny proportion of the prison population in

63 Nemitz, *supra* note 38, p. 98.

64 Meijer, *supra* note 55, p. 149.

65 Holá *et al.*, *supra* note 61, p. 351.

66 Kai Ambos, 'Determinate and indeterminate sentences of imprisonment in international criminal justice' in Roisin Mulgrew and Denis Abels, *Research Handbook on the International Penal System* (Edward Elgar Publishing, 2016), p. 100.

any given prison in Europe, and so there can be no focus on these offenders in particular. Moreover, the enforcement States often lack the financial means or the willingness to attempt to rehabilitate these individuals, partly because they will not settle in the country in which they are serving their sentence upon their release. This burden falls upon the post-conflict state. As such, the suitability of placing international offenders in different countries needs to be considered in light of the need to focus on rehabilitation at the imprisonment stage.

I would suggest the balancing of rights by giving offenders a positive right to rehabilitation, by considering what type of rehabilitation programme could be introduced for these specific offenders and a chance of dialogue where this is desirable. If we accept that rehabilitation means providing assistance and help to the offenders, this includes helping offenders to come to terms with their crimes and to prepare for an eventual return to the post-conflict society.[67] In fact, one way of understanding rehabilitation is as mediation between the victim and the convicted individual, which focuses on the victim's needs to be heard and to understand, as well as the need for the offender to return to society without being a threat to the stability of that society.[68] This would allow the victims to voice the harm that they have incurred, as well as giving the offender a chance to understand the human impact of his or her crimes, offer an explanation as to what happened and why, and perhaps even utter some words of remorse.[69] This would not be suitable or desirable in all circumstances, particularly where the offender refuses to admit what happened in the conflict, or what happened to the victims and their families. Nevertheless, there are individuals convicted by the ICTY whose meeting with victims could be beneficial and useful to both parties. The ICTY should have considered, and the IRMCT should consider, this part of its mandate rather than leaving it up to enforcement states to decide upon and regulate. As such, victims and offenders would both have the same rights irrespective of which enforcement State the offender had been incarcerated in. Admittedly, this would be a very demanding practice both practically and financially,[70] but if a court such as the ICTY, or now the IRMCT, is to have a reconciliatory impact, it must be willing to take this broader objective seriously and take actions and adopt practices that help it to achieve its broader objectives. Needless to say, mediation could not nor should not ever be forced on individuals, but it could be made a clear option for both parties as part of the offender's rehabilitation process. Another method for placing emphasis on rehabilitation is by making early release conditional on a demonstration of rehabilitation, for example by setting specific

67 Gert Vermeulen and Eveline De Wree, *Offender Reintegration and Rehabilitation as a Component of International Criminal Justice?* (Maklu Publishers, 2014), p. 73.

68 Jessica M. Kelder, Barbora Holá and Joris van Wijk, 'Rehabilitation and Early Release of Perpetrators of International Crimes: A Case Study of the ICTY and ICTR', 14 *International Criminal Law Review* (2014) 1177, p. 1201.

69 Jonathan Doak, 'The Therapeutic Dimension of Transitional Justice: Emotional Repair and Victim Satisfaction in International Trials and Truth Commissions', 11 *International Criminal Law Review* (2011) 263, pp. 295–6.

70 Ibid.

conditions that can be measured and taken into account by the President of the Tribunal.[71]

The ICTY would nevertheless have needed to adapt its methods for rehabilitation to the specific offender and to each context; the court would be acting responsively to needs rather than prescriptively.[72] However rehabilitation is practiced, the macro-level and micro-level objectives are connected through rehabilitation.[73] At the micro-level, rehabilitation is an important punishment objective, particularly as it links to reconciliation and the reparation of social bonds in the post-conflict state.[74] As I have already stated, the micro-level objectives should imperatively facilitate the promotion of the broader objectives, and reconciliation in particular.[75] This includes the need for post-conviction practices, in particular imprisonment and early release decisions to be practiced in a manner that further reconciliation.[76]

Conclusion

In conclusion, the aim of this chapter was to add to the debate on balancing the rights of the victims with those of the offender, in the pursuit of international criminal justice. The focus of this chapter has been on the ICTY and its successor, the IRMCT, but the discussion is also relevant for other international criminal tribunals and courts, as they will be faced with the same question of how to achieve domestic criminal justice objectives, as well as the broader objective of promoting peace and reconciliation. The importance of balancing the rights of different stakeholders in international criminal justice is particularly pertinent to the court's ability to achieve these micro and macro level objectives. This chapter has suggested one solution – attempting to promote the macro level objective by focusing on a micro level objective: rehabilitation.

The balancing of different rights is an important topic of discussion for international criminal justice because the ICTY, as with other international courts and tribunals, was integrally linked to the restoration of peace and thus to the promotion of reconciliation. It is therefore important to consider how this macro level objective could be achieved. Whilst the ICTY could never hope to achieve reconciliation – even to promote it actively is an ambitious objective for a court of law – it nevertheless had to attempt to do so. This notion of adapting to a

71 Ibid.

72 Luke Moffett, 'Realising Justice for Victims before the International Criminal Court' *International Crimes Database Brief* (6 September 2014), p. 2.

73 Antonio Cassese (ed) *The Oxford Companion to International Criminal Justice* (Oxford University Press, 2009), pp. 509–510.

74 William Schabas, 'Sentencing by International Tribunals', *7 Duke Journal of Comparative and International Law* (1997) 503.

75 James Meernik, 'Sentencing Rationales and Judicial Decision Making at the International Criminal Tribunals' 92(3) *Social Science Quarterly* (2011) 594.

76 Roisin Mulgrew, *Towards the Development of the International Penal System* (Cambridge University Press, 2013), p. 215.

more reasonable expectation – promotion rather than achievement – is itself an important step in the right direction. International courts of law, including the ICTY and now the IRMCT, must firstly remain true to their mandate, that of a court of law, and secondly to achieving their overarching reason for being – the promotion of peace, and thereby reconciliation.

Although there are tensions between reconciliation and retributive justice, they are not incompatible; it is more the way in which these objectives are promoted that causes tension.[77] Throughout this chapter, I have emphasised the need for balance: balance between the macro and micro-level objectives, and balance between the rights of one party against those of the other. This means that reconciliation, although an overarching objective, cannot be given prominence over the more direct micro-level objectives of domestic criminal justice, which come into play when trying, sentencing, and deciding on the release of offenders. Thus, this chapter has argued for the promotion of reconciliation through punishment with the caveat of respecting the rights of the offender to individualisation of his or her guilt and sentencing him or her appropriately. I have suggested that the rights of the victims and those of the offender can be respected whilst nonetheless promoting reconciliation, by focusing on the offender's rehabilitation and reintegration into the post-conflict society. Although a very challenging task, the state of international penal policy is such that rehabilitation is a recognised objective of imprisonment, and a particularly important one in view of the heinous and destructive nature of mass crimes.

It is clear that time and resources need to be devoted to conceptualising rehabilitation in the context of international criminal justice and just how it can be promoted, but this is not a matter of choice; there is no option for international courts to abandon rehabilitation, just as it cannot abandon some form of outreach and communication, despite the contentions of some scholars.[78] The question is not whether, but how. The next step is to consider just how rehabilitation can be put into practice in the context of international criminal justice. Rehabilitative programmes are an absolute necessity, however inadequate they may well prove to be, we simply have no other choice.

77 Vasiliev, *supra* note 33, p. 204.
78 Holá and van Wijk, *supra* note 56, p. 295.

9 The politics of victim participation in the International Criminal Court

Does politically motivated victim participation have an impact on the legitimacy of the proceedings?

Kirsten Bowman

Introduction: the entry of victim participation in international criminal law

The central provision within the Rome Statute[1] concerning victim participation is Article 68(3), which allows for victims to participate when appropriate and when not impacting the rights of the accused. Rule 85 of the International Criminal Court (ICC) Rules of Procedure and Evidence[2] defines 'victim' as natural persons who have suffered harm (Rule 85(a)), or organisations or institutions which have suffered (direct) harm (Rule 85(b)). In interpreting Rule 85, the Chambers of the ICC have further enumerated the criteria necessary to claim the status of victim within the ICC proceedings. The applicant must first demonstrate that they are a natural person, organisation, or institution. Second, they must show that a crime within the jurisdiction of the Court has been committed. Third, they must show that they have suffered harm, and fourth, such harm must have arisen as a result of the alleged crime within the jurisdiction of the Court.[3]

Within these boundaries, it has been left largely to the Chambers to judicially interpret and build the framework under which victim participation within the ICC proceedings will advance. When doing so, the Chambers of the ICC were unable to refer to the procedures followed by other international courts and tribunals. At previous international criminal tribunals, victims were treated solely as witnesses, called to support the Prosecution's case and without an independent voice of their own. While various State practices in domestic criminal proceedings could provide clues, it is a cumbersome and clumsy task to use comparative

1 Rome Statute of the International Criminal Court (adopted 17 July 1998, entered into force 1 July 2002), 2187 UNTS 90 (Rome Statute).

2 International Criminal Court, Rules of Procedure and Evidence, U.N. Doc. PCNICC/2000/1/Add.1 (2000).

3 ICC-01/04-101-tEN-Corr, Decision on the Applications for Participation in the Proceedings of VPRS1, VPRS2, VPRS3, VPRS4, VPRS5, and VPRS 6 (17 January 2006), para. 79.

domestic proceedings to implement a new international justice norm. Thus, the ICC has been faced with the difficult task of developing a framework which benefits victims, while ensuring the right of the accused to a fair and efficient process.

While this shift to include victims in the proceedings has been argued to show that restorative justice, rather than simply retribution, is of growing importance to international justice,[4] it has also been noted that the ultimate goal of the Court remains criminal in nature. Thus, the fundamental application of criminal proceedings must be foremost in the minds of the participants to the proceedings.[5]

However, there are many ways in which the participation of victims in the proceedings can be argued to be beneficial to the pursuit of justice. The early jurisprudence of the Court suggests that victims have an interest in unveiling the truth and can 'bring clarity about what indeed happened; and close possible gaps between the factual findings resulting from the criminal proceedings and the actual truth'.[6] In support of this, in both the *Lubanga* and *Bemba* cases, victims were able to make important contributions, shedding light on issues such as the use of names and social conventions in the case of *Lubanga* and the Democratic Republic of Congo;[7] and on the local languages spoken in the case of *Bemba* and the Central African Republic.[8]

At the ICC, victims are participants rather than parties to the proceedings prior to the reparations phase, and thus their role, and that of their Representative, is different to the role of the Prosecution and Defence. Upon authorization of the competent ICC Chamber, they may introduce evidence in Court which relates to the guilt or innocence of the accused person, but, in contrast to the Prosecution and Defence who are looking primarily at evidence which specifically provides insight into the guilt or innocence of the accused, the victim participant may introduce information which provides context and fills important gaps in the understanding of truth for the judges in the case.

For example, in the case of *Lubanga*, the Chamber itself was quite moved during the presentation of evidence which focused on crimes of sexual violence, though the Prosecutor had chosen not to include charges of sexual violence in the indictment.[9] The Victim's Representatives made a motion to the Chamber

4 Pena, Mariana and Carayon, Gaelle, 'Is the ICC Making the Most of Victim Participation', 7(3) *International Journal of Transitional Justice*, 1 November 2013, p. 519.

5 Brady, Helen and Guariglia, Fabricio, 'An Insider's View: Consistency and Transparency While Preserving Prosecutorial Discretion', *International Criminal Justice Today*, 15 December2016,availableatwww.international-criminal-justice-today.org/arguendo/an-insiders-view/

6 Decision on the Set of Procedural Rights Attached to Procedural Status of Victims at the Pre-Trial Stage of a case *Prosecutor v. Katanga and Ngudjolo*, (ICC-01/04-01/07-474), 13 May 2008, paras. 31-36.

7 Analyse Relative à l'Attribution et aux Composants du Nom en République Démocratique du Congo, *Prosecutor v. Lubanga*, (ICC-01/04-01/06-1793), 20 March 2009.

8 Transcript of the Confirmation of Charges Hearing, *Prosecutor v. Bemba*, (ICC-01/05-01/08-T-12-ENG), 15 January 2009, paras. 97-98. See Pena, Mariana and Carayon, Gaelle, *supra* note 4, p. 519.

9 Warrant of Arrest, *Prosecutor v Lubanga* (ICC – 01/04-01/06-2-tEN), 10 February 2006.

to request that sexual violence charges be added under Regulation 52.[10] The Chamber, in a majority decision, with Judge Fulford dissenting, attempted to add charges under this regulation. The Trial Chamber Decision was appealed, and the Appeals Counsel agreed with Judge Fulford's minority opinion that, under Article 74(2) of the Rome Statute, this revision would be illegal as the Trial Judgment could not 'exceed the facts and circumstances described in the charges'.[11] Though the victim's application could not withstand the scrutiny of the Appeals Chamber, it can be argued that, in this case, the victims' presentation was effective in swaying the Trial Chamber judges, and it is to be noted that the Prosecutor later added sexual violence charges to the arrest warrant for Ntaganda, Lubanga's co-Accused.[12]

Along with this important role in assisting in informing the Chamber and helping unveil the truth, it is recognized, most notably in the creation of a victims' reparation system by the ICC, that the effects of atrocity crimes on the victims should be a piece of the puzzle. Thus, the victims themselves become an entity which must be considered within the scope of participation rights at the ICC.

Very little consideration has been given to the political interests of the victims. However, this may be an oversight on the part of the Court, as can be seen in more recent events within court proceedings and the participation of victims. This chapter aims to consider the implications of a victim's politics in the proceedings, and to further hypothesize as to whether the Court should take a different approach based on this political reality. In this way, this chapter considers how to balance a victim's right to agency with the needs and premises of the Court to find both truth and justice through the proceedings. The following sections of the chapter first consider the assumption and realities of the politics of victims and their participation in the proceedings. The analysis then moves to two case studies, one in Sudan and the other in the Kenya situation in order to explore examples of how the participation of victims in the proceeding may be impacted by political realities. Applying this analysis, the chapter then moves to consider whether the political reality of victims' participation has an impact on the fairness and efficiency of the proceedings and finally considers some possible ways in which the Court may want to address the issues at hand.

10 Regulation 52(c) allows the charging document to be changed by a 'legal characterisation of the facts to accord both with the crimes under Articles 6, 7, or 8 and the precise form of participation under Articles 25 and 28.' Joint Application of the Legal Representatives of the Victims for the Implementation of the Procedure Under Regulation 55 of the Regulations of the Court, *Prosecutor v. Lubanga Dyilo*, (ICC-01/04-01/16-1891-tENG), 22 May 2009.

11 For a full discussion on this situation, see War Crimes Research Office, 'Defining the Case Against an Accused Before the International Criminal Court: Whose Responsibility is it?', Dec. 2009, available at: www.wcl.american.edu/warcrimes/icc/documents/WCRO_Report_on_Defining_Case_Nov2009.pdf?rd=1.

12 Decision on the Prosecutor's Application under Article 58, *Prosecutor v. Ntaganda*, (ICC-01/04-02/06-36-Red), 13 July 2012.

The politics of victims' participation: assumptions and realities

While there has been little in the way of research, discussion or debate on the topic of the political implications of victims' participation, the political nature of the ICC hearings and their impact on victims' participation, or even the politics of victim participation itself, is a subject ripe for greater scrutiny. Understanding the difference between the politics that arguably are part and parcel of international justice and the politicization of international justice, in which politics manipulates the judicial process, is key. Beyond the politicization of international justice, a discussion on the framework of politics and victims and how they interact and exist in tandem is important in order to reflect on the outcomes which these systems may influence.

The politics of international justice

It is argued that the process of international criminal law is political in nature.[13] While, not created in the same way as the *ad hoc* Tribunals, the establishment of the ICC was a political process in and of itself. Furthermore, the Court has jurisdiction over crimes that are often connected with politics, and it must rely on political will to enforce its mandate and any decisions emanating from it.[14] The work of war crimes tribunals exists in a space which circles around the political currents of the societies that are involved, as well as within the larger global political space. This relationship between politics and law – international justice and war crimes – has been referred to as 'political justice', differing from 'politicization' of the process.[15] The politicization of the judicial process has been defined as '[t]he manipulation of the judicial process by politics, not the manipulation of politics to serve the judicial process, or the apolitical administration of justice to serve a political goal'.[16] In arguing that the international criminal courts are not necessarily politicized, Kerr has written of the International Criminal Tribunal for the former Yugoslavia (ICTY) that:

> The question of politicization is not a straightforward one. The decision to establish the tribunal [ICTY] was political, and it was established for a political purpose, but its internal mandate was to deliver justice. Thus, while politics permeated every aspect of the tribunal's operation, including its establishment, proceedings had to be conducted in a political vacuum. On a conceptual level, while this form of justice is inherently political, the judicial process is not necessarily 'politicized'. On a practical level, the interaction

13 For a greater discussion on this, see Sarah M.H. Nouwen and Wouter G. Werner, 'Doing Justice to the Political: The International Criminal Court in Uganda and Sudan', 21 *European Journal of International Law* (2010) 941.

14 Ibid.

15 Rachel Kerr, *The International Criminal Tribunal for the Former Yugoslavia: An Exercise in Law, Politics, and Diplomacy*, (Oxford and New York: Oxford University Press, 2004), p. 3.

16 Ibid.

> of politics and law was central to the tribunal's ability to perform its judicial function, it did so independently of politics, which was crucial for its success as a tool for the restoration and maintenance of peace and security.[17]

Beyond this debate between politics and politicization, it is hard to escape the fact that politics is a strong influencer within the context of international criminal courts and tribunals. For example, the very issue of who is prosecuted, and who is excluded from prosecution, is an inherently political process.[18] The selective application of international criminal law, for example, results in 'not a rule of law but a subordination of law to the dictates of power'.[19]

Politics and victims

It is within this framework of political justice that the introduction of victims into the proceedings comes. It has been argued that 'political trials emerge from the criminalization of enemies',[20] and that the ICC has the capacity to 'contribute to the construction of the international community's friends and enemies'.[21] The ICC should be aware that it can, in fact, become a tool for warring parties to use – a type of warfare, or lawfare, as it were.

One of the major novelties of the Rome Statute is that the drafters strove to blend elements of the Romano-Germanic and the common law traditions found within various Western legal systems around the globe.[22] While not found as a common attribute in common law systems, victim participation in criminal proceedings is more familiar to the Romano-Germanic, inquisitorial legal traditions. In common law countries, it is more likely that a victim would seek recourse from the perpetrator in a separate civil law proceeding. In an effort to create a hybrid legal traditional within the Rome Statute, the drafters decided to include a victim participation scheme that is more in line with proceedings from the Romano-Germanic tradition.

The problem with this essentially political compromise is that rules were taken out of each system, but the safeguards which protected the rights, fairness and efficiency of the proceedings were not always incorporated into the ICC legal

17 Ibid., p. 2.
18 Moghalu and Kingsley, *Rwanda's Genocide: The Politics of Global Justice*, (MacMillan, 2005), p. 4
19 Mahmood and Mandani, *Saviors and Survivors: Darfur, Politics and the War on Terror*, (Random House, 2009), p. 284.
20 Gerry Simpson, *Law, War and Crime: War Crimes Trials and the Reinvention of International Law* (Polity, 2007), p. 14.
21 Nouwen and Werner, *supra* note 13, p. 956.
22 See Otto Trifterer and Kai Ambos (eds), *The Rome Statute of the International Criminal Court: A Commentary*, 3rd edn. (C.H. Beck, Hart, Nomos, 2016); Antonio Cassese, Paola Gaeta, John R.W.D. Jones (eds), *The Rome Statute for an International Criminal Court: A Commentary* (Oxford, 2002); Michael J. Struett, *The Politics of Constructing the International Criminal Court: NGOs, Discourse and Agency* (Palgrave Macmillan, 2008).

system. Similar to a jigsaw puzzle, the drafters took pieces of each system and placed them together in a new system, without necessarily taking into account whether the system would become unfair or imbalanced with each new addition. This challenge is further emphasised when looking at the Rome Statute as a whole, and recognizing that the final outcome strongly favours the common law, adversarial system. The ICC more closely resembles a common law court, that has incorporated additional features[23] from the Romano-Germanic system. As John Jackson has noted, this hybrid system has resulted in a 'skewed procedure'.[24]

The drafters of the Rome Statute understood and had concerns about how the addition of victim participation might affect the efficiency and fairness of the proceedings. In order to address these concerns they required that the Court manage victim participation in a way that ensures efficiency and fairness in the proceedings, especially with respect to the rights of the accused.[25] The addition of a victim participation regime in such an adversarial process means that the Court itself is required to use exceptional caution when trying to implement a system of victim participation, in order to ensure that the rights of the accused are not infringed upon during the process.[26]

Within the framework of the realities under which the victim participation scheme was created, another layer of victim and politics should be observed that has, until recently, been overlooked. Recent activity concerning several situations and cases at the ICC has raised the issue of the politics of international criminal law, and its impact on victim participation and the construction of the definition of victim within the ICC context.

One question that has been raised is to what extent, if any, should the politics of the victim themselves be a factor when determining victim eligibility. This question was raised most strongly in the case of *Banda/Jerbo* from the Darfur, Sudanese situation, where the political leanings of two victims came under close scrutiny, as their participation tested the possible assumptions of the Court.[27]

23 For example, the blending of systems in the law of evidence within the ICC, which created challenges for parties and Judges as to how to implement such a system. See Michele Caianiello, 'Law of Evidence at the International Criminal Court: Blending Accusatorial and Inquisitorial Models', 36 *North Carolina Journal of International Law and Commercial Regulation* (2010) 287.

24 John Jackson, 'Finding the Best Epistemic Fit for International Criminal Tribunals: Beyond the Adversarial-Inquisitorial Dichotomy', 7 *Journal of International Criminal Justice* (2009) 17.

25 Article 68(3) of the Rome Statute states: 'Where the personal interests of the victims are affected, the Court shall permit their views and concerns to be presented and considered at stages of the proceedings determined to be appropriate by the Court and in a manner which is not prejudicial to or inconsistent with the rights of the accused and a fair and impartial trial. Such views and concerns may be presented by the legal representatives of the victims where the Court considers it appropriate, in accordance with the Rules of Procedure and Evidence.'

26 See Judge Blattmann's dissent, para. 10 (and the dissent more generally) in Decision on Victims' Participation *Prosecutor v Lubanga*, (ICC-01/04-01/06-1119), 18 January 2008.

27 Decision on Victims' Participation at the Hearing on the Confirmation of Charges, *Prosecutor v. Banda/Jerbo*, (ICC-02/05-03/09), 29 October 2010.

Ultimately, as discussed below, the Court decided to side-step any direct mention of the politics of the victims involved in the case, thereby avoiding the issue altogether. However, avoidance of the issue may not always be a tenable solution.

Another question regarding politics and victim status is raised in the Kenya situation, namely that of how the politics in a country affects the participation of victims at the Court. In a report on the Kenya situation and victim participation, it was noted that lack of state cooperation was a challenge to victim participation, because the Kenyan government created obstacles for victims to participate, despite it having an obligation to assist and facilitate participation.[28] Another observation from the same report noted that politics affects victims' understanding and support for the ICC, and thus the political environment in the country had significant effects on victims' support and participation.[29] These issues will be the focus of the following analysis, beginning with the *Banda/Jerbo* case in Darfur, Sudan, where 89 victims were accepted and had common representation, but two victims had interests which were vastly different to the others in the class.

Case study: *Banda/Jerbo* case and victims' participation

The *Banda/Jerbo* case arose out of the Prosecutor's investigations into three rebel commanders, Abdallah Banda Abakaer Nourain, Saleh Mohammed Jerbo Jamus and Bahar Idriss Abu Garda, in Darfur who were accused of targeting peacekeepers and aid workers. They were leaders of rebel groups and were accused of committing war crimes during an attack on an African Union (AU) compound which killed 12 AU peacekeepers and wounded many more.[30] The compound was destroyed, which the Prosecution argued affected 'aid and security for millions of people of Darfur who are in need of protection'.[31]

At the confirmation of charges hearing in December 2010, 89 victims were recognized as victim participants.[32] Two of these victims, originally represented by Sir Geoffrey Nice QC and Rodney Dixon, were separate from the other 87 victims.[33] These two victims differed from the other participating victims as they were both local residents and civilian workers who were employed by the

28 Thomas Obel, Research Report, 'In the Shadow of Politics: Victim Participation in the Kenyan ICC Cases', June 2016, p. 33, available at www.impunitywatch.org/docs/IW_Report_Victim_Participation_in_Kenya_(June_2016).pdf

29 Ibid.

30 See, Document Containing the Charges, *Prosecutor v Banda and Jerbo*, (ICC-02/05-03/09) 11 November 2010.

31 Office of the Prosecutor of the ICC, '"Attacks on Peacekeepers Will Not Be Tolerated", ICC Prosecutor Presents Evidence in Third Case in Darfur', (ICC-OTP-20081120-PR373), 20 November 2008.

32 Decision on Victims' Participation at the Hearing on the Confirmation of the Charges, *Prosecutor v. Banda/Jerbo*, (ICC-02/05-03/09), 29 October 2010.

33 They also represented three other applicants in *Banda/Jerbo* (a/6000/11, a/6001/11 and a/6002/11): see, e.g., Decision on the Application for Leave to Appeal the 'Decision on Common Legal Representation, *Prosecutor v Banda/Jerbo*, Trial Chamber IV (ICC-02/05-03/09), 13 July 2012) ('Decision on Leave to Appeal').

peacekeeping mission and present in the compound during the attack.[34] The other participating victims were members of the international peacekeeping forces, or were connected to them.[35]

The victim participation scheme established by the Pre-Trial Chamber in the case required that in order to be eligible to participate at trial, victims had to establish a link to the specific crimes charged. The nature and specificity of the charges necessarily left out many of the Darfuri victims, for example those whose homes were burned during the attack.[36] The two civilian worker victims were recognized by the Pre-Trial Chamber as having suffered psychological harm from both the threat to their own lives and from being a witness to the atrocities suffered by the AU peacekeepers.[37]

In organizing the victims' representation, Trial Chamber VI accepted the Registry's nomination of a single common representative for all 89 accepted victims, including the two Darfuri victims. This assignment of one common legal representative led to a great deal of litigation, with Nice and Dixon, the two Darfuri victims' original legal representatives, arguing that the two Darfuri victims had interests sufficiently distinct from the other victims that justified their separate representation. The arguments put forth by Nice and Dixon included an analysis of the law. Rule 90 of the Rules of Procedure and Evidence allows for victims to make their own selection of common legal representation with the assistance of the Registry, allowing the Registry and the Chamber to make appointments only in the event that the victims are unable to do so in a timely fashion. Rule 90(4) requires the court to 'take all reasonable steps to ensure that in the selection of common legal representatives, the distinct interests of the victims [. . .] are represented and that any conflict of interest is avoided'.[38]

Ultimately Trial Chamber VI rejected Nice and Dixon's arguments. The chamber was reluctant to accept the position that the two victims had separate and distinct interests from the other victims, and decided to appoint one common legal

34 Emily Haslam and Rod Edmunds, 'Victim Participation, Politics and the Construction of Victims at the International Criminal Court: Reflections on Proceedings in Banda/Jerbo', 14 *Melbourne Journal of International Law* (2013) 727, p. 732.

35 For example, family members of peacekeepers killed in the attack on the compound.

36 For a more thorough understanding of this issue see *supra* note 34. See also, Decision on the Joint Submission Regarding the Contested Issues and the Agreed Facts, *Prosecutor v Banda/Jerbo*, Trial Chamber IV, (ICC-02/05-03/09, 28 September 2011), where the Trial Chamber disagreed with the argument of the Darfuri Victims that the scope of their concerns would be limited.

37 See Participation at Confirmation *Prosecutor v Banda/Jerbo,* Pre-Trial Chamber I, (ICC-02/05-03/09), 29 October 2010.

38 It is also important to note that Rule 90(1) provides that victims shall be free to choose a legal representative. However, Rule 90(2) does allow that, '[w]here there are a number of victims, the Chamber may, for the purposes of ensuring the effectiveness of the proceedings, request the victims or particular groups of victims, if necessary with the assistance of the Registry, to choose a common legal representative or representatives'.

representative for all victims, illustrating the balance of resource management and fair representation which is often required of the Court.[39,40]

This case was peppered with concerns about the political leanings of the victims in the case, and was infused with the geopolitics surrounding the situation itself. The potential of the larger political issues to interfere in the proceedings, created an atmosphere which was ripe for mistrust and uncertainty regarding the legal proceedings.

The politics infused in the Banda/Jerbo case

Not only did the *Banda/Jerbo* case take place within the context of a necessarily political forum, it also took place within the complex political atmosphere of the conflict in Darfur, and the controversial decision of the Prosecutor to indict President Al Bashir.[41] This particular move by the Prosecutor changed the relationship that the Government of Sudan had with the Court. There had been a short period of engagement and limited cooperation by the Sudanese Government, which ended when the ICC issued its arrest warrant for Al Bashir. The Sudanese government refused to hand him over to the Court, and this ultimately sparked a, still ongoing, conflict with the AU, Arab and African States and negatively affected these entities' relationship with the Court.[42]

A situation was created whereby Jerbo and Banda, who were rebel leaders who fought against the Sudanese Government, recognized the jurisdictional competence of the ICC and voluntarily appeared before the Court; while the Government of Sudan refused to recognize the Court's jurisdiction (despite the UNSC referral under its Chapter VII powers). The interests of the accused rebels were at odds with the interests of the Sudanese Government and Al Bashir. It was argued that the 'ICC has the capacity to contribute to the construction of the international community's "friends and enemies"',[43] and that by cooperating with

39 Decision on Common Legal Representation, *Prosecutor v. Banda/Jerbo*, (ICC-02/05-03/09), 25 May 2012; Decision on Leave to Appeal, *Prosecutor v. Banda/Jerbo*, (ICC-02/05-03/09), 13 July 2012.

40 Realistically, victim participation must be limited by cost; the practicability of proceedings and issues of fairness and efficiency, *supra*, note 34, p. 734.

41 Warrant of Arrest, *Prosecutor v. Al Bashir*, (ICC-02/05-01/09), 4 March 2009.

42 For further discussion on this topic see, Dapo Akande, 'The Legal Nature of Security Council Referrals to the ICC and Its Impact on Al Bashir's Immunities' 7 *Journal of International Criminal Justice* (2009) 333 and Paola Gaeta, 'Does President Al Bashir Enjoy Immunity from Arrest?' 7 *Journal of International Criminal Justice* (2009) 315. For a debate on the issue, see Alex de Waal and Gregory H Stanton, 'Should President Omar al-Bashir of Sudan be Charged and Arrested by the International Criminal Court?: An Exchange of Views' 4 *Genocide Studies and Prevention* (2009) 329. Referring to some of the political consequences in Sudan in the wake of the ICC's warrant against Al Bashir, Mark Drumbl notes the lack of certainty as to whether indictments actually aid the position of victims: see Mark Drumbl, 'International Criminal Law: Taking Stock of a Busy Decade' 10 *Melbourne Journal of International Law* (2009) 38, 41.

43 Nouwen and Werner, *supra* note 13, p. 941.

the ICC, the rebel defendants have sought to portray themselves as 'partners in the fight against genocidaires'.[44] The rebel movements in Darfur have, in fact, presented themselves as allies of the ICC, and the Prosecutor has also presented the rebels as friends of the ICC, in contrast to its relationship with the Sudanese Government.[45]

The politics of the Sudanese situation and its impact in the Banda/Jerbo victim participation

It has been asserted that the participation of the two Darfuri victims was politically motivated and used to advance the agenda of the Sudanese Government.[46] In truth, the actual politics, views and sympathies of the Darfuri victims did not come to light during the proceedings.[47] However, Nice and Dixon's pursuit for separate representation of the victims, as well as the involvement of two related intermediaries with close connections to Nice and Dixon, created a cloud of suspicion over the proceedings.[48] Both the Prosecution and Defence expressed concerns related to the involvement of the Sudanese Workers' Trade Union Federation (SWTUF)[49] and the Sudanese International Defence Group (SIDG)[50] with the two Darfuri victims.[51] The use of intermediaries within the victim participation scheme is common, as the Court relies heavily on them to help it connect with the affected communities. But, these two particular organizations

44 Ibid., p. 956; Emily Haslam and Rod Edmunds, *supra* note 34, p. 727.

45 Nouwen and Werner, *supra* note 13, pp. 956–8; Luis Moreno-Ocampo, 'How Prosecution Can Lead to Prevention' 29 *Law and Inequality* (2011) 477, p. 489.

46 Defence Application to Restrain Legal Representatives for the Victims a/1646/10 and a/1647/10 from Acting in Proceedings and for an Order Excluding the Involvement of Specified Intermediaries, *Prosecutor v. Banda/Jerbo*, (ICC-02/05-03/09), 6 December 2010.

47 Emily Haslam and Rod Edmunds, *supra* note 34, p. 743.

48 Ibid., p. 738.

49 The Sudanese Workers' Trade Union Federation presented itself to the ICC as a 'union of all trade unions of Sudan with affiliates from 25 state unions and 22 professional federations', with a membership that 'covers the vast majority of the organised working people of Sudan comprising about two million citizens from the government, private and informal sectors': Application under Rule 103 in respect of Prosecution Appeal against Decision on the Prosecution's Application for a Warrant of Arrest against Omar Hassan Ahmed Al Bashir, *Prosecutor v Al Bashir* Appeals Chamber, (ICC-02/05-01/09), 20 July 2009 para 8.

50 The Sudanese International Defence Group describes itself as 'a non-governmental committee of Sudanese citizens established out of concern for the negative effects that ICC arrest warrants could have for the peace process in Sudan and for the ordinary people of this country'. *Prosecutor v Al Bashir*, ibid., para. 8.

51 Other cases have similarly raised questions about the interference of intermediaries in the proceedings, including the *Bemba* case in which L'Organisation pour la Compassion et le Development des Families en Detresse (OCODEFAD) assisted a number of victim applicants and the *Bemba* Defence team raised concerns about the organization, noting that it was established by one of Bemba's political rivals and claiming that they may have used unethical methods in their assistance. See Public Redacted Version of Mr. Bemba's Reply Brief, *Prosecutor v Bemba*, Trial Chamber III, (ICC-01/05-01/08), 22 April 2016.

caused concerns. SIDG was established after the Al Bashir warrant was issued. Furthermore, the then President of SIDG publicly declared his opposition to the ICC and introduced Nice and Dixon to the Darfuri victims, served as their main point of contact, and arranged for their removal from Darfur for security reasons.[52] A further link between the two organizations and the proposed victim representatives, Dixon and Nice, caused the parties in the *Banda/Jurbo* case concern. Both SIDG and SWTUF had unsuccessfully sought to present an *amicus curiae* application, contesting the ICC's jurisdiction, in the *Al Bashir* proceedings, using Nice and Dixon as their legal representatives.[53] Both the Prosecution and the Defence requested the removal of Nice and Dixon as Victim Representatives at the pre-trial stage, while the Defence asked the ICC to prohibit SIDG and SWTUF from any future involvement in the proceedings.[54]

Whether the assessments by the Prosecution and Defence were indeed correct, whether the Darfuri victims were indeed politically aligned with the Sudanese Government, or whether they were unintentionally caught in a political battle, the perception of political manipulation in the proceedings is a clear cause of concern for observers interested in maintaining the judicial integrity of the proceedings.

Case study: *Kenyatta* case and victim participation

Following the Kenyan presidential election in December 2007, the outcome was disputed, both parties claimed victory and areas of the country erupted into

52 Prosecution Objection to the Continued Representation of Victims a/1646/10 & a/1647/10 by Messrs Geoffrey Nice and Rodney Dixon, *Prosecutor v Bemba*, Pre-Trial Chamber I, (ICC-02/05-03/09), 6 December 2010, para. 7.

53 Decision on Application under Rule 103, *Situation in Darfur, The Sudan*, Pre-Trial Chamber I, (ICC-02/05), 4 February 2009; Decision on the Application for Leave to Appeal the Decision on Application under Rule 103, *Situation in Darfur, The Sudan*, Pre-Trial Chamber I, (ICC-02/05), 19 February 2009.

54 Prosecution Objection to the Continued Representation of Victims a/1646/10 and a/1647/10 by Messrs Geoffrey Nice and Rodney Dixon, *Situation in the Darfur, Sudan*, Pre-Trial Chamber I, (ICC-02/05-03/09)6 December 2010, paras. 27–31; Defence Application to restrain legal representatives for the victims a/1646/10 and 16470/10 from acting in proceedings and for an order excluding the involvement of specified intermediaries, *Situation in the Darfur, Sudan*, Pre-Trial Chamber I, (ICC-02/05-03/09), 6 December 2010. 'The Prosecutor argued that the previous lack of success on the part of SIDG and SWTUF when they intervened as amicus curiae in the Al Bashir case led them to turn to victim participants in Banda/Jerbo as "new proxies". For the Defence, the SIDG's founding statement demonstrated that it was a "front" for the Sudanese Government and Al Bashir and that moreover the victims were effectively being used to advance the political agenda of others. The Defence maintained that victim participation provided a platform for SIDG to advance Al Bashir's views and an opportunity to utilise the courtroom to remove enemies that the Government of Sudan had been unable to remove in battle. It questioned SIDG's and SWTUF's suitability as "honest brokers" and reliable intermediaries in ensuring both the flow of information to the victims about the proceedings and from the victims to the ICC, describing the role of the intermediaries to be both "untenable" and "dangerous"' Emily Haslam and Rod Edmunds, *supra* note 34, pp. 740–1.

violence.[55] The violence lasted for several weeks, over a thousand Kenyans were killed, thousands were raped and injured, and hundreds of thousands were displaced.[56] A Commission of Inquiry into the post-election violence found that what had started as spontaneous rioting and protests by supporters of Presidential candidate Odinga began to take on more organized forms, including premeditated attacks against ethnic groups.[57] It was also discovered that the violence had in fact been organized and planned in advance of the elections by the political leaders themselves.[58]

In November of 2009, the ICC Prosecutor, *proprio motu,* opened an investigation into the Kenya Situation.[59] As a result of that investigation, six suspects were summoned, but charges were only confirmed by the Pre-Trial Chamber for four of the six, and eventually, in March of 2013, the Trial Chamber withdrew the charges against one of those four, citing a lack of evidence.[60]

In August of 2011, 233 victims were granted participation rights in the case against Muthaura and Kenyatta, and a single Victim's Representative was assigned to all participating victims in the case.[61] In the case against Ruto and Sang, 327

55 In particular the Rift Valley region and the slums of Nairobi.

56 Commission of Inquiry into the Post-Election Violence (CIPEV) 'Report of the Commission of Inquiry into the Post-Election Violence', (2008), available at www.dialoguekenya.org/docs/PEV%20Report.pdf

57 Ibid.

58 For example, Human Rights Watch stated, '[i]n many cases the chief architects of post-election violence were prominent and well-known individuals [. . .] including politicians, counsellors and business people'. Ibid., pp. 38–9.

59 In relying on his *proprio motu* powers, on 26 November 2009 the Prosecutor applied to the Pre-Trial Chamber for authorization to open an investigation, as required under Article 15 of the Rome Statute. Corrigendum of the Decision Pursuant to Article 15 of the Rome Statute on the Authorization of an Investigation into the Situation in the Republic of Kenya, (ICC-01/09-19), 31 March 2010.

60 The original six suspects included William Samoei Ruto (Ruto), Henry Kiprono Kosgey (Kosgey), Joshua Arap Sang (Sang), Uhuru Muigai Kenyatta (Kenyatta), Francis Kirimi Muthaura (Muthaura) and Mohammed Hussein Ali (Ali). Decision on the Prosecutor's Application for Summons to Appear for William Samoei Ruto, Henry Kiprono Kosgey and Joshua Aarp Sang, *Prosecutor v. Ruto, Kosgey and Sang*, Pre-Trial Chamber II, (ICC-01/09-01/11-01), 8 March 2011; Decision on the Prosecutor's Application for Summonses to Appear for Francis Kirimi Muthaura, Uhuru Muigai Kenyatta and Mohammed Hussein Ali, Prosecutor v. Muthaura, Kenyatta and Hussein Ali, Pre-Trial Chamber II, (ICC-01/09-02/11-01), 8 March 2011. The confirmed accused included Ruto, Sang, Kenyatta and Muthaura. Decision on the Confirmation of Charges Pursuant to Article 61(7)(a) and (b) of the Rome Statute, *Prosecutor v. Ruto and Sang*, Pre-Trial Chamber II, (ICC-01/09-01/11-373), 4 February 2012; Decision on the Confirmation of Charges Pursuant to Article 61(7)(a) and (b) of the Rome Statute, *Prosecutor v. Kenyatta*, Pre-Trial Chamber II, (ICC-01/09-02/11-382-Red), 29 January 2012. Trial Chamber V withdrew the charges against Muthaura in March of 2013. Decision on the withdrawal of charges against Mr Muthaura, *Prosecutor v. Kenyatta*, Trial Chamber V, (ICC 01/09-02/11-696), 18 March 2013.

61 Decision on Victims' Participation at the Confirmation of Charges Hearing and in the Related Proceedings, *Prosecutor v. Muthaura, Kenyatta and Hussein Ali*, Pre-Trial Chamber II, (ICC-01/09-02/11-267), 26 August 2011.

victims were granted participation rights. Again, one Representative was assigned to all the victim participants.[62] The politics of victims participation were strongly at work in this case as well, though it was not the agency of the victims politics that was at question, but the way in which the Accused were able to use politics to manipulate the proceedings and the potential influence which politics may have had on the proceedings.

The political dimension of the Kenyan situation within the framework of the court

The Kenya situation cases were infused with controversy from the start. However, the political situation for the Court took on new heights of difficulty when, in 2013, Kenyatta and Ruto ran on a joint presidential ticket in Kenya and won the election. This emboldened the accused in their actions within the context of the Court. The new leaders of Kenya were further buoyed by the AU opposition to the prosecution of sitting heads of State, similar to the *Al Bashir* case in Darfur, Sudan.

On 22 December 2010, the Kenyan Parliament passed a motion requiring the Government to take action to withdraw Kenya from the Rome Statute.[63,64] In early 2011, the Kenyan Government launched diplomatic efforts aimed at obtaining a UN Security Council (UNSC) deferral of the Kenyan ICC cases under Article 16 of the Statute, and then made a formal request to the UNSC for a deferral of the case, which was not acted upon by the UNSC.[65] The Kenyan government also challenged the admissibility of the case, with Pre-Trial Chamber II rejecting the challenge. That decision was upheld upon appeal by the Kenyan Government.[66]

Additionally, the Kenyan Government consistently failed to cooperate with the Court.[67] They worked to portray the Court as politically motivated against the

62 Decision on Victims' Participation at the Confirmation of Charges Hearing and in the Related Proceedings, *Prosecutor v. Ruto and Sang*, Pre-Trial Chamber II, (ICC-01/09-01/11-249), 5 August 2011.

63 T.O. Hansen., 'Transitional Justice in Kenya? An Assessment of the Accountability Process in Light of Domestic Politics and Security Concerns', 42(1) *California Western International Law Journal* (2011) 1, pp. 10–12.

64 Article 127(1) of the Rome Statute requires cooperation with pending cases in the event of a withdrawal.

65 Obel, *supra* note 28, p. 15.

66 Judgment on the appeal of the Republic of Kenya against the decision of Pre-Trial Chamber II of 30 May 2011 entitled, "Decision on the Application by the Government of Kenya Challenging the Admissibility of the Case Pursuant to Article 19(2)(b) of the Statute", (ICC-01/09-01/11-307), Appeals Chamber, 30 August 2011. For a wider discussion on the various ways in which the Kenyan Government sought to legally end the ICC Kenyan cases, see Obel, *supra* note 28, pp. 15–17.

67 For example see Prosecution notice regarding the provisional trial date, *Prosecutor v. Kenyatta*, Trial Chamber V(B), (ICC-01/09-02/11-944), 5 September 2014; Kenya's Cabinet Secretary for Foreign Affairs Amina Mohamed called a Human Rights Watch report which alleged non-cooperation 'outrageous and incomprehensible', and further stated that claims that 'the country was not cooperating with the ICC is not true at all', Bosire Boniface, Kenya: Human Rights Watch Report Critical of Kenya's Commitment to fighting impunity,

sovereignty of Kenya, and advanced the notion that the Court unfairly targeted African countries. This campaign against the Court was eventually successful. Charges against all accused in the Kenya Situation have either been withdrawn or vacated.[68]

Victims and politics infused in the Kenyan situation

Trial Chamber V issued a Victim Participation Decision on 3 October 2012 which applied to both of the Kenyan cases and differed from earlier victim participation decisions in some significant ways. For one thing, victims who did not want to appear in person at the ICC were not required to submit a detailed application, due to the large number of victims and the 'unprecedented security concerns and other difficulties' in the Kenyan cases.[69] The Chamber noted that the registration process for the victims who were not participating directly and in person in the proceedings should be much less demanding and less onerous, and should not be subject to an individual assessment of their application by the Chamber, as had been done in other cases and situations.[70] The Chamber further decided to delegate its functions in terms of assessing and managing victim participation, by assigning the common Legal Representatives for the victims in the proceedings the task of representing the views and concerns of all victims in the case including:

> 1) those who would follow the application procedure set out in Rule 89; 2) those who would simply 'register' with the Court; and 3) those who either chose not to or were unable to register but whom the LRV [Legal Representative of Victims] should determine who qualifies as victims in the cases.[71]

This decision allowed the Legal Representatives to have a great deal more knowledge of the victims in the case than the Chambers themselves did. It also allowed for a more relaxed scheme of evaluating the victims themselves. While the Legal Representative was tasked with representing the victims' interests, the

---

27 January 2014, available at https://allafrica.com/stories/201401281433.html; Decision on Prosecution's applications for a finding of non-compliance pursuant to Article 87 (7) and for an adjournment of the provisional trial date, *Prosecutor v. Kenyatta*, Trial Chamber V(b), (ICC-01/09-02/11-908), 31 March 2014.

68 For an in-depth understanding of what happened in each of the cases to lead to the conclusion of the proceedings, see Obel, *supra* note 28, pp. 63–7.

69 The Chamber also emphasized the need to strike a 'balance between the need to allow for the presentation and consideration of victims' views and concerns, on the one hand, and to safeguard the rights of the accused and a fair and impartial trial, on the other'. Decision on victims' representation and participation, *Prosecutor v. Ruto and Sang*, Trial Chamber V, (ICC-01/09-01/11-460), 9 October 2012, paras 24, 29; Decision on victims' representation and participation, *Prosecutor v. Ruto and Sang*, Trial Chamber V, (ICC-01/09-02/11-498), 6 October 2012, paras 23, 28.

70 Ibid., (ICC-01/09-01/11-460,) para 25; Ibid., (ICC-01/09-02/11-498), para 24

71 Obel, *supra* note 28, p. 21.

Chamber had no way of evaluating what those interests were and if they would have an impact on the fairness and efficiency of the proceedings.

The security of the victims was also a huge problem that may have had an impact on the proceedings and was directly linked to the political situation of the country. Victims were often targeted and 'received threats from goons allied to the suspects at the Court [. . .] victims have been misconceived to be witnesses therefore they have been subjected to violent attacks'.[72] One NGO reported, 'fewer victims now want to participate because of the security risks' and that 'victims have to oppose the ICC to not be affected by security risks'.[73] In corroboration, the Human Rights Center of UC Berkeley School of Law concluded that 'instances of intimidation and witness disappearances led victim participants to fear that the accused could use the apparatus of the state to target them' and therefore many victims chose to withdraw and to no longer participate as victims in the case.[74]

Beyond the security problems, the political actors in the Kenya cases sought to confuse and conflate the language of victims, equating themselves with the victims of the post-election violence. For example, Ruto made a statement at a pre-trial status conference which appeared to place him in the group of victims.[75] The politicization of the trials at the ICC by the Kenyan accused was acknowledged by the Office of the Prosecutor who sought to reframe their efforts as trying to obtain justice for victims and to ensure that impunity was not allowed.[76]

In the end, the various factors of this case, when taken together, created a situation in which the integrity of the victim participation scheme could be called into question. The politicization of the case and the intermixing of victims in the political language, coupled with known victim intimidation and the delegation of victim management by the Chamber, regardless of intent or reasoning, created a situation ripe for potential political influence and interference in the legitimacy

72 Ibid., p. 53.

73 Ibid.

74 Human Rights Center, UC Berkeley School of Law 'The Victims' Court? A Study of 622 Victim Participants at the International Criminal Court', (2015), available at www.law.berkeley.edu/wp content/uploads/2015/04/VP_report_2015_final_full2.pdf

75 '[T]he circumstances surrounding these matters has produced two sets of victims, which I am very passionate about. Post-election violence victims, whose lives and property were destroyed and deserve justice and truth, and another set of victims, which I belong to. Victims of a syndicate of falsehood, and a conspiracy of lies choreographed by networks that are obviously against truth and justice.' Transcript of 14 May 2013, *Prosecutor v. William Samoei Ruto and Joshua Arap Sang*, (ICC-01/09-01/11), Trial Chamber V(A).

76 At the opening of the case against Ruto and Sang, ICC Prosecutor Fatou Bensouda addressed these perceptions directly: 'This is not a trial of Kenya or the Kenyan people. It is not about vindicating or indicating – indicting one or other ethnic group or political party. It is not about meddling in African affairs. This trial, Mr President, Your Honors, is about obtaining justice for the many thousands of victims of the post-election violence and ensuring that there is no impunity for those responsible, regardless of power or position.' Transcript of 10 September 2013, *Prosecutor v. William Samoei Ruto and Joshua Arap Sang*, (ICC-01/09-01/11), Trial Chamber V(A), paras. 19–20.

and foundations of the criminal trial itself. This should sound the alarm for a situation similar to that in the Darfur victim situation. The interests of the government of the country involved in the situation being investigated may find a way to influence the proceedings through the participation of victims, flying under the radar of the Chambers and potentially at odds with the fairness and efficiency rules required to ensure fair proceedings at the ICC.

Analysis: do the politics of victims' participation impact the fundamental rights of the Defence and the legitimacy of the Court?

> [T]he victim is considered 'worthy of humanitarian support as long as he remains a helpless victim – but turns into a danger the moment he seeks to liberate himself'. As individual human beings, victims (in sharp contrast to 'The Victims') are inherently political persons. As a political person – with interests and relationships and strategies – a victim carries a political narrative of the past and a vision for the future that may fit uneasily in the courtroom process, and indeed in the project of international criminal law more broadly. Victims as political persons may even oppose the use of international criminal law in response to the harms they have suffered, preferring other solutions to conflicts and alternate avenues of redress.[77]

As Nouwen and Kendall point out, victims are humans, each with their own set of values, norms, ideas and interests, which may or may not fit into the same ideals and interests as the Court. However, it may be assumed by the Court and those facilitating victim participation that victims are, or should be, politically neutral.[78] In arguing for the rights of the Darfuri victims to participate with their full interests and views being represented, Nice and Dixon stated that the Darfuri victims' status as independent agents would not be compromised.[79]

But the larger question is, so what? Should the Court care, consider, or take steps to limit the intervening of politics with victims in the proceedings? If, after all, one of the benefits of victim participation is to bring further nuance and understanding to the bench, does it matter that those participating in the process have their own agendas? Critics of Nice and Dixon's approach may be concerned that the accused's right to a fair trial, free of political interference, would be in jeopardy if the politics of participants were allowed to affect the proceedings.

77 S. Kendall and S. Nouwen, 'Representational Practices at the International Criminal Court: The Gap between Juridified and Abstract Victimhood', 76 *Law and Contemporary Problems* (2014) 259.

78 For further thoughts, see the discussion on 'the ideal victim' in Haslam and Edmunds, *supra* note 31, pp. 734–44.

79 Submission by Legal Representatives for Victims a 1646110 and a11647110 in light of Urgent Prosecution Objection, *Prosecutor v Banda and Jerbo*, (ICC-02/05-03/09), Pre-Trial Chamber I, 7 December 2010, para 26.

It is not clear that the Court or the Rome Statute drafters considered these issues when envisioning, drafting or implementing a victim participation scheme at the ICC. Perhaps the framers and implementers assumed that victims should not be looked upon as individuals, but as a class of persons with a common interest. However, as became clear in the *Banda/Jerbo* case, this class of persons may contain individuals who do not always have the same common interests. There are various approaches that the Court may take to address the issue of politics and the politicization of victim participation within ICC proceedings.

No acknowledgement of the politics involved

The Court could continue to proceed as it has done, ignoring the concept of politics and the risk of politicization, in a way, staying above the fray and only considering the judicial rules and norms in the proceedings. They attempted this in the *Banda/Jerbo* case by relying on formal legal tests and references to the rules. However, by not addressing the elephant in the room, the Chamber missed an opportunity to recognize the challenge being presented to the Court and to take steps to clarify and address these challenges. Essentially, the Chamber kicked the can down the road. The refusal to face an uncomfortable truth does not make it any less a truth, and may put proceedings in jeopardy as more governments and outside intermediaries learn how to harness the power of victim participation to achieve victories for their individual interests.

Recognition and understanding of victims' political views and the allowance of representation that responds to those views and concerns

Perhaps it is fair to recognize that individual victims have the right to a political view,[80] and even that they might participate in proceedings before the Court with those political views and interests in mind, but that, in order for the truth to prevail and for the case to not be swayed by political leanings, the Chambers must become more aware of who the participants really are and what their agendas might be. This would require that future Chambers do not delegate the laborious work of requiring and reviewing victims' applications to others. It might even require the addition of answers on the applications that would provide the Chamber with some insight into whether the victim applicant has political agendas at stake in their interest in participating in the proceedings. The additional burden of taking on the political ideologies of the victims participating in the case may have a serious impact upon the Chamber's ability to efficiently organize the case, thereby impacting the rights of the Defence. In practical terms, perhaps this would be a role that the Registry could assume,

80 For a fuller discussion on the right of victims to individual political identities, see generally Nouwen and Werner, *supra* note 13.

but practical issues such as budget, staffing and time constraints could make this alternative challenging.

Recognition of victims' political views and concerns while limiting the victims' ability to impact court proceedings by politicization of the court

This solution may attempt to balance autonomy and agency in terms of seeing victims as individuals rather than a class of 'idealized victims', with the adherence to the principles of fairness, essential to international criminal law, that must remain at the forefront of the proceedings. However, this approach would take a bold Chamber willing to directly address the political element and would require the Chamber to engage in a delicate balancing act. It is likely that it would take time for the Court to strike the right balance, creating a precedent as to how the Court wanted to recognize and allow for the individuality of victims to be recognized, while maintaining fairness and efficiency in the proceedings.

Strict scrutiny and systems put in place to filter political leanings and politicisation out of the proceedings

As has been pointed out, '[t]he attempt to prevent victim participants from becoming willing or unwilling proxies for other political interests may run the risk of denying victims their political agency'.[81] However, the counter argument here was made at the beginning of this chapter, that while a shift in judicial proceedings to include victims highlights the growing importance of restorative justice, the ultimate goal of the Court remains criminal in nature, and criminal law proceedings must remain the focus of the proceedings. Thus, the argument can be made that while victim participation has been an added component to the criminal proceedings at the Court, it is neither the Court's responsibility nor its duty to take into account the politicization of victims in the proceedings, and with respect to its duty to uphold fairness and efficiency principles, it must take measures to ensure the integrity of the proceedings and disallow political interference.

Conclusion

Has victim participation within the ICC framework been compromised, or 'politicised' to such a degree that it affects the fairness of the proceedings? This question remains to be answered. The Chamber chose to sidestep the question in the *Banda/Jerbo* case, and the Kenyan cases were ended without ever addressing the political interference in victim participation which may or may not have had a real effect on the outcome of those cases.

81 Haslam and Edmunds, *supra* note 34, p. 744.

What we can see clearly is that there is the potential for political victims or the politicization of victim participation to have an influencing impact upon the proceedings. What this might mean for the right of the accused to a fair and impartial trial is a concern. It is also fair to address the rights of the victim as an individual human being with agency and freedom of thought to participate in proceedings in a way that is authentic to their needs and beliefs. With this insight and no guiding principles from the Rome Statute to follow, it would behoove the Court to address the issue sooner rather than later. By developing a clear policy as to how to address, understand, and balance the individual political underpinnings of different cases, the Court may be able to prevent further problems as it develops its victim participation scheme so as to fully integrate the fairness and efficiency of Court proceedings to address both the rights of the accused and the rights of the victim.

10 Protecting victims who testify before the ICC

Tensions and balances with the defendants' right to a fair trial

Rossella Pulvirenti

Introduction

Victims have been the centre of attention at the International Criminal Court (ICC), since the Rome Statute both allows their participation in the proceedings when their personal interests are affected, and sets up a system of reparation in case of any damage, loss or injury.[1] This revived interest in victims' participation and reparation is also clear from the significantly large body of literature on this topic.[2]

Conversely, little attention has been dedicated to victims when they testify as witnesses (hereinafter, victims) in front of the ICC, although they play a central role in the ICC's evidentiary system. Since the ICC sits in The Hague and the majority of its investigations are conducted outside Europe, the ICC has been experiencing logistic and administrative difficulties in accessing documentary sources or forensic evidence, which are readily available at the crime scene, but spatially separated from the seat of the ICC.[3] For this reason, it has, *inter alia*,

1 Rome Statute of the International Criminal Court (adopted 17 July 1998, entered into force 1 July 2002) 2187 (p. 3) UNTS 1-38544 (Rome Statute), Arts. 68(3) and 75.

2 Chistine Van den Wyngaert, 'Victims before the ICC: Some Views and Concerns of an ICC Trial Judge' 44 *Case Western Reserve Journal of International Law* (2001) 475; Marianna Tonellato, 'The Victim's Participation at a Crossroads: How the International Criminal Court Could Devise a Meaningful Victims' Participation While Respecting the Rights of the Defendant' 19 *European Journal of Crime Criminal Law and Criminal Justice* (2012) 315; Maria Elander, 'The Victim's Address: Expressivism and the Victim at the Extraordinary Chambers in the Courts of Cambodia' 7 *International Journal of Transitional Justice* (2013) 95; Povel Singh, 'Victim Protection and Criminal Justice System in 21st Century', 48 *Civil and Military Law Journal on Rule of Law, Military Jurisprudence, and Legal Aid* (2012) 176; Brianne L McGonigle, 'Victim Oriented Measures at International Criminal Institutions: Participation and Its Pitfalls' 12 *International Criminal Law Review* (2012) 375; Conor McCarthy, 'Victim Redress and International Criminal Justice: Competing Paradigms, or Compatible Forms of Justice' 10 *Journal of International Criminal Justice* (2012) 325; Conor McCarthy, *Reparations and victim support in the International Criminal Court* (Cambridge University Press, 2012).

3 At the time of the writing, the ICC has only opened one investigation within Europe, namely, the Georgia investigation which was opened on 27 January 2016. Currently, the other investigations focus on the Democratic Republic of Congo, Uganda, Sudan (Darfur), Central African Republic, Kenya, Libya, Cote d'Ivoire, Mali, Central African Republic II and Burundi.

relied on the testimony of victims of crime since they can more easily travel to the seat of the ICC.[4] As testimony may be instrumental in determining the innocence of the accused, victims of crimes may be threatened, bribed, injured or even killed due to their participation in the proceedings. In addition to this, appearing as a witness before the ICC can demand considerable courage, because the alleged perpetrators are often the neighbours of victims.[5] Thus, protecting victims' identity, whereabouts and, more generally, their privacy is a key element in ensuring their safety and their willingness to participate in the ICC proceedings. Furthermore, some victims of the most heinous crimes such as sexual violence may also experience isolation, rejection and stigmatization from their families and communities, if the details of these crimes are publicly revealed.[6]

In order to address this gap, and in line with the main topic of this book on ensuring and balancing the rights of victims and defendants in international criminal justice, this chapter asks whether the ICC safeguards victims' privacy during their testimony, according to Article 68(1) of the Rome Statute. Furthermore, in accordance with the dichotomous aim of this book on the rights of both victims and defendants, this chapter aims to verify whether the ICC has correctly balanced victims' rights with the accused's right to a fair trial. Indeed, the application of these measures restricts several aspects of the defendant's right to a fair trial, such as the right to have a public hearing; the right to cross-examine or to have witnesses examined; and the right to have adequate time and facilities to prepare a defence.

Before proceeding with the human rights analysis, the next section focuses upon the scope of victims' right to privacy within the Rome Statute, relying on an original definition of this right, which departs from its general understanding under international human rights law. This definition of privacy shapes the content of the human rights analysis, since it defines which protective measures are used by the ICC to protect the privacy of the victims who decide to testify before the ICC. The following section focuses on the limitations of this right to privacy

---

See ICC, 'Situations under investigation' (ICC, 2019) available at www.icccpi.int/Pages/Situations.aspx accessed 29 March 2019.

4 International Bar Association, 'Evidence Matters in ICC Trials: An International Bar Association International Criminal Court & International Criminal Law Programme report providing a comparative perspective on selected evidence matters of current importance in ICC trial practice', August 2016; American University Washington College War Crimes Research Office, 'Expediting Proceedings at the International Criminal Court', June 2011, p. 20.

5 Cody S Smith, Alexa Koenig and Erik Stover, 'Witness Testimony, Support, and Protection at the ICC' in K M Clarke, A S Knottnerus, E de Volder (eds) *Africa and the ICC: Perceptions of Justice* (Cambridge University Press, 2016), p. 301.

6 Anne-Marie De Brouwer, *Supranational Criminal Prosecution of Sexual Violence: the ICC and the Practice of the ICTY and ICTR* (Intersentia, 2005), p. 234; Sandra Ka Hon Chu, Anne-Marie de Brouwer and Renée Römkens, 'Survivors of Sexual Violence in Conflict: Challenges in Prevention and International Criminal Prosecution in Victimological Approaches to International Crimes: Africa', in R Letschert and others (eds) *Prevention and International Criminal Prosecution in Victimological Approaches to International Crimes* (Intersentia, 2011), pp. 527, 535–9.

against the right to a fair trial. Following this general introduction on the scope of the right to privacy and right to fair trial within the Rome Statute, the next section analyses the ICC's case-law and transcripts. It focuses on the first investigation opened by the ICC in the Democratic Republic of Congo (DRC). More specifically, it deals with the cases against Lubanga, who was convicted by Trial Chamber I for the war crimes of enlisting and conscripting children under the age of 15 years and using them to participate actively in hostilities; Katanga, who was found guilty by Trial Chamber II of crimes against humanity and war crimes; Ngudjolo Chui, who was acquitted by the very same Chamber; and Ntaganda, who is still under trial for war crimes and crimes against humanity.[7] Furthermore, the analysis includes two cases from the Central African Republic. The first one is the case against Bemba, found guilty by Trial Chamber III of two counts of crimes against humanity and three counts of war crimes.[8] The second case was against Bemba and his co-accused for offences against the administration of justice under Article 70 of the Rome Statute.[9] Among the Kenyan cases, this chapter focuses on the *Ruto and Sang* trial, which was terminated by Trial Chamber V(A) on 5 April 2016 for lack of evidence, and on the case against Kenyatta, Muthaura and Ali, where the charges were withdrawn by the Office of the Prosecutor (OTP) because of interferences with witnesses.[10] Finally, this chapter focuses on the case against Gbagbo and Ble' Goude' in Côte d'Ivoire.[11] Following the human rights analysis of these cases, the final secion produces some recommendations for the ICC in order to make its practice more respectful of victims' right to privacy without infringing defendants' right to fair trial.

Protecting victims' privacy under the Rome Statute

The obligation upon the ICC to protect victims stems from Article 68(1) of the Rome Statute, which establishes an obligation upon the ICC to adopt appropriate measures to protect victims' privacy.[12] While scholarship agrees on the

7 Judgment pursuant to Article 74 of the Statute, *Prosecutor v Lubanga*, (ICC-01/04-01/06-2842), Trial Chamber I, 14 March 2012; Judgment pursuant to Article 74 of the Statute, *Prosecutor v Katanga* (ICC-01/04-01/07-3436-tENG), Trial Chamber II, 7 March 2014; Judgment pursuant to Article 74 of the Statute, *Prosecutor v Ngudjolo Chui* (ICC-01/04-02/12-3-tENG) Trial Chamber II, 26 December 2012.

8 Judgment pursuant to Article 74 of the Statute, *Prosecutor v Bemba,* (ICC-01/05-01/08-3343), Trial Chamber III, 21 March 2016.

9 Decision on Sentence pursuant to Article 76 of the Statute, *Prosecutor v Bemba*, (ICC-01/05-01/08-3399), Trial Chamber III, 21 June 2016 and Public Redacted Version of Judgment pursuant to Article 74 of the Statute, *Prosecutor v Bemba* et al, (ICC-01/05-01/13-1989-Red), Trial Chamber VII, 19 October 2016.

10 ICC, www.icc-cpi.int/kenya accessed 29 March 2019.

11 ICC, www.icc-cpi.int/cdi/gbagbo-goude accessed 29 March 2019.

12 David Donat-Cattin, 'Article 68' in O Triffterer (eds), *Commentary on the Rome Statute of the ICC: Observers Notes, Article by Article* (Hart Publishing, 2008) pp. 1275, 1277; J Fernandez and X Pacreau (eds), *Statut de Rome de la Cour pénale internationale. Commentaire article par article* (Pedone, 2012), p. 1550.

existence of such an obligation, different views exist as to whether victims who testify as witnesses hold a right, or a mere interest, to be protected. For instance, Zappalà believes that 'the expectation of witnesses to obtain protection do not really amount to a formal right to make application to the Court for measures to be taken'.[13] Unfortunately, Zappalà does not provide any further explanation as to why he believes victims are not the beneficiaries of a proper right, but just of a mere expectation. Conversely, Donat-Cattin believes that Article 68 affords a non-derogable right of victims to protection while testifying.[14] The view of Donat-Cattin is based on the idea that to each obligation established by law, a corresponding right exists.[15]

Additionally, it must be noted that the Rome Statute not only grants victims a so called 'status right' to be protected for the fact of testifying at the trial, but it also directly protects their right to privacy as a 'universally-accepted human right'.[16] This view is also confirmed in the ICC's case-law. In *Prosecutor v Bemba et al.*, a case involving several charges for witness tampering under Article 70 of the Rome Statute, Trial Chamber VII was called upon to decide on whether the way in which some Western Union Documents were provided by the Austrian authorities was in violation of the defendant's right to privacy.[17] In concluding that no violation could be envisaged in that circumstance, Trial Chamber VII stated that '[t]he right to privacy is an internationally recognised human right'.[18] In a footnote linked to this statement, Trial Chamber VII clarified that this view was based on the fact that the right is enshrined in several conventional sources, such as Article 8 of the European Convention on Human Rights, Article 17 of the International Covenant for Civic and Political Rights, Article 11 of the American Convention on Human Rights, Article 12 of the Universal Declaration of Human Rights and Article 21 of the Arab Charter of Human rights. The approach of the ICC in considering the right to privacy as an 'internationally recognised human right' in light of Article 21(3) of the Rome Statute, finds further corroboration in several domestic constitutions and provisions with

13 Salvatore Zappala', *Human Rights in International Criminal Proceedings* (Oxford University Press, 2003), p. 239.

14 Otto Triffterer and Kai Ambos, *The Rome Statute of the International Criminal Court: A Commentary* (Hart, 2016), p. 1683.

15 Ibid.

16 Yvonne McDermott, *Fairness in International Criminal Trials* (Oxford University Press, 2016), p. 120.

17 Decision on Requests to Exclude Western Union Documents and other Evidence Pursuant to Article 69(7), *The Prosecutor v Jean-Pierre Bemba Gombo, Aimé Kilolo Musamba, Jean-Jacques Mangenda Kabongo, Fidèle Babala Wandu And Narcisse Arido*, (ICC-01/05-01/13-1854), Trial Chamber VII, 29 April 2016, para. 46.

18 Decision on Requests to Exclude Western Union Documents and other Evidence Pursuant to Article 69(7), *The Prosecutor v Jean-Pierre Bemba Gombo, Aimé Kilolo Musamba, Jean-Jacques Mangenda Kabongo, Fidèle Babala Wandu And Narcisse Arido*, (ICC-01/05-01/13-1854), Trial Chamber VII, 29 April 2016, para. 46.

constitutional force, which demonstrate that the right to privacy is protected throughout the world.[19]

This 'status' of the right of privacy as an 'internationally recognised human right' has three main consequences. First, the ICC is bound to respect the right to privacy when interpreting and applying the provisions on protective measures. Second, this obliges the ICC to interpret the very same right to privacy in consonance with international human rights law, and, finally, since international human rights law establishes that the right to privacy is a qualified right, it follows that it can be limited under certain circumstances. The latter point will be discussed in the next section. Here, it is important to consider the content of the right to privacy, since it determines which protective measures should be used and, thus, the scope of this chapter.

The right to privacy is an amorphous right according to the Human Rights Committee (HRC) and the European and Inter-American Human Rights Courts (respectively, ECtHR and IACtHR), since it is the right to live how one wishes without any interference from the outside world.[20] For instance, the right to privacy might also protect an individual's physical and psychological integrity and well-being.[21] From this perspective, the interpretation of the right to privacy in

19 Among others, see Articles 44 and 45 of the Afghan Constitution, Article 18 of the Argentinian Constitution, Article 37 of the Albanian Constitution, Article 40 of the Algerian Constitution, Article 15 of the Andorra Constitution, Article 1 of the Austrian Constitution, Article II, 3 (f) of the Bosnia and Herzegovina Constitution, Article 40 of Cambodia Constitution, Article 19(5) of Chile Constitution, Articles 23 and 24 of Costa Rica Constitution, Article 72 of the Denmark Constitution, Articles 20 and 24 of the El Salvador Constitution, Article 18(2) of the Ghana Constitution, Article 12 of the Guinea Constitution, Article 59(1) of the Hungary Constitution, Article 71 of the Iceland Constitution, Article 14 of the Italy Constitution, Article 38 of the Kuwait Constitution, Article 16 of the Liberia Constitution, Article 13 of the Madagascar Constitution, Article 21 of the Malawi Constitution, Article 6 of the Mali Constitution, Article 16 of the Mexico Constitution, Article 16(3) of the Mongolia Constitution, Article 104 of the Mozambique Constitution, Article 13(1) of the Namibia Constitution, Article 22 of the Nepal Constitution, Article 21 of the New Zeeland Constitution, Articles 27-30 of the Oman Constitution, Articles 34-36 Paraguay Constitution, Article 22 of the Rwanda Constitution, Article 24 of São Tomé and Príncipe, Article 221(1) of Sierra Leone Constitution, Articles 29-30 of the Somalia Constitution, Article 29 of the Sudan Constitution, Article 6 of the Sweden Constitution, Article 13(1) of the Switzerland Constitution, Articles 28-29 of the Togo Constitution, Article 9 of the Tunisia Constitution, Article 27 of the Uganda Constitution and Chapter 7 of the Uzbekistan Constitution.

20 For the ECtHR see *X v Iceland*, (App no 6825/74), ECHR, 18 May 1976; *Niemietz v Germany*, (App no 13710/88), ECHR, 16 December 1992. For the IACtHR see *Ituango Massacres v Colombia*, Preliminary Objections, Merits, Reparations and Costs, Inter-American Court of Human Rights, Series C No.148, 1 July 2006 and *Massacres of El Mozote and Nearby Places v El Salvador*, Merits, Reparations, and Costs, Inter-American Courts of Human Rights, Series C No. 252, 25 October 2012. For the HRC see *Toonen v Australia*, Communication no 488/1992, UN Doc CCPR/C/50/D/488/1992 (1994).

21 For the ECtHR see *A, B AND C v Ireland*, (App no 25579/05), ECHR, 16 December 2010. For the IACtHR see *Rivas Quintanilla v El Salvador*, Preliminary Objections, Merits, Reparations and Costs, Inter-American Court of Human Rights, Series C No. 37, 25 October

the Rome Statute according to international standards poses some difficulties, because some of the elements, such as psychological well-being, encompassed under the umbrella term of 'privacy' under international human rights, are interests protected by Article 68 of the Rome Statute. The *travaux préparatoires* of the Rome Statute do not provide any insight into why only these aspects have been included in Article 68.[22] However, since they are listed in Article 68, it could be presumed that the drafters have consciously chosen that these aspects are not synonymous, despite being related to each other. However, although it is clear that the drafters lacked attention in highlighting the differences among these elements, it cannot be excluded that these interests blur into each other. This might expand the scope of the right to privacy to include the other non-synonymous elements contained in Article 68, such as psychological well-being. However, by doing that the presence of 'psychological well-being' in Article 68 of the Rome Statute would be made completely redundant. However, since this provision should be interpreted in line with Article 21(3) of the Rome Statute and 'internationally recognised human rights', a broad interpretation of the right to privacy should be used. Notwithstanding this, the wide meaning should be narrower and exclude well-being in order not to make all the elements contained in Article 68 of the Rome Statute redundant.

In light of this definition, the ICC can use different measures to protect victims' privacy. Rule 87 of the Rule off Procedure and Evidence (RPE), entitled 'protective measures', contains a non-exhaustive list of measures that can be applied within the courtroom to protect victims' and witnesses' right to privacy. These are, for instance, to expunge the name of the victim, witness, or other person at risk on account of testimony from the public records; the prohibition from disclosing such information to a third party; the testimony may be presented by electronic or other special means, which are able to alter the pictures or voice of the witness; the use of audio-visual technology, in particular videoconferencing and closed-circuit television, and the exclusive use of sound media; the use of a pseudonym, and, finally, the possibility of conducting the proceedings *in camera*.[23] While Rule 87(3) is echoed by Articles 68(2) and 69(2) of the Rome Statute and Regulation 21(2) of Regulation of the Court,[24] which refer to the same

2012 and *Y v Argentina*, Merits, Reparations, and Costs, Inter-American Courts of Human Rights, Series C No. 38, 15 October 1996. For the HRC see Manfred Nowak, *UN Covenant on Civil and Political Rights: CCPR Commentary* (Engel, 2005) 385; Sofia Gruskin and Aart Hendriks, 'The Right to Privacy: Some implications for Confidentiality in the Context of HIV/AIDS', in T S Orlin, A Rosas and M Scheinin (eds), *The Jurisprudence of Human Rights Law: A Comparative Interpretative Approach* (Institute for Human Rights, 2000), p. 227.

22 United Nations 'Preparatory Committee on the Establishment of an International Criminal Court' (UN Doc. A/AC.249/1997/L.8/Rev.1), 14 August 1997, 204; Decisions Taken by the Preparatory Committee at its Session Held from 4 to 15 August 1997, (UN doc. A/AC.249/1997/L.8/Rev1), 14 August 1997, pp. 36–7.

23 Rule 87, Rules of Procedure and Evidence of the International Criminal Court, ICC-ASP/1/3, at 10, and Corr. 1 (2002), U.N. Doc. PCNICC/2000/1/Add.1 (2000).

24 International Criminal Court, Doc. ICC-BD/01-01-04, adopted by the International Criminal Court on 26 May 2004 and modified (ICC-BD/01-01-04/Rev.01-05) on 9 March 2005.

measures, Regulation 94 of the Registry Regulation adds a further protective measure of private sessions, which is not mentioned elsewhere.[25] In addition to these measures, Regulation 94 of the Regulation of the Registry adds that the ICC might apply 'any combination of the protective measures listed above or any modification of a measure ordered by the Chamber which is technically feasible'. This last sentence gives judges some flexibility in deciding which measures to implement. They may either combine protective measures, or modify any of the existent measures as far as is technically achievable.

Against this background, the next section focuses on the limitations upon victims' right to privacy in the Rome Statute.

Limitations to victims' right to privacy: the right to a fair trial

Although the right to privacy under international human rights law is a qualified right, the Rome Statute does not expressly prescribe a limitation to victims' right to privacy.[26] Conversely, it establishes an indirect limitation to such a right when applying protective measures, because Article 68(1) of the Rome Statute states that '[protective] measures shall not be prejudicial to or inconsistent with the rights of the accused and a fair and impartial trial'. The scope of the right to a fair and impartial trial for the purposes of the Rome Statute is clarified by Article 67, which includes a set of minimum guarantees, such as the right to have adequate time and facilities for the preparation of the defence; to be tried without undue delay; to conduct the defence in person; and to examine, or to have examined, the witness against him or her.

Thus, although the respect for fair trials norms is explicitly listed in the Rome Statute, it is difficult to set the right applicable standard. On the one hand, it has been argued that the ICC should adopt the highest standards of fairness. This view was endorsed by the Ad Hoc Committee of the General Assembly which, by commenting on the ILC Draft Statute for the ICC, stated that '[the ICC] should be bound to apply the highest standards of justice, integrity and due process'.[27] This approach has also been shared by some scholars, such as McDermott, who believes that this would enhance the ICC's legitimacy and the respect for the rule of law world-wide.[28] However, on the other hand, Damaška argued that the

25 Regulation of the Registry, entered into force on 6 March 2006 on revised on 25 September 2006, ICC-BD/03-01-06-Rev1.

26 For instance, under Article 8(2) of the ECHR, limitations to the right to privacy must fulfil 3 requirements: they must be prescribed by law, be necessary in a democratic society and should pursue a legitimate aim, as stated in the exhaustive list of Article 8(2) of the ECHR. According to Article 17 of the ICCPR '[n]o one shall be subjected to arbitrary or unlawful interference with his privacy'. Article 11 of the IACHR reads that '[n]o one may be the object of arbitrary or abusive interference with his private life'.

27 UNGA, Report of the Ad Hoc Committee on the Establishment of an International Criminal Court (UN Doc. A/50/22) 1995, 129.

28 McDermott, *supra* note 16, p. 147.

highest standard of fairness might be too high for international criminal trials and suggests that the process should be just 'fair enough'.[29]

The practice of the ICC seems to suggest that judges lean towards the first option because, although they may combine protective measures according to regulation 94, they cannot modify the existing protective measures to allow witnesses to testify in full anonymity. Indeed, not only was a proposal of the Italian delegation to allow anonymity for witnesses not accepted by the Assembly of State Parties,[30] but also the ICC has several times rejected the idea that anonymous victims, who enjoy the dual status of victims-witnesses, should maintain their anonymous status when testifying. For instance, in *Lubanga*, Pre-Trial Chamber I ruled that anonymous victims are subjected to some restrictions, such as an absolute ban on submitting evidence during the proceedings.[31] A more lenient approach was endorsed by Trial Chamber I, which overruled the Pre-Trial Chamber's decision. It stated that anonymous victims could never testify as witnesses, explaining that the difficulties in accepting anonymous victims are related to the accused's right to fair trial.[32] Thus, it concluded that whether victims can testify anonymously should be decided on a case-by-case basis.[33]

Although, in this first decision, Trial Chamber I left it to the discretion of the judges as to whether anonymous victims could testify, later decisions were clearer on the matter that the ICC should prohibit anonymous victims' testimony. For example, Trial Chamber II in the *Katanga* and *Ngudjolo Chui* case, ruled that victims might be allowed to testify under certain circumstances, but '[u]nder no circumstances the Chamber will allow victims to testify anonymously vis-à-vis the Defence'.[34] The same approach was shared in the *Bemba* case.[35] Here, Trial Chamber III, referring back to the decision of Trial Chamber II in the *Katanga and Chui* case, ruled that victims are not allowed to testify anonymously.[36] The prohibition

29 Mirjan R Damaška, 'Reflections on Fairness in International Criminal Justice' 10 *Journal of International Criminal Justice* (2012) 611, p. 616.

30 Guido Acquaviva and Mikaela Heikkilä, *'Protective and Special Measures for Witnesses', in* Goran Sluiter and others (eds) *International Criminal Procedure: Principles and Rules* (Oxford University Press, 2013) 818, p. 844; Michael E Kurth, 'Anonimity witness before the International Criminal Court: Due process in dire straits', in C Stahn and G Sluiter, *The Emerging Practice of the International Criminal Court* (Martinus Hijhoff Publishers, 2009), p. 615.

31 Decision on the Arrangements for Participation of Victims a/0001/06, a/0003/06 and a/0003/06 at the Confirmation Hearing, *Prosecutor v Lubanga,* (ICC-01/04-01/06-462-tEN), Pre-Trial Chamber I, 22 September 2006, para. 6–8.

32 Decision on victims' participation, *Prosecutor v Lubanga* (ICC-01/04-01/06-1119), Trial Chamber I, 18 January 2008, para. 130–1.

33 Ibid.

34 Directions for the conduct of the proceedings and testimony in accordance with rule 140, *Prosecutor v Katanga and Ngudjolo Chui,* (ICC-01/04-01/07-1665-Corr), Trial Chamber II, 1 December 2009, para. 22.

35 Decision on the supplemented applications by the legal representatives of victims to present evidence and the views and concerns of victims, *Prosecutor v* Bemba, (ICC-01/05-01/08-2138), Trial Chamber III, 22 February 2012.

36 Ibid., para. 23.

of victims' anonymity is so ingrained in the ICC that in the *Laurent Gbagbo and Charles Blé Goudé* case, the Office of Public Counsel for Victims requested that only victims who present their views and concerns should maintain their anonymity.[37] Conversely, the Common Legal Representatives of Victims recognised that victims who appear as witnesses before the ICC must reveal their identities.[38]

While the boundaries of the application of the right to a fair trial are clear, it remains difficult to strike the right balance between the different rights at stake. In the absence of any clear benchmark by the ICC, a useful guidance can be found in Art 21(3) of the Rome Statute, which establishes that the ICC should interpret and apply the law in conformity with internationally recognised human rights.[39] Since the right to a fair and impartial trial is an 'internationally recognized human right', judges should ensure that the international human right standards are applied and, with it, the relevant case-law which aims to counterbalance victims' against defendants' rights. In the remainder of this chapter, these standards will be applied to the ICC's case law in order to analyse whether the ICC has fully respected victims' right to privacy when testifying, without undermining the right of a defendant to a fair and impartial trial.

An analysis of the ICC's case-law

Protective measures, such as pseudonyms, voice and face distortion, redaction from public transcripts, closed or private sessions, can be used to preserve victims' privacy, identity and whereabouts and to keep some information revealed during testimony confidential. These measures have been used in all the proceedings before the ICC to protect both prosecution and defence witnesses, but to different extents. However, since the focus of this chapter is on victims, the following sections will only analyse whether, in interpreting and applying protective measures, the ICC has safeguarded the right to privacy of victims who testify at trial and whether it has successfully counterbalanced it with the defendant's right to a fair and public trial.

Prosecutor v Lubanga

The first trial before the ICC, *Lubanga*, was characterised by an extensive use of protective measures. Victims testified with facial and voice distortion, under

37 Further Submissions on the Modalities of Victims' Participation at Trial, *Prosecutor v Gbagbo and Blé Goudé,* (ICC-02/11-01/15-75), Trial Chamber I, 21 May 2015, para. 15.

38 Ibid.

39 Rebecca Young, 'Internationally Recognised Human Rights' Before the International Criminal Court' 60 *International Criminal Law Review* (2011) 189, p. 202. See also Alain Pellet, 'Applicable Law' in A Cassese, P Gaeta and J R W D Jones (eds), *The Statute of the International Criminal Court: A Commentary* (Oxford University Press, 2002); Lorenzo Gradoni, 'The Human Rights Dimension of International Criminal Procedure', in G Sluiter and others (eds), *International Criminal Procedure: Principles and Rules* (Oxford University Press, 2013), pp. 74, 80–5, 93; Dapo Akande, 'Sources of International Criminal Law' in A Cassese (eds), *The Oxford Companion to International Criminal Justice* (Oxford University Press, 2009), pp. 41, 47.

a pseudonym, and in a closed or private session to protect their identities. For instance, these measures were granted to Witness 11, a former child soldier trained in one of the Lubanga military camps,[40] and to Witness 10, a female witness, who was enlisted in Lubanga's army and was, like most of the other kidnapped young girls, raped.[41]

The widespread use of measures to protect OTP victims' privacy can be justified under several grounds in the *Lubanga* case. First, it is certainly linked to the type of charges Lubanga was facing. Since he was indicted for having enlisted, conscripted and used child soldiers, it was to be expected that many of the victims testifying were going to be former child soldiers. Protecting their identity was of the utmost importance for the ICC. Second, the situation in Ituri in DRC, where many victims were from, was still volatile at the time they were heard. Thus, preserving their identities and whereabouts was necessary not only to protect their privacy, but also their safety. Finally, the *Lubanga* case was the first case held before the ICC. The ICC was struggling to establish its credibility as a reliable institution and in order to attract more victims to testify before its benches, it was necessary to show that the ICC was actually protecting their privacy.

The Defence was very critical of the use of protective measures during the entire *Lubanga* trial.[42] However, Lubanga's Defence team was able to cross-examine all the victims who testified as witnesses, although partially in closed sessions.[43] International human rights standards establish that any handicap under which the defence team is working must be counterbalanced by some procedures put in place by the judiciary. This principle was clearly stated by the ECHR in *Doorson v Netherlands* and, subsequently, *Van Mechelen v Netherlands*, where the accused were convicted on the basis of anonymous testimonies.[44] Here, in line with the previous and subsequent case-law, the ECHR observed that 'the handicaps under which the defence labours [should] be sufficiently counterbalanced by the procedures followed by the judicial authorities'.[45]

40 Transcript, *Prosecutor v Lubanga,* (ICC-01/04-01/06-T-139-Red2-ENG), Trial Chamber I, 3 March 2009.

41 Transcript, *Prosecutor v Lubanga,* (ICC-01/04-01/06-T-144-Red2-ENG), Trial Chamber I, 5 March 2009.

42 International Justice Monitor, 'Lubanga Defense To Call 'Around 30 Witnesses' (International Justice Monitor, 5 January 2010) www.ijmonitor.org/2010/01/lubanga-defense-to-call-around-30-witnesses/ accessed 29 March 2019 and International Bar Association, 'Report on Witness before the International Criminal Court', July 2013, 31.

43 Transcript, *Prosecutor v Lubanga,* (ICC-01/04-01/06-T-145-Red3-ENG), Trial Chamber I, 6 March 2009.

44 *Doorson v Netherlands,* (App no 20524/92), ECHR, 26 March 1996 and *Van Mechelen v The Netherlands,* (Apps nos 21363/93, 21364/93, 21427/93), ECHR, 17 April 1997. See also *Kok v The Netherlands,* (App no 43149/98), ECHR, 4 July 2000 para. 54; *Visser v The Netherlands,* (App No 26668/95), ECHR, 14 February 2002, paras. 45-46 and *Lucà v Italy,* (Application no 43870/04), ECHR, 24 September 2013, para. 40.

45 *Van Mechelen v The Netherlands,* (Apps nos 21363/93, 21364/93, 21427/93), ECHR, 17 April 1997, para. 54. See also *Kok v The Netherlands,* (App no 43149/98) ECHR, 4 July 2000, para. 54; *Visser v The Netherlands,* (App No 26668/95), ECHR, 14 February 2002,

Furthermore, the ECtHR has elaborated a 'sole or decisive rule', which provides that a conviction based 'solely or to a decisive extent' on anonymous witnesses infringes the accused's right to a fair trial.[46] Some authors believe that little consistency on the 'solely or to a decisive extent' principle exists within the ECtHR cases.[47] Indeed, as clarified by Judge van Dijk in *Van Mechelen v Netherlands* this rule

> is difficult to apply, because if the testimony of an anonymous witness is used by the court as part of the evidence, it will always be because the court considers it a 'decisive' part of that evidence, making the proof complete or at least sufficient.[48]

In its later case-law, the ECtHR has further developed the notion of 'counterbalancing' the defendant's right to a fair trial against the right to be protected, and has developed a three-prong test.[49] According to this test, first a court must verify what reasons justify the non-attendance of the victim who needs to testify as a witness, and whether all reasonable steps were taken to secure his/her attendance at trial. Second, the court must apply the 'sole or decisive' test, and, finally, it is necessary to ascertain whether enough measures were taken to counterbalance the handicap under which the defence labours.

In light of this case-law, it is clear that Lubanga's right to a fair trial was not infringed, since sufficient measures, such as cross-examination, were taken to counterbalance the handicap under which the defence was working.

Furthermore, even when cross-examining victims who testify as witnesses, the ICC and the relevant parties were careful to protect their privacy. This happened, for instance, when the Lubanga Defence team cross-examined one of the intermediaries used by the OTP to contact victims in the DRC, and asked several questions on the allegations that this intermediary had bribed some of the OTP victims who were supposed to testify against Lubanga.[50] The Defence team requested that the cross-examination be held in a closed session and argued that this was justified by the fact that the names of many protected victims and witnesses were going to be mentioned during cross-examination.[51] Similarly, the

---

paras. 45-46 and *Lucà v Italy*, (Application no 43870/04), ECHR, 24 September 2013, para. 40; *Windisch v Austria*, (App no 12489/86), ECHR, 27 September 1990, para. 31; *Unterpertinger v Austria,* (App no 9120/80), ECHR, 24 November 1986.

46 Doorson, *supra* note 44, p. 76; *Windsch*, *supra* note 31; *Unterpertinger*, *supra* note 45.

47 Tim Welch and others, 'Witness Anonymity at The International Criminal Court: Due Process For Defendants, Witnesses Or Both?' 23 *Denning Law Journal* (2011), pp. 29, 40.

48 *Van Mechelen, supra* note 45, p. 88.

49 *Schatschschwili v Germany*, (App no 9154/10), ECtHR, 15 December 2015, paras. 110–11.

50 Transcript, *Prosecutor v Lubanga*, (ICC-01/04-01/06-T-317-Red2-ENG), Trial Chamber I, 25 October 2010; Transcript, *Prosecutor v Lubanga*, (ICC-01/04-01/06-T-319-Red-ENG), Trial Chamber I, 27 October 2010.

51 Transcript, *Prosecutor v Lubanga*, (ICC-01/04-01/06-T-317-Red2-ENG), Trial Chamber I, 25 October 2010, p 38 l 14.

week after, the Defence Counsel requested that the cross-examination of Witness 321 be carried out in closed session. The cross-examination lasted for four days, throughout which the entire public and media were completely excluded from the proceedings.[52] Well aware that this could undermine the right to a fair trial of Lubanga since no public sessions were carried out, Presiding Judge Fulford requested the Defence to conduct the cross-examination of Witness 316 in open trial, as far as possible. He pointed out that:

> [r]egrettably with the last witness effectively all of his evidence was held in private session. If there is any way of being able to deliver at least part of this evidence in open session, I would ask you please to construct your questions in such a way as to make that a real opportunity, that the Court can avail itself of, but I imagine you're going to want to start in private session so that the witness can give his name and his present circumstances.[53]

It is questionable whether the protracted use of closed or private sessions affected Lubanga's right to a public trial. This right is not absolute according to international human rights standards, but some exceptions can be introduced if the 'interest(s) of [. .] the private life of the parties so require, or to the extend strictly necessary on the opinion of the court in special circumstances where publicity would prejudice the interests of justice'.[54] Furthermore, according to the ECtHR's case law, it is necessary to consider the proceedings as a whole. This principle was expressed in *Axen*, where the applicant claimed that his right to a public trial was violated because, while the trial in first instance was heard in public, the appeal phase was all conducted *in camera*.[55] Here, no violation was found because the trial, taken as a whole, could be regarded as public.[56] It therefore seems clear that Lubanga's right to a public trial was not infringed by the use of protective measures, since Judge Fulford urged the Defence team to conduct the cross-examination in open trial and, at the time of writing, the relevant documents have been reclassified as open, as the security concerns, which led to the application of protected measures, changed, and some measures were lifted.[57]

52 Transcript, *Prosecutor v Lubanga,* (ICC-01/04-01/06-T-320-Red2-ENG), Trial Chamber I, 1 November 2010; Transcript, *Prosecutor v Lubanga,* (ICC-01/04-01/06-T-321-Red2-ENG), Trial Chamber I, 2 November 2010; Transcript, *Prosecutor v Lubanga,* (ICC-01/04-01/06-T-322-Red2-ENG), Trial Chamber I, 2 November 2010; Transcript, *Prosecutor v Lubanga,* (ICC-01/04-01/06-T-323-Red2-ENG), Trial Chamber I, 3 November 2010; Transcript, *Prosecutor v Lubanga,* (ICC-01/04-01/06-T-324-Red2-ENG), Trial Chamber I, 4 November 2011; Transcript, *Prosecutor v Lubanga,* (ICC-01/04-01/06-T-325-Red2-ENG), Trial Chamber I, 4 November 2011.

53 Transcript, *Prosecutor v Lubanga,* (ICC-01/04-01/06-T-327-Red2-ENG), Trial Chamber I, 8 November 2010, p 9, ll 4–9.

54 *P and B v United Kingdom,* (Apps nos 36337/97 and 35974/97), ECtHR, 24 April 2001.

55 *Axen v Germany,* (App no 8273/88), ECtHR, 8 December 1983.

56 Ibid.

57 All of these were reclassified as open apart from this: Transcript, *Prosecutor v Lubanga,* (ICC-01/04-01/06-T-327-Red2-ENG), Trial Chamber I, 8 November 2010.

Having said that, if a formal human rights violation could not be found, the protracted use of protective measures which excluded the public, had the potential to undermine the reliability and legitimacy of the ICC, which was already the target of open criticism. This did not diminish in the following cases.

Prosecutor v Katanga and Ngudiolo Chui

Fewer closed or private sessions characterised the *Katanga and Ngudjolo Chui* trial. Indeed, at least 90 percent of the hearings were held in public sessions.[58] The OTP called a total of 26 victims to testify as witnesses on the events which happened on 24 February 2003 during an attack in Bogoro, a village in the DRC Ituri Region.[59] In order to keep victims' identity, whereabouts and other relevant information confidential, the ICC mainly relied on facial and/or voice distortion, redaction of the transcripts, or relocation through the International Criminal Court Protection Programme.[60] For instance, with a pseudonym and his voice and image distorted, OTP Witness 250, a former soldier who fought at Bogoro within the ranks of the *Front des Nationalistes et Intégrationnistes*, took the stand on 27 January 2010.[61] OTP Witness 250 was also considered vulnerable and, for this reason, some special measures were also applied so that the witness was not supposed to have visual contact with the two accused and a psychologist was present.[62]

Nevertheless, few private or closed sessions were held in the case. For example, in the first part of his testimony, OTP Witness 233 was granted image and voice distortion in order to preserve his identity, and he gave part of his testimony in private session to keep his identity and whereabouts confidential.[63] Similarly,

58 J Easterday, 'International Justice Monitor, Q&A with Eric MacDonald, Senior Trial Lawyer for the ICC: Part II' (International Justice Monitor, 2 June 2011) available at www.ijmonitor.org/2011/06/qa-with-eric-macdonald-senior-trial-lawyer-for-the-icc-part-ii/ accessed 29 March 2019.

59 J Algueró Llop, 'Katanga-Ngudjolo Trial Poised to Resume' (International Justice Monitor, 21 February 2011) available at www.ijmonitor.org/2011/02/katanga-ngudjolo-trial-poised-to-resume/ accessed 16 October 2017.

60 J Easterday, 'International Justice Monitor, Q&A with Eric MacDonald, Senior Trial Lawyer for the ICC: Part II' (International Justice Monitor, 2 June 2011) available at www.ijmonitor.org/2011/06/qa-with-eric-macdonald-senior-trial-lawyer-for-the-icc-part-ii/ accessed 29 March 2019.

61 Transcript, *Prosecutor v Katanga and Ngudjolo Chui,* (ICC-01/04-01/07-T-91-Red-ENG), Trial Chamber II, 27 January 2010, p. 1 ll 21–5, p. 2, ll 1-2.

62 Ibid., p. 2 ll 9-14.

63 Transcript, *Prosecutor v Katanga and Ngudjolo Chui,* (ICC-01/04-01/07-T-83-Red-ENG),Trial Chamber II, 26 November 2009, pp. 5–12; Transcript, *Prosecutor v Katanga and Ngudjolo Chui,* (ICC-01/04-01/07-T-84-Red-ENG), Trial Chamber II, 27 November 2009, pp. 3–7; Transcript, *Prosecutor v Katanga and Ngudjolo Chui,* (ICC-01/04-01/07-T-86-Red2-ENG), Trial Chamber II, 27 November 2009, pp. 9–10 and 13-22; Transcript, *Prosecutor v Katanga and Ngudjolo Chui,* (ICC-01/04-01/07-T-87-Red-ENG), Trial Chamber II, 30 November 2009, pp. 20–3. For the reasons used to request private sessions, see Transcript, *Prosecutor v Katanga and Ngudjolo Chui,* (ICC-01/04-01/07-T-84-Red-ENG), Trial Chamber II, 27 November 2009, pp. 3, ll 17–19.

OTP Witness 161, who unexpectedly accused the two defendants of being present at the crime scene, provided part of his testimony in private session.[64]

The fact that many of the hearings were held in public and that the Defence team was able to cross-examine the victims who testified as witnesses called by the other party posed no threat to Katanga's and Ngudjolo's right to a fair trial. Conversely, as emerged from an interview with the senior trial lawyer for the ICC, Eric MacDonald, cross-examination might undermine victims' right to privacy, because sometimes there are slip-ups, for example, when questioning some of them, it has happened that they have been named by their first name.[65] For this reason, Trial Chamber II ordered that the transcript or the recording of the hearings be redacted.[66]

Against this background, it is clear that the ICC protected the right to privacy-of the victims who testified as witnesses. Nevertheless, given the limited application of judicial protective measures, and the small number of private or closed hearings, the ICC judges fully safeguarded Katanga's and Ngudjolo's right to a fair and public trial. However, a different picture emerged in the *Bemba* case.

Prosecutor v Bemba

In the *Bemba* trial, the use of protective measures was massive. For instance, among the 40 OTP witnesses, only the expert witnesses testified in open court without any protective measures.[67] As explained below in this section, all the remaining OTP witnesses, both victims (who were crime-based witnesses, such as children, women and men, who had been raped and sodomised by Bemba's troops) and insider witnesses (who were members of President Ange-Félix Patassé's armed forces) testified with protective measures.[68] The privacy of victims who

64 Transcript, *Prosecutor v Katanga and Ngudjolo Chui,* (ICC-01/04-01/07-T-84-Red-ENG), Trial Chamber II, 27 November 2009, pp. 3–9, 16–21; 38–42, 44–5.

65 J Easterday, 'International Justice Monitor, Q&A with Eric MacDonald, Senior Trial Lawyer for the ICC: Part II' (International Justice Monitor, 2 June 2011) available at www.ijmonitor.org/2011/06/qa-with-eric-macdonald-senior-trial-lawyer-for-the-icc-part-ii/ accessed 29 March 2019.

66 Ibid.

67 The experts were: Dr. Adeyinka Akinsulure-Smith, who is an expert on post-traumatic stress disorder affecting victims of sexual violence perpetuated by Bemba's militia, Transcript, *Prosecutor v Bemba,* (ICC-01/05-01/08-T-38-ENG),Trial Chamber III, 29 November 2010; Samarin, a professor of linguistics and anthropology at the University of Toronto, Transcripts, *Prosecutor v Bemba,* (ICC-01/05-01/08-T-88-ENG), Trial Chamber III, 24 March 2011; Transcripts, *Prosecutor v Bemba,* (ICC-01/05-01/08-T-89-Red2-ENG), Trial Chamber III, 25 March 2011; Transcripts, *Prosecutor v Bemba* (ICC-01/05-01/08-T-90-Red2-ENG), 28 March 2011; Transcripts, *Prosecutor v Bemba* (ICC-01/05-01/08-T-91-Red2-ENG), Trial Chamber III, 29 March 2011; and Dr. André Tabo, the Head of the psychiatry department at Centre National Hospitalier Universitaire de Bangui in the CAR, Transcripts, *Prosecutor v Bemba,* (ICC-01/05-01/08-T-91-Red2-ENG), Trial Chamber III, 29 March 2011.

68 For example, see Witness 178, Transcripts, *Prosecutor v Bemba,* (ICC-01/05-01/08-T-154-Red2-ENG), Trial Chamber III, 6 September 2011 and Transcripts, *Prosecutor v Bemba,* (ICC-01/05-01/08-T-157-Red2-ENG), Trial Chamber III, 8 September 2011. For Witness 33 see Transcripts, *Prosecutor v Bemba,* (ICC-01/05-01/08-T-158-Red2-ENG),

decided to appear as witnesses was fully protected. First, their identities were not known by the public and media since all of them were attributed pseudonyms.[69] Furthermore, in testifying before Trial Chamber III, those victims were granted a further set of protective measures, including face and voice distortion, and total or partial private or closed sessions to protect their security, dignity and privacy.[70]

Following the accusation that Bemba and his defence team tried to bribe some victims to falsify their testimony, a new investigation and prosecution was launched against Bemba; Aimé Kilolo-Musamba, his lead counsel at the time the charges were issued; Jean-Jacques Mangenda Kabongo, the case manager; Narcisse Arido, a defense witness; and Fidèle Babala Wandu, a member of the Congolese parliament. For this reason, Trial Chamber III ordered that the presentation

---

Trial Chamber III, 9 September 2011; Transcripts, *Prosecutor v Bemba,* (ICC-01/05-01/08-T-159-Red2-ENG), Trial Chamber III, 12 September 2011. For Witness 32, Transcripts, *Prosecutor v Bemba,* (ICC-01/05-01/08-T-165-Red2-ENG), Trial Chamber III, 23 September 2011; Transcripts, *Prosecutor v Bemba* (ICC-01/05-01/08-T-166-Red2-ENG), Trial Chamber III, 26 September 2011; Transcripts, *Prosecutor v Bemba* (ICC-01/05-01/08-T-167-Red2-ENG), Trial Chamber III, 27 September 2011. For Witness 65 see Transcripts, *Prosecutor v Bemba,* (ICC-01/05-01/08-T-168-Red2-ENG), Trial Chamber III, 11 October 2011; Transcript, *Prosecutor v Bemba,* (ICC-01/05-01/08-T-169-Red2-ENG), Trial Chamber III, 4 October 2011; Transcript, *Prosecutor v Bemba,* (ICC-01/05-01/08-T-170-Red2-ENG), Trial Chamber III, 5 October 2011; Transcript, *Prosecutor v Bemba,* (ICC-01/05-01/08-T-171-Red2-ENG), Trial Chamber III, 6 October 2011. For testimony both in closed session and via video-link see Transcript, *Prosecutor v Bemba,* (ICC-01/05-01/08-T-171-Red2-ENG), Trial Chamber III, 6 October 2011; Transcript, *Prosecutor v Bemba,* (ICC-01/05-01/08-T-214-Red2-ENG), Trial Chamber III, 14 March 2012; Transcript, *Prosecutor v Bemba,* (ICC 01/05-01/08-T-215-Red2-ENG), Trial Chamber III, 15 March 2012; Transcript, *Prosecutor v Bemba,* (ICC-01/05-01/08-T-216-Red2-ENG), Trial Chamber III, 16 March 2011; Transcript, *Prosecutor v Bemba,* (ICC-01/05-01/08-T-217-Red2-ENG), Trial Chamber III, 19 March 2012.

69 For example, for Witness 38, see Transcript, *Prosecutor v Bemba,* (ICC-01/05-01/08-T-34-Red2-ENG), Trial Chamber III, 24 November 2010. For Witness 22 see Transcript, *Prosecutor v Bemba,* (ICC-01/05-01/08-T-40-Red2-ENG), Trial Chamber III, 30 November 2010; Transcript, *Prosecutor v Bemba,* (ICC-01/05-01/08-T-41-Red2-ENG), Trial Chamber III, 1 December 2010; Transcript, *Prosecutor v Bemba,* (ICC-01/05-01/08-T-41-Red2-ENG), Trial Chamber III, 1 December 2010. For Witness 87 see Transcript, *Prosecutor v Bemba,* (ICC-01/05-01/08-T-44-Red3-ENG), Trial Chamber III, 11 January 2011. For Witness 23 see Transcript, *Prosecutor v Bemba,* (ICC-01/05-01/08-T-48-Red2-ENG), Trial Chamber III, 17 January 2011; Transcript, *Prosecutor v Bemba,* (ICC-01/05-01/08-T-49-Red2-ENG), Trial Chamber III, 18 January 2011; Transcript, *Prosecutor v Bemba,* (ICC-01/05-01/08-T-51-Red2-ENG), Trial Chamber III, 21 January 2011. For Witness 81 see Transcript, *Prosecutor v Bemba,* (ICC-01/05-01/08-T-55-Red2-ENG), Trial Chamber III, 27 January 2011; Transcript, *Prosecutor v Bemba,* (ICC-01/05-01/08-T-56-Red2-ENG), Trial Chamber III, 28 January 2011; Transcript, *Prosecutor v Bemba,* (ICC-01/05-01/08-T-57-Red2-ENG), Trial Chamber III, 31 January 2011; Transcript, *Prosecutor v Bemba,* (ICC-01/05-01/08-T-162-Red2), Trial Chamber III, 15 September 2011; Transcript, *Prosecutor v Bemba,* (ICC-01/05-01/08-T-164-Red-ENG), Trial Chamber III, 19 September 2011.

70 Corrigendum to "Prosecution's Request for Protective and Special Measures for Prosecution Witnesses at Trial", *Prosecutor v Bemba,* (ICC-01/05-01/08-800-Conf-Exp-Corr), Trial Chamber III, 6 July 2010, para. 10.

of evidence be reopened.[71] During this phase, some of the victims who had been previously heard were called back to testify concerning the offences against the administration of justice, according to Article 70 of the Rome Statute, for '[c]orruptly influencing a witness, obstructing or interfering with the attendance or testimony of a witness, retaliating against a witness forgiving testimony or destroying, tampering with or interfering with the collection of evidence.'[72] In recalling these witnesses, Trial Chamber III kept the previous protective measures in place granting witnesses pseudonyms and allowing witnesses to testify in closed or private sessions with the use of voice and/or facial distortion.[73]

Furthermore, the ICC has also safeguarded the right to privacy of victims who testified as witnesses from third parties. For instance, in order to protect Witness 22's privacy, judges of Trial Chamber III rejected the Defence request to disclose to third parties confidential documents carrying information on the health status of Witness 22 provided by an HIV specialist doctor.[74] Considering that no public information is available, it can be easily concluded that the ICC has fully protected victims' right to privacy from unwanted intrusions by the public and media, although this makes the study of this topic quite challenging.

Against this background, it seems that the ICC has correctly balanced the necessity to protect the right to privacy of the victims who were called by the OTP as witnesses, with Bemba's right to a fair and public trial. With reference to international human rights standards, according to which the handicap under which the defence team is working must be counterbalanced by some procedures put in place by the judiciary, it seems that the judges have successfully balanced the two rights at stake. There are a few points to note. First, not all the testimonies were held in private or closed sessions, Trial Chamber III switched to open sessions when no sensitive information was discussed. Second, all the victims who testified as witnesses were cross-examined by the *Bemba* Defence team, although these cross-examination sessions were often held in private or closed sessions.[75] Finally, as happened in

71 Notice of limited reopening of the presentation of evidence and rescheduling of closing statements', *Prosecutor v Bemba* (ICC-01/05-01/08-3155), Trial Chamber III, 2 October 2014.

72 Art. 70(1)(c), Rome Statute.

73 For Witness 242 see Transcript, *Prosecutor v Bemba* (ICC-01/05-01/13-T-37-Red-ENG) Trial Chamber III, 13 November 2015; for Witness D21-3 Transcript, *Prosecutor v Bemba* (ICC-01/05-01/13-T-40-Red2-ENG), Trial Chamber III, 2 March 2016. For Witness D21-P-0003 also testifying via video link see Transcript, *Prosecutor v Bemba* (ICC-01/05-01/13-T-40-Red2-ENG) Trial Chamber III, 2 March 2016.

74 Transcript, *Prosecutor v Bemba* (ICC-01/05-01/08-T-42-Red2-ENG), Trial Chamber III, 2 December 2010, p. 7, ll. 4-8.

75 For Transcript, *Prosecutor v Bemba*, (ICC-01/05-01/08-T-156-Red-ENG), Trial Chamber III, 7 September 2011, which became public pursuant to Trial Chamber III 's Second Order (ICC-01/05-01/08-2223), dated 4 June 2012, and the instructions in the email dated 24 September 2013, from p. 22; for Witness 87, Transcript *Prosecutor v Bemba* (ICC-01/05-01/08-T-44-Red-ENG) and (ICC-01/05-01/08-T-47-Red2-ENG), Trial Chamber III, 14 January 2011, which became public pursuant to Trial Chamber III 's Second Order (ICC-01/05-01/08-2223) dated 4 June 2012, and the instructions in the email dated 7 October 2013; For Witness 68 see Transcript *Prosecutor v Bemba*,

the *Lubanga* and *Katanga* and *Ngudiolo* trials, most of the transcripts have been reclassified as open, meaning that the risks for victims' privacy are no longer so serious, with the result that some information can be realised publicly.[76]

(ICC-01/05-01/08-T-50-Red2-ENG), Trial Chamber III, 20 January 2011, which became public pursuant to Trial Chamber III 's Second Order (ICC-01/05-01/08-2223) dated 4 June 2012, and the instructions in the email dated 4 November 2013. For Witness 23 see Transcript, *Prosecutor v Bemba* (ICC-01/05-01/08-T-53-Red2-ENG), Trial Chamber III, 25 January 2011, which became public pursuant to Trial Chamber III 's Orders ICC-01/05-01/08-2223 and ICC-01/05-01/08-3038, and the instructions in the email dated 4 November 2013.

76 For Witness 38, see Transcript, *Prosecutor v Bemba*, (ICC-01/05-01/08-T-34-Red2-ENG), Trial Chamber III, 24 November 2010, which became public pursuant to Trial Chamber III 's Second Order, ICC-01/05-01/08-2223, dated 4 June 2012, and the instructions in the email dated 9 October 2013; for Witness 22 see Transcript *Prosecutor v Bemba*, (ICC-01/05-01/08-T-40-Red2-ENG), Trial Chamber III, 30 November 2010, which became public pursuant to Trial Chamber III 's Second Order, ICC-01/05-01/08-2223, dated 4 June 2012, and the instructions in the email dated 24 September 2013 and Transcript, *Prosecutor v Bemba* (ICC-01/05-01/08-T-41-Red2-ENG) Trial Chamber III, which became public pursuant to Trial Chamber III's Second Order, (ICC-01/05-01/08-2223), dated 4 June 2012, and the instructions in the email dated 24 September 2013; Transcript, *Prosecutor v Bemba*, (ICC-01/05-01/08-T-41-Red2-ENG), Trial Chamber III, 1 December 2010, which became public pursuant to Trial Chamber III 's Second Order, ICC-01/05-01/08-2223, dated 4 June 2012, and the instructions in the email dated 24 September 2013. For Witness 87 see Transcript, *Prosecutor v Bemba*, (ICC-01/05-01/08-T-44-Red3-ENG), Trial Chamber III, 11 January 2011, which became public pursuant to Trial Chamber III 's Second Order, ICC-01/05-01/08-2223, dated 4 June 2012, and the instructions in the email dated 7 October 2013. For Witness 23 see Transcript, *Prosecutor v Bemba*, (ICC 01/05-01/08-T-48-Red2-ENG), Trial Chamber III, 17 January 2011, which became public pursuant to Trial Chamber III 's Orders, ICC-01/05-01/08-2223 and ICC-01/05 01/08 3038, dated 4 June 2012, and the instructions in the email dated 4 November 2013 and Transcript, *Prosecutor v Bemba*, (ICC-01/05-01/08-T-49-Red2-ENG), Trial Chamber III, 18 January 2011, which became public pursuant to Trial Chamber III 's Orders, ICC-01/05-01/08-2223 and ICC-01/05-01/08-3038, dated 4 June 2012, and the instructions in the email dated 4 November 2013; Transcript, *Prosecutor v Bemba*, (ICC-01/05-01/08-T-51-Red2-ENG), Trial Chamber III, 21 January 2011, which became public pursuant to Trial Chamber III's Orders, ICC-01/05-01/08-2223 and ICC-01/05-01/08-3038, and its instructions in the email dated 29 November 2013. For Witness 81 see Transcript, *Prosecutor v Bemba* (ICC-01/05-01/08-T-55-Red2-ENG), Trial Chamber III, 27 January 2011, which became public pursuant to Trial Chamber III 's Orders, ICC-01/05-01/08-2223 and ICC-01/05-01/08-3038, and the instructions in the email dated 9 September 2013; Transcript, *Prosecutor v Bemba* (ICC-01/05-01/08-T-56-Red2-ENG), Trial Chamber III, 28 January 2011, which became public pursuant to Trial Chamber III 's Orders, ICC-01/05-01/08-2223 and ICC-01/05-01/08-3038, and the instructions in the email dated 9 September 2013; Transcript, *Prosecutor v Bemba* (ICC-01/05-01/08-T-57-Red2-ENG,) Trial Chamber III, 31 January 2011, which became public pursuant to Trial Chamber III 's Orders, ICC-01/05-01/08-2223 and ICC-01/05-01/08-3038, and the instructions in the email dated 9 September 2013. For Witness 178, Transcript, *Prosecutor v Bemba* (ICC 01/05 01/08-T-154-Red2-ENG), Trial Chamber III, 6 September 2011, made public pursuant to Trial Chamber III 's Orders, ICC-01/05-01/08-2223 and ICC-01/05-01/08-3038, and its instructions in the email dated 6 February 2014. Among those private sessions which were not reclassified as public see for Witness 32, Transcript, *Prosecutor v*

Despite this, although the right to a fair and public trial was not unduly restricted in *Bemba*, it is necessary to note that all the victims called by the OTP as witnesses testified with protective measures, which contradicts the view that protective measures have an exceptional nature. With this in mind, we can turn to the Kenyan cases, where even greater use was made of exceptional measures.

The Kenyan cases

The OTP faced several challenges in prosecuting those alleged responsible for the 2007–2008 post-election violence in Kenya. One of the challenges was to keep identity of victims and witnesses confidential during the proceedings. Interference reached such systematic and alarming levels that the Prosecutor, Fatou Bensouda, while commenting on the killing of a defence witness, Meshak Yebey, announced that '[p]rosecution witnesses in this case have been under siege.'[77]

In the Confirmation of Charges Hearings in the *Ruto and Sang* and *Muthaura, Kenyatta and Ali* cases, no one testified, since the OTP preferred to maintain victims' and witnesses' identities and their whereabouts confidential.[78] Thus, the OTP used the statements of several victims, who were granted protection as witnesses, to uphold the charges.[79] While the use of statements *per se* remains outside the scope of this chapter, this technique has been heavily criticised by the Defence team, because not only it did not have the opportunity to test victims' honesty, credibility, reliability and accuracy, but also because the statements were heavily redacted to preserve victims' privacy. According to Article 61(5) of the Rome Statute, the OTP is not obliged to rely on testimony at the hearing of the confirmation of charges, but it may rely on documentary or summary evidence. Furthermore, the Defence does not know the identity of those victims who agreed to testify as witnesses, who are *de facto* anonymous witnesses.[80] This

---

Bemba (ICC-01/05-01/08-T-166-Red2-ENG), Trial Chamber III, 26 September 2011; for Witness 178, Transcript, *Prosecutor v Bemba* (ICC-01/05-01/08-T-156-Red-ENG), Trial Chamber III, 7 September 2011.

77 Office of the Prosecutor, 'Statement of the Office of the Prosecutor regarding the reported abduction and murder of Mr Meshak Yebei', 9 January 2015 available at www.icc-cpi.int/Pages/item.aspx?name=otp-stat-09-01-2015&ln=en accessed 29 March 2019.

78 For the *William Samoei Ruto and Joshua Arap Sang* case, see for instance Transcript, *Prosecutor v Ruto and Sang* (ICC-01/09-01/11-T-6-Red-ENG), Pre-Trial Chamber II, 2 September 2011, p. 6 ll. 5–19; p. 9, ll. 12–21; p. 10, ll. 20-25; p. 11, ll. 2-7. See also Transcript, *The Prosecutor v Francis Kirimi Muthaura, Uhuru Muigai Kenyatta and Mohammed Hussein Ali* case *Prosecutor v Muthaura, Kenyatta and Ali* (ICC-01/09-02/11-T-5-Red-ENG), Pre-Trial Chamber II, 22 September 2011, p. 12 ll. 13-19, pp. 13–14, ll. 23–25, ll. 1–10, p. 14, ll. 11–19; Transcript, *Prosecutor v Ruto and Sang* (ICC-01/09-02/11-T-6-ENG), Pre-Trial Chamber II, 23 September 2011, p. 6, ll. 16–21, p. 7, ll. 23-25; p. 8, ll. 1–3.

79 Ibid.

80 For Ruto and Sang see Transcript, *Prosecutor v Ruto and Sang*, (ICC-01/09-02/11-T-6-ENG), Pre-Trial Chamber II, 23 September 2011, p. 110, ll. 5–11; p. 111 ll. 23–24; p. 112, ll. 10–18. For *The Prosecutor v Francis Kirimi Muthaura, Uhuru Muigai Kenyatta and*

posed a great disadvantage to the Defence, which was not counterbalanced by the judiciary.

The charges against Muthaura and Kenyatta were quickly dropped,[81] as victims of the crimes refused to testify because they were intimidated or bribed, and the Kenyan Government did not disclose the relevant documentation as requested by the ICC.[82] Thus, no victims appeared to testify before Trial Chamber V(b), and the focus on the defendants' right to fair trial in this respect, was soon removed.

Conversely, charges against Ruto and Sang were confirmed.[83] In these two cases, significant use of protective measures to safeguard victims' identity and privacy was made, because the OTP was working in a very difficult environment. For this reason, all the victims who testified were called by a pseudonym in order to safeguard their identity. Furthermore, in order to preserve their privacy, Trial Chamber V(a) made frequent use of closed or private sessions; heavily redacted transcripts of the hearings; pixilation; voice distortion; and use of some curtains.[84]

Mohammed Hussein Ali case see Transcript, *Prosecutor v Muthaura, Kenyatta and Ali* (ICC-01/09-02/11-T-10-ENG), Pre-Trial Chamber II, 28 September 2011, p. 27, ll. 14–19, p. 29, ll. 19-21.

81 Prosecution notification of withdrawal of the charges against Francis Kirimi Muthaura, *Prosecutor v Muthaura, Kenyatta and Ali* (ICC-01/09-02/11-687), Trial Chamber V(B), 11 March 2013; Notice of withdrawal of the charges against Uhuru Muigai Kenyatta, *Prosecutor v Muthaura, Kenyatta and Ali* (ICC-01/09-02/11-983), Trial Chamber V(B), 5 December 2014.

82 Public redacted version of the Prosecution request for protective measures and protections against self-incrimination for its first ten witnesses, *Prosecutor v Kenyatta* (ICC-01/09-02/11-823-Red2), Trial Chamber V(B), 11 October 2013; Public redacted version of the 16 July 2013 Prosecution notification of withdrawal of witnesses, *Prosecutor v Kenyatta* (ICC-01/09-02/11-773-Red), Trial Chamber V(B), 16 July 2013; Notification of the removal of a witness from the Prosecution's witness list and application for an adjournment of the provisional trial date, *Prosecutor v Kenyatta* (ICC-01/09-02/11-875), Trial Chamber V(B), 19 December 2013; Prosecution appeal against the 'Decision on Prosecution's application for a finding of non-compliance under Article 87(7) of the Statute, *Prosecutor v Kenyatta* (ICC-01/09-02/11-100), Trial Chamber V(B), 20 March 2015; Decision on Prosecution request to add P-548 and P-66 to its witness list, *Prosecutor v Kenyatta* (ICC-01/09-02/11-832), Trial Chamber V(B), 23 October 2013.

83 Decision on the Confirmation of Charges Pursuant to Article 61(7)(a) and (b) of the Rome Statute, *Prosecutor v. William Samoei Ruto and Joshua Arap Sang* (ICC-01/09-01/11-373), Pre-Trial Chamber II, 4 February 2012.

84 For Witness P-536 see Transcript, *Prosecutor v Ruto and Sang* (ICC-01/09-01/11-T-29-Red3-ENG), Trial Chamber V(A), 17 September 2013; Transcript, *Prosecutor v Ruto and Sang* (ICC-01/09-01/11-T-33-Red-ENG), Trial Chamber V(A), 24 September 2013; Transcript, *Prosecutor v Ruto and Sang* (ICC-01/09-01/11-T-34-Red2-ENG), Trial Chamber V(A), 20 September 2013. For testimony almost entirely in private session see Transcript, *Prosecutor v Ruto and Sang* (ICC-01/09-01/11-T-39-Red-ENG), Trial Chamber V(A), 2 October 2013, pp. 5–36, 38–56, 72–86, 87–94; Transcript, *Prosecutor v Ruto and Sang* (ICC-01/09-01/11-T-41-Red2-ENG), Trial Chamber V(A), 3 October 2013; Transcript, *Prosecutor v Ruto and Sang* (ICC-01/09-01/11-T-41-Red2-ENG), Trial Chamber V(A), 3 October 2013. For witness P-326, see Transcript, *Prosecutor v Ruto and Sang* (ICC-01/09-01/11-T-43-Red2-ENG), Trial Chamber V(A), 7 October; Transcript, *Prosecutor v Ruto and Sang* (ICC-01/09-01/11-T-44-Red2-ENG), Trial Chamber V(A), 8 October 2013,

However, the fact that several victims who testified as crime-based witnesses were bribed or intimidated and their names were revealed to third parties, shows that more effort should have been invested in protecting those individuals.[85]

As far as the right to a fair trial is concerned, the main issue was represented by the disclosure of victims' identities to the Defence teams.[86] However, the OTP did not disclose these identities in advance for security reasons, missing the effective deadline of 9 January 2013 fixed by the judges of Trial Chamber V(a). Despite this, the judges decided that the identities of the victims who were supposed to testify should have been disclosed on a rolling basis closer to the date of their testimony and, in order to mitigate any prejudice to the accused resulting from delayed disclosure, the OTP should have provided to the Defence summaries of witnesses' statements.[87] However, the Defence did not agree with the OTP's point of view, according to which the summaries would give the Defence team enough time to investigate the case, because the deadline of 9 January was missed.[88]

In truth, the concerns of Ruto's and Sang's Defence Teams can be justified in light of international human rights standards. Indeed, no violation could be envisaged in the process of disclosing evidence, since international human rights standards require that the prosecution must consult trial judges should they wish to withhold evidence in their possession. In this case, judges were consulted. Conversely, the principles of equality of arms and to have adequate time and facilities for the preparation of the defence was affected.[89] Although some scholars believe that the delayed disclosure of evidence is a 'necessary evil',[90] this forced the defence to work under more disadvantageous conditions than the other parties in the proceedings.[91]

Finally, in order to demonstrate that the Defence was bribing the victims called by the OTP as witnesses, the OTP relied on prior recorded testimonies, which

---

which was heavily redacted because in closed sessions pp. 29–46; Transcript, *Prosecutor v Ruto and Sang* (ICC-01/09-01/11-T-44-Red2-ENG), Trial Chamber V(A), 8 October 2013; Transcript, *Prosecutor v Ruto and Sang* (ICC-01/09-01/11-T-45-Red-ENG), Trial Chamber V(A), 9 October 2013; Transcript, *Prosecutor v Ruto and Sang*, ICC-01/09-01/11-T-46-Red-ENG, Trial Chamber V(A), 10 October 2013; Transcript, *Prosecutor v Ruto and Sang* (ICC-01/09-01/11-T-47-Red2-ENG), Trial Chamber V(A), 11 October 2013; Transcript, *Prosecutor v Ruto and Sang* (ICC-01/09-01/11-T-48-Red2-ENG), Trial Chamber V(A), 14 October 2013.

85 ICC, available at www.icc-cpi.int/Pages/item.aspx?name=pr941&ln=en accessed 29 March 2019.

86 For *William Samoei Ruto and Joshua Arap Sang* case see Transcript, *Prosecutor v Ruto and Sang* (ICC-01/09-01/11-T-19-ENG), Trial Chamber V(A), 14 February 2013, p. 8, ll. 1–25 and 9, ll. 1–2.

87 Ibid., p. 9, ll. 3–13, pp. 10–13.

88 Ibid., p. 9, ll. 17–25.

89 *Rowe v Davis*, (App no 28901/95), ECHR, 16 February 2000; *Jasper v UK*, (App no 27052/95), ECHR, 16 February 2000; *Fitt v UK*, (App 29777/96), ECHR, 16 February 2000.

90 Sangkul Kim, 'The Witness Protection Mechanism of Delayed Disclosure at the Ad Hoc International Criminal Tribunals', 1 *Journal of East Asia and International Law* (2016) 53, p. 87.

91 *Edwards and Lewis v UK*, (Apps nos 39647/98 and 40461/98), ECHR, 27 October 2004.

were deemed admissible by Trial Chamber V(a).[92] However, this decision highlights that the ICC did not strike the right balance between the obligation to protect witnesses' right to privacy and the opposed right of the accused to a fair and impartial trial for several reasons. First, Trial Chamber V(a) erred in defining 'prior recorded testimonies'. Indeed, the OTP requested that the Chamber admit unsworn 'formal statements made by any person who is questioned in connection with an investigation or with proceedings', as understood under Rule 111 and 112 of the ICC RPE. The judges considered that the unsworn formal statements could qualify as prior recorded testimonies and be admitted as evidence in line with the new Rule 68, which reads that the Trial Chamber may 'allow the introduction of previously recorded audio or video testimony of a witness, or the transcript or other documented evidence of such testimony, provided that this would not be prejudicial to or inconsistent with the rights of the accused'.[93] However, this chapter agrees with the Separate, Partly Concurring Opinion of Judge Eboe-Osuji on the 'Decision on Prosecution Request for Admission of Prior Recorded Testimony' (hereinafter 'Separate, Partly Concurring Opinion'), according to which 'testimony [is] as an oral or written statement under oath or affirmation.'[94]

Furthermore, Trial Chamber V(a) concluded that the interests of justice were served because these statements are necessary to understand whether any crime against the administration of justice has been committed on the accused person's behalf, and because the Defence was able to use cross examination.[95] While it is true that the ICC has the material jurisdiction to investigate any offences against justice under Article 70 of the Rome Statute, this chapter does not consider that the right to fair trial has been respected. This point was clearly highlighted, once again, by Judge Eboe-Osuji in his Separate, Partly Concurring Opinion, when he clarified that it is true that the witnesses were examined and cross-examined in court under an oath.[96] However, neither the OTP nor the Defence questioned the witnesses on the specific issues, which were of particular interest to the OTP and which were contained in the witnesses' out-of-court statements. For this reason, Judge Eboe-Osuji believes that

> only the evidence of these witnesses to the extent of those questions and answers (including questions and answers connected to documentary and

92 Decision on Prosecution Request for Admission of Prior Recorded Testimony, *Prosecutor v Ruto and Sang*, (ICC-01/09-01/11-1938-Red-Corr), Trial Chamber V(a), 19 August 2015.

93 Ibid., paras. 28–33.

94 Separate, Partly Concurring Opinion of Judge Eboe-Osuji on the Decision on Prosecution Request for Admission of Prior Recorded Testimony, *Prosecutor v Ruto and Sang*, (ICC-01/09-01/11-1938-Anx-Red), Trial Chamber V, 19 August 2015, para. 19.

95 *Prosecutor v Ruto and Sang*, (ICC-01/09-01/11-1938-Red-Corr), *supra* note 92, para. 57.

96 Public Redacted Version of Decision on Prosecution Request for Admission of Prior Recorded Testimony, *Prosecutor v Ruto and Sang*, (ICC-01/09-01/11-1938-Anx-Red), Trial Chamber V(a), 19 August 2019, para. 48.

other materials put to the witness while on the stand) may be considered for the truth of their content.[97]

Since Trial Chamber V(a) admitted this evidence without giving the Defence the possibility to cross-examine the witnesses on specific and relevant points, this chapter argues that in these circumstances the ICC infringed the right to a fair trial of Ruto and Sang.

Prosecutor v Ntaganda

The *Ntaganda* case dealt with some crimes committed in the Ituri region in the DRC and, for this reason, shared the same investigative background as the *Lubanga* and the *Katanga and Ngudiolo* cases. As with the preceding cases, it did not experience challenging situations in protecting victims who testified as witnesses, and successfully protected their privacy and balanced the different concurring interests at stake.

In order to preserve their privacy within the courtroom, Trial Chamber VI confirmed the same protective measures (pseudonym, facial and voice distortion) previously applied to 11 witnesses who testified at the *Lubanga* Trial.[98] More specifically, Trial Chamber VI was of the view that 'the in-court protective measures ordered by Trial Chamber I in relation to the Witnesses are directly applicable to the *Ntaganda* case'.[99] In addition to these measures, the majority of the victims who were called by the OTP as witnesses also testified in private or *ex parte* hearings.[100] Once again, the

97 Ibid., 48.

98 Decision on Prosecution request for in court protective measures, *Prosecutor v Bosco Ntaganda*, (ICC-01/04-02/06-774-Red), Trial Chamber VI, 10 August 2015.

99 Ibid., 4. Footnote omitted.

100 For example, for private hearings see Transcript, *Prosecutor v Ntaganda* (ICC-01/04-02/06-T-36-Red2-ENG), Trial Chamber VI, 22 October 2015, pp. 7–22, 24–51; Transcript, *Prosecutor v Ntaganda* (ICC-01/04-02/06-T-39-Red-ENG), Trial Chamber VI, 27 October 2015, pp. 3–12, 14–31, 35–40, 43–50, 66–88; Transcript, *Prosecutor v Ntaganda* (ICC-01/04-02/06-T-40-Red-ENG), Trial Chamber VI, 28 October 2015, pp. 13–32, 33–62, 68–80; Transcript, *Prosecutor v Ntaganda* (ICC-01/04-02/06-T-41-Red-ENG) Trial Chamber VI, 30 October 2015, pp. 3–9; 12–18; Transcript, *Prosecutor v Ntaganda* (ICC-01/04-02/06-T-43-Red-ENG), Trial Chamber VI, 30 October 2015, pp. 2–13; Transcript, *Prosecutor v Ntaganda* (ICC-01/04-02/06-T-44-Red-ENG), Trial Chamber VI, 3 November 2015, pp. 11–14, 23–6; Transcript, *Prosecutor v Ntaganda* (ICC-01/04-02/06-T-45-Red-ENG), Trial Chamber VI, 4 November 2015, pp. 26–36, 54–61; Transcript, *Prosecutor v Ntaganda*, ICC-01/04-02/06-T-46-Red-ENG, Trial Chamber VI, 10 November 2015, pp. 7–18, 44–9, 52–5; Transcript, *Prosecutor v Ntaganda* (ICC-01/04-02/06-T-53-Red-ENG), Trial Chamber VI, 18 January 2016, pp. 9–11; 14–20, 25–7, 33–5, 44–63; Transcript, *Prosecutor v Ntaganda* (ICC-01/04-02/06-T-54-Red-ENG), Trial Chamber VI, 19 January 2016, pp. 5–12, 19–21, 30–8, 43–5, 46–52, 64–8, 70–3; Transcript, *Prosecutor v Ntaganda*, ICC-01/04-02/06-T-54-Red-ENG), Trial Chamber VI, 19 January 2016, pp 2–6; Transcript, *Prosecutor v Ntaganda*, ICC-01/04-02/06-T-104-Red-ENG, Trial Chamber VI, 17 June 2016. For *ex parte*

widespread use of private hearings was heavily criticised by the Defence Team for Ntaganda, because no one outside the courtroom could understand the content of each testimony.[101]

Against this background, the few exceptions where protective measures were denied can be explained by a correct balancing exercise of Trial Chamber VI judges. For instance, the use of facial and voice distortion for Witness P-886 and Witness P-39 was denied.[102] In both examples, the judges believed that the objectively justifiable risk was missing. The lack of this element in conjunction with the uncertainty of the level of risk at the early stage of proceedings encouraged the judges that less stringent protective measures were needed.[103] Despite this, Witness P-886 decided to testify in the *Ntaganda* case without the use of these measures, while Witness P-39 refused to continue cooperating with the ICC.[104] While no particular challenges characterised the *Ntaganda* case, a different scenario can be envisaged in the *Gbagbo* case.

Prosecutor v Gbagbo

Gbagbo, the former president of Côte d'Ivoire, was indicted by the ICC for crimes against humanity committed after the presidential election between 28 November 2010 and 19 September 2012. As had happened in several other cases, protective measures such pseudonyms, voice and facial distortions and testified in closed or private hearings were granted.[105]

At a hearing on 5 February 2016 before Trial Chamber I, some witnesses were promised protective measures, such as face and voice distortion. During a closed session called by the Presiding Judge Cuno Tarfusser, the lead prosecutor Eric

---

hearing, see Transcript, *Prosecutor v Ntaganda* (ICC-01/04-02/06-T-42-Red-ENG), Trial Chamber VI, 30 October 2010.

101 W Wakabi, 'Q&A with Stéphane Bourgon, Lawyer Representing Bosco Ntaganda: Part II' (International Justice Monitor, 23 August 2016) available at www.ijmonitor.org/2016/08/qa-with-stephane-bourgon-lawyer-representing-bosco-ntaganda-part-ii/ accessed 29 March 2019.

102 For Witness P-39, see Decision on Prosecution's request for in-court protective measures for Witness P-0039, *Prosecutor v Ntaganda*, (ICC-01/04-02/06-956-Red), Trial Chamber VI, 28 October 2015. For witness P-886 see Transcript, *Prosecutor v Ntaganda* (ICC-01/04-02/06-T-36-Red2-ENG), Trial Chapter VI, 22 October 2015, p. 56, ll. 24–25; p. 57, ll. 1–8.

103 Ibid.

104 For Witness P-886 Transcript, *Prosecutor v Ntaganda* (ICC-01/04-02/06-T-36-Red2-ENG), Trial Chamber VI, 22 October 2015, p. 61, ll. 12–13. For Witness P-39, see Transcript, *Prosecutor v Ntaganda* (ICC-01/04-02/06-T-40-Red-ENG), Trial Chamber VI, 28 October 2015, p. 82 ll. 3–5.

105 For Witness P-547 see Transcript, *Prosecutor v Gbagbo and Blé Goudé* (ICC-02/11-01/15-T-15-Red2-ENG), Trial Chamber I, 5 February 2016; Transcript, *Prosecutor v Gbagbo and Blé Goudé* (ICC-02/11-01/15-T-18-Red2-ENG), Trial Chamber I, 8 February 2016; Transcript, *Prosecutor v Gbagbo and Blé Goudé* (ICC-02/11-01/15-T-19-Red-ENG), Trial Chamber I, 9 February 2016.

MacDonald, listed the names of some protected witnesses. However, due to an error made by the Registry, who are responsible for the non-judicial aspects of the administration and servicing of the ICC, the microphones were still on.[106] Thus, the public present in the ICC public gallery heard witnesses' names. A transcript of the hearing is not currently available but, following the incident, a clip of the hearing with the names of the protected witnesses circulated on YouTube.[107]

Presiding Judge Tarfusser described the accident as being 'of (the) utmost gravity', saying that:

> because what happened is really incredible, and in order to find out exactly what happened and who is responsible for what and how is the situation is now, we have to – we're making a closed session just ex parte, Prosecutor and Registry only, in order just to find out and to find out what is also the security issues which have to be put in place or whatever, we will hear.[108]

Ultimately, the judges of Trial Chamber I had to take extreme measures to protect witnesses' identities in the case. The measures adopted at trial did not reach the desired effect however, as speculations over witnesses' identities on the internet became very serious. Unfortunately, the speculations did not cease and, after having threatened the parties with holding the proceedings *in camera*, on 9 June 2016, the judges of Trial Chamber I decided to introduce prior recorded testimonies for 28 crime-based witnesses and 11 insider witnesses.[109] Although Trial Chamber I was publicly challenged on the impact of this decision on the right to a fair and impartial trial, the judges considered 'that introduction of prior recorded testimony under Rule 68(3) of the Rules typically carries a lower risk of interfering with the fair trial rights of the accused, because the witness still appears before the Chamber and is available for examination, including by the Defence'.[110] Thus, the restrictions on the right to a fair trial were not justified since the judges correctly concluded that sufficient safeguards were established.

106 Art. 43(1), Rome Statute.

107 See the comments to the video on YouTube available at www.youtube.com/watch?v=Bzo_RZH093s accessed 12 February 2016. AFP, 'ICC to probe 'outing' of secret witnesses in Gbagbo case' (*Daily Mail*, 6 February 2016) available at www.dailymail.co.uk/wires/afp/article-3434827/ICC-probe-outing-secret-witnesses-Gbagbo-case.html accessed 29 March 2019.

108 Transcript, *Prosecutor v Gbagbo and Blé Goudé*, (ICC-02/11-01/15-T-16-ENG), Trial Chamber I, 8 February 2016, pp. 1, ll 19–23.

109 Lesser public redacted version of "Public redacted version of Prosecution's consolidated application to conditionally admit the prior recorded statements and related documents of various witnesses under rule 68 and Prosecution's application for the introduction of documentary evidence under paragraph 43 of the directions on the conduct of proceedings relating to the evidence of Witnesses P-0087 and P-0088", *Prosecutor v Gbagbo and Blé Goudé*, (ICC-02/11-01/15-829-Red2), Trial Chamber I, 8 June 2017.

110 Ibid., para. 18; Decision on the Prosecutor's application to introduce prior recorded testimony under Rules 68(2)(b) and 68(3), *Prosecutor v Gbagbo and Blé Goudé*, (ICC-02/11-01/15-573-Red), Trial Chamber I, 9 June 2016, para. 24; Judgment on the

Findings and recommendations

This analysis of the ICC's case-law has revealed that the information on which judges rely to decide whether to grant protective measures is confidential given the sensitive nature of the rights at stake. Recognising that confidentiality in this matter is necessary, this chapter recommends that the ICC should be as transparent as possible in sharing information on protective measures in full respect of the rights of victims who testified as witnesses. This would guarantee an independent evaluation of the protection system, which can lead to its enhancement.

Furthermore, the analysis has showed that, although the ICC has an appropriate legal system to protect the privacy of the victims who testify within its courtroom, some confidential information was revealed to the public and the media. This chapter urges parties to check in advance for any possible risks to victims' privacy in order to choose the correct measures in advance and avoid expunging *ex post* any confidential information from the public transcripts. In order to prevent other macroscopic mistakes, as occurred in the *Gbagbo* case where the Registry did not switch off the microphone, some internal rules should be changed. Following this incident, it is unclear whether a new procedure to check that protective measures are correctly applied in court has been established, although the ICC launched an internal investigation to identify those responsible.

In addition, the ICC should improve its compliance concerning respect for the defendants' right to a fair, impartial and public trial, while applying judicial protective measures which safeguard witnesses' privacy. International human right standards establish that the handicap under which the defence works should be compensated with sufficient guarantees. Since all the victims who testified in person or via video-link before the ICC judges have been cross-examined, it is easy to conclude that the ICC judges have struck the right balance between the opposing rights at stake. However, some concerns still remain. For instance, the widespread and, in some cases, disproportionate use of closed and/or private sessions has the potential to undermine both the defendants' right to a public trial and the very same principle under which protective measures were created: their exceptional nature. Although the ICC alternates open sessions with closed or private sessions, and periodically reclassifies the transcripts and the decisions as public, it has been very difficult for the public and the media to follow what is happening, for instance, in the *Bemba* and Kenyan cases.

Also, the analysis of the ICC's practice in the Kenyan cases highlighted that identities of some victims who were supposed to testify were kept confidential during the confirmation of charges hearing, but were later disclosed to the other parties during the actual trial. If this way of proceeding was justified by the incredible difficulties the OTP was encountering at the time, due to several

appeals of Mr Laurent Gbagbo and Mr Charles Blé Goudé against the decision of Trial Chamber I of 9 June 2016 entitled "Decision on the Prosecutor's application to introduce prior recorded testimony under Rules 68(2)(b) and 68(3), *Prosecutor v Gbagbo and Blé Goudé,* (ICC-02/11-01/15-744), Trial Chamber I, 1 November 2016, para. 28.

victims being bribed, intimidated or even killed, it also impaired the right of the defendants to equality of arms and to have adequate time and facilities to prepare their defence.

In this regard, the ICC could solve this problem using some alternatives to testimony, such as documentary forensic or digital evidence. The International Bar Association, in a report entitled 'Witnesses before the International Criminal Court', proposed such changes to ICC practice and launched an app called eye-Witness.[111] Such an option has a positive impact on witnesses' rights, as it would solve the problem at its roots: victims would not be involved as witnesses in ICC proceedings and their rights would not be put at risk.

Also, the OTP released a Strategic Plan for 2016-2018, which lists among its strategic goals that of prioritising alternative forms of evidence, or preferring to use victims as witnesses with a low-risk profile.[112] From this perspective, it should be noted that the ICC has lately been relying on digital evidence, defined as 'data [. . .] that is created, manipulated, stored or communicated by any device, computer or computer system or transmitted over a communication system, that is relevant to the proceedings', in some of its recent cases.[113] For instance, in the *Al -Mahdi* case, after the confirmation of charges, the accused pled guilty and admitted to being responsible for the war crime of destroying ten of Timbuktu's mausoleums and mosques between June and July 2012.[114] More specifically, in order to corroborate the plea of guilty pursuant to Article 65(1)(c) of the Rome Statute, the OTP used only 3 witnesses, together with a significant amount of digital evidence. The OTP clarified that:

> [i]n view of the guilty plea entered, the public must understand, therefore, today that the Prosecution does not intend to deal with each of the 700 pieces of evidence that have been filed before the Court, we will deal only with specific aspects; namely, starting with an interactive platform, the Prosecution will use satellite images, photographs, videos and other material gleaned from the Internet which are included on the list of our evidence material to show the situation of the mausoleums before, during and after the destruction, including the participation of the accused.[115]

In addition to these sources, the OTP used open source evidence, such as Google Earth satellite images, to demonstrate the status of the buildings before,

111 International Bar Association, 'Report on Witness before the International Criminal Court', July 2013, pp. 8, 18, 36. See Eye Witness Project available at www.eyewitnessproject.org/ accessed 29 March 2019.

112 Office of the Prosecutor, Strategic Plan, 6 July 2015.

113 Stephen Mason, *International Electronic Evidence* (British Institute of International and Comparative Law, 2008), xxxv.

114 Judgment and Sentence, *Prosecutor v Al Mahdi,* (ICC-01/12-01/15-171), Trial Chamber VIII, 27 September 2016.

115 Transcript, *Prosecutor v Al Mahdi,* (ICC-01/12-01/15-T-4-Red-ENG), Trial Chamber VIII, 22 August 2016, p. 41 ll. 4–10.

during and after the attacks; videos taken from YouTube where the accused and his soldiers were shown destroying religious buildings; and videos of Timbuktu residents uploaded on public websites.[116]

Similarly, in *Bemba et al*, in order to prove that Bemba and his affiliates bribed some witnesses, the OTP relied on alternative types of evidence, such as some Western Union documents (obtained by the Austrian authorities) indicating money transfers between Bemba and some witnesses. Additionally, the OTP used telephone communications, including data records on the use of telephones by the accused, and some digital audio-recordings of communications between the parties.

Following this trend, in the *Al-Werfalli* case, the OTP mainly relied on open-source evidence.[117] It presented seven videos of executions published on Facebook and other social media websites, which resulted in an arrest warrant being issued for Al-Werfalli, a commander within the Al-Saiqa Brigade, who allegedly ordered 33 murders in the area of Benghazi.[118]

Some authors, such as Freeman, argue that the use of digital evidence in the above-mentioned cases does not constitute an 'anomal[y] or temporary deviation [. . .] but rather the first in a growing trend'.[119] Similarly, this chapter recognises the necessity of integrating witness testimony with digital data, but it is more cautious than Freeman.

The use of digital evidence is deeply linked to the typology of facts that must be proven during the trial. For instance, in the *Al-Mahdi* case, it was necessary to prove the destruction of certain religious buildings in the area of Timbuktu. Proving the existence of these buildings and their consequent destructions through the use of Google Earth images might be a good example if the OTP wants to have access to satellite imagery to demonstrate the burning and destruction of villages and the movement of populations. However, the *Bemba* case cannot be considered as a good example, because the accused was in the ICC's detention facilities and certain a type of evidence was readily available to the investigation team. Furthermore, this case was closer to a national public corruption type of case rather than an investigation into war crimes.[120] In addition to this, it has to be noted that in both the *Al Werfalli* and the *Al-Mahdi* cases, the indicted persons were the direct perpetrators of the alleged crimes. Digital evidence has not been yet used by the OTP to demonstrate the existence of a chain of command, and it remains to be seen whether these different types of evidence are economically sustainable.

116 *Prosecutor v Al Mahdi*, (ICC-01/12-01/15-171), *supra* note 114, ft 79–89.

117 Public Warrant of Arrest, *Prosecutor v Al-Werfalli,* (ICC-01-11-01/17-2), Trial Chamber VIII, 15 August 2017.

118 Ibid.

119 Lindsay Freeman, 'Digital Evidence and War Crimes Prosecutions: The Impact of Digital Technologies on International Criminal Investigations and Trials', 41 *Fordham International Law Journal* (2018) 283, p. 333.

120 Ibid., p. 322.

In conclusion, the ICC should continue its work in granting measures to protect witnesses' privacy while balancing, on a case-by-case basis, the defendants' conflicting right to a fair, impartial and public trial, in line with the obligation contained in Article 68 of the Rome Statute.

Conclusion

While this book took inspiration from the idea that the ICC should ensure victims' rights and balance them with the defendants' rights, in the current legal debate, little attention has been given to victims' rights when they testify as witnesses before the ICC. For this reason, this chapter specifically focused on the measures implemented by the ICC to safeguard victims' right to privacy when they testify. This obligation, which stems from Article 68 of the Rome Statute, shall not be prejudicial to, or inconsistent with, the rights of the accused and a fair and impartial trial.

This chapter has demonstrated that the ICC's practice in granting protective measures is generally consistent with the right to privacy of victims who decide to testify as witnesses before the ICC. Thus, the ICC should continue its good work in granting protective measures on a case-by-case basis when this is justified by the necessity of protecting victims' privacy. Furthermore, although the ICC has an appropriate legal system to protect and safeguard the privacy of victims and witnesses in its courtrooms, some confidential information was revealed to the public and media in the *Lubanga* and *Gbagbo* cases. Following the latter incident, it is unclear whether a new procedure that ensures that protective measures are correctly applied in court has been established. Although the ICC has since launched an internal investigation, at the time of the incident, it was not using all appropriate and reasonable means to protect the rights of those involved in the proceedings.

This chapter has also suggested that the ICC should be as transparent as possible in sharing information on protective measures, since the analysis of protective measures depended on publicly available case-law and transcripts. Many relevant documents which discuss sensitive topic are confidential and not accessible for further assessment. For instance, the circumstances and reasons which determine the decision as to whether to grant protective measures are always expunged.

In addition, the ICC should improve its compliance with respecting the defendant's right to a fair, impartial and public trial while applying judicial protective measures, because the sum of all protective measures can create a substantial disadvantage for the Defence. In light of international human rights standards, which establish that the handicap under which the Defence works should be compensated with sufficient guarantees, this chapter highlighted some concerns about the wide-spread use of closed and/or private sessions. Furthermore, it stressed that this practice contravenes the same nature of protective measures as exceptional measures, which should not be used routinely. Rather, the ICC should continue to alternate open sessions with closed or private sessions and to periodically reclassify the transcripts and the decisions as open. Furthermore, the

ICC should limit, when possible, the use of closed or private sessions. Finally, following several cases of witness tampering, witnesses' identities were kept confidential during the confirmation of charges hearing, before being disclosed to the other parties during the actual trial, impairing the rights of defendants to have adequate time and facilities to prepare their defence. In future, the ICC should carefully balance the necessity of protecting victims who testify before the ICC, with ensuring that the defence is provided with enough time to read the relevant material and adequately prepare.

Finally, this chapter recommends that the ICC pursue additional forms of evidence, such as written statements and new electronic evidence. In addition to forensic evidence, for instance, the ICC could temper witness testimonies with new digital and video technologies, cyber investigations, satellite imaging or remote sensing. The ICC has heavily relied on live testimony, because this is necessary to assess witnesses' reliability and to preserve the defendant's right to a fair trial. Using alternative forms of evidence and, more specifically, digital evidence, as in the recent cases of *Prosecutor v Bemba et al.*, *Prosecutor v Al Mahdi* and *Prosecutor v Al-Werfalli,* would relieve victims from the burden of testifying, while allowing the prosecutor to base her cases on reliable evidence.

11 The legal effect of a reparations order and the rights of those persons subject to it[1]

Anthony Abato

Reparations in the *Bemba* case: Act one

It was not long before the mix of elation and disappointment in the room would turn into a fog of confusion. In front of a public gallery, Jean-Pierre Bemba's conviction had been reversed by the Appeals Chamber of the International Criminal Court (ICC). As a result of the decision, Mr Bemba could be assured that the joint sentence of 18 years imprisonment would certainly be overturned. But how would his acquittal impact his liability for reparations to victims? Are reparations even permitted under the circumstances? In search of an answer, Trial Chamber III, seized of the reparations phase, invited written submissions from the parties and participants in the case.[2]

Perhaps the call for submissions was inspired by the looming presence of an unprecedented number of participating victims. More than 5,000 victims took part in the criminal trial, one of whom was Jane Doe.[3] During the attacks of 2003, she was at home with her two sisters in a city in the Central African Republic (CAR). She and her family fled their home during the attacks, and when they returned home, several days later, they were arrested by Mr Bemba's soldiers. Her sisters were kidnapped and taken to the base of the *Mouvement de Libération du Congo* (MLC) where they were forced to cook and were raped by the soldiers. Jane Doe remained in her home where she was also forced to cook and was raped three times by an armed man. Before leaving her home, the soldiers set her house on fire. During the following years, her sisters died from HIV infections. In her application for participation, Jane Doe indicated that several members of the group carried out the vicious attacks, and that Ange-Félix Patassé and Jean-Pierre Bemba were also responsible.[4]

1 The views expressed in this essay are the author's own.

2 Order inviting submissions following the Appeals Decision, *Prosecutor v Jean-Pierre Bemba Gombo*, (ICC-01/04-01/07-3639) Trial Chamber III, 13 June 2018.

3 A pseudonym is used for reasons of confidentiality.

4 Corrigendum to Annex A of the Decision on the participation of victims in the trial and on 86 applications by victims to participate in the proceedings, *Prosecutor v Jean-Pierre Bemba Gombo*, (ICC-01/05-01/08-807-Anx-Corr-Red), Trial Chamber III, 11 July 2013, pp. 93–4.

Like Jane Doe, many other victims named Mr Bemba as the person responsible for the harm they endured in the attacks which took place from 26 October 2002 up to 15 March 2003. Many victims also named Ange-Félix Patassé, who gave orders for Mr Bemba's soldiers to intervene in the CAR. Some victims complained of attacks that may have been instigated by groups other than the MLC.[5] And some complained of attacks not included in the charges against Mr Bemba.[6] In seeking compensation on behalf of victims, the victims' legal representative argued that it is essential that reparations not be perceived by victims as a donation, but rather as a right that is recognised by virtue of the harm they suffered.[7] According to the legal representative, all of the victims preferred individual monetary compensation over other forms of reparations.

Trial Chamber III's call for submissions was intriguing. There was no doubt, even in spite of the acquittal, that mortifying crimes took place under Mr Bemba's watch during the period in question.[8] Certainly, as a matter of negligence in private law, Mr Bemba would be responsible for the harm as a tort (*responsabilité délictuelle*). For that matter, Mr Patassé would likely also be responsible. Does this offer victims a second chance to obtain justice? Or is their 'right' to reparations, as alleged, contingent upon criminal responsibility?

This chapter builds upon the theme of this book by looking at reparations in international criminal law from two perspectives: that of the victims and that of the convicted person. Through four ICC cases[9] and several courses of pleadings, it has now become clear that victims have high expectations and their expectations are premised upon rights that are sometimes difficult to pinpoint. The question raised by Trial Chamber III in the *Bemba* case is but one example among many wherein legal representatives for victims and the convicted person appear to fundamentally disagree as to the rights and obligations of participants in a reparations proceeding. This chapter will explore the expectations of participants as to the outcome of a reparations proceeding, and it will present an important discussion about ensuring and balancing the rights of those persons subject to a reparations order.

The right to reparations in context

The confusion in the *Bemba* case is symptomatic of a larger issue. In the course of the determination of a person's rights, that person will invariably have expectations

5 Ibid., pp. 15–16.

6 Ibid., p. 12.

7 Observations de la Représentante légale des victimes relativement aux réparations, *Prosecutor v Jean-Pierre Bemba Gombo*, (ICC-01/05-01/08-3459-Red), Legal Representative of Victims, 25 November 2016, para. 121.

8 See the references to crimes in footnote 15 of: Final decision on the reparations proceedings, *Prosecutor v Jean-Pierre Bemba Gombo*, (ICC-01/05-01/08-3653), Trial Chamber III, 3 August 2018.

9 *Prosecutor v Jean-Pierre Bemba Gombo, Prosecutor v Thomas Lubanga Dyilo, Prosecutor v Germain Katanga, Prosecutor v Ahmad Al Faqi Al Mahdi.*

as to the scope of their rights. Such a person would expect that their claim will be heard and that the procedure for determination of their claim will be fair, as would his or her opponent. But beyond that, both parties may disagree as to each and every step taken along the way on account of what they perceive as 'fair' or 'unfair'. In a reparations proceeding following a conviction under international criminal law, an applicant for reparations will have a different set of expectations as to what is fair and what is unfair depending upon whether the applicant is a party to, or simply a participant in, the proceedings. It is this contrast that exists between the rights of a party and those of a participant that must be explored in order to address what lies at the heart of the question raised by Trial Chamber III in the *Bemba* case.

The labels 'party' and 'participant' are separated by more than just semantics. They carry significant meaning for victims. In domestic courts, a victim is a 'party' to a proceeding in pursuing compensation for a violation of his or her rights. As a party, the victim may initiate an action in which harm is assessed and compensation is awarded on an individualised basis. As a party, the victim may avail himself or herself of protective measures, and after a judgment is rendered, he or she may initiate the execution of a judgment in his or her own name. Finally, as a party, the victim may appeal the award in his or her own right to be reviewed by at least one judicial body on errors of either law, fact, or both.

By contrast, a participant has a passive role in legal proceedings. He or she does not participate as of right, but rather by prescription. Examples of participants are witnesses in criminal trials. And while reasonable people may quibble over the precise contours of 'party' and 'participant', one fundamental difference persists: while a party benefits from the requirements of due process in the determination of his or her rights, a participant does not.

In the context of an international crime, a victim will invariably endure a violation of his or her rights – whether they are rights of a personal, economic or material nature – which gives rise to a 'civil claim' in domestic law.[10] The pursuit of such a claim has widely attracted the protection of due process guarantees in the laws of States. Where the procedural rights in domestic law fall short, a victim also enjoys a measure of due process as a matter of international human rights law.[11]

Due process in the pursuit of a claim in this sense gives meaning to every stage of the proceeding. Victims can expect to enjoy equality of arms in the sense that they will have every reasonable opportunity to present their case under

10 Liesbeth Zegveld, 'Victims' Reparations Claims and International Criminal Courts', 8 *Journal of International Criminal Justice* (2010) 79, pp. 85–6.

11 Art. 6, Convention for the Protection of Human Rights and Fundamental Freedoms (European Convention on Human Rights, as amended) (ECHR); Art .7(1), African Charter on Human and Peoples' Rights (adopted 27 June 1981, entered into force 21 October 1986) (1982) 21 ILM 58 (African Charter); Art. 14(2), International Covenant on Civil and Political Rights (adopted 16 December 1966, entered into force 23 March 1976) 999 UNTS 171 (ICCPR).

conditions that do not place them at a substantial disadvantage vis-à-vis the opponent.[12] This also includes the principle that proceedings should be adversarial, meaning that, 'within the context of proceedings on a civil right to which persons belonging to that circle are a party, those persons must as a rule be guaranteed free access to the observations of the other participants in these proceedings and a genuine opportunity to comment on those observations'.[13] A separate, but closely related, right of parties in the pursuit of a civil claim is access to justice.[14] Framed as an obligation of States, victims must possess the right to bring a claim before an appropriate tribunal and have it adjudicated.[15] Both of these fundamental procedural rights presuppose that there is an underlying substantive 'right' at issue.[16]

Many jurisdictions allow victims to pursue civil claims as parties in criminal proceedings. The *action civile* present in the criminal procedure of many States following the Romano-Germanic tradition, allows victims to 'constitute' themselves as parties and to initiate an investigation. *Parties civiles* may also lead evidence during the trial and appeal a final decision in the event of an acquittal.[17] Where a person joins a criminal proceeding as a *partie civile* in order to obtain a remedy, the European Court of Human Rights has found that this aspect of the proceeding gives rise to a right to compensation.[18] If the claim is successful, *parties civiles* may obtain compensation or restitution assessed on an individual basis.

On the other hand, many jurisdictions do not allow such claims in the course of criminal proceedings. States following the common law tradition discharge the duty under human rights law to provide rules to protect victims' rights by maintaining a national tort system.[19] While victims enjoy the full spectrum of rights as parties in civil proceedings, they are mere participants in criminal trials as witnesses or interlocutors. They do not enjoy a right to compensation or restitution in criminal trials. Many common law jurisdictions have recognised that there exists a gap between public prosecutions, wherein there is no access to reparations; and private lawsuits, wherein remedies may be difficult to access for want of resources and expertise. To bridge this gap, the last few decades have brought a rise in awards of

12 Dinah Shelton, *Remedies in International Human Rights Law* (Oxford University Press, 2015), p. 105.

13 European Court of Human Rights (ECtHR), Judgment, *Ruiz Mateos v Spain* (App no 12952/87), 23 June 1993, paras 15, 61, 63, 65.

14 Art 2(3), ICCPR; Art. 25, African Charter; Art. 13, ECHR.

15 Shelton, *supra* note 12, p. 96.

16 UN Human Rights Committee (HRC), 'General Comment 32, Article 14, Right to equality before courts and tribunals and to fair trial, Right to equality', 23 August 2007, CCPR/C/GC/32; Judgment, *James and others v The United Kingdom* (ECtHR, App no 8793/79), 21 February 1986, para. 81.

17 eg Christine Van den Wyngaert, 'Belgium' in Desmond Greer (ed.), *Compensating Crime Victims: A European Survey* (Freiburg im Breisgau, 1996), pp. 69–72.

18 Judgment, *Perez v France*, (ECtHR, App no 47287/99), 12 February 2004, paras 70-71; Judgment, *Gorou v Greece*, (ECtHR, App no 9747/94), 11 January 2007, paras 25–6.

19 Cees van Dam, *European Tort Law* (Oxford University Press, 2013), pp. 24–5.

State compensation following criminal convictions.[20] State-funded compensation is available to some degree in civil law jurisdictions as well.[21]

The practice varies among States, but State-funded compensation is typically seen as an administrative matter. The State itself becomes a party in the assessment of compensation, and the procedure is not necessarily dependent upon the application of a victim.[22] The victim has no right to request the freezing of assets, and after compensation is awarded the victim has no right to enforce its execution. Practices also vary as to whether 'compensation' is assessed in the same way as civil damage awards, or whether there are other considerations that inform the calculation of the award. For example, in the USA, 'pain and suffering' damages are not included in State-funded compensation.[23]

The victim's interest in the criminal trial has received increasing emphasis in many States, which has led to an increase in special legislation for the protection of victims of crime.[24] However, there remain fundamental concerns that have stood in the way of full adoption of the *action civile* model across the globe. Some argue that including a civil claim in a criminal trial complicates the task of a judge, who in one and the same case must consider what may be conflicting interests – those of society and those of the victim. This can in turn lead to a distortion of the criminal trial,[25] which may adversely affect the rights of the accused person.[26] For this reason, among others, Kilchling reports that the mechanism for civil actions in criminal proceedings in Germany (*adhäsionsverfahren*) is rarely used.[27] Zegveld observes that, in her experience, there is a general preference in domestic criminal law to refer victims' claims to civil courts. She finds that 'national judges have been hesitant or even outright reluctant to examine complex civil law matters related to victims' claims'.[28]

This concern is magnified in prosecutions of mass crimes,[29] and practice has demonstrated that the civil action model can be awkward in such situations.

20 Council of Europe, European Convention on the Compensation of Victims of Violent Crimes (European Treaty Series No 116, 1983)

21 Van den Wyngaert, *supra* note 17, paras. 76–84; François Lombard, 'France' in Desmond Greer (ed.), *Compensating Crime Victims: A European Survey* (Freiburg im Breisgau, 1996), pp. 227–39.

22 Lucia Zedner, 'England' in Albin Eser and Susanne Walther (Hrsg), *Reparation in Criminal Law: International Perspectives*, volume 1 (Max-Planck-Institut, 1996), pp. 170–1.

23 Emily Silverman, 'United States' in Albin Eser and Susanne Walther (Hrsg), *Reparation in Criminal Law: International Perspectives*, volume 2 (Max-Planck-Institut, 1996), pp. 66–8.

24 Desmond Greer, 'Concluding Observations' in Desmond Greer (ed.), *Compensating Crime Victims: A European Survey* (Freiburg im Breisgau 1996), p. 690; Stefan Trechsel, *Human Rights in Criminal Proceedings* (Oxford University Press, 2006), p. 38.

25 Lombard, *supra* note 21, p. 215; Greer, *supra* note 24, p. 693.

26 Salvatore Zappalà, 'The Rights of Victims v. the Rights of the Accused', 8 *Journal of International Criminal Justice* (2010) 137, p. 143.

27 Michael Kaiser and Michael Kilchling, 'Germany' in Desmond Greer (ed.), *Compensating Crime Victims: A European Survey* (Freiburg im Breisgau, 1996), p. 266.

28 Zegveld, *supra* note 10, p. 93.

29 Anne-Marie de Brouwer and Mikaela Heikkilä, 'Victim Issues: Participation, Protection, Reparation, and Assistance' in Göran Sluiter et al. (eds), *International Criminal Procedure: Principles and Rules* (Oxford University Press, 2013), pp. 1339–41.

There are few examples of civil claims in domestic proceedings arising from mass crimes that have been determined in a way perceived as fair and expeditious. Tort claims in the United States following mass crimes require protracted and costly litigation to overcome numerous legal hurdles, such as class certification and enforcement.[30] Rwanda's *gacaca* system of adjudication, created in response to the 1994 genocide, has had difficulty providing fair trials to the parties.[31]

Thus, at present, the precise contours of a victim's role in the criminal trial are by no means settled. As a matter of State practice, common law jurisdictions have not embraced the role of victims as parties in criminal proceedings, and even among civil law jurisdictions the spectrum of rights and obligations of *parties civiles* is nuanced and far from standardised.[32] International human rights law has accorded certain participatory rights to victims, such as access to the dossier during a criminal investigation.[33] But beyond the most basic rights regarding notice and participation in sentencing, there is still great variation among jurisdictions.[34] For instance, there is no generally recognised right of victims to pursue compensation against an individual, whether the accused person or an accomplice, in criminal proceedings. Neither is there a general right of victims to a fair trial in criminal law. Rather, as part of the broader obligation to provide access to justice, States enjoy discretion as to the appropriate judicial (or quasi-judicial) mechanism for the determination of individual claims for compensation. In the context of gross and systemic violations of human rights, it is not impermissible (nor uncommon) for States to process mass claims through administrative programs or special, non-criminal tribunals.[35]

In parallel with victims' rights movements in domestic law, victims' advocates have also been successful in the last few decades in developing and giving meaning to the right to reparations in international law. Different from the civil injustices actionable under domestic law, which are usually disputes among

30 Beth Van Schaack, 'Unfulfilled Promise: The Human Rights Class Action' (2003) *University of Chicago Legal Forum* 279, pp. 288, 291.

31 Lars Waldorf, 'Goats & Graves: Reparations in Rwanda's Community Courts' in Carla Ferstman, et al. (eds), *Reparations for Victims of Genocide, War Crimes and Crimes Against Humanity* (Brill Nijhoff, 2009), p. 519. In response to the claims against more than 500,000 individuals accused of murder following the massacre of the Rwandan Tutsi minority in 1994, thus overwhelming the conventional court system, the government established community criminal courts, or *gacaca*. The *gacaca* courts were empowered to award restitution, and victims could become parties in the trials. In his observation of *gacaca* trials, Waldorf reports that participation of victims was lower than expected, and the trials were seen to be one-sided, falling short of international fair trial standards.

32 Juan-Pablo Pérez-León-Acevedo, *Victims' Status at International and Hybrid Criminal Courts* (Åbo Akademi University Press, 2014), p. 59; cf. Recommendation No. R (85) 11 on the position of the victim in the framework of criminal law and procedure, adopted by the Committee of Ministers on 28 June 1985.

33 Ibid., pp. 41–3.

34 De Brouwer and Heikkilä, *supra* note 29, pp. 1339, 1372.

35 Shelton, *supra* note 12, p. 96.

private persons, the right to reparations arises in response to gross or systemic violations of international human rights and the laws of armed conflict.[36] Under human rights treaties, States must provide effective remedies for human rights violations, which include investigations into criminal acts. Furthermore, the UN General Assembly's Basic Principles and Guidelines on the Right to a Remedy and Reparation for Victims of Gross Violations of International Human Rights Law and Serious Violations of International Humanitarian Law (2005) encourage States to provide access to justice against individual perpetrators of gross and systemic human rights and humanitarian law violations. But although this represents an important step for access to justice, human rights treaties and soft law instruments do not stipulate that States must provide mechanisms for victims to claim reparations against individuals or that reparations must be available through criminal courts.[37] Rather, the responsibility to provide reparations has fallen solely upon States.[38]

What does this mean for victims' expectations for the criminal trial? There is no doubt that the right to pursue a civil claim as a party is protected by human rights law. But the question as to whether a victim of crime may have access to the criminal trial to pursue such a claim will depend entirely upon where the wrongful act occurred. In the conventional world of criminal law, administered by each State in accordance with its long-standing legal traditions, it was a relatively simple matter for victims to determine, on their own or through legal counsel, which venue would be appropriate to hear a claim, and what his or her rights would be there. This rather pedestrian level of certainty has all but disappeared with the advent of international criminal trials.

36 Christine Evans, *The Right to Reparation in International Law for Victims of Armed Conflict* (Cambridge University Press, 2012), pp. 42–3.

37 De Brouwer and Heikkilä, *supra* note 29, p. 1349; *Basic Principles and Guidelines on the Right to a Remedy and Reparation for Victims of Gross Violations of International Human Rights Law and Serious Violations of International Humanitarian Law*, 19 April 2005, E/CN.4/2005/L.10/Add.11, adopted and proclaimed by General Assembly resolution 60/147 of 16 December 2005, principle 15.

38 This is true for several reasons. First, the right to reparations often arises in a transitioning State wherein the courts have collapsed or cannot provide access for victims (Jared Watkins, 'The Right to Reparations in International Human Rights Law and the Case of Bahrain' 34 *Brook Journal of International Law*, (2009) 559, 570–3). Second, the decision to mobilise public resources involves discretion of the executive and law makers involving political considerations and matters of social policy (Birte Timm, 'The Legal Position of Victims in the Rules of Procedure and Evidence' in Horst Fischer et al. (eds), *International and National Prosecution of Crimes Under International Humanitarian Law* (BWV Berliner Wissenschafts-Verlag, 2004), p. 303, observing that the UN Basic Principles deal with State responsibility and they refer to many restorative measures which can only be taken by the State and will be outside the power of an individual convicted person). Finally, as a conceptual matter, States are responsible for protecting individuals from such violations, and States therefore have the obligation to provide adequate remedies (Arturo Carrillo, 'Justice in Context: the Relevance of Inter-American Human Rights Law and Practice to Repairing the Past' in Pablo DeGreiff (ed.), *The Handbook of Reparations* (Oxford University Press, 2006), p. 511).

The legal effect of a reparations order and the rights of victims

Consensus was in the air in Rome in the summer of 1998. By all accounts, the notion of meaningful participatory rights for victims enjoyed broad support during the drafting of the Statute of the International Criminal Court. The exclusionary, retribution-focused models of the former International Military Tribunals following World War II, and of the United Nations' ad hoc tribunals of the 1990s, seemed like vestiges of the past.[39] The new approach at the ICC would be restorative, and victim-friendly. Since that summer in Rome, several new hybrid tribunals have been created, all of which place greater focus on victim participation and reparations.[40]

The judge presiding over a modern international or hybrid criminal trial will sometimes look to human rights principles for interpretation when grappling with difficult issues involving victims' rights.[41] However, human rights law has only limited import. The point has been argued in this chapter that the right of access to justice does not provide a general right to reparations in domestic criminal courts. It follows that victims cannot rely on any established body of law or general practice among States that would give rise to a right to reparations before international criminal courts and tribunals.[42] Furthermore, victims' right to reparations as interpreted in human rights jurisprudence has developed in the context of State responsibility. Often the procedures taken are rather broad and ill-suited for criminal proceedings.[43]

Thus, the victims' 'bill of rights', so to speak, in a reparations proceeding is left for statutory interpretation – it has no normative content. Such an interpretation is not too difficult in the circumstances of the Extraordinary Chambers in the Courts of Cambodia (ECCC). The participation regime in the Internal Rules of the ECCC is based upon the *action civile* known in civil law jurisdictions. Victims may 'constitute' themselves as parties and make claims for reparations. Similarly, the Extraordinary African Chambers[44] (EAC) derived its participatory regime from Senegalese law and provided for *actions civiles* and reparations in the form of monetary compensation. However, despite the fact that victims participating in

39 Aurélien-Thibault Lemasson, *La victime devant la justice pénale internationale* (Pulim, 2011), pp. 28–37.

40 E.g., Extraordinary Chambers in the Courts of Cambodia (2003), Special Tribunal for Lebanon (2007), Chambres Africaines Extraordinaires (2012).

41 E.g. Annex A to Judgment on the appeals against the 'Decision establishing the principles and procedures to be applied to reparations' of 7 August 2012 order for reparations (amended), *Prosecutor v Thomas Lubanga Dyilo*, (ICC-01/04-01/06-3129-AnxA (A A2 A3)), Appeals Chamber, 3 March 2015, paras 37–40.

42 In the context of reparations awarded on an individual basis, see Judgment on the appeals against the 'Decision establishing the principles and procedures to be applied to reparations' of 7 August 2012, *Prosecutor v Thomas Lubanga Dyilo*, (ICC-01/04-01/06-3129 (A A2 A3)), Appeals Chamber, 3 March 2015, para. 155.

43 ECCC, Judgment, *Case 001* (Doc No F28), Appeals Chamber, 3 February 2012, paras 431–5, 652.

44 Now dissolved.

proceedings in these tribunals may enjoy rights that are closely linked with those in *actions civiles*, participation is still *sui generis*.[45] The judges of both tribunals have construed the types of remedies available to victims narrowly, engaging in strict statutory interpretation. In the ECCC, victims are entitled only to symbolic and moral reparations, and not to individual compensation. Conversely, in the EAC, victims could not claim collective and moral reparations, and were entitled only to compensation.[46]

The reparations regime in the Statute of the ICC has a different character altogether. Article 75 of the Statute, read together with Rules 94 and 95 of the Rules of Procedure and Evidence, creates a request procedure for reparations, available in the form of restitution, compensation, and rehabilitation.[47] Rule 97(3) of the Rules, under the heading 'assessment of reparations', requires that in all cases, the 'Court must respect the rights of victims and the convicted person'. There is no further explanation in the Statute, the Rules, or the Regulations of the Court as to what these 'rights' may be. Taking, first, the perspective of the victim: where can one look for an interpretation of his or her rights? This chapter has presented the argument that human rights law and State practice do not prescribe any such 'rights'. So, what should victims expect to encounter in the course of a reparations proceeding at the ICC? Has the Statute itself bestowed victims with the status of 'party'?

As a principle of treaty interpretation, the Statute must be interpreted 'in good faith in accordance with the ordinary meaning to be given to [its terms] in their context and in the light of its object and purpose'.[48] The context of a provision is 'defined by the particular sub-section of the law read as a whole in conjunction with the section of an enactment in its entirety'.[49] Following this formula, the conclusion can be drawn that the reparations regime is well integrated into the Statute's overall framework of victim participation, rather than a unique and separate stage disconnected from the trial itself. This can be illustrated in several points.

First, the reparations regime in Article 75 of the Statute falls under Part 6 of the Statute, entitled 'The Trial'. One could also look to the definition of 'victims' in Rule 85 of the Rules. Although it is itself rather benign as a matter of interpretation,[50] what is telling is that the definition makes no distinction as to the interpretation of

45 In reference to the ECCC, see De Brouwer and Heikkilä, *supra* note 29, p. 1343.

46 EAC, Judgment, *Le Procureur Général c Hissein Habré*, 27 April 2017, paras 857–75.

47 The Appeals Chamber in *Lubanga* has added to this list, including reparations with a symbolic, preventative or transformative value (ICC-01/04-01/06-3129-AnxA), *supra* note 41, para. 34.

48 Judgment on the Prosecutor's Application for Extraordinary Review of Pre-Trial Chamber I's 31 March 2006 Decision Denying Leave to Appeal, *Situation in the Democratic Republic of the Congo*, (ICC-01/04-168), Appeals Chamber, 13 July 2006, para. 33, referring to Vienna Convention on the Law of Treaties, Art. 31(1).

49 Ibid.

50 Rule 85(a) of the Rules of Procedure and Evidence, 'Definition of Victims', says that victims are 'natural persons who have suffered harm as a result of the commission of any crimes with the jurisdiction of the Court'.

'victims' in the various stages of the case, whether pre-trial, trial, sentencing, or reparations.[51] Moreover, Rule 94(2) of the Rules provides that requests for reparations must be notified to the convicted person at the commencement of the trial. Regulation 56 of the Regulations of the Court provides for hearing evidence relevant to reparations during the trial,[52] and Article 76(3) of the Statute allows for oral submissions on reparations to be heard together with those on sentencing.

The context, then, illustrates that the reparations regime is an integrated part of the trial as a whole. In this regard, the role of victims in the pre-trial and trial stages has been described as that of a 'participant', falling short of a full 'party' to the litigation.[53] This makes sense, as victims participate not as of right, but with the leave of the Court, where their personal interests are affected.[54] If victims are 'participants' in the trial, one could reasonably infer, as Article 75 of the Statute is literally found in the section entitled 'The Trial', that victims are also 'participants', as opposed to 'parties', in the stage of the trial devoted to reparations. Further support for this argument is found in the procedure for hearing evidence relevant to reparations, which may take place during the trial or during sentencing.

In terms of a purposive interpretation, it is worth repeating that Article 75 of the Statute creates a request procedure only.[55] Trial chambers 'may' make an order under Article 75(2) of the Statute, but it does not appear that they are required to do so.[56] Trial chambers also have discretion to make an assessment of harm that goes beyond the representations received,[57] to make awards other than the types of reparations requested, and to award reparations on an individual or collective basis, or both.[58] Victims do not have the right to initiate proceedings against an individual,[59] to appeal decisions of the Prosecutor to close the investigation, or to continue a reparations proceeding after an acquittal. These features of the ICC legal framework appear to place discretion in the hands of the Court, and to stray from the role of the victim as claimant in the civil sense.

The reparations order itself, once it has been rendered, also does not appear to recognise victims as parties, either individually or collectively. Victims are not

51 Decision on the admissibility of the appeals against Trial Chamber I's 'Decision establishing the principles and procedures to be applied to reparations' and directions on the further conduct of the proceedings, *Prosecutor v Thomas Lubanga Dyilo*, (ICC-01/04-01/06-2953 (A A2 A3 OA21)), Appeals Chamber, 14 December 2012, para. 70.

52 Rule 91(4) of the Rules of Procedure and Evidence also allows for the testimonies of witnesses and experts to be heard.

53 Zappalà, *supra* note 26, p. 154.

54 Article 68(3) of the Statute; see also Articles 15(3) and 19(3) of the Statute.

55 But see Rule 218(1) of the Rules, referring to a 'claim' under Article 75 of the Statute.

56 Luke Moffett, *Justice for Victims before the International Criminal Court* (Routledge, 2014), p. 162.

57 Article 75(3) of the Statute; see also Judgment on the appeals against the order of Trial Chamber II of 24 March 2017 entitled 'Order for Reparations pursuant to Article 75 of the Statute', *Prosecutor v Germain Katanga*, (ICC-01/04-01/07-3778 (A3 A4 A5), Appeals Chamber, 8 March 2018, paras 146–7.

58 Rule 97(2) of the Rules of Procedure and Evidence.

59 De Brouwer and Heikkilä, *supra* note 29, p. 1317.

listed in the 'style of cause' in a reparations order like they are in domestic civil actions. The cover page of the order features the convicted person, the Prosecutor, and not a single victim either in name or in pseudonym. This is not surprising, as the enforcement regime for reparations orders is not focused on individual victims. Only those victims who will receive individual reparations of a 'financial nature' must be identified for the purposes of enforcement by States with jurisdiction.[60] The procedure for enforcement, in fact, follows the same procedure as fines and forfeiture orders under Article 109(1) of the Statute.[61] States are to 'give effect' to the order in accordance with national law. In a study of European States on the implementation of the Rome Statute, most States reported implementation of the reparations provisions in a way that recognises the order as a penal sanction.[62] Under such a procedure, individual victims are not parties in the sense that they would be entitled to personally bring enforcement proceedings.

Based upon the foregoing analysis of the reparations provisions in the context of the Statute as a whole and in light of their object and purpose, it is far from clear that Article 75 of the Statute creates a party-proceeding like a traditional civil action. Birte Timme was a German representative on the preparatory commission for drafting the Rules. He observes that neither the Statute nor the Rules provides the victim with a classic 'claim' for reparations with legally defined conditions for the award.[63] Timme's analysis seems to fit comfortably with Article 75(6) of the Statute, which specifically contemplates that the outcome of the reparations proceeding will not in any way prejudice the rights of victims in separate proceedings, including in civil claims in national courts should they choose to pursue them.[64] That is, Article 75(6) of

60 Rule 218(3)(b) and (4) of the Rules of Procedure and Evidence.

61 Article 75(5) of the Statute.

62 Bruce Broomhall and Claus Kreβ, 'Implementing Cooperation Duties under the Rome Statute' in Claus Kreβ et al. (eds), *The Rome Statute and Domestic Legal Orders: Volume II* (Baden-Baden: Nomos, 2005), pp. 539–540: 'In this scenario the victims do not have to go through the trouble of, first, locating the State where assets are present and, second, going through burdensome, time-consuming and costly (civil) court proceedings'.

63 Timm, *supra* note 38, p. 303.

64 In Schabas' estimation, this provision does not seem to be addressed to the Court. Rather, he says, 'it is a message to other tribunals, before whom the reparations mechanism of the Court might be invoked in opposition to other claims' (William Schabas, *The International Criminal Court: A Commentary on the Rome Statute* (2nd ed, Oxford University Press 2016), p. 883). This provision may have been inspired by the ILC Draft Statute, in which its members recognised, in relation to the limited nature of the provisions of the Draft Statute which allow fines to be transferred to a fund for the benefit of victims, that those measures 'are not intended in any way to substitute for reparation or to prevent any action which victims may take to obtain reparation through other courts or on the international plane' (ILC, Draft Statute for an International Criminal Court with commentaries, 46th session (1994) Yearbook of the International Law Commission, vol II, Part Two, page 60), as well as by Security Council Resolution 827 (UNSC Res 827 (25 May 1993) UN Doc S/RES/827), adopting the Statute of the ICTY, wherein the Security Council decided that 'the work of the International Tribunal shall be carried out without prejudice to the right of victims to seek, through appropriate means, compensation for damages incurred as a result of violations of international humanitarian law'.

the Statute appears to indicate that the reparations regime does not stand in the place of a victim's civil claim.[65]

It is difficult to say that the intent of the drafters of the Statute was to bestow victims with party status, and by the same token it is difficult to say otherwise. Although a consensus was reached about reparations as a general premise, none of the finer details were reduced to writing in the final draft and, instead, the Court itself was left to establish 'principles' in its jurisprudence.[66] There was no overarching design to the reparations regime – it was not built on the basis of any one particular model, and it, in fact, has elements of many different types of domestic compensation schemes, whether criminal, civil, or administrative.[67] Some State delegates and NGOs that propounded the rights of victims argued that because a right to reparations for victims of mass atrocities is recognised under international human rights law, it must equally be recognised under international criminal law.[68] Nevertheless, State delegates approached the negotiating table with preconceptions about reparations that they were familiar with in domestic legal frameworks.[69] The concept of giving victims a right to reparations in criminal law still remained foreign to many delegates.[70]

Once Article 75 of the Statute reached an acceptable form, the elaboration of victims' rights was left to the Preparatory Commission for the Rules of Procedure and Evidence. This was not an easy task. Friman recalls that

> some delegations saw reparations as a method for victims to enforce their civil claims through the Court. [. . .] Other delegations took a different view of the process. For them reparations were another form of sanction imposed by the Court, specifically tailored to the needs of victims, and were not a means of satisfying civil debts. [. . .] Yet a third view was that whereas the Court should have the flexibility to make individual or collective awards, reparations were very much a matter of trying to address the needs of victims and for this reason victims should have a say in how any resources were used.[71]

65 In the intervention of the French delegation for the Preparatory Committee on the creation of the ICC, it was explained that the intention is that this provision 'laisse ouverte toute possibilité aux victimes: en effet la loi nationale peut leur ouvrir des droits plus importants dont elles pourront bien entendu bénéficier' (Réparations dues aux victimes: Intervention de la France. Sixième session du Comité préparatoire sur la création d'une Cour Criminelle Internationale, available on Legal Tools Database: www.legal-tools.org/en/doc/39f4ea/ last accessed on 15 January 2019).

66 Art. 75(1) of the Statute.

67 Christoph Sperfeldt, 'Rome's Legacy: Negotiating the Reparations Mandate of the International Criminal Court' 17 *International Criminal Law Review* (2017) 351, p. 352.

68 Ibid., p. 367.

69 Ibid., p. 368.

70 Christian Muttukumaru, 'Reparations for Victims' in Roy Lee (ed.), *The International Criminal Court: The Making of the Rome Statute* (Kluwer Law International, 1999), p. 263.

71 Peter Lewis and Håkan Friman, 'Victims and Witnesses' in Roy Lee (ed.), *The International Criminal Court: Elements of Crimes and Rules of Procedure and Evidence* (Transnational Publishers, 2001), p. 483.

Given this philosophical debate, the rules that were ultimately adopted do not reflect one prevailing view as to what victims' procedural rights must entail.[72] The rules on reparations in Section III, subsection 4, read together with Article 75 of the Statute, represent a series of compromises, skilfully drafted in spite of dramatically diverging views as to the meaning of reparations in criminal law.

Taking stock of the debates, the text, bracketed text, drafts, and footnotes, and the various attempts at domestic implementation, it is submitted here that what results is a proceeding that is more an adjunct to the criminal trial than it is a separate civil action.[73] The language of Article 75(1) and (2) of the Statute, in fact, bears a striking resemblance to the compensation order that was available in British criminal courts at the time that Article 75 of the Statute was drafted.[74] Zedner explains that the British regime is seen as analogous to a civil measure imposed via the criminal process. However, there is no procedure in British courts whereby victims can make civil claims during criminal proceedings. A 'request' from a victim during a criminal proceeding, explains Zedner, 'should be clearly differentiated from a "claim" in civil law'.[75]

The compensation order issued against a convicted person in the criminal courts of common law jurisdictions, such as that in the United Kingdom, is not a perfect analogy. One could argue that the Trust Fund for Victims at the ICC, as a body which may fund reparations at the discretion of its Board, seems to steer reparations towards the model of domestic compensation schemes administered and funded by States. But although these comparisons may appear apt, Mégret rightly cautions against the hasty comparison with domestic compensation models. He explains that the proper role for domestic compensation schemes is still very much in flux. Therefore, 'their transposition to the international plane creates an additional hurdle'.[76] In the end, the ICC and the Trust Fund operate in an 'environment that is fundamentally different from that of domestic society, even as they may be part of an effort to emulate some of its features'.[77]

72 See Gilbert Bitti, 'Les droits procéduraux des victims devant la Cour pénale internationale' 44 *Criminologie* (2011) 63, pp. 96–7, for a discussion about the compromises reached for victims' participation in the trial and pre-trial stages.

73 Timm estimates that 'the model of the reparation as a compensatory type of criminal sanction also serves best to explain the legal nature of the award for reparations under the Statute and Rules' (Timm, *supra* note 38, 308).

74 The 'Compensation orders against convicted persons' in the Powers of the Criminal Courts Act (1973) in the United Kingdom states, in pertinent part, that 'a court by or before which a person is convicted of an offence [. . .] may, on application or otherwise, make an order [. . .] requiring him to pay compensation for any personal injury, loss or damage resulting from that offence' (available at www.legislation.gov.uk/ukpga/1973/62/section/35/1992-10-01?timeline=true last accessed on 15 January 2019).

75 Zedner, *supra* note 22, p. 183.

76 Frédéric Mégret, 'Justifying Compensation by the International Criminal Court's Victims Trust Fund: Lessons from Domestic Compensation Schemes', 36 *Brooklyn Journal of International Law* (2010) 123, p. 142.

77 Ibid., p. 142.

Scholars refer to the system of victim participation at the ICC as *sui generis*, meaning that it does not follow any single approach known in domestic law.[78] Victim participation in reparations proceedings is no exception. Indeed, victims have important procedural guarantees in the ICC's reparations regime. To name a few, victims i) may request reparations, ii) may be invited to make representations, iii) have a right to be notified, iv) may request protective measures, v) may request the appointment of experts, and vi) may appeal the order. But even these 'rights', which resemble rights familiar in domestic party-proceedings, are nonetheless *sui generis* in the Statute. One example is the right to appeal a reparations order. This is not in all circumstances intended as a right of a single victim to bring his or her own appeal. Rather, some delegations expressed the view that, when there are more than a few victims, individual victims could not file separate appeals, and the number of victims who could appeal would be limited.[79] Another example is the successor's right to claim reparations. A victim's claim based on succession has been rejected in the jurisprudence of the Court, only allowing participation based upon a victim's own right.[80]

78 De Brouwer and Heikkilä, *supra* note 29, 1343; Zegveld describes victims' claims as being of a 'mixed private-public law character' (Zegveld, *supra* note 10, p. 101).

79 'Report to the Committee of the Whole', 13 July 1998, A/CONF.183/C.1/WGPM/L.2/Add 7, p 5. Article 82(4) of the Statute permits appeals only through a legal representative, and in appellate practice groups of victims are jointly represented. The Appeals Chamber has held in the *Lubanga* case that victims are parties in appeals of a reparations order (Decision on the admissibility against Trial Chamber I's 'Decision establishing the principles and procedures to be applied to reparations' and directions on the further conduct of proceeding, *Prosecutor v Lubanga,* (ICC-01/04-01/06-2953 (A A2 A3 OA21)), Appeals Chamber, 14 December 2012, para. 67. On the one hand, as a matter of human rights law, victims would then be fully entitled to the protection of due process in appeals proceedings (see Judgment, *Delcourt v Belgium*, (ECtHR, App no 2689/65), 17 January 1970, paras 25-26). However, the Appeals Chamber in *Katanga* granted the appeals of individual victims 'bearing in mind that the number of applications [. . .] is low' (Judgment on the appeals against the order of Trial Chamber II of 24 March 2017 entitled 'Order for Reparations pursuant to Article 75 of the Statute', *Prosecutor v Katanga,* (ICC-01/04-01/07-3778-Red (A3 A4 A5)), 8 March 2018, para. 260). This appears to suggest that victims have something less than an absolute right to access and enjoy a fair trial in appeals proceedings.

80 Pre-Trial Chamber I (Single Judge), *Situation in the Democratic Republic of the Congo*, 'Corrigendum to the 'Decision on the Applications for Participation Filed in Connection with the Investigation in the Democratic Republic of the Congo by a/0004/06 to a/0009/06, a/0016/06 to a/0063/06, a/0071/06 to a/0080/06 and a/0105/06 to a/0110/06, a/0188/06, a/0128/06 to a/0162/06, a/0199/06, a/0203/06, a/0209/06, a/0214/06, a/0220/06 to a/0222/06, a/0224/06, a/0227/06 to a/0230/06, a/0234/06 to a/0236/06, a/0240/06, a/0225/06, a/0226/06, a/0231/06 to a/0233/06, a/0237/06 to a/0239/06 and a/0241/06 to a/0250/06', 31 January 2008, ICC-01/04-423-Corr-tENG, paras 23-25; Pre-Trial Chamber I (Single Judge), *Situation in Darfur, Sudan*, 'Corrigendum to Decision on the Applications for Participation in the Proceedings of Applicants a/0011/06 to a/0015/06, a/0021/07, a/0023/07 to a/0033/07 and a/0035/07 to a/0038/07', ICC-02/05-111-Corr, 14 December 2007, para. 35; cf Pre-Trial Chamber III, *Prosecutor v Jean-Pierre Bemba Gombo*, 'Fourth Decision on Victims' Participation', ICC-01/05-01/08-320, 12 December 2008, paras 44–8.

What is left, then, is a *sui generis* model of reparations linked to the criminal conviction and administered at the discretion of trial chambers. It provides an important role for victims to play in the determination of the award, but it remains an adjunct to the criminal trial and sentencing procedure. This conclusion will no doubt strike some as controversial.[81] Indeed, there are authoritative statements to the contrary. In the context of a broader discussion about Article 36(10) of the Statute and the mandate of judges, the Presidency of the Court determined in an internal memorandum (later made public) that, in reparations proceedings,

> victims receive an enhanced procedural role in that they become parties to the proceedings, thereby altering the nature and focus of proceedings from punitive to reparative. The Appeals Chamber has held that 'reparations proceedings are a distinct stage of the proceedings.[82]

Furthermore, as discussed, there were vociferous advocates in Rome among NGOs and State delegates in favour of the right of victims to launch civil claims. However, one must consider whether such advocacy is paving a road that leads towards an unachievable mandate for an international organisation such as the ICC. Reparations proceedings at the ICC are not capable of returning compensation for all victims in all cases. Civil claims in domestic proceedings, when numbering in the hundreds or thousands, can take years to adjudicate. Proceedings are fully adversarial, and parties often hire numerous experts schooled in science and statistical modelling. Even in representative actions, where findings of liability may be extrapolated and applied to the class of victims as a whole, due process still requires individual determinations of causation and damages in some cases.[83] At the ICC, given the possibility for evidence relevant to reparations to be heard during trial,[84] how could a trial chamber entertain party-proceedings and still produce a timely judgment in the criminal phase? Would this not simply transfer the difficulties faced by domestic criminal courts to the international plane?

If victims are to adopt realistic expectations for the reparations proceeding, the constraints on the Court must not be taken lightly. Time, money and expertise are all prohibitive of returning full compensation to victims. The Appeals Chamber has explained that compensation may not be the ideal modality of reparations

81 See Zappalà, *supra* note 26, p. 157, concluding that '[t]he recognition in the ICC Statute of the right of victims to seek reparation from the convicted person implies that victims have a claim which belongs to them and entitles them to be *party to proceedings against the convicted person*' (emphasis in original).

82 Annex I to decision replacing two judges in Trial Chamber II, *Prosecutor v Germain Katanga*, (ICC-01/04-01/07-3468-AnxI), Presidency, 16 April 2014, para. 6.

83 USA, *Cimino v. Raymark Industries, Inc.*, 151 F.3d 297 (1998), pp. 311–21.

84 In addition to regulation 56 of the Regulations of the Court, see ASP Res. ICC-ASP/10/Res.3, 7th Plenary, 20 December 2011, para. 4, 'evidence concerning reparations may be taken during trial hearings so as to ensure that the judicial phase is streamlined and does not result in any delay thereof'.

when resources are scarce.[85] Nevertheless, practice has shown that trial chambers of the ICC have a fondness for aggregating monetary damages, calculated on a per-victim basis. In the practice of the Inter-American Court of Human Rights, material and moral damages paid out may range from USD150,000 to 200,000 per victim.[86] But such awards reflect a State's liability for failing to fulfil its duty to prevent human rights violations – a form of liability significantly broader than individual liability. And drawing on precedents from human rights courts may not be realistic given that every Article 75 reparations order to date has been issued against an insolvent convicted person.[87] Nor is it sustainable for the Trust Fund given its limited resources.

The trouble is, victims' advocates seem to treat 'party' status as being victim-friendly. But great care should be taken before importing principles from party proceedings into reparations. In addition to rights, parties in civil proceedings also have obligations. Party proceedings are adversarial and, as such, one of the fundamental obligations of litigants on both sides is to preserve and disclose evidence.[88] At present, victims in reparations proceedings at the ICC have not been held to any such requirement. The Appeals Chamber has been clear that the only obligation of disclosure in the Statute belongs to the Prosecutor during the criminal phase.[89] While victims may disclose whatever evidence they choose in support of their application for reparations under Rule 94 of the Rules, they are under no obligation to preserve and disclose mitigating evidence. In the *Katanga* case, victims were able to benefit from an evidentiary presumption of a standard amount of material loss even where the evidence they had produced demonstrated the loss of less than the standard amount.[90] Rather than treating disclosure of evidence – whether exculpatory or inculpatory – as an obligation,

85 Annex A to Judgment on the appeals against the 'Decision establishing the principles and procedures to be applied to reparations' of 7 August 2012 order for reparations (amended), *Prosecutor v Thomas Lubanga Dyilo*, (ICC-01/04-01/06-3129-AnxA (A A2 A3)), Appeals Chamber, 3 March 2015, para. 37.

86 Pablo De Greiff, 'Justice and Reparations' in Pablo De Greiff (ed.), *The Handbook of Reparations* (Oxford University Press, 2006), p. 456. Interestingly, the European Court of Human Rights has explained that it will make awards based upon equity, as it does not 'have the capacity, nor is it appropriate to its function as an international court, to adjudicate on large numbers of cases which require the finding of specific facts or the calculation of monetary compensation – both of which should, as a matter of principle and effective practice, be the domain of domestic jurisdictions', Judgment (Just satisfaction), *Chiragov et al. v Armenia*, (ECtHR, App no 13216/05), 12 December 2017, paras 50–8.

87 Carrillo, *supra* note 38, p. 530.

88 Parties in civil proceedings are also, in some cases, obliged to take steps to mitigate the damage they have endured if they have the opportunity to do so. It is questionable that this principle is something that can be enforced in reparations proceedings.

89 Judgment on the appeal of Mr Katanga Against the Decision Trial Chamber II of 22 January 2010 entitled 'Decision on the Modalities of Victim Participation at Trial', *Prosecutor v Germain Katanga*, (ICC-01/04-01/07-2288 (OA 11)), Appeals Chamber, 16 July 2010, paras 75, 82–7.

90 Order for Reparations pursuant to Article 75 of the Statute, *Prosecutor v. Germain Katanga*, (ICC-01/04-01/07-3728-tENG), Trial Chamber II, 24 March 2017, para. 105.

the procedure taken in *Katanga* appears to be that the evidence produced by a victim is only taken into account if beneficial to the victim.

Furthermore, the importation of principles of civil liability may lead to significant legal and practical difficulties.[91] For example, victims' advocates uniformly argue for the adoption of the principle of liability *in solidum* in ICC reparations proceedings.[92] Such a move would be unworkable for several reasons. First, liability *in solidum* is typically applied in domestic courts to determine a person's responsibility for monetary damages. However, under the Statute, trial chambers have discretion in awarding individual or collective reparations and in selecting appropriate modalities. The application of the principle of *in solidum* liability would require trial chambers to assess harm individually, and to identify the monetary damages to which each victim is entitled. The convicted person would then be jointly liable to each victim for this amount, and victims would have a right to monetary compensation. Therefore, a strict application of liability *in solidum* cannot live side by side with non-monetary remedies and the broad discretion enjoyed by trial chambers.[93]

Second, once rendered, how would States with jurisdiction give effect to an order made pursuant to the principle of liability *in solidum*? We have seen that many States have implemented the reparations provisions in domestic law in a way that recognises the order as some form of a criminal sanction, enforced by State authorities. It would be unusual if an order based upon liability *in solidum* was enforced by the State when rendered by the ICC, but enforced by the victim when rendered in domestic civil courts. And it must be kept in mind that liability *in solidum* connotes that, in simple terms, a person is liable to another person. Who would a convicted person at the ICC be liable *in solidum* to? Would the reparations order list every victim who is bound by the order, and the individual amounts of damages? And would those victims who are bound by the order then be precluded from seeking civil remedies in domestic courts? This would cause numerous difficulties for victims, and it certainly would not sit comfortably with Article 75(6) of the Statute.

Third, there are many iterations of liability *in solidum*, or joint and several liability, in domestic law. Which iteration do advocates propose for adoption? In

91 For a discussion in the context of the ECCC, see Appeal Judgment, *Case 001*, (Doc No F28), 3 February 2012, para. 644.

92 E.g., TFV, Observations on Reparations Procedure, *Prosecutor v Germain Katanga*, (ICC-01/04-01/07-3548), 13 May 2015, paras 32-36; The Redress Trust, Observations by the Redress Trust pursuant to Article 75(3) of the Statute and Rule 103 of the Rules, *Prosecutor v Jean-Pierre Bemba Gombo*, (ICC-01/05-01/08-3448), 18 October 2016, paras 26–30.

93 Donat-Cattin writes that reparations in the Statue is a 'broad and flexible concept, which has been introduced in the Statute to allow the judges to decide upon the widest possible range of means of remedy to victims' rights violations. It follows that, especially in cases of mass or collective victimization, 'reparation' may be better achieved through means other than restitution or monetary compensation' (David Donat-Cattin, 'Article 75' in Otto Triffterer and Kai Ambos (eds), *The Rome Statute of the International Criminal Court: A Commentary* (C.H. Beck, Hart, Nomos, 2016), 1859).

this regard, the International Law Commission's comment, though made on the plurality of responsible States and not individuals, is apt:

> It is important not to assume that internal law concepts and rules in this field can be applied directly to international law. Terms such as 'joint', 'joint and several' and 'solidary' responsibility derive from different legal traditions and analogies must be applied with care.[94]

At the ICC, is the Court prepared to deliver a nuanced understanding of this principle as it applies in reparations proceedings? One can imagine a situation where a pronouncement by the Court, without more, that liability *in solidum* applies in ICC reparations proceedings would lead to more confusion than clarity.

Finally, and most importantly, the adoption of the principle of liability *in solidum* may have the undesirable effect of misleading victims. A key principle upon which liability *in solidum* is based in domestic systems is that a claimant can choose to pursue the wrongdoer with the 'deepest pockets'. Therefore, a victim who goes through the trouble of participating in arduous litigation will take solace in the fact that the defendant is solvent and capable of paying compensation of the whole amount of the harm. At the ICC, investigations and subsequent arrest warrants are initiated by a decision of the Prosecutor, and to date the solvency of the suspect has not been one of the selection criteria.[95] Therefore, reparations orders based upon liability *in solidum* may in fact lead to monumental awards that neither the Trust Fund nor the convicted person could ever fulfil.[96] Stating that liability *in solidum* applies, ostensibly in the victims' best interests, would create unwanted expectations, and it may even be misleading as to the rights of victims.

Reparations in the *Bemba* case: Act two

After a few weeks of written submissions, Trial Chamber III delivered the 'Final decision on the reparations proceedings' in the *Bemba* case. The decision refers to the determination in the *Ruto and Sang* joint trial, wherein Judge Fremr, writing separately, explained that 'a criminal court can only address compensation for harm suffered as a result of crimes if such crimes have been found to have taken place and the person standing trial for his or her participation in those crimes is found

94 Draft Articles on the Responsibility of States for Internationally Wrongful Acts, with commentaries (2001) Yearbook of the International Law Commissions, vol II, Part Two, as corrected, Article 47, comment 3.

95 OTP, 'Policy Paper on Case Selection and Prioritisation', 15 September 2016, pp. 12–18 (available at www.icc-cpi.int/itemsDocuments/20160915_OTP-Policy_Case-Selection_Eng.pdf last accessed on 15 January 2019).

96 Not to mention the unfairness that would result to convicted persons due to, among other things, inability to seek contribution against others. Concepts related to the rights of the convicted person are explored later in this chapter.

guilty'.[97] As Mr Bemba's conviction was reversed, the Court found that 'no reparations order can be made against Mr Bemba under Article 75 of the Statute'.[98]

Trial Chamber III's decision confirms that, unlike domestic courts, the ICC will not ensure an effective remedy for victims of human rights violations. Victims do not have a right of access, and they are not parties capable of initiating proceedings. And even when proceedings have already been initiated by the Prosecutor (as was the case in *Bemba*), victims do not have claims that exist independent of the criminal trial. Victims' claims live and die with the Prosecutor's case. They cannot continue their claims either against the acquitted person or against others.

This spells the end for Jane Doe and her family. Impunity has prevailed. The legally inclined will no doubt seize the opportunity to lay blame with the Court, with victims' counsel, or with the Prosecutor. Although there may have been technical failings, legal oversights, or peculiarities in the trial that could have been avoided, it is hoped that at least some of the energy will be spent on addressing the rights of victims. If victims' rights in reparations proceedings were, from the very beginning – that is, at the time of first contact with a legal officer or agent of the Court – ascertainable and realistic, rather than undefined and illusory, then perhaps the blow of an acquittal after such an investment of trust would have been softened, albeit slightly.

In a public press release, the Trust Fund made a commitment to augment its assistance activities following the acquittal.[99] Hopefully Jane Doe and others will be in a position to take advantage of it. But as the decision of Trial Chamber III was made as a final decision in the reparations phase, is it an 'order', and therefore appealable, pursuant to Article 82(4) of the Statute?[100] Fitting that the reparations proceeding should end with yet another ambiguity.

The legal effect of a reparations order and the rights of the convicted person

There is no parallel in criminal trials to the throngs of NGOs, jurists and academics in the international community who have thrown their support behind

97 Decision on Defence Applications for Judgments of Acquittal, *Prosecutor v William Samoei Ruto and Jushua Arap Sang*, (ICC-01/09-01/11-2027-Red-Corr), Trial Chamber V(A), 5 April 2016, para. 149; Decision on the Requests regarding Reparations, *Prosecutor v William Samoei Ruto and Jushua Arap Sang*, (ICC-01/09-01/11-2038), Trial Chamber V(A), 1 July 2016, para. 7.

98 Final decision on the reparations proceedings, *Prosecutor v Jean-Pierre Bemba Gombo*, (ICC-01/05-01/08-3653), Trial Chamber III, 3 August 2018, para. 3.

99 Available at www.trustfundforvictims.org/en/news/press-release-following-mr-bemba%E2%80%99s-acquittal-trust-fund-victims-icc-decides-accelerate-launch last accessed on 15 January 2019.

100 Gideon Boas et al, 'Appeals, Reviews, and Reconsideration' in Göran Sluiter et al. (eds), *International Criminal Procedure: Principles and Rules* (Oxford University Press, 2013), p. 955, 'It is also not expressly stated that an appeal can be filed against a decision *refusing* to make an order for reparations, although one would expect this to be the case'; Christopher Staker, 'Appeal and Revision' in O Triffterer and Kai Ambos (eds), *Rome Statute of the International Criminal Court: A Commentary* (C.H. Beck, Hart, Nomos, 2016), p. 1480.

victims. A glance at the roster of groups invited to make submissions in reparations proceedings at the ICC would reveal that the convicted person speaks only with his own voice. Opposing his views may be victims' legal representatives, the Office of Public Counsel for Victims, the Trust Fund for Victims, the Prosecutor, *amici curiae*, and experts invited pursuant to Rules 97(3) and 103 of the Rules. This is not surprising. The concerns of victims draw an enormous amount of sympathy. Due to marginalisation, lack of resources and an inability to gather evidence and navigate the criminal justice system, victims can use all the support that the international community can muster. The ascertainment of victims' rights should be everyone's concern.

Conversely, a person convicted under international law has been found guilty of crimes ranging from the reprehensible to the grotesque. He is no longer protected by the presumption of innocence in the reparations proceeding and doubts as to facts are no longer resolved in his favour. So, who cares about protecting the procedural rights of the convicted person in reparations proceedings? Why not just adopt all the principles that are pro-victim and ignore the procedural safeguards that are pro-defendant?

There are two sides to every coin; even in reparations proceedings. When a reparations order is issued against a convicted person, that order is transferred to States with jurisdiction pursuant to chapter 12, section IV of the Rules. Those States must give effect to the order pursuant to Article 109 of the Statute, which may result in the State authorities using whatever means are legally at their disposal for the enforcement of the order and the recuperation of funds and assets. Whether or not a convicted person has the ability to pay the award, a judgment recognised by national courts and registered against a person has a significant effect. In theory, a judgment debtor has a financial obligation, and he carries this obligation for the rest of his life until it is completely discharged.

As borne out in the judgments of the ICC and EAC,[101] individual financial liability can be astronomical. In a judgment of a reparations chamber a person can suddenly find himself responsible for repairing all the harm caused in the course of armed conflict through the involvement of militias of men and well-funded paramilitary groups often with access to State resources. What has typically been the responsibility of States to repair has fallen on the shoulders of a single person. At the time of writing, Thomas Lubanga Dyilo has been ordered to pay USD 10 million.[102] Even the most heinous criminals have rights in the determination of their sentence and the conditions of their detention. There should be no exception for convicted persons in reparations proceedings. On the contrary, given the 'restorative' goals in reparations proceedings, including reconciliation and the reintegration of offenders in communities,[103] it would make sense to allow the

101 As mentioned, chambers of the ECCC are not empowered to award reparations of a financial nature against convicted persons.

102 This award is currently under appeal.

103 Shelton, *supra* note 12, p. 23.

convicted person to have meaningful participation in the determination of the sanction. This participation is not possible if his rights are completely discarded.

Save for a few exceptions, references to procedural rights of convicted persons in the jurisprudence of international and hybrid tribunals are scarce. Thus, the field of procedural rights is still open. At the ICC, Rule 97(3) of the Rules requires respect for the rights of the convicted person. This was an afterthought,[104] and its meaning is still open to interpretation. Though it is clear that a convicted person must enjoy *some* rights, the question remains as to which rights must be recognised for a proceeding to be considered fair? How much protection is enough? As with victims' rights, the answer will inevitably depend upon the nature of the proceeding and the interests at stake.

At the ECCC, reparations awards are largely symbolic and take into account the availability of funds for the proposed projects.[105] Although convicted persons would have an interest in the outcome of the proceedings, they do not face crippling financial liability. The EAC, on the other hand, was designed for the purpose of bringing one man, former Chadian dictator Hissein Habré, to justice. The trial resulted in a conviction, confirmed on appeal, and the reparations proceeding saw an award of compensation in favour of more than 7,000 victims totalling approximately 124 million euros.[106] The reparations proceeding was fully adversarial, resembling something of a trial in a Senegalese domestic court exercising universal jurisdiction.[107] Habré's liability was set using rather opaque methodology, as the Chambre d'Assises took into account victims' submissions and then reduced them to 'fair proportions'.[108]

Judges presiding over reparations proceedings at the ICC have the discretion to award a broad spectrum of remedies, from full monetary compensation at one end to symbolic reparations at the other. Although reparations chambers have adopted a practice to ignore the financial solvency of the convicted person,[109] very few other principles have been adopted in setting the size of the potential award. A reparations award must be 'proportionate to the harm', which in collective awards is set according to the cost of repair.[110] This means, in the first place, that the monetary component of the award must not exceed what is determined

104 Lewis and Friman, *supra* note 71, p. 484.

105 ECCC, Appeal Judgment, *Case 001*, (Doc No F28), 3 February 2012, paras 667–8.

106 Nader Iskandar Diab, 'Challenges in the Implementation of the Reparation Award against Hissein Habré' 16 *Journal of International Criminal Justice* (2018) 141, p. 152.

107 Ibid., 144.

108 EAC, *Le Procureur Général c Hissein Habré*, 29 July 2016, pp 62, 65, 68 (author's translation).

109 Judgment on the appeals against the 'Decision establishing the principles and procedures to be applied to reparations' of 7 August 2012, *Prosecutor v Thomas Lubanga Dyilo*, (ICC-01/04-01/06-3129 (A A2 A3)), Appeals Chamber, 3 March 2015, paras 102–5.

110 Judgment on the appeals against the order of Trial Chamber II of 24 March 2017 entitled 'Order for Reparations pursuant to Article 75 of the Statute', *Prosecutor v Germain Katanga*, (ICC-01/04-01/07-3778-Red (A3 A4 A5)), Appeals Chamber, 8 March 2018, paras 71–2, 178.

to be the cost of repair, otherwise it cannot be considered 'proportionate'. It can also be inferred from the Appeals Chamber's judgment in *Katanga* that a convicted person has a right to be free of 'double punishment', and an award may be considered 'double punishment' if it exceeds the cost of repair given that it is imposed against a person already convicted and sentenced.[111] There is also support for the notion that a reparations award could be substantially less than the monetary amount of harm. Rule 97(1) of the Rules states that an order should be made 'taking into account the scope and extent of any damage, loss or injury', rather than 'solely based upon' or 'in accordance with' that harm.[112] However, there are no other criteria given as a basis for reducing the amount of liability.[113]

This focus on the harm itself could justify ignoring certain factors that are personal to the convicted person, such as inability to pay. On the other hand, as a matter of logic, the focus on harm should tend to take account of other factors. In fairness, the focus on harm must be blind, and not only applied to the detriment of the accused. For example, if the damage caused as a result of the crimes has been substantially reduced subsequent to the events in question, the 'cost to repair' must account for that reduction. This, regardless of whether the mitigation of damage was at the instance of the convicted person himself, the victims, the Trust Fund, or some other third party. When a party other than the convicted person has taken such steps, that person may have recourse against the convicted person in separate proceedings.[114]

111 Ibid., para. 185.

112 There are seven other occurrences of the words 'taking into account' in the Rules of Procedure and Evidence. One example is found in rule 88 of the Rules, where a chamber is permitted to, 'taking into account the views and concerns of the victim or witness', order special measures for that victim or witness to facilitate their testimony. Another example is rule 185 of the Rules, which requires a chamber to, under certain circumstances, make arrangements for the transfer of a prisoner, 'taking into account' the views of that person. Similarly, under rule 191 of the Rules, a chamber may decide, after 'taking into account the views of the Prosecutor and the witness or expert concerned', to provide assurances to a witness or expert. Therefore, it appears that the words 'taking into account' are used to indicate a factor, perhaps among many, that a chamber should have consideration of when ruling on a related issue. It is submitted that rule 97(1) of the Rules does not require a trial chamber to hold a convicted person liable for the full extent of the injury, loss, or damage.

113 Although the word 'gravity' was included in the 'Report on the international seminar on victims' access to the ICC', 6 July 1999, a decision appears to have been taken not to adopt that criterion as it does not appear in the text of rule 97(1) of the Rules.

114 Although it has only been the subject of passing mention, the Appeals Chamber has suggested that the Trust Fund may be able to recover funds advanced from its 'other resources' from a convicted person (Annex A to Judgment on the appeals against the 'Decision establishing the principles and procedures to be applied to reparations' of 7 August 2012 order for reparations (amended), *Prosecutor v Thomas Lubanga Dyilo*, (ICC-01/04-01/06-3129-AnxA (A A2 A3)), 3 March 2015, para. 62). Bodies such as the Trust Fund in domestic jurisdictions make advances on an *ex gratia* basis (Kate Warner, 'Australia' in Albin Eser and Susanne Walther (Hrsg), *Reparation in Criminal Law: International Perspectives*, volume 2 (Max-Planck-Institut, 1996), p. 253), and there are mixed practices as to whether they enjoy a right to subrogate claims of victims. Following a reparations order under Article 75(2) of the Statute, it would seem difficult for a body that has advanced funds to claim a right of

However, this has not been the practice. The *Al Mahdi* reparations chamber received reports that the mausoleums that were the subject of the attacks in question had been restored at the expense of UNESCO and private parties.[115] Nevertheless, in the section entitled 'Damage to the Protected Buildings', Trial Chamber VIII held that the repairs should have 'no impact' on Mr Al Mahdi's liability:

> Remedial efforts by a third party in the time elapsed between the destruction and the issuance of the reparations order do not alter the amount of damage originally done. To place undue weight on this fact would be to understate the amount of harm actually caused and the corresponding reparations required to remedy it.[116]

If the reparations proceeding is truly reparative, it would seem illogical to hold a person responsible for the cost of repairing harm that has already been repaired. To assign liability based primarily upon the fact that a convicted person had engaged in certain bad behaviour, irrespective of whether there continues to be a cost associated with its repair, appears to focus more on reprimanding the convicted person than it does on repairing the harm to victims. Perhaps, then, despite the principles established in previous jurisprudence, the reparations award at the ICC does have a punitive element.

Furthermore, under a reparative theory of liability, the logic of Trial Chamber VIII could be criticised as creating a risk of double recovery. Suppose for a moment that instead of repairing the mausoleums, UNESCO had chosen to simply give monetary awards as 'reparations' to persons affected by their destruction. Could this be ignored in the same way that Trial Chamber VIII ignored reparations to victims in-kind?

Of course, due to the difficulty in processing a high volume of applications and the challenges regarding access to evidence in certain regions, the quantification of harm may sometimes be elusive. Therefore, reparations proceedings must have an element of flexibility in favour of victims. This has led to the widespread use of factual presumptions. However, a review of UN and State compensation programs reveals that, in practice, the burden on victims can be eased 'less by lowering the requisite degree of probability and more by widely accepting other means of evidence'.[117] Factual presumptions must therefore still be proved to the requisite standard,[118] and judges of international and hybrid criminal chambers

---

subrogation where victims are not specifically listed in the order. A further legal difficulty for the Trust Fund is that it has consistently argued that its decisions to complement awards are entirely discretionary, and not based upon any obligation like that of an insurance fund.

115 Reparations Order, *Prosecutor v Ahmad Al Faqi Al Mahdi*, (ICC-01/12-01/15-236), Trial Chamber VIII, 17 August 2017, para. 65.

116 Ibid.

117 ECCC, Appeal Judgment, *Case 001*, (Doc No F28), 3 February 2012, para. 525.

118 Judgment on the appeals against the order of Trial Chamber II of 24 March 2017 entitled 'Order for Reparations pursuant to Article 75 of the Statute', *Prosecutor v Germain*

have recognised that factual presumptions drawn to the detriment of a convicted person must not be arbitrary and must be open to meaningful challenge.[119] For certain novel heads of damage, harm caused must have been reasonably foreseeable to an offender.[120]

Although there are clear policy reasons for the use of factual presumptions in the assessment of harm, they allow for a reversal of the burden of proof and as such they must be used with caution. Presumptions should be adopted only where a victim has demonstrated an inability to produce evidence for reasons beyond his or her control. As noted in the ECCC's Supreme Court Chamber, trial chambers should give notice to a convicted person before the adoption of presumptions giving him the opportunity to design his defence strategy.[121] Moreover, victims should not benefit from a presumption of harm where there is reason to believe that they experienced harm amounting to something less than the presumed harm. Put simply, factual presumptions must be rebuttable.

Finally, in particular regarding moral harm, where presumptions are drawn in the absence of medical evidence and extrapolated to an entire class of victims in the absence of statistical sampling of qualified experts, those presumptions of harm cannot be the basis of individualised monetary damages akin to civil damage awards. The assessment of individual civil damages in mass claims proceedings is a complex and lengthy process, meant for expert witnesses and experienced counsel.[122] The complexity is endured out of fairness to the person who faces the steep monetary liability that results from individualised damage awards. The presumption used in the *Katanga* case – that all relatives, near or distant, suffered psychological harm from the loss of a direct victim – resulted in the assessment of more than USD 2.7 million in moral damages for the 297 victim-applicants. However, it did so without any supporting evidence aside from the victims' written applications. As suggested in the Appeals Chamber's judgment,[123] fairness would require that an aggregation of damages of this magnitude would result only from a full adversarial process, with opposing experts and rebuttal evidence.

Katanga, (ICC-01/04-01/07-3778-Red (A3 A4 A5)), Appeals Chamber, 8 March 2018, para. 75.

119 ECCC, Appeal Judgment, *Case 001*, (Doc No F28), 3 February 2012, paras 437-438; Judgment on the appeals against the order of Trial Chamber II of 24 March 2017 entitled 'Order for Reparations pursuant to Article 75 of the Statute', *Prosecutor v Germain Katanga*, (ICC-01/04-01/07-3778-Red (A3 A4 A5)), Appeals Chamber, 8 March 2018, paras 75, 91.

120 Decision on the Matter of the Transgenerational Harm Alleged by Some Applicants for Reparations Remanded by the Appeals Chamber in its Judgment of 8 March 2018, *Prosecutor v Germain Katanga*, (ICC-01/04-01/07-3804-Red-tENG), Trial Chamber II, 19 July 2018, para. 17.

121 ECCC, Appeal Judgment, *Case 001*, (Doc No F28), 3 February 2012, para. 438.

122 Zegveld, *supra* note 10, pp. 98–9.

123 Judgment on the appeals against the order of Trial Chamber II of 24 March 2017 entitled 'Order for Reparations pursuant to Article 75 of the Statute', *Prosecutor v Germain Katanga*, (ICC-01/04-01/07-3778-Red (A3 A4 A5)), Appeals Chamber, 8 March 2018, paras 122–3.

However, fairness may not require a full adversarial process if the outcome is more symbolic than compensatory. Presumptions of this nature could be used to define the heads of harm more generally, or to define the scope of victims eligible for collective reparations. This is precisely how they were used in the practice of the ECCC.[124]

Conclusion

In the beginning, probably before Jane Doe was even born, the concept of reparations was seen as being incompatible with international criminal justice. In the Draft Statute for an International Criminal Court (1994), the ILC considered empowering the court to order forfeiture and restitution of property – which would have required ruling on the claims of victims – but '[o]n balance the Commission considered that these issues were best left to national jurisdictions and to international judicial cooperation agreements'.[125] Around the same time, Amnesty International suggested that 'an international civil court or claims commission should be established', arguing that 'this body might be better suited [than the ICC] to grant relief to victims'.[126] The delegates in Rome courageously planted reparations into Article 75 of the Statute, but they did so in spite of the concerns about its efficacy. The negotiations were carried by a wave of support for moving beyond the old model of retributive criminal justice. However, after the Statute was signed and the Rules were prepared, the reparations regime as a whole remained precarious.[127] And despite all of the energy expended on reparations at the ICC, and subsequently at the ECCC and the EAC, there are still calls for an international civil court.[128]

The *Bemba* case has awoken us to the 'expectations gap' that was created in 1998 and lay dormant for 20 years. Now that it has presented itself, the international community must seize the opportunity rather than let it slide by. The procedure for reparations at the ICC must be clarified. Convicted persons must be able to know what their liability will be based upon, and the presumptions employed by reparations chambers must not result in an aggregation of civil

124 Even still, they were accompanied by expert evidence (see ECCC, Appeal Judgment, *Case 001*, (Doc No F28), 3 February 2012, para. 449).

125 ILC, Draft Statute for an International Criminal Court with commentaries, 46th session (1994) Yearbook of the International Law Commission, vol II, Part Two, Article 47, comment 3.

126 Sperfeldt, *supra* note 67, p. 360, fn 38.

127 Sperfeldt writes that, '[i]n the end, a broad human-rights inspired concept of reparations was introduced into a system that strictly adhered to the bedrock of criminal law – the notion of individual criminal responsibility – that translated in the reparations realm to individual liability for the harm that resulted from crimes adjudicated before the Court. This imbalance constitutes one of the main challenges today. 'Such a model is at risk of raising expectations among victims of a potential of reparations that are at odds with the means and resources at the Court's disposal' (Sperfeldt, *supra* note 67, p. 373).

128 Zegveld, *supra* note 10, 110–111; Mark Gibney, 'On the need for an international civil court', 26 Fletcher Forum for World Affairs (2002) 47.

damages. Victims must be able to know their rights so they can be fully informed about what to expect and, on that basis, pursue remedies in other venues. The rights of both parties must be clearly identified, perhaps in a document adopted by the Assembly of States Parties.[129]

Ultimately, clarity can only be achieved if reparations proceedings in international criminal law have a broader sense of purpose in the array of remedies available to victims under international and national law.[130] For the reasons explored in this chapter, reparations proceedings should not (and cannot) supplant States' responsibility to provide effective remedies. Instead, reparations must complement what may be available in domestic and regional courts.[131] Moreover, international and hybrid criminal tribunals are not appropriate venues for returning civil remedies. Expectations of international courts must be tempered given the problems encountered in civil proceedings at the national level,[132] and advocates must focus on pinning liability on States and corporations to obtain full monetary compensation for victims.[133] As was so eloquently stated by the Supreme Court Chamber of the ECCC, an international criminal tribunal should not be 'overloaded with utopian expectations that would ultimately exceed the attainable goals of transitional justice'.[134] Rather, reparations should be based upon an 'award that is modest but tailored to what is in practical terms attainable'.[135]

129 See Bitti, *supra* note 72, p. 97, calling for 'une codification des droits des victimes'; De Brouwer and Heikkilä, *supra* note 29, 1347–8, 1368, explaining that 'to meet expectations, victims' rights must be clearly explained'.

130 Lorna MacGregor, 'An Integrated System of National and International Remedies for Crimes under International Law', 14 *Journal of International Criminal Justice* (2016) 239, p. 245.

131 'Responsibility for reparations should maintain an element of state responsibility, as those considered to have carried the greatest responsibility for serious violations may have exercised functions of state authority. There are inherent dangers in shifting responsibility of States towards individuals. While the shift towards recognising victims and their right to reparation in international criminal law is welcome and positive, ideally this should operate alongside measures to establish state responsibility vis-à-vis victims' (Evans, *supra* note 36, p. 86).

132 See Zegveld, *supra* note 10, pp. 80–1, 'these courts should pay attention to the imperfect functioning of remedies for victims in domestic criminal courts. Problems emanate from the parallel hearing of the criminal case and civil compensation case by a criminal court, each case being of a distinctly different nature, based on different branches of law. The fact that civil claims have a subordinate nature to the criminal proceedings, prohibiting the court from spending sufficient time on the civil claim, adds to the frustration of reparation for victims in domestic criminal courts. Incapable or unwilling to deal with the complex issues relating to civil claims, these courts are inclined to refer victims to civil courts to submit their request for damage. While remedies for victims before international criminal courts are not an exact copy of domestic procedures, it is legitimate to ask what may be expected from international criminal courts in view of the problems encountered at the national level'.

133 'Extensive victim participation can delay proceedings, and sentences against individuals cannot comprehensively address the questions relating to institutional and state responsibility that victims wish to explore' (Evans, *supra* note 36, p. 123).

134 ECCC, Appeals Judgment, *Case 001*, 3 February 2012, para. 655.

135 Ibid., para. 668.

The importance of ensuring and balancing the rights of victims and the convicted person in reparations proceedings is growing with the emergence of new hybrid tribunals. Looking ahead, the statute of the Kosovo Specialist Chambers also contains provisions on reparations. There have not yet been reparations proceedings, but the statute allows a trial panel to make an order specifying 'appropriate reparation' against a convicted person,[136] and the rules allow the trial panel to appoint experts for the assessment of harm.[137] Elsewhere, the Special Criminal Court in CAR is taking shape. Civil society groups have made a concrete proposal to include a reparations provision in the Court's rules of procedure.[138] Indeed, the reparations order is a relatively new phenomenon which will be inherent in criminal trials in international and hybrid courts for many years to come. The proceedings leading to the order must offer concrete participatory rights that are well-suited to the reparations order that is ultimately produced. This is essential if reparations proceedings are ever to bridge the gap between expectations and outcomes.

136 Article 22(8) of the Law on Specialist Chambers and Specialist Prosecutor's Office.
137 Rule 168 of the Rules of Procedure and Evidence.
138 'Le droit à la réparation dans le Règlement de Procédure et de Preuve de la Cour Pénale Spéciale', October 2017, available at www.asf.be/wp-content/uploads/2017/10/ASF-REDRESS-FIDH_CPS_Reparations_201710.pdf last accessed on 15 January 2019.

12 Final reflections on defendants and victims in international criminal proceedings

Juan-Pablo Pérez-León-Acevedo and Joanna Nicholson

Defendants and victims lie at the very heart of the international criminal justice process. The presence of defendants at international and hybrid criminal courts and tribunals (ICTs) corresponds to the very nature of and mandate of this type of judicial institution, in that ICTs are international level courts which determine the criminal liability of individuals who perpetrated crimes under the court's jurisdiction. The legal frameworks of ICTs contain sets of rights held and exercised by those who are suspected, accused or convicted of international offences. These rights have been extensively interpreted and applied by ICTs in the main procedural stages of the criminal process, namely, investigation, pre-trial, trial, appeals, sentencing and, where applicable, reparations proceedings. Naturally, defendants assume a prominent role at ICTs, and alongside the prosecutor, they are generally the main parties to the diverse array of proceedings which take place at these institutions. Moreover, ICTs are mainly guided by retributive and punitive justice paradigms, which require particular attention to be paid to the protection of defendants' rights.

In this context, the increasing role of victims and their related procedural rights at ICTs have brought new challenges and issues. The need for introducing some reparative and restorative justice elements to international criminal justice underlies the evolution of the role of victims at ICTs. They are no longer only witnesses, but have been empowered to hold an autonomous participatory role to voice their own views and concerns and, at some ICTs, they have become authentic parties to the cases, even claiming reparations. The normative instruments and judicial practices of ICTs evidence important developments which have overall enhanced the role of victims within the criminal justice process. Nevertheless, the realisation of the rights of victims has often resulted in tension or conflict with the realisation of the rights of defendants.

When balancing the conflicting rights of defendants and victims, ICTs have relied on a number of alternatives which have mainly included some restrictions on the exercise of certain rights of victims, or the implementation of specific modalities of exercising these rights, so that the rights of the defendants are better protected and fully guaranteed. Whether these practices should follow case-by-case approaches, or whether the ICTs should aim to standardise their judicial decisions, is also open to debate. When balancing the rights of defendants and victims, close attention should be paid to the concrete circumstances of the respective case or issue, but it is also important that ICTs become more consistent in their judicial practices when addressing similar issues for the sake of coherence and predictability.

A key common ground underlying the situation of defendants and victims at ICTs, concerns the human rights of these different individuals, and how to realise and balance these rights. The mandate and nature of ICTs is different from other international courts, such as the International Court of Justice which determines state liability in state vs state litigation, and regional human rights courts which find state liability in individual vs state litigation. Human rights, in particular the rights of defendants and victims, are, however, embedded within the international criminal justice process for several reasons.

To begin with, international crimes committed by defendants against victims constitute serious violations of human rights. The legal instruments of ICTs contain rights of defendants and victims. When it comes to the rights of the defendants, the origin of these normative provisions can be traced to major universal and regional human rights treaty provisions on the right to a fair trial.[1] In turn, the normative provisions of ICTs on the rights of victims[2] reflect important developments that have taken place in the field of human rights. This does not involve an automatic transplant of international human rights law to international criminal justice institutions, however. In order to appropriately ensure and balance the human rights of the defendants and victims at ICTs, judges and other actors need to adapt international human rights principles and standards to the particular characteristics of, and challenges at, ICTs. Indeed, these judicial bodies have, to a larger or lesser extent, engaged in this process of adaptation, which may be considered as a factor when evaluating the level of success ICTs have had when endeavouring to ensure and balance the rights of defendants and victims.

In any event, ICTs, as with other international level institutions, are generally bound by international human rights law. A clear example of such an obligation is Article 21(3) of the Rome Statute, which states that: 'application and interpretation of [International Criminal Court (ICC)] law [. . .] must be consistent with internationally recognized human rights'. International practice, including that of the United Nations Secretary General, recognises that respect for international human rights constitutes one of the fundamental pillars of the modern

1 International Covenant on Civil and Political Rights, Article 14; European Convention for the Protection of Human Rights and Fundamental Freedoms, Article 6; American Convention on Human Rights, Articles 8 and 25; African Charter on Human and Peoples' Rights, Article 7.

2 UN General Assembly, *Declaration of Basic Principles of Justice for Victims of Crime and Abuse of Power*: resolution / adopted by the General Assembly, 29 November 1985, A/RES/40/34; UN General Assembly, *Basic Principles and Guidelines on the Right to a Remedy and Reparation for Victims of Gross Violations of International Human Rights Law and Serious Violations of International Humanitarian Law*: resolution / adopted by the General Assembly, 21 March 2006, A/RES/60/147.

international legal system.[3] In turn, diverse legal approaches and theories, such as global constitutionalism[4] and the goal-based approach,[5] acknowledge human rights as being an important standard by which to assess critical aspects such as the legitimacy and effectiveness of international courts, including ICTs. During times when there is a growing hostility or scepticism towards the work of international courts, the contributions of ICTs to ensuring and balancing the rights of defendants and victims may play a part in powerfully illustrating that international law and its judicial institutions have an important role to play in today's global society.

In his opening address at the Nuremberg Trial, chief prosecutor Robert H. Jackson famously stated that 'To pass these defendants a poisoned chalice is to put it to our own lips as well' – the effects of a defendant not being accorded a fair trial are ultimately suffered by us all. His argument applies with equal force today: if ICTs are to be legitimate institutions, in the sense of being both normatively legitimate, in that they possess a 'right to rule', and sociologically legitimate, in that they are perceived as having a right to rule,[6] then the protection of the fair trial rights of defendants must stand as an, or perhaps even *the*, absolute priority in international criminal law. While a fair trial may not be sufficient in itself to legitimise a court, an unfair trial will almost always do so,[7] and the ramifications of an unfair trial have the potential to detrimentally affect the whole system. Thus, ensuring that a defendant receives a fair trial should always take centre stage during court processes.

To this end, the fair trial rights of defendants are firmly embedded within the legislative and procedural framework of ICTs, and these institutions have continually been at pains to emphasise their commitment to ensuring and protecting these rights. However, the reality of interpreting fair trial rights is complex and raises challenging questions. One debate surrounds the larger role played by ICTs when interpreting fair trial rights. Some argue that ICTs should be leading institutions when it comes to the interpretation and implementation of fair trial rights, setting standards for others to follow. This view has been expressed by

3 For example, see: Secretary-General, United Nations, *The Rule of Law and Transitional Justice in Conflict and Post-Conflict Societies* (2004) UN Doc. S/2004/616; Secretary General, United Nations, *The rule of law and transitional justice in conflict and post-conflict societies: Report of the Secretary-General to the Security Council* (S/2011/634); and General Assembly of the United Nations, *Resolution on the Rule of Law at the National and International Levels* (2012) A/RES/67/97.

4 For example, see: Jan Klabbers, Anne Peters, and Geir Ulfstein (eds.), *The Constitutionalization of International Law* (Oxford University Press 2011); Antje Wiener and others, "Global Constitutionalism: Human Rights, Democracy and the Rule of Law" (2012) 1 *Global Constitutionalism* 1.

5 For example, see: Yuval Shany, *Assessing the Effectiveness of International Courts* (Oxford University Press 2016).

6 Allen Buchanan and Robert O. Keohane, 'The Legitimacy of Global Governance Institutions', 20(4) *Ethics and International Affairs* 405.

7 Asad Kiyani, 'The antinomies of legitimacy: On the (im)possibility of a legitimate International Criminal Court', 8 *African Journal of Legal Studies* (2015) 1, p. 27.

the courts themselves: the International Criminal Tribunal for Rwanda (ICTR), for example, described itself as providing a 'model of fairness'[8] for other legal systems to emulate; the International Criminal Tribunal for the Former Yugoslavia (ICTY) stated that it set the 'highest standards of justice'.[9] This desire that ICTs set the highest standards has been echoed by other organisations, including NGOs,[10] and within scholarship.[11] However, others have suggested that while fair trial rights are vitally important to the defendant and to the overall legitimacy of ICTs, continually aiming for the highest standards of fairness is not necessarily always the best course of action.[12] For example, what is the benchmark which is to be used when aiming for the highest standards of fair trial rights?[13] Although international human rights standards may seem pertinent, they were not formulated with the unique context of ICTs in mind, raising questions as to the precise relevance of human rights law and decisions from international human right bodies in an international criminal law arena. If, on the other hand, the benchmark is other ICTs, each ICT functions within its own unique framework, and direct comparisons may not always be possible or desirable. For those who conceive of ICTs as standard setting institutions when it comes to fair trial rights, the fact that each court operates in a particular context with a very particular jurisdiction and structure, also raises questions as to whether they can be conceived as suitable standard setting institutions for other ICTs or for national courts.

Another issue is how defendants' fair trial rights should be balanced and weighted throughout the trial process. A balancing exercise needs to take place both *vis-à-vis* the defendant's individual fair trial rights and the defendant's right to a fair trial *vis-à-vis* the rights of other actors in the criminal justice process. Thus, ICTs must balance different individual facets of a defendant's right to a fair trial with other facets, for example, ensuring that their right to self-representation

8 Separate Opinion of Judge Pavel Dolenc, Judgment, Ntagerura et al. (ICTR-99-46-T), Trial Chamber, 25 February 2004, x 5.

9 Decision on the objection of the Republic of Croatia to the Issuance of Subpoenae Duces Tecum, *Blakić* (IT-95-14-T), TrialChamber, 18 July 1997, para. 61.

10 Remarks of Kenneth Roth, Human Rights Watch, Assembly of State Parties, 9 September 2002, available online at http://pantheon.hrw.org/legacy/campaigns/icc/docs/ken-icc0909.htm and Amnesty International, States Must Strengthen, Not Abandon, Only Route to Justice for Millions of Victims, 15 November 2016, available online at www.amnesty.org/en/latest/news/2016/11/icc-states-must-not-abandon-only-route-to-justice-for-millions-of-victims/ Also see International Bar Association, Report on Fair Trials and Complementarity: An Experts' Roundtable Discussion Addressing Practice, Challenges and Future Perspectives, 19 September 2017, pp. 15–16.

11 Yvonne McDermott, *Fairness in International Criminal Tribunals* (Oxford University Press, 2017), pp. 140–1 and Colin Warbrick, 'International Criminal Courts and Fair Trial', 3 *Journal of Armed Conflict Law* (1998) 45, p. 49.

12 Joanna Nicholson, 'Too High', 'Too Low', or 'Just Fair Enough'? Finding Legitimacy Through the Accused's Right to a Fair Trial', 17 *Journal of International Criminal Justice* (2019) 351.

13 Sergey Vasiliev, 'Fairness and Its Metric in International Criminal Procedure' (2013), available online at https://papers.ssrn.com/sol3/papers.cfm?abstract_id1/42253177

does not prejudice the fundamental right to a fair, public and expeditious trial.[14] Over-emphasising one aspect of fair trial rights can affect the overall fairness of the trial for the defendant, and the fairness of the trial as a whole.

Furthermore, the defendant's fair trial rights must be balanced against the interests of other participants in the international criminal justice system, including victims, and the prosecutor.[15] It remains controversial as to whether the prosecutor and victims can be said to have a right to a fair trial. Some court decisions have held that the prosecutor has such a right,[16] whereas others incline to the view that the important factor is whether there is an equality of arms between the defence and the prosecution.[17] This issue will likely remain unresolved for some time to come. Courts need to undertake a difficult balancing act when weighing the defendant's right to a fair trial against the interests of other participants in the process and ensuring that the proceedings are undertaken in a way that is fair and expeditious to all. However, as Damaška writes, 'The ghost of innocent men convicted must continue to hover over international criminal justice.'[18] Ultimately, what should never be lost sight of is that it is the defendant who has most to lose if a trial process is unfair and a miscarriage of justice occurs.

As for victims at international criminal justice institutions, the rights held and exercised by them as witnesses, victim participants/civil parties or reparations claimants are necessary in their search for justice and redress. Protective measures ordered in favour of victims mainly when they intervene as witnesses; procedural rights or participation modalities exercised by victims in their procedural status of victim participants or civil parties; and the possibility to claim and receive reparations awards at ICTs, constitute concrete manifestations of victims' general rights to protection, participation and reparations related to criminal proceedings. These rights have long been recognised in international human rights law as well as in domestic practices. However, their successful realisation at ICTs is particularly challenging for the following two reasons: First, due to the large scale of atrocities committed, there are normally high numbers of victims at ICTs, yet, these courts and tribunals possess limited resources. Such a proportionally inverse relationship can lead to quite restrictive situations and outcomes concerning in particular victim participation and reparations for victims. The fact that a number of victims' rights are exercised through common legal representatives at ICTs clearly indicates this problematic situation. Second, to ensure the rights of

14 W. Schombourg, 'The Role of International Criminal Tribunals in Promoting Respect for Fair Trial Rights', 8 *Northwestern Journal of International Human Rights* (2009) 1, p. 16.

15 McDermott, *supra* note 11, pp. 109–116.

16 Decision on Prosecution Motion to Amend its Exhibit List and Oneissi Defence Request to Stay the Proceedings, *Ayyash* et al., (STL-11-01/T/TC), Trial Chamber, 3 April 2015, para. 47.

17 G. McIntyre, 'Equality of Arms: Defining Human Rights in the Jurisprudence of the International Criminal Tribunal for the former Yugoslavia', 16 *Leiden Journal of International Law* (2003) 269.

18 M. Damaška, 'Reflections on Fairness in International Criminal Justice', 10 *Journal of International Criminal Justice* (2012) 611, p. 615.

victims in their different procedural roles at ICTs in a feasible manner, human rights and legitimate interests and concerns of other important actors such as defendants must be taken into account. The rights of victims at ICTs do not work in isolation, but in direct interaction with other rights and needs. The rights of the accused may be affected or jeopardised by an (excessive) enhancement of the dimensions of the procedural role of victims at ICTs. The right to a fair and impartial trial may be affected by, for example, closed sessions, anonymity of witnesses, and certain procedural rights of victims which make them assume roles similar to those of additional or auxiliary prosecutors. The defendant's right to timely proceedings may also be affected by a steady increase in both the number of victims and victim participation instances. Conversely, should victims see their rights excessively limited or constrained for the sake of the rights of the defendants or in the face of limited resources, the expectations of victims and their perceptions about ICTs will be severely affected. Not only may this cause secondary victimization or re-victimization, but it may also negatively undermine the legitimacy and legacy of international criminal justice institutions as a whole.

Nevertheless, ICTs overall constitute viable and important judicial platforms to realise the rights of victims as witnesses, victim participants/civil parties and reparations claimants. As the most serious international crimes committed against large numbers of victims and their communities fall under the jurisdiction of ICTs, the balanced realisation of the rights of victims in several procedural dimensions is both logical and necessary. In order to achieve workable and meaningful levels of realisation of the rights of victims at ICTs, judicial exercises of balancing and reconciling the rights of victims with the rights of the defendant need to be conducted carefully and always in light of the limited mandate and resources of ICTs. It is noticed that international criminal justice institutions have arguably and continuously examined diverse options to enforce the rights of victims in international criminal proceedings. In these processes, each court has paid attention to not only its own mistakes and limitations, but also ('best') practices from similar judicial institutions, which should continue in the future.

Ensuring the human rights of victims and balancing these rights against the rights of defendants at international criminal justice institutions has become increasingly necessary. This is because of the general trend whereby the role of victims at ICTs is no longer limited to their status as witnesses, which was the case at the ICTY, the ICTR and the Special Court for Sierra Leone, but now incorporates dimensions involving participation in proceedings as participants or civil parties and reparations claims, which has been the situation with the establishment of the ICC and has been followed by hybrid criminal courts such as the Special Tribunal for Lebanon, the Extraordinary Chambers in the Courts of Cambodia and the Extraordinary African Chambers as well as the prospective first regional criminal court, namely, the International Criminal Law Section of the ACJHPR. These expanded roles attributed to victims and related procedural rights also correspond to long-standing national traditions, in particular the civil law countries and their procedural inquisitorial model.

This trend should arguably guide the constitution of future ICTs in order to fully realise the rights of victims of atrocities in criminal proceedings, but always with the adoption of necessary safeguards, mechanisms and guarantees to make the role of victims workable. Moreover, this trend corresponds to the thirst for justice that victims in many instances cannot quench at the national level, either in national criminal courts or other transitional justice mechanisms, because the respective national jurisdictions or mechanisms are unwilling or unable to deliver proper justice for victims. Careful consideration of the procedural roles of victims and their respective rights is fundamental to design proceedings and adopt coherent normative and jurisprudential practices at ICTs, so that victims can exercise their rights in a manner whereby not only the victims themselves can obtain benefits, but also the rights of the defendants and other legitimate interests are respected within the limited legal and material frameworks of these international judicial bodies.

The fact that proceedings ensure the rights of victims in full respect of the rights of the defendants should also by itself have a positive impact on victims. An effective and balanced exercise of the rights of victims as witnesses, participants/civil parties and reparations claimants can provide an important quota of reparative or restorative justice to international criminal proceedings. Under no circumstances does this deny that ICTs fall short of being a panacea for problems of victims of the most serious international crimes. Conversely, these courts should ideally work on a coordinated basis with a wide array of other transitional justice mechanisms, such as truth and reconciliation commissions, national reparations programmes, and domestic criminal investigations and trials.

Despite their limitations and deficits, ICTs have become important platforms where defendants and victims of international crimes exercise their rights in international criminal proceedings. In any event, one of the major challenges encountered by current and future ICTs is to fully ensure and balance the rights of the defendants and victims. In turn, academia can and should accompany and contribute to the efforts to better handle such a challenge.

Index

For Product Safety Concerns and Information please contact our EU
representative GPSR@taylorandfrancis.com
Taylor & Francis Verlag GmbH, Kaufingerstraße 24, 80331 München, Germany

www.ingramcontent.com/pod-product-compliance
Ingram Content Group UK Ltd.
Pitfield, Milton Keynes, MK11 3LW, UK
UKHW011004180926
475701UK00004B/545
9781032236216